Virtual Reality

Virtual reality (VR) is a powerful technology that promises to transform our lives. This balanced and interdisciplinary text blends key components from computer graphics, perceptual psychology, human physiology, behavioral science, media studies, human–computer interaction, optical engineering, and sensing and filtering, showing how each contributes to engineering perceptual illusions. Steven LaValle draws on his unique experience as a teacher, researcher, and co-creator of the Oculus Rift to demonstrate how the best practices and insights from industry are built on fundamental principles. Topics include media history, geometric modeling, optical systems, displays, eyes, ears, low-level perception, neuroscience of vision, graphical rendering, tracking systems, interaction mechanisms, audio, evaluating VR systems, and mitigating side effects. Students, researchers, and developers will gain a clear understanding of timeless foundations and new applications, enabling them to make innovative contributions to this growing field as scientists, engineers, business developers, and content makers.

Steven LaValle is Professor of Computer Science and Engineering at the University of Oulu and Professor of Computer Science at the University of Illinois at Urbana-Champaign. He was an early founder and chief scientist of Oculus VR, where he developed patented tracking technology for consumer VR and led a team of perceptual psychologists to provide principled approaches to virtual reality system calibration, health and safety, and the design of comfortable user experiences. He has also served as Vice President and Chief Scientist of VR/AR/MR at Huawei. He has conducted research for over three decades, publishing over 150 articles and two books, *Planning Algorithms* and *Sensing and Filtering*.

Virtual Reality

Steven M. LaValle

University of Oulu, Finland

CAMBRIDGE
UNIVERSITY PRESS

CAMBRIDGE
UNIVERSITY PRESS

Shaftesbury Road, Cambridge CB2 8EA, United Kingdom

One Liberty Plaza, 20th Floor, New York, NY 10006, USA

477 Williamstown Road, Port Melbourne, VIC 3207, Australia

314–321, 3rd Floor, Plot 3, Splendor Forum, Jasola District Centre,

New Delhi – 110025, India

103 Penang Road, #05–06/07, Visioncrest Commercial, Singapore 238467

Cambridge University Press is part of Cambridge University Press & Assessment,
a department of the University of Cambridge.

We share the University's mission to contribute to society through the pursuit of
education, learning and research at the highest international levels of excellence.

www.cambridge.org
Information on this title: www.cambridge.org/9781107198937

DOI: 10.1017/9781108182874

First published 2023

Printed in the United Kingdom by TJ Books Limited, Padstow Cornwall

A catalogue record for this publication is available from the British Library.

A Cataloging-in-Publication data record for this book is available from the Library of Congress.

ISBN 978-1-107-19893-7 Hardback

For my family, Anna, Alexander, Ethan, Rose, and Petri

Contents

CONTENTS

Preface

The Rebirth of Virtual Reality

Virtual reality (VR) is a powerful technology that promises to change our lives unlike any other. By artificially stimulating our senses, our bodies become tricked into accepting another version of reality. Virtual reality is like a waking dream that could take place in a magical cartoon-like world or could transport us to another part of the Earth or universe. It is the next step along a path that includes many familiar media, from paintings to movies to video games. We can even socialize with people inside of new worlds, which could be real or artificial.

At the same time, VR bears the stigma of unkept promises. The hype and excitement has often far exceeded the delivery of VR experiences to match it, especially for people without access to expensive laboratory equipment. This was particularly painful in the early 1990s when VR seemed poised to enter mainstream use but failed to catch on (outside of some niche markets). Decades later, we are witnessing an exciting rebirth. The latest technological components, mainly arising from the smartphone industry, have enabled high-resolution, low-cost, portable VR headsets to provide compelling VR experiences. From 2014 onward, this has mobilized leading technology companies to invest billions of dollars into growing a VR ecosystem that includes art, communication, entertainment, enhanced work productivity, and social interaction. At the same time, a new generation of technologists is entering the field with fresh ideas. Online communities of hackers and makers, along with college students around the world, are excitedly following the rapid advances in VR and are starting to shape it by starting new companies, working to improve the technology, and making new kinds of experiences.

The whole ecosystem is growing at a steady pace, while some particular use cases such as industry training are rapidly expanding. A current challenge is to introduce advanced hardware that is not simply derived from other markets. The greatest need for innovation is in visual displays that are particularly designed for VR. Distinctions with other technologies such as augmented reality (AR) and mixed reality (MR) are becoming less significant as the technology progresses because they can all be handled by the same or similar devices. At the time of writing, the relatively new term extended reality (XR) has become popular to represent this unification; however, this book will refer to these as variations of VR.

The Intended Audience

The book grew out of material for an undergraduate course on VR that I introduced at the University of Illinois in 2015. I have never in decades of teaching seen students so excited to take a course. We could not offer enough slots to come even close to meeting the demand. Therefore, the primary target of this book is undergraduate students around the world. This book would be an ideal source for starting similar VR courses at other universities. Although most of the interested students have been computer scientists, the course at the University of Illinois has attracted students from many disciplines, such as psychology, music, kinesiology, engineering, medicine, and economics. Students in these other fields come with the most exciting project ideas because they can see how VR has the potential to radically alter *their* disciplines. To make the course accessible to students with such diverse backgrounds, I have made the material as self-contained as possible. There is no assumed background in software development or advanced mathematics. If prospective readers have at least written some scripts before and can remember how to multiply matrices together, they should be ready to go.

In addition to students who are studying VR in university courses, this text is also targeted at developers in industry, hobbyists on the forums, and researchers in academia. The book appears online so that it may serve as a convenient reference for all of these groups. To provide further assistance, there are also accompanying materials online, including lecture slides (prepared by Anna Yershova LaValle) and recorded lectures (provided online for free by NPTEL of India).

Why Am I Writing This Book?

I enjoy teaching and research, especially when I can tie the two together. I have been a professor and have taught university courses for over two decades. Robotics has been my main field of expertise; however, in 2012, while on a sabbatical in Oulu, Finland, I started working at Oculus VR a few days after its Kickstarter campaign. I left the university and became their chief scientist, working on head tracking methods, perceptual psychology, health and safety, and numerous other problems. I was struck by how many new challenges arose during that time because engineers and computer scientists (myself included) did not recognize human perception problems that were disrupting our progress. I became convinced that for VR to succeed, perceptual psychology must permeate the design of VR systems. As we tackled some of these challenges, the company rapidly grew in visibility and influence, eventually being acquired by Facebook. Oculus VR is largely credited with stimulating the most recent rebirth of VR [111].

I quickly returned to the University of Illinois with a new educational mission: teach a new generation of students, developers, and researchers the fundamentals of VR in a way that fuses perceptual psychology with engineering. Furthermore, this book focuses on principles that do not depend heavily on the particular technology of today. The goal is to improve the reader's *understanding* of how VR systems work, what limitations they have, and what can be done to improve them. One important component is that even though technology rapidly evolves, humans who use it do not. It is therefore crucial to understand how our sensory systems function, especially when matched with artificial stimulation. The intent is to provide a useful foundation as the technology evolves. In many cases, open challenges remain. This book does not provide the solutions to them, but instead supplies the background to begin researching them.

Online Materials

Pointers to additional materials, including lecture videos and slides, are available online at the following link:

`http://lavalle.pl/vr/`

Suggested Use

This text may be used for a one-semester course by spending roughly one week per chapter, with the exception of Chapter 3, which may require two weeks. The book can also be used to augment other courses such as computer graphics, interfaces, and game development. Selected topics may also be drawn for a short course or seminar series.

Depending on the technical level of the students, the mathematical concepts in Chapter 3 might seem oppressive. If that is the case, students may be advised to skim over it and jump to subsequent chapters. They can understand most of the later concepts without the full mathematical details of Chapter 3. Nevertheless, understanding these concepts will enhance their comprehension throughout the book and will also make them more comfortable with programming exercises.

Lab Component

From 2015, we have used high-end consumer VR headsets on PCs with graphics cards that were specifically designed for VR. Development on many other platforms is possible, including all-in-one VR headsets, but one must be careful to ensure that the performance requirements for projects and exercises are met by the particular choice of platform. For software, almost all students develop VR projects using Unity 3D. Alternatives may be Unreal Engine and CryEngine, depending on their level of technical coding skills. Unity 3D is the easiest, because knowledge of C++ and associated low-level concepts is unnecessary. Students with strong programming and computer graphics skills may instead want to develop projects "from scratch," but they should be aware that implementation times may be much longer.

Acknowledgments

I am very grateful to many students and colleagues who have given me extensive feedback and advice in developing this text. It evolved over many years through development and teaching at the University of Illinois at Urbana-Champaign (UIUC), starting in early 2015. The biggest thanks goes to Anna Yershova LaValle, who has also taught the virtual reality course at the University of Illinois and University of Oulu, and collaborated on the course development. We also worked side by side at Oculus VR since the earliest days. We continue to work together at the University of Oulu in Finland.

I am grateful to the College of Engineering and Computer Science Department at the University of Illinois for their support of the course. Furthermore, Oculus/Facebook has generously supported the lab with headset donations. I am also grateful to the Indian Institute of Technology (IIT) Madras in Chennai, India, for their hospitality and support while I taught a short version of the course. I also appreciate the efforts of my colleagues at the University of Oulu, who in 2018 recruited me and supported me in building the Perception Engineering Laboratory, which investigates fundamental VR issues. Most of the thanks goes to Timo Ojala and the Center for Ubiquitous Computing. Finally, I am extremely grateful to the hundreds of students who have served as test subjects for the course and book while they were under development. Their endless enthusiasm and questions helped shape this material.

Among many helpful colleagues, I especially thank Alan B. Craig, Ian Bailey, Henry Fuchs, Don Greenberg, Jukka Häkkinen, T. Kesh Kesavadas, Paul Mac-Neilage, M. Manivannan, Betty Mohler, Aaron Nichols, Timo Ojala, Yury Petrov, Dan Simons, and Richard Yao for their helpful insights, explanations, suggestions, feedback, and pointers to materials.

I sincerely thank the many more people who have given me corrections and comments on early drafts of this book. These include Lawrence Angrave, Frank Dellaert, Blake J. Harris, Jamin Hu, Evgeny Klavir, Cameron Merrill, Katherine J. Mimnaugh, Peter Newell, Matti Pouke, Yingying (Samara) Ren, Matthew Romano, Tish Shute, Killivalavan Solai, Karthik Srikanth, Markku Suomalainen, Jiang Tin, David Tranah, Ilija Vukotic, Chris Widdowson, Kan Zi Yang, and Xu (Richard) Yu.

Finally, thanks to Lauren Cowles, Deborah Nicholls, Becca Grainger, Reshma Venkatachalapathy, Bret Workman, Adam Warkoczewski, and the team at Cambridge University Press for all their help in preparing this manuscript for publication.

CHAPTER ONE

Introduction

1.1 What Is Virtual Reality?

Virtual reality (VR) technology is evolving rapidly, making it undesirable to define VR in terms of specific devices that may fall out of favor in a year or two. In this book, we are concerned with fundamental principles that are less sensitive to particular technologies and therefore survive the test of time. Our first challenge is to consider what VR actually means in a way that captures the most crucial aspects in spite of rapidly changing technology. The concept must also be general enough to encompass what VR is considered today and what we envision for its future.

We start with two thought-provoking examples: (1) A human having an experience of flying over virtual San Francisco by flapping his own wings (Figure 1.1); (2) a gerbil running on a freely rotating ball while exploring a virtual maze that appears on a projection screen around the gerbil (Figure 1.2). We want our definition of VR to be broad enough to include these examples and many more, which are coming in Section 1.2. This motivates the following.

Definition of VR: Inducing targeted behavior in an organism by using artificial sensory stimulation, while the organism has little or no awareness of the interference.

Four key components appear in the definition:

1. *Targeted behavior:* The organism is having an "experience" that was designed by the creator. Examples include flying, walking, exploring, watching a movie, and socializing with other organisms.
2. *Organism:* This could be you, someone else, or even another life form such as a fruit fly, cockroach, fish, rodent, or monkey. (Scientists have used VR technology on all of these!)
3. *Artificial sensory stimulation:* Through the power of engineering, one or more senses of the organism become co-opted, at least partially, and their ordinary inputs are replaced or enhanced by artificial stimulation.
4. *Awareness:* While having the experience, the organism seems unaware of the interference, thereby being "fooled" into feeling immersed in a virtual world. This unawareness may lead to a sense of *presence* in an altered or alternative world. It is accepted as being natural.

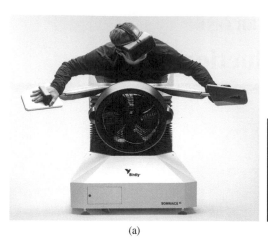

(a)   (b)

Figure 1.1   In the Birdly experience from the Zurich University of the Arts, the user, wearing a VR headset, flaps his wings while flying over virtual San Francisco. A motion platform and fan provide additional sensory stimulation. The figure on the right shows the stimulus presented to each eye.

You have probably seen optical illusions before. A VR system causes a *perceptual illusion* to be maintained for the organism. For this reason, human physiology and perception represent a large part of this book.

Testing the Boundaries

The examples shown in Figures 1.1 and 1.2 clearly fit the definition. Anyone donning a modern VR headset[1] and enjoying a session should also be included. How far does our VR definition allow one to stray from the most common examples? Perhaps listening to music through headphones should be included. What about watching a movie at a theater? Clearly, technology has been used in the form of movie projectors and audio systems to provide artificial sensory stimulation. Continuing further, what about a portrait or painting on the wall? The technology in this case involves paints and a canvass. Finally, we might even want reading a novel to be considered as VR. The technologies are writing and printing. The stimulation is visual but does not seem as direct as a movie screen and audio system. In this book, we do not worry too much about the precise boundary of our VR definition. Good arguments could be made either way about some of these borderline cases, but it is more important to understand the key ideas for the core of VR. The boundary cases also serve as a good point of reference for historical perspective, which is presented in Section 1.3.

Who Is the Fool?

Returning to the VR definition, the idea of "fooling" an organism might seem fluffy or meaningless; however, this can be made surprisingly concrete using research from neurobiology. When an animal explores its environment, neural structures composed of *place cells* are formed that encode spatial information about its surroundings [239, 243]; see Figure 1.3(a). Each place cell is activated precisely when the organism

---

[1] This is also referred to as a *head-mounted display* or *HMD*.

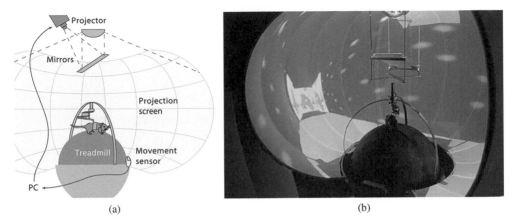

(a)   (b)

Figure 1.2 (a) An experimental setup used by neurobiologists at LMU Munich to present visual stimuli to a gerbil while it runs on a spherical ball that acts as a treadmill [330]. (b) The gerbil appears to be in a panoramic movie theater.

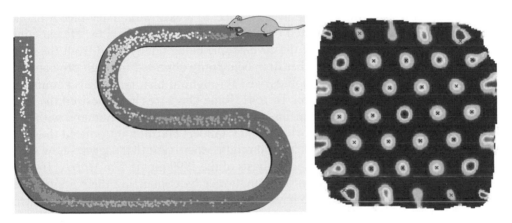

Figure 1.3 (a) We animals have neurons assigned as *place cells*, which fire when we return to specific locations. This figure depicts the spatial firing patterns of eight place cells in a rat's brain as it runs back and forth along a winding track (figure by Stuart Layton). (b) We even have *grid cells*, which fire in uniformly, spatially distributed patterns, apparently encoding location coordinates.

returns to a particular location that is covered by it. Although less understood, *grid cells* even encode locations in a manner similar to Cartesian coordinates [227] (Figure 1.3(b)). It has been shown that these neural structures may form in an organism even when having a VR experience [2, 44, 114]. In other words, our brains may form place cells for places that are not real! This is a clear indication that VR is fooling our brains, at least partially. At this point, you may wonder whether reading a novel that meticulously describes an environment that does not exist will cause place cells to be generated.

We also cannot help wondering whether we are always being fooled and some greater reality has yet to reveal itself to us. This problem has intrigued the greatest philosophers over many centuries. One of the oldest instances is the *Allegory of the Cave*, presented by Plato in *Republic*. In this, Socrates describes the perspective of

Figure 1.4 A VR thought experiment: the brain in a vat, by Gilbert Harman in 1973.

people who have spent their whole lives chained to a cave wall. They face a blank wall and only see shadows projected onto the walls as people pass by. He explains that the philosopher is like one of the cave people being finally freed from the cave to see the true nature of reality rather than being only observed through projections. This idea has been repeated and popularized throughout history, and also connects deeply with spirituality and religion. In 1641, René Descartes hypothesized the idea of an *evil demon* who has directed his entire effort at deceiving humans with the illusion of the external physical world. In 1973, Gilbert Harman introduced the idea of a *brain in a vat* (Figure 1.4), which is a thought experiment that suggests how such an evil demon might operate. This is the basis of the 1999 movie *The Matrix*. In that story, machines have fooled the entire human race by connecting their brains to a convincing simulated world, while harvesting their real bodies. The lead character, Neo, must decide whether to face the new reality or take a memory-erasing pill that will allow him to comfortably live in the simulation without awareness of the ruse.

Terminology Regarding Various "Realities"
The term *virtual reality* dates back to eighteenth-century philosopher Immanuel Kant [342], although its use did not involve technology. Kant introduced the term to refer to the "reality" that exists in someone's mind, as differentiated from the external physical world, which is also a reality. The modern use of the VR term was popularized by Jaron Lanier in the 1980s. Unfortunately, the name *virtual reality* itself seems to be self-contradictory, which is a philosophical problem rectified in [34] by proposing the alternative term *virtuality*. While acknowledging this issue, we will nevertheless continue with the term *virtual reality*. The following distinction, however, will become important: the *real world* refers to the physical world that contains the user at the time of the experience, and the *virtual world* refers to the perceived world as part of the targeted VR experience.

   Although the term VR is already quite encompassing, several competing terms related to VR are in common use at present. The term *virtual environments* predates widespread usage of VR and is preferred by most university researchers [109]. It is typically considered to be synonymous with VR; however, we emphasize in this book that the perceived environment could be a photographically captured "real" world just as well as a completely synthetic world. Thus, the perceived environment presented in VR need not seem "virtual." *Augmented reality* (*AR*) refers to systems in which most of the visual stimuli are propagated directly through glass or cameras to the eyes, and some additional structures, such as text and graphics, appear to be superimposed onto the user's world. The term *mixed reality* (*MR*) is sometimes used to refer to an entire spectrum that encompasses VR, AR, and ordinary reality [216]. People have realized that these decades-old terms and distinctions have eroded away in recent years, especially as unifying technologies have rapidly advanced. Therefore, attempts have been made to hastily unify them back together again under the headings *XR*, *extended reality*, *VR/AR*, *AR/VR*, *VR/AR/MR*, and so on.

The related notion of *telepresence* refers to systems that enable users to feel like they are somewhere else in the real world; if they are able to control anything, such as a flying drone, then *teleoperation* is an appropriate term. For our purposes, virtual environments, augmented reality, mixed reality, telepresence, and teleoperation will all be considered as perfect examples of VR.

The most important idea of VR is that the user's perception of reality has been altered through engineering, rather than whether the environment they believe they are in seems more "real" or "virtual." A perceptual illusion has been engineered. Thus, another reasonable term for this area, especially if considered as an academic discipline, could be *perception engineering*, whereby engineering methods are being used to design, develop, and deliver perceptual illusions to the user. Figure 1.5 illustrates the ingredients of perception engineering, which also motivates the topics of book, and are a mixture of engineering and human psysiology and perception.

Interactivity
Most VR experiences involve another crucial component: *interaction*. Does the presented experience depend on actions taken by the organism? If the answer is "no," then the VR system is called *open-loop*; otherwise, it is *closed-loop*. In the case of closed-loop VR, the organism has partial control over the presented experience, which could vary as a result of body motions, including eyes, head, hands, or legs. Other possibilities include voice commands, heart rate, body temperature, and skin conductance (indicates whether the user is sweating).

First- versus Third-Person
Some readers of this book might want to develop VR systems or experiences. In this case, pay close attention to this next point! When a scientist designs an experiment for an organism, as shown in Figure 1.2, then the separation is clear: the laboratory subject (organism) has a *first-person* experience, while the scientist is a *third-person* observer. The scientist carefully designs the VR system as part of an experiment that will help to resolve a scientific hypothesis. For example, would turning off a few neurons in a rat's brain affect its navigation ability? On the other hand, when engineers or developers construct a VR system or experience, they are usually targeting themselves and people like them. They feel perfectly comfortable moving back and forth between being the "scientist" and the "lab subject" while evaluating and refining

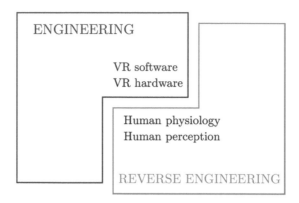

Figure 1.5 When considering a VR system, it is tempting to focus only on the traditional engineering parts: hardware and software. However, it is equally important, if not more important, to understand and exploit the characteristics of human physiology and perception. Because we did not design ourselves, these fields can be considered as reverse engineering. All of these parts tightly fit together to form *perception engineering*.

their work. As you will learn throughout this book, this is a bad idea! The creators of the experience are heavily biased by their desire for it to succeed without having to redo their work. They also know what the experience is supposed to mean or accomplish, which provides a strong bias in comparison to a fresh tester. To complicate matters further, the creator's body will physically and mentally adapt to whatever flaws are present so that they may soon become invisible. You have probably seen these kinds of things before. For example, it is hard to predict how others will react to your own writing. Also, it is usually harder to proofread your own writing in comparison to that of others. In the case of VR, these effects are much stronger and yet elusive to the point that you must force yourself to pay attention to them. Take great care when co-opting the senses that you have trusted all of your life. This will most likely be uncharted territory for you.

More Real Than Reality?
How "real" should the VR experience be? It is tempting to try to make it match our physical world as closely as possible. This is referred to in Section 10.1 as the *universal simulation principle*: Any interaction mechanism in the real world can be simulated in VR. Our brains are most familiar with these settings, thereby making them seem most appropriate. This philosophy has dominated the video game industry at times, for example, in the development of highly realistic first-person shooter (FPS) games that are beautifully rendered on increasingly advanced graphics cards. In spite of this, understand that extremely simple, cartoon-like environments can also be effective and even preferable. Examples appear throughout history, as discussed in Section 1.3.

If you are a creator of VR experiences, think carefully about the task, goals, or desired effect you want to have on the user. You have the opportunity to make the experience *better than reality*. What will they be doing? Taking a math course?

Experiencing a live theatrical performance? Writing software? Designing a house? Maintaining a long-distance relationship? Playing a game? Having a meditation and relaxation session? Traveling to another place on Earth, or in the universe? For each of these, think about how the realism requirements might vary. For example, consider writing software in VR. We currently write software by typing into windows that appear on a large screen. Note that even though this is a familiar experience for many people, it was not even possible in the physical world of the 1950s. In VR, we could simulate the modern software development environment by convincing the programmer that she is sitting in front of a screen; however, this misses the point that we can create almost *anything* in VR. Perhaps a completely new interface will emerge that does not appear to be a screen sitting on a desk in an office. For example, the windows could be floating above a secluded beach or forest. Furthermore, imagine how a debugger could show the program execution trace. In all of these examples, it will be important to determine the *perception-based criteria* that need to be satisfied for the perceptual illusions to be convincingly and comfortably maintained for the particular VR experience of interest.

Synthetic versus Captured

Two extremes exist when constructing a virtual world as part of a VR experience. At one end, we may program a *synthetic* world, which is completely invented from geometric primitives and simulated physics. This is common in video games and such virtual environments were assumed to be the main way to experience VR in earlier decades. At the other end, the world may be *captured* using modern imaging techniques. For viewing on a screen, the video camera has served this purpose for over a century. Capturing panoramic images and videos and then seeing them from any viewpoint in a VR system is a natural extension. In many settings, however, too much information is lost when projecting the real world onto the camera sensor. What happens when the user changes her head position and viewpoint? More information should be captured in this case. Using depth sensors and SLAM (Simultaneous Localization And Mapping) techniques, a 3D representation of the surrounding world can be captured and maintained over time as it changes. It is often difficult, however, to construct an accurate and reliable representation, unless the environment is explicitly engineered for such capture (for example, a motion capture studio).

As humans interact, it becomes important to track their motions, which is an important form of capture. What are their facial expressions while wearing a VR headset? Do we need to know their hand gestures? What can we infer about their emotional state? Are their eyes focused on me? Synthetic representations of ourselves called *avatars* enable us to interact and provide a level of anonymity, if desired in some contexts. The attentiveness or emotional state can be generated synthetically. We can also enhance our avatars by tracking the motions and other attributes of our actual bodies. A well-known problem is the *uncanny valley*, in which a high degree of realism has been achieved in an avatar, but its appearance makes people feel uneasy. It seems almost right, but the small differences are disturbing. There is currently no easy way to make ourselves appear to others in a VR experience exactly as we do in the real world, and in most cases, we might not want to.

Health and Safety

Although the degree of required realism may vary based on the tasks, one requirement remains invariant: the health and safety of the users. Unlike simpler media such as radio or television, VR has the power to overwhelm the senses and the brain, leading to fatigue or sickness. This phenomenon has been studied under the heading of *simulator sickness* for decades; in this book we will refer to adverse symptoms from VR usage as *VR sickness*. Sometimes the discomfort is due to problems in the VR hardware and low-level software; however, in many cases, it is caused by a careless developer who misunderstands or disregards the side effects of the experience on the user. This is one reason why human physiology and perceptual psychology are large components of this book. To engineer comfortable VR experiences, one must understand how these factor in. In many cases, fatigue arises because the brain appears to work harder to integrate the unusual stimuli being presented to the senses. In some cases, inconsistencies with prior expectations, and outputs from other senses, even lead to dizziness and nausea.

Another factor that leads to fatigue is an interface that requires large amounts of muscular effort. For example, it might be tempting to move objects around in a sandbox game by moving your arms around in space. This quickly leads to fatigue and an avoidable phenomenon called *gorilla arms*, in which people feel that the weight of their extended arms is unbearable. However, by following the principle of the computer mouse, it may be possible to execute large, effective motions in the virtual world by small, comfortable motions of a controller. Over long periods of time, the brain will associate the motions well enough for it to seem realistic while also greatly reducing fatigue. This will be revisited in Section 10.1.

1.2 Modern VR Experiences

The current generation of VR systems was brought about by advances in display, sensing, and computing technology from the smartphone industry. From Palmer Luckey's 2012 Oculus Rift design to building a viewing case for smart phones [123, 244, 312], the world has quickly changed as VR headsets are mass produced and placed onto the heads of millions of people. This trend is similar in many ways to the home computer and web browser revolutions; as a wider variety of people have access to the technology, the set of things they do with it substantially broadens.

This section provides a quick overview of what people are doing with VR systems, and provides a starting point for searching for similar experiences on the Internet. Here, we can only describe the experiences in words and pictures, which is a long way from the appreciation gained by experiencing them yourself. This printed medium (a book) is woefully inadequate for fully conveying the medium of VR. Perhaps this is how it was in the 1890s to explain in a newspaper what a movie theater was like! If possible, it is strongly recommended that you try many VR experiences yourself to form first-hand opinions and spark your imagination to do something better.

Video Games

People have dreamed of entering their video game worlds for decades. By 1982, this concept was already popularized by the Disney movie Tron. Figure 1.6 shows several video game experiences in VR. Most gamers currently want to explore large,

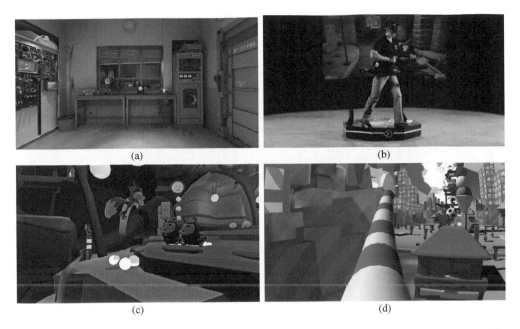

Figure 1.6 (a) Valve's Portal 2 demo, which shipped with The Lab for the HTC Vive headset, is a puzzle-solving experience in a virtual world. (b) The Virtuix Omni treadmill for walking through first-person shooter games. (c) Lucky's Tale for the Oculus Rift maintains a third-person perspective as the player floats above her character. (d) In the Dumpy game from DePaul University, the player appears to have a large elephant trunk. The purpose of the game is to enjoy this unusual embodiment by knocking things down with a swinging trunk.

realistic worlds through an avatar. Figure 1.6(a) shows Valve's Portal 2 for the HTC Vive headset. Figure 1.6(b) shows an omnidirectional treadmill peripheral that gives users the sense of walking while they slide their feet in a dish on the floor. These two examples give the user a *first-person* perspective of his character. By contrast, Figure 1.6(c) shows Lucky's Tale, which instead yields a comfortable *third-person* perspective as the user seems to float above the character that she controls. Figure 1.6(d) shows a game that contrasts with all the others in that it was designed to specifically exploit the unique opportunities of VR.

Immersive Cinema

Hollywood movies continue to offer increasing degrees of realism. Why not make the viewers feel like they are part of the scene? Figure 1.7 shows an immersive short story. Movie directors are entering a fascinating new era of film. The tricks of the trade that were learned across the twentieth century need to be reinvestigated because they are based on the assumption that the cinematographer controls the camera viewpoint. In VR, viewers can look in any direction, and perhaps even walk through the scene. What should they be allowed to do? How do you make sure they do not miss part of the story? Should the story be linear, or should it adapt to the viewer's actions? Should the viewer be a first-person character in the film, or a third-person observer who is invisible to the other characters? How can a group of friends experience a VR film together? When are animations more appropriate versus the capture of real scenes?

Figure 1.7 In 2015, Oculus Story Studio produced Emmy-winning *Henry*, an immersive short story about an unloved hedgehog who hopes to make a new friend, the viewer.

Figure 1.8 The Virtual Movie Theater. Viewers can choose their seats in the theater and watch various movies.

It will take many years to resolve these questions and countless more that will arise. In the meantime, VR can also be used as a kind of "wrapper" around existing movies. Figure 1.8 shows the Virtual Movie Theater application, which allows the user to choose any seat in a virtual movie theater. Whatever standard movies or videos that are on the user's hard drive can be streamed to the screen in the theater. These could be 2D or 3D movies. A projector in the back emits flickering lights

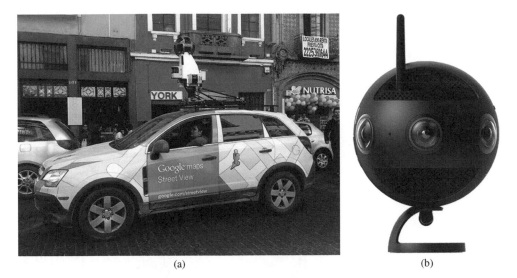

(a)   (b)

Figure 1.9 An important component for achieving telepresence is to capture a panoramic view. (a) A car with cameras and depth sensors on top, used by Google to make Street View. (b) The Insta360 Pro 2 captures and streams omnidirectional videos.

and the audio is adjusted to mimic the acoustics of a real theater. This provides an immediate way to leverage all content that was developed for viewing on a screen, and bring it into VR. Many simple extensions can be made without modifying the films. For example, in a movie about zombies, a few virtual zombies could enter the theater and start to chase you. In a movie about tornadoes, perhaps the theater rips apart. You can also have a social experience. Imagine having "movie night" with your friends from around the world, while you sit together in the virtual movie theater. You can even have the thrill of misbehaving in the theater without getting thrown out.

Telepresence
The first step toward feeling like we are somewhere else is capturing a panoramic view of the remote environment (Figure 1.9). Google's Street View and Earth apps already rely on the captured panoramic images from millions of locations around the world. Simple VR apps that query the Street View server directly enable the user to feel like he is standing in each of these locations, while easily being able to transition between nearby locations (Figure 1.10). Panoramic video capture is even more compelling. Figure 1.11 shows a frame from an immersive rock concert experience. Even better is to provide *live* panoramic video interfaces, through which people can attend sporting events and concerts. Through a live interface, interaction is possible. People can take video conferencing to the next level by feeling present at the remote location. By connecting panoramic cameras to robots, the user is even allowed to move around in the remote environment (Figure 1.12). Current VR technology allows us to virtually visit faraway places and interact in most of the ways that were previously possible only while physically present. This leads to improved opportunities for telecommuting to work. This could ultimately help reverse the urbanization trend

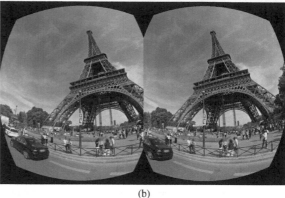

(a)   (b)

Figure 1.10 A simple VR experience that presents Google Street View images through a VR headset. (a) A familiar scene in Paris. (b) Left- and right-eye views are created inside the headset, while also taking into account the user's looking direction.

sparked by the nineteenth-century Industrial Revolution, leading to *deurbanization* as we distribute more uniformly around the Earth.

Virtual Societies

Whereas telepresence makes us feel like we are in another part of the physical world, VR also allows us to form entire societies that remind us of the physical world but are synthetic worlds that contain avatars connected to real people. Figure 1.13 shows a Second Life scene in which people interact in a fantasy world through avatars; such experiences were originally designed to view on a screen but can now be experienced through VR. Groups of people could spend time together in these spaces for a variety of reasons, including common special interests, educational goals, or simply an escape from ordinary life.

Empathy

The first-person perspective provided by VR is a powerful tool for causing people to feel *empathy* for someone else's situation. The world continues to struggle with acceptance and equality for others of different race, religion, age, gender, sexuality, social status, and education, while the greatest barrier to progress is that most people cannot fathom what it is like to have a different identity. Figure 1.14 shows a VR project sponsored by the United Nations to yield feelings of empathy for those caught up in the Syrian crisis of 2015. Some of us may have compassion for the plight of others, but it is a much stronger feeling to understand their struggle because you have been there before. Figure 1.15 shows a VR system that allows men and women

Figure 1.11 A panoramic camera on a stage provides a VR experience where users feel like they were on stage with rock stars (in this case, the band Queen).

(a)   (b)

Figure 1.12 Examples of robotic avatars. (a) The DORA robot from the University of Pennsylvania mimics the user's head motions, allowing him to look around in a remote world while maintaining a stereo view. (Panoramas are monoscopic.) (b) The PlexiDrone, a flying robot that is designed for streaming panoramic video.

to swap bodies. Through virtual societies, many more possibilities can be explored. What if you were 10 cm shorter than everyone else? What if you teach your course with a different gender? What if you were the victim of racial discrimination by the police? Using VR, we can imagine many "games of life" where you might not get as far without being in the "proper" group.

Education

In addition to teaching empathy, the first-person perspective could revolutionize many areas of education. In engineering, mathematics, and the sciences, VR offers the chance to visualize geometric relationships for difficult concepts or data that are hard to interpret. Furthermore, VR is naturally suited for practical training because skills developed in a realistic virtual environment should transfer naturally to the real environment. The motivation is particularly high if the real environment is costly to provide or poses health risks. One of the earliest and most common examples of training in VR is *flight simulation* (Figure 1.16). Other examples include

Figure 1.13 Virtual societies develop through interacting avatars that meet in virtual worlds that are maintained on a common server. A snapshot from Second Life is shown here.

Figure 1.14 In *Clouds Over Sidra*, 2015, film producer Chris Milk offered a first-person perspective on the suffering of Syrian refugees.

firefighting, nuclear power plant safety, search-and-rescue, military operations, and medical procedures.

Beyond these common uses of VR, perhaps the greatest opportunities for VR education lie in the humanities, including history, anthropology, and foreign language acquisition. Consider the difference between reading a book on the Victorian era in England versus being able to roam the streets of nineteenth-century London, in a simulation that has been painstakingly constructed by historians. We could even visit important cultural heritage sites, past or present (Figure 1.17). Fascinating possibilities exist for either touring *physical* museums through a VR interface or scanning

Figure 1.15 In 2014, BeAnotherLab, an interdisciplinary collective, created "The Machine to Be Another" where you can swap bodies with the other gender. Each person wears a VR headset that has cameras mounted on its front. Each person therefore sees the world from the approximate viewpoint of the other person. They are asked to move their hands in coordinated motions so that they see their new body moving appropriately.

Figure 1.16 A flight simulator in use by the US Air Force. The user sits in a physical cockpit while being surrounded by displays that show the environment.

Figure 1.17 A VR experience that visits the ancient Dunhuang caves in western China, developed by Tsinghua University and the Dunhuang Academy.

and exhibiting artifacts directly in *virtual* museums. These examples fall under the heading of *digital heritage*.

Virtual Prototyping

In the real world, we build prototypes to understand how a proposed design feels or functions. Thanks to 3D printing and related technologies, this is easier than ever. At the same time, *virtual prototyping* enables designers to inhabit a virtual world that contains their prototype (Figure 1.18). They can quickly interact with it and make modifications. They also have opportunities to bring clients into their virtual world so that they can communicate their ideas. Imagine you want to remodel your kitchen. You could construct a model in VR and then explain to a contractor exactly how it should look. Virtual prototyping in VR has important uses in many businesses, including real estate, architecture, and the design of aircraft, spacecraft, cars, furniture, clothing, and medical instruments.

Health Care

Although health and safety are challenging VR issues, the technology can also help to improve our health. There is an increasing trend toward distributed medicine, in which doctors train people to perform routine medical procedures in remote communities around the world. Doctors can provide guidance through telepresence, and also use VR technology for training. In another use of VR, doctors can immerse themselves in 3D organ models that were generated from medical scan data (Figure 1.19). This enables them to better plan and prepare for a medical procedure by studying the patient's body shortly before an operation. They can also explain medical options to the patient or his family so that they may make more informed decisions. In yet another use, VR can directly provide therapy to help patients. Examples include overcoming phobias and stress disorders through repeated exposure, improving or maintaining cognitive skills in spite of aging, and improving motor skills to overcome balance, muscular, or nervous system disorders. VR systems could also one day improve longevity by enabling aging people to virtually travel, engage in fun physical therapy, and overcome loneliness by connecting with family and friends through an interface that makes them feel present and included in remote activities.

Figure 1.18 Architecture is a prime example of where a virtual prototype is invaluable. This demo, called Ty Hedfan, was created by IVR-NATION. The real room is shown in the upper photo and the virtual room in the lower one.

Augmented and Mixed Reality

In many applications, it is advantageous for users to see the live, real world with some additional graphics superimposed to enhance its appearance; see Figure 1.20.

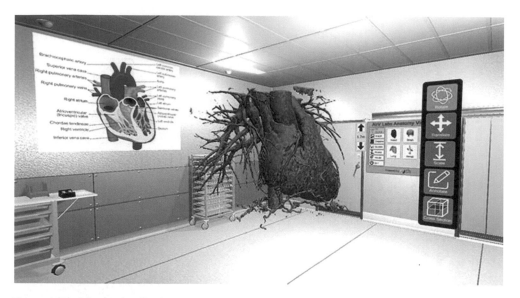

Figure 1.19 A heart visualization system based on images of a real human heart. This was developed by the Jump Trading Simulation and Education Center and the University of Illinois.

Recall that this is often referred to as AR or MR (both of which we consider to be part of VR in this book). By placing text, icons, and other graphics into the real world, the user could leverage the power of the Internet to help with many operations such as navigation, social interaction, and mechanical maintenance. Many applications to date are targeted at helping businesses to conduct operations more efficiently. Imagine a factory environment in which workers see identifying labels above parts that need to assembled, or they can look directly inside a machine to determine potential replacement parts.

These applications rely heavily on advanced computer vision techniques, which must identify objects, reconstruct shapes, and identify lighting sources in the real world before determining how to draw virtual objects that appear to be naturally embedded. Achieving a high degree of reliability becomes a challenge because vision algorithms make frequent errors in unforeseen environments. The real-world lighting conditions must be estimated to determine how to draw the virtual objects and any shadows they might cast onto real parts of the environment and other virtual objects. Furthermore, the real and virtual objects may need to be perfectly aligned in some use cases, which places strong burdens on both tracking and computer vision systems.

Several possibilities exist for visual displays. A fixed screen should show images that are enhanced through 3D glasses. A digital projector could augment the environment by shining light onto objects, giving them new colors and textures, or by placing text into the real world. A handheld screen, which is part of a smartphone or tablet, could be used as a window into the basis of the popular Nintendo Pokemon Go basis of the Nintendo Pokemon Go game; see Figure 1.21. The cases more relevant for this book involve mounting the display on the head. In this case, two main

Figure 1.20 The Microsoft Hololens, first generation, uses advanced see-through display technology to superimpose graphical images onto the ordinary physical world, as perceived by looking through the glasses.

approaches exist. In a *see-through display*, the users see most of the real world by simply looking through a transparent material, while the virtual objects appear on the display to disrupt part of the view. Headsets with advanced see-through display technology include Google Glass, Microsoft Hololens, and Magic Leap. Achieving high resolution, wide field of view, and the ability to block out incoming light remain significant challenges for affordable consumer-grade devices; however, it may well be solved within a few years. An alternative is a *pass-through display*, which sends images from an outward-facing camera to a standard screen inside the headset. Pass-through displays overcome current see-through display problems, but sometimes suffer from latency, optical distortion, color distortion, and limited dynamic range.

New Human Experiences

Finally, the point of VR might be to simply provide a new human experience. Through telepresence, people can try experiences through the eyes of robots or other people. However, we can go further by giving people experiences that are impossible (or perhaps deadly) in the real world. Most often, artists are the ones leading this effort. The Birdly experience of human flying (Figure 1.1) was an excellent example. Figure 1.22 shows two more. What if we change our scale? Imagine being 2 mm tall and looking ants right in the face. Compare that to being 50 m tall and towering over a city while people scream and run from you. What if we simulate the effect of drugs in your system? What if you could become your favorite animal? What if you became a piece of food? The creative possibilities for artists seem to be endless. We are limited only by what our bodies can comfortably handle. Exciting adventures lie ahead!

Figure 1.21 Nintendo Pokemon Go is a geolocation-based game from 2016 that allows users to imagine a virtual world that is superimposed on the real world. They can see Pokemon characters only by looking "through" their smartphone screen.

(a)   (b)

Figure 1.22 (a) In 2014, Epic Games created a wild roller-coaster ride through a virtual living room. (b) A guillotine simulator was made in 2013 by Andre Berlemont, Morten Brunbjerg, and Erkki Trummal. Participants were hit on the neck by friends as the blade dropped, and they could see the proper perspective as their heads rolled.

1.3 History Repeats

Staring at Rectangles

How did we arrive at VR as it exists today? We start with a history that predates what most people would consider to be VR, but includes many aspects crucial to VR that have been among us for tens of thousands of years. Long ago, our ancestors

Figure 1.23 (a) A 30,000-year-old painting from the Bhimbetka rock shelters in India (photo by Archaeological Survey of India). (b) An English painting from around 1470 that depicts John Ball encouraging Wat Tyler rebels (unknown artist). (c) A painting by Hans Vredeman de Vries in 1596. (d) *Impression, Sunrise* by Claude Monet in 1872.

were trained to look at the walls and imagine a 3D world that is part of a story. Figure 1.23 shows some examples, such as cave paintings, such as the one in Figure 1.23(a) from 30,000 years ago. Figure 1.23(b) shows a painting from the European Middle Ages. Similar to the cave painting, it relates to military conflict, a fascination of humans regardless of the era or technology. There is much greater detail in the newer painting, leaving less to the imagination; however, the drawing perspective is comically wrong. Some people seem short relative to others, rather than being further away. The rear portion of the fence looks incorrect. Figure 1.23(c) shows a later painting in which the perspective has been meticulously accounted for, leading to a beautiful palace view that requires no imagination for us to perceive it as "3D." By the nineteenth century, many artists had grown tired of such realism and started the controversial *impressionist* movement, an example of which is shown in Figure 1.23(d). Such paintings leave more to the imagination of the viewer, much like the earlier cave paintings.

Moving Pictures

Once humans were content with staring at rectangles on the wall, the next step was to put them into motion. The phenomenon of *stroboscopic apparent motion* is the

Figure 1.24 This 1878 *Horse in Motion* motion picture by Eadweard Muybridge was created by evenly spacing 24 cameras along a track and triggering them by trip wire as the horse passed. The animation was played on a zoopraxiscope, which was a precursor to the movie projector but was mechanically similar to a record player.

basis for what we call *movies* or *motion pictures* today. Flipping quickly through a sequence of pictures gives the illusion of motion, even at a rate as low as two pictures per second. Above ten pictures per second, the motion even appears to be continuous, rather a series of individual pictures. One of the earliest examples of this effect is the race horse movie created by Eadweard Muybridge in 1878 at the request of Leland Stanford (yes, that one!); see Figure 1.24.

Motion picture technology quickly improved, and by 1896, a room full of spectators in a movie theater screamed in terror as a short film of a train pulling into a station convinced them that the train was about to crash into them (Figure 1.25(a)). There was no audio track. Such a reaction seems ridiculous for anyone who has been to a modern movie theater. As audience expectations increased, so did the degree of realism produced by special effects. In 1902, viewers were inspired by *A Trip to the Moon* (Figure 1.25(b)), but many years later, an extremely high degree of realism seemed necessary to keep viewers believing (Figure 1.25(c) and 1.25(d)).

At the same time, motion picture audiences have been willing to accept lower degrees of realism. One motivation, as for paintings, is to leave more to the imagination. The popularity of *animation* (also called *anime* or *cartoons*) is a prime example (Figure 1.26). Even within the realm of animations, a similar trend has emerged as

Figure 1.25 A progression of special effects. (a) *Arrival of a Train at La Ciotat Station*, 1896. (b) *A Trip to the Moon*, 1902. (c) The movie *2001*, from 1968. (d) *Gravity*, 2013.

with motion pictures in general. Starting from simple line drawings in 1908 with Fantasmagorie (Figure 1.26(a)), greater detail appears in 1928 with the introduction of Mickey Mouse (Figure 1.26(b)). By 2003, animated films achieved a much higher degree of realism (Figure 1.26(c)); however, excessively simple animations have also enjoyed widespread popularity (Figure 1.26(d)).

Toward Convenience and Portability
Further motivations for accepting lower levels of realism are cost and portability. As shown in Figure 1.27, families were once willing to gather in front of a television to watch free broadcasts in their homes, even though they could go to theaters and watch high-resolution, color, panoramic, and 3D movies at the time. Such tiny, blurry, black-and-white television sets seem comically intolerable with respect to our current expectations. The next level of portability is to carry the system around with you. Thus, the progression is from (1) having to go somewhere to watch it, to (2) being able to watch it in your home, to (3) being able to carry it anywhere. Whether pictures, movies, phones, computers, or video games, the same progression continues. We can therefore expect the same for VR systems. At the same time, note that the gap is closing between these levels: the quality we expect from a portable device is closer than ever before to the version that requires going somewhere to experience it.

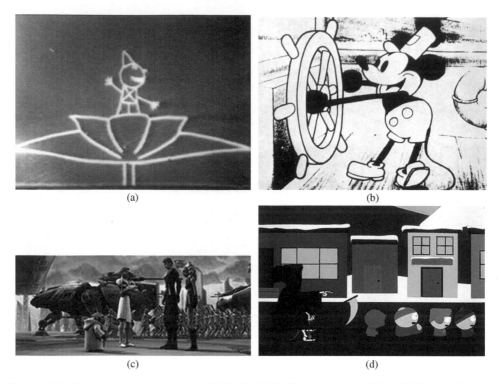

(a)

(b)

(c)

(d)

Figure 1.26 A progression of cartoons. (a) Emile Cohl, *Fantasmagorie*, 1908. (b) Mickey Mouse in *Steamboat Willie*, 1928. (c) *Star Wars: The Clone Wars*, 2008. (d) *South Park*, 1997.

Video Games

Motion pictures yield a passive, third-person experience, in contrast to video games, which are closer to a first-person experience by allowing us to interact with them. Recall from Section 1.1 the differences between open-loop and closed-loop VR. Video games are an important step toward closed-loop VR, whereas motion pictures are open-loop. As shown in Figure 1.28, we see the same trend from simplicity to improved realism and then back to simplicity. The earliest games, such as Pong and Donkey Kong, left much to the imagination. *First-person shooter (FPS)* games such as Doom gave the player a first-person perspective and launched a major campaign over the following decade toward higher-quality graphics and realism. Assassin's Creed shows a typical scene from a more realistic video game. At the same time, wildly popular games have emerged by focusing on simplicity. Angry Birds looks reminiscent of games from the 1980s, and Minecraft allows users to create and inhabit worlds composed of coarse blocks. Note that reduced realism often leads to simpler engineering requirements; in 2015, an advanced FPS game might require a powerful PC and graphics card, whereas simpler games would run on a basic smartphone. Repeated lesson: don't assume that more realistic is better!

Beyond Staring at a Rectangle

The concepts so far are still closely centered on staring at a rectangle that is fixed on a wall. Two important steps come next: (1) Presenting a separate picture to each eye

Figure 1.27 Although movie theaters with large screens were available, families were also content to gather around television sets that produced a viewing quality that would be unbearable by current standards, as shown in this photo from 1958.

to induce a 3D effect. (2) Increasing the field of view so that the user is not distracted by the display boundary. One way our brains infer the distance of objects from our eyes is by *stereopsis*. Information is gained by observing and matching features in the world that are visible to both the left and right eyes. The differences between their images on the retina yield cues about distances; keep in mind that there are many more such cues, which are explained in Section 6.1. The first experiment that showed the 3D effect of stereopsis was performed in 1838 by Charles Wheatstone in a system called the *stereoscope* (Figure 1.29(a)). By the 1930s, a portable version became a successful commercial product known to this day as the View-Master (Figure 1.29(b)). Pursuing this idea further led to Sensorama, which added motion pictures, sound, vibration, and even smells to the experience (Figure 1.29(c)). An unfortunate limitation of these designs is requiring that the viewpoint is fixed with respect to the picture. If the device is too large, then the user's head also becomes fixed in the world. An alternative has been available in movie theaters since the 1950s. Stereopsis was achieved when participants wore special glasses that select a different image for each eye using polarized light filters. This popularized *3D movies*, which are viewed the same way in the theaters today.

Another way to increase the sense of immersion and depth is to increase the field of view. The Cinerama system from the 1950s offered a curved, wide field of view that is similar to the curved, large LED (Light-Emitting Diode) displays offered today (Figure 1.29(d)). Along these lines, we could place screens all around

INTRODUCTION

Figure 1.28 A progression of video games. (a) Atari's Pong, 1972. (b) Namco's Pac-Man, 1980. (c) id Software's Doom, 1993. (d) Ubisoft's Assassin's Creed Unity, 2014. (e) Rovio Entertainment's Angry Birds, 2009. (f) Markus "Notch" Persson's Minecraft, 2011.

us. This idea led to one important family of VR systems called the *CAVE*, which was introduced in 1992 at the University of Illinois [49] (Figure 1.30(a)). The user enters a room in which video is projected onto several walls. The CAVE system also offers stereoscopic viewing by presenting different images to each eye using polarized light and special glasses. Often, head tracking is additionally performed to allow viewpoint-dependent video to appear on the walls.

VR Headsets
Once again, the trend toward portability appears. An important step for VR was taken in 1968 with the introduction of Ivan Sutherland's *head-mounted display*, which

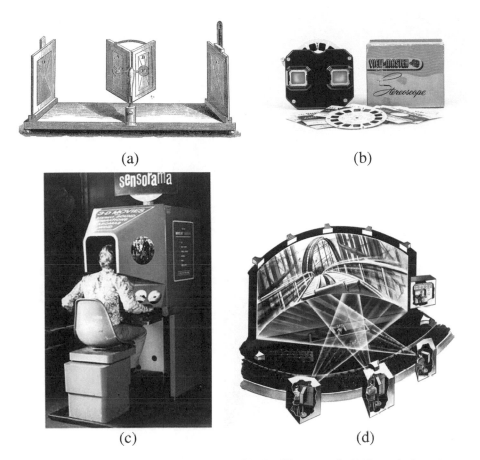

(a)

(b)

(c)

(d)

Figure 1.29 (a) The first stereoscope, developed by Charles Wheatstone in 1838, used mirrors to present a different image to each eye; the mirrors were replaced by lenses soon afterward. (b) The View-Master is a mass-produced stereoscope that has been available since the 1930s. (c) In 1957, Morton Heilig's Sensorama added motion pictures, sound, vibration, and even smells to the experience. (d) In competition to stereoscopic viewing, Cinerama offered a larger field of view. Larger movie screens caused the popularity of 3D movies to wane in the 1950s.

leveraged the power of modern displays and computers (Figure 1.30(b)) [321, 322]. He constructed what is widely considered to be the first VR headset. As the user turns his head, the images presented on the screen are adjusted to compensate so that the virtual objects appear to be fixed in space. This yielded the first glimpse of an important concept in this book: the *perception of stationarity*. To make an object appear to be stationary while you move your sense organ, the device producing the stimulus must change its output to compensate for the motion. This requires sensors and tracking systems to become part of the VR system. Commercial VR headsets started appearing in the 1980s with Jaron Lanier's company VPL, thereby popularizing the image of *goggles and gloves*; see Figure 1.30(c). In the 1990s, VR-based video games appeared in arcades (Figure 1.30(d)) and in home units (Figure 1.30(e). The experiences were not compelling or comfortable enough to attract mass interest. However, the current generation of VR headsets leverages the widespread availability of high-resolution screens and sensors, due to the smartphone industry, to offer

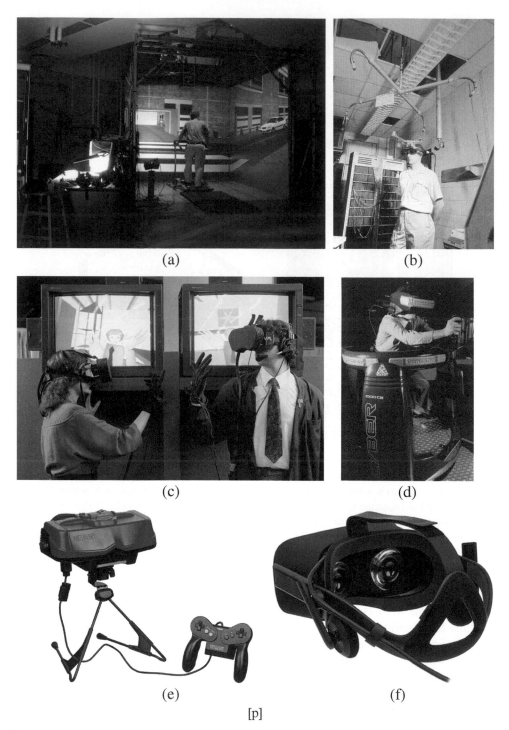

Figure 1.30 (a) CAVE virtual environment, Illinois Simulator Laboratory, Beckman Institute, University of Illinois at Urbana-Champaign, 1992 (photo by Hank Kaczmarski). (b) Sutherland's head-mounted display, Harvard University, 1968. (c) VPL Eyephones, 1980s. (d) Virtuality gaming, 1990s. (e) Nintendo Virtual Boy, 1995. (f) Oculus Rift, 2016.

Figure 1.31 Second Life was introduced in 2003 as a way for people to socialize through avatars and essentially build a virtual world to live in. Shown here is the author giving a keynote address at the 2014 Opensimulator Community Conference. The developers build open source software tools for constructing and hosting such communities of avatars with real people behind them.

lightweight, low-cost, high-field-of-view headsets, such as the Oculus Rift (Figure 1.30(f)). This has greatly improved the quality of VR experiences while significantly lowering the barrier of entry for developers and hobbyists. This also caused a flood of interest in VR technology and applications.

Bringing People Together

We have so far neglected an important aspect, which is human-to-human or social interaction. We use formats such as a live theater performance, a classroom, or a lecture hall for a few people to communicate with or entertain a large audience. We write and read novels to tell stories to each other. Prior to writing, skilled storytellers would propagate experiences to others, including future generations. We have communicated for centuries by writing letters to each other. More recent technologies have allowed us to interact directly without delay. The audio part has been transmitted through telephones for over a century, and now the video part is transmitted as well through videoconferencing over the Internet. At the same time, simple text messaging has become a valuable part of our interaction, providing yet another example of a preference for decreased realism. Communities of online users who interact through text messages over the Internet have been growing since the 1970s. In the context of games, early Multi-User Dungeons (MUDs) grew into Massively Multiplayer Online Games (MMORPGs) that we have today. In the context of education, the PLATO system from the University of Illinois was the first computer-assisted instruction system, which included message boards, instant messaging, screen sharing, chat rooms, and emoticons. This was a precursor to many community-based, online learning systems, such as the Khan Academy and Coursera. The largest amount of online social interaction today occurs through Facebook or similar apps, which involve direct communication through text along with the sharing of pictures, videos, and links.

Returning to VR, we can create *avatar* representations of ourselves and "live" together in virtual environments, as is the case with Second Life and Opensimulator 1.31. Without being limited to staring at rectangles, what kinds of societies will emerge with VR? Popular science fiction novels have painted a thrilling, yet dystopian future of a world where everyone prefers to interact through VR [47, 96, 314]. It remains to be seen what the future will bring.

As the technologies evolve over the years, keep in mind the power of simplicity when making a VR experience. In some cases, maximum realism may be important; however, leaving much to the imagination of the users is also valuable. Although the technology changes, one important invariant is that humans are still designed the same way. Understanding how our senses, brains, and bodies work is crucial to understanding the fundamentals of VR systems.

Further Reading

Each chapter of this book concludes with pointers to additional, related literature that might not have been mentioned in the preceding text. Numerous books have been written on VR. A couple of key textbooks that precede the most recent VR push are *Understanding Virtual Reality* by W. R. Sherman and A. B. Craig, 2002 [294] and *3D User Interfaces* by D. A. Bowman et al., 2005 [31]. Books based on more recent technology include [137, 186]. For a survey of the concept of reality, see [357]. For coverage of *augmented reality* that is beyond the scope of this book, see [286].

A vast amount of research literature has been written on VR. Unfortunately, there is a considerable recognition gap in the sense that current industry approaches to consumer VR appear to have forgotten the longer history of VR research. Many of the issues being raised today and methods being introduced in industry were well addressed decades earlier, albeit with older technological components. Much of the earlier work remains relevant today and is therefore worth studying carefully. An excellent starting place is the *Handbook on Virtual Environments*, 2015 [109], which contains dozens of survey articles and thousands of references to research articles. More recent works can be found in venues that publish papers related to VR. Browsing through recent publications in these venues may be useful: IEEE Virtual Reality (IEEE VR), IEEE International Conference on Mixed and Augmented Reality (ISMAR), ACM SIGGRAPH Conference, ACM Symposium on Applied Perception, ACM SIGCHI Conference, IEEE Symposium of 3D User Interfaces, *Journal of Vision, Presence: Teleoperators and Virtual Environments*.

CHAPTER TWO

Bird's-Eye View

This chapter presents an overview of VR systems from hardware (Section 2.1) to software (Section 2.2) to human perception (Section 2.3). The purpose is to quickly provide a sweeping perspective so that the detailed subjects in the remaining chapters will be understood within the larger context. Further perspective can be gained by quickly jumping ahead to Section 12.2, which provides recommendations to VR developers. The fundamental concepts from the chapters leading up to that will provide the engineering and scientific background to understand why the recommendations are made. Furthermore, readers of this book should be able to develop new techniques and derive their own recommendations to others so that the VR systems and experiences are effective and comfortable.

2.1 Hardware

The first step to understanding how VR works is to consider what constitutes the entire *VR system*. It is tempting to think of it as being merely the hardware components, such as computers, headsets, and controllers. This would be woefully incomplete. As shown in Figure 2.1, it is equally important to account for the organism, which in this chapter will exclusively refer to a human *user*. The hardware produces stimuli that override the senses of the user. In the head-mounted display from Section 1.3 (Figure 1.30(b)), recall that tracking was needed to adjust the stimulus based on human motions. The VR hardware accomplishes this by using its own sensors, thereby *tracking* motions of the user. Head tracking is the most important, but tracking also may include button presses, controller movements, eye movements, or the movements of any other body parts. Finally, it is also important to consider the surrounding physical world as part of the VR system. In spite of stimulation provided by the VR hardware, the user will always have other senses that respond to stimuli from the real world. She also has the ability to alter her environment through body motions. The VR hardware might also track objects other than the user, especially if interaction with them is part of the VR experience. Through a robotic interface, the VR hardware might also change the real world. One example is teleoperation of a robot through a VR interface.

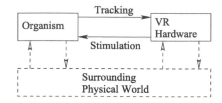

Figure 2.1 A third-person perspective of a VR system. It is wrong to assume that the engineered hardware and software are the complete VR system: the organism and its interaction with the hardware are equally important. Furthermore, interactions with the surrounding physical world continue to occur during a VR experience.

Sensors and Sense Organs

How is information extracted from the physical world? Clearly this is crucial to a VR system. In engineering, a *transducer* refers to a device that converts energy from one form to another. A *sensor* is a special transducer that converts the energy it receives into a signal for an electrical circuit. This may be an analog or digital signal, depending on the circuit type. A sensor typically has a *receptor* that collects the energy for conversion. Organisms work in a similar way. The "sensor" is called a *sense organ*, with common examples being eyes and ears. Because our "circuits" are formed from interconnected neurons, the sense organs convert energy into *neural impulses*. As you progress through this book, keep in mind the similarities between engineered sensors and natural sense organs. They are measuring the same things and sometimes even function in a similar manner. This should not be surprising because we and our engineered devices share the same physical world: the laws of physics and chemistry remain the same.

Configuration Space of Sense Organs

As the user moves through the physical world, her sense organs move along with her. Furthermore, some sense organs move relative to the body skeleton, such as our eyes rotating within their sockets. Each sense organ has a *configuration space*, which corresponds to all possible ways it can be transformed or configured. The most important aspect of this is the number of *degrees of freedom* or *DOFs* of the sense organ. Chapter 3 will cover this thoroughly, but for now note that a rigid object that moves through ordinary space has six DOFs. Three DOFs correspond to its changing position in space: (1) side-to-side motion, (2) up-down motion, and (3) closer–further motion. The other three DOFs correspond to possible ways the object could be rotated; in other words, exactly three independent parameters are needed to specify how the object is oriented. These are called yaw, pitch, and roll, and are covered in Section 3.2.

As an example, consider your left ear. As you rotate your head or move your body through space, the position of the ear changes, as well as its orientation. This yields six DOFs. The same is true for your right eye, but it is also capable of rotating independently of the head. Keep in mind that our bodies have many more degrees of freedom, which affect the configuration of our sense organs. A tracking system may be necessary to determine the position and orientation of each sense organ that receives artificial stimuli, which will be explained shortly.

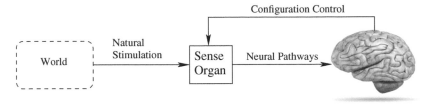

Figure 2.2 Under normal conditions, the brain (and body parts) control the configuration of sense organs (eyes, ears, fingertips) as they receive natural stimulation from the surrounding physical world.

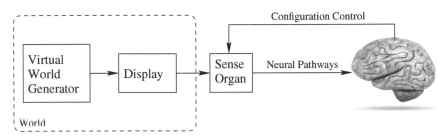

Figure 2.3 In comparison to Figure 2.2, a VR system stimulates each sense by replacing the natural stimulation with artificial stimulation that is provided by hardware called a display. Using a computer, a virtual world generator maintains a coherent virtual world. Appropriate "views" of this virtual world are rendered to the display.

An Abstract View

Figure 2.2 illustrates the normal operation of one of our sense organs without interference from VR hardware. The brain controls its configuration, while the sense organ converts natural stimulation from the environment into neural impulses that are sent to the brain. Figure 2.3 shows how it appears in a VR system. The VR hardware contains several components that will be discussed shortly. A *Virtual World Generator (VWG)* runs on a computer and produces "another world," which could be many possibilities, such as a pure simulation of a synthetic world, a recording of the real world, or a live connection to another part of the real world. The human perceives the virtual world through each targeted sense organ using a *display*, which emits energy that is specifically designed to mimic the type of stimulus that would appear without VR. The process of converting information from the VWG into output for the display is called *rendering*. In the case of human eyes, the display might be a smartphone screen or the screen of a video projector. In the case of ears, the display is referred to as a *speaker*. (A display need not be visual, even though this is the common usage in everyday life.) If the VR system is effective, then the brain is hopefully "fooled" in the sense shown in Figure 2.4. The user should believe that the stimulation of the senses is natural and comes from a plausible world, being consistent with at least some past experiences.

Aural: World-Fixed versus User-Fixed

Recall from Section 1.3 the trend of having to go somewhere for an experience, to having it in the home, and then finally to having it be completely portable. To understand these choices for VR systems and their implications on technology, it will be helpful to compare a simpler case: audio or *aural* systems.

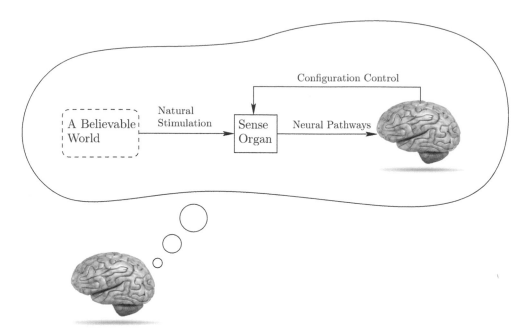

Figure 2.4 If done well, the brain is "fooled" into believing that the virtual world is in fact the surrounding physical world and natural stimulation is resulting from it.

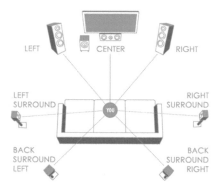

Figure 2.5 In a surround-sound system, the aural displays (speakers) are world-fixed while the user listens from the center.

Figure 2.5 shows the speaker setup and listener location for a Dolby 7.1 Surround Sound theater system, which could be installed at a theater or a home family room. Seven speakers distributed around the room periphery generate most of the sound, while a subwoofer (the "1" of the "7.1") delivers the lowest frequency components. The aural displays are therefore *world-fixed*. Compare this to a listener wearing headphones, as shown in Figure 2.6. In this case, the aural displays are *user-fixed*. Hopefully, you have already experienced settings similar to these many times.

What are the key differences? In addition to the obvious portability of head-phones, the following quickly come to mind:

- In the surround-sound system, the generated sound (or stimulus) is far away from the ears, whereas it is quite close for the headphones.

- One implication of the difference in distance is that much less power is needed for the headphones to generate an equivalent perceived loudness level compared with distant speakers.
- Another implication based on distance is the degree of privacy allowed by the wearer of headphones. A surround-sound system at high volume levels could generate a visit by angry neighbors.
- Wearing electronics on your head could be uncomfortable over long periods of time, causing a preference for surround sound over headphones.
- Several people can enjoy the same experience in a surround-sound system (although they cannot all sit in the optimal location). Using headphones, they would need to split the audio source across their individual headphones simultaneously.
- They are likely to have different costs, depending on the manufacturing difficulty and available component technology. At present, headphones are favored by costing much less than a set of surround-sound speakers (although one can spend a large amount of money on either).

All of these differences carry over to VR systems. This should not be too surprising because we could easily consider a pure audio experience to be a special kind of VR experience based on our definition from Section 1.1.

While listening to music, close your eyes and imagine you are at a live performance with the artists surrounding you. Where do you perceive the artists and their instruments to be located? Are they surrounding you, or do they seem to be in the middle of your head? Using headphones, it is most likely that they seem to be inside your head. In a surround-sound system, if recorded and displayed properly, the sounds should seem to be coming from their original locations well outside of your head. They probably seem constrained, however, into the horizontal plane that you are sitting in.

This shortcoming of headphones is not widely recognized, but nevertheless represents a problem that becomes much larger for VR systems that include visual displays. If you want to have accurate perception of where sounds are coming from, then headphones would need to take into account the configurations of your ears in space to adjust the output accordingly. For example, if you nod your head back and forth in a "no" gesture, then the sound being presented to each ear needs to be adjusted so that the simulated sound source is rotated in the opposite direction. In the surround-sound system, the speaker does not follow your head and therefore does not need to rotate. If the speaker rotates with your head, then a counterrotation is needed to "undo" your head rotation so that the sound source location is perceived to be stationary.

Visual: World-Fixed versus User-Fixed

Now consider adding a visual display. You might not worry much about the perceived location of artists and instruments while listening to music, but you will quickly notice if their locations do not appear correct to your eyes. Our vision sense is much more powerful and complex than our sense of hearing. Figure 2.7(a) shows a CAVE system, which parallels the surround-sound system in many ways. The user again sits in the center while displays around the periphery present visual stimuli

Figure 2.6 Using headphones, the displays are user-fixed, unlike the case of a surround-sound system.

(a)   (b)

Figure 2.7 (a) A CAVE VR system developed at Teesside University, UK. (b) A 90-year-old woman (Rachel Mahassel) wearing the Oculus Rift DK1 headset in 2013.

to his eyes. The speakers are replaced by video screens. Figure 2.7(b) shows a user wearing a VR headset, which parallels the headphones.

Suppose the screen in front of the user's eyes shows a fixed image in the headset. If the user rotates his head, then the image will be perceived as being attached to the head. This would occur, for example, if you rotate your head while using the Viewmaster (recall Figure 1.29(b)). If you would like to instead perceive the image as part of a fixed world around you, then the image inside the headset must change to compensate as you rotate your head. The surrounding virtual world should be counterrotated, the meaning of which will be made more precise in Section 3.4. Once we agree that such transformations are necessary, it becomes a significant engineering challenge to estimate the amount of head and eye movement that has occurred and apply the appropriate transformation in a timely and accurate manner. If this is not handled well, then users could have poor or unconvincing experiences. Worse yet, they could fall prey to VR sickness. This is one of the main reasons why the popularity of VR headsets waned in the 1990s. The component technology was not good enough yet. Fortunately, the situation is much improved at present. For audio, few seemed to bother with this transformation, but for the visual counterpart, it is absolutely critical. One final note is that tracking and applying transformations also becomes necessary in CAVE systems if we want the images on the screens to be altered according to changes in the eye *positions* inside of the room.

Now that you have a high-level understanding of the common hardware arrangements, we will take a closer look at hardware components that are widely available for constructing VR systems. These are expected to change quickly, with costs decreasing and performance improving. We also expect many new devices to appear in the marketplace in the coming years. In spite of this, the fundamentals in this book remain unchanged. Knowledge of the current technology provides concrete examples to make the fundamental VR concepts clearer.

The hardware components of VR systems are conveniently classified as follows:

- **Displays (output):** Devices that each stimulate a sense organ.
- **Sensors (input):** Devices that extract information from the real world.
- **Computers:** Devices that process inputs and outputs sequentially.

Displays

A display generates stimuli for a targeted sense organ. Vision is our dominant sense, and any display constructed for the eye must cause the desired image to be formed on the retina. Because of this importance, Chapters 4 and 5 will explain displays and their connection to the human vision system. For CAVE systems, some combination of digital projectors and mirrors is used. Due to the plummeting costs, an array of large-panel displays may alternatively be employed. For headsets, a smartphone display can be placed close to the eyes and brought into focus using one magnifying lens for each eye. Screen manufacturers have produced custom displays for VR headsets by leveraging the latest LED and LCD display technology from the smartphone industry. Some are targeting one display per eye with frame rates above 90 Hz and over two megapixels per eye. Reasons for this are explained in Chapter 5.

Now imagine displays for other sense organs. Sound is displayed to the ears using classic speaker technology. Bone conduction methods may also be used, which vibrate the skull and propagate the waves to the inner ear; this method appeared with Google Glass. Chapter 11 covers the auditory part of VR in detail. For the sense of touch, there are *haptic displays*. Two examples are pictured in Figure 2.8. Haptic feedback can be given in the form of vibration, pressure, or temperature. More details on displays for touch, and even taste and smell, appear in Chapter 13.

Sensors

Consider the input side of the VR hardware. A brief overview is given here, until Chapter 9 covers sensors and tracking systems in detail. For visual and auditory body-mounted displays, the position and orientation of the sense organ must be tracked by sensors to appropriately adapt the stimulus. The orientation part is usually accomplished by an *inertial measurement unit* or *IMU*. The main component is a *gyroscope*, which measures its own rate of rotation; the rate is referred to as *angular velocity* and has three components. Measurements from the gyroscope are integrated over time to obtain an estimate of the cumulative change in orientation.

(a)   (b)

Figure 2.8 Two examples of haptic feedback devices. (a) The Touch X system by 3D Systems allows the user to feel strong resistance when poking into a virtual object with a real stylus. A robot arm provides the appropriate forces. (b) Some game controllers occasionally vibrate.

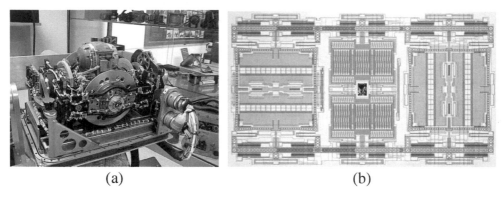

(a)   (b)

Figure 2.9 Inertial measurement units (IMUs) have gone from large, heavy mechanical systems to cheap, microscopic MEMS circuits. (a) The LN-3 Inertial Navigation System, developed in the 1960s by Litton Industries. (b) The internal structures of a MEMS gyroscope, for which the total width is less than 1 mm.

The resulting error, called *drift error*, would gradually grow unless other sensors are used. To reduce drift error, IMUs also contain an *accelerometer* and possibly a *magnetometer*. Over the years, IMUs have gone from existing only as large mechanical systems in aircraft and missiles to being tiny devices inside smartphones; see Figure 2.9. Due to their small size, weight, and cost, IMUs can be easily embedded in wearable devices. They are one of the most important enabling technologies for the current generation of VR headsets and are mainly used for tracking the user's head orientation.

Digital cameras provide another critical source of information for tracking systems. Like IMUs, they have become increasingly cheap and portable due to the smartphone industry, while at the same time improving in image quality. Cameras enable tracking approaches that exploit line-of-sight *visibility*. The idea is to identify features or markers in the image that serve as reference points for a moving object or a stationary background. Such *visibility constraints* severely limit the possible object positions and orientations. Standard cameras passively form an image by focusing the light through an optical system, much like the human eye. Once the camera calibration parameters are known, an observed marker is known to lie along a ray in

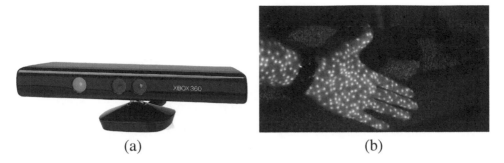

(a)   (b)

Figure 2.10 (a) The Microsoft Kinect sensor gathers both an ordinary RGB image and a depth map (the distance away from the sensor for each pixel). (b) The depth is determined by observing the locations of projected IR dots in an image obtained from an IR camera.

space. Cameras are commonly used to track eyes, heads, hands, entire human bodies, and any other objects in the physical world. One of the main challenges at present is to obtain reliable and accurate performance without placing special markers on the user or objects around the scene.

As opposed to standard cameras, *depth cameras* work actively by projecting light into the scene and then observing its reflection in the image. This is typically done in the infrared (IR) spectrum so that humans do not notice; see Figure 2.10.

In addition to these sensors, we rely heavily on good-old mechanical switches and potientiometers to create keyboards and game controllers. An optical mouse is also commonly used. One advantage of these familiar devices is that users can rapidly input data or control their characters by leveraging their existing training. A disadvantage is that they might be hard to find or interact with if their faces are covered by a headset.

Computers

A computer executes the virtual world generator (VWG). Where should this computer be? Although unimportant for world-fixed displays, the location is crucial for body-fixed displays. If a separate PC is needed to power the system, then fast, reliable communication must be provided between the headset and the PC. This connection is sometimes made by wires, leading to an awkward tether; however, wireless speeds are improving rapidly. As you have noticed, most of the needed sensors exist on a smartphone, as well as a moderately powerful computer. Therefore, a smartphone can be dropped into a case with lenses to provide a VR experience with little added cost (Figure 2.11). The limitation, though, is that the VWG must be simpler than in the case of a separate PC so that it runs on less-powerful computing hardware. There are also wireless, all-in-one headsets which contain all of the essential parts of smartphones for delivering VR experiences. These eliminate unnecessary components of smartphones (such as the additional case), and instead have customized optics, microchips, and sensors for VR.

In addition to the main computing systems, specialized computing hardware may be utilized. Graphical processing units (GPUs) have been optimized for quickly rendering graphics to a screen and they are currently being adapted to handle the specific performance demands of VR. Also, a display interface chip converts an

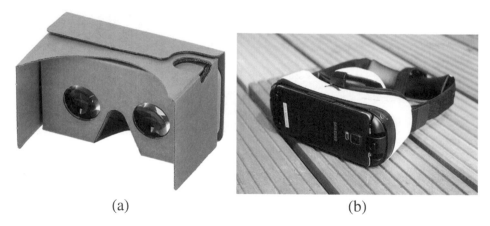

(a)   (b)

Figure 2.11 Two headsets that create a VR experience by dropping a smartphone into a case. (a) Google Cardboard works with a wide variety of smartphones. (b) Samsung Gear VR is optimized for one particular smartphone (in this case, the Samsung S6).

Figure 2.12 Disassembly of the Oculus Rift DK2 headset

input video into display commands. Finally, microcontrollers are frequently used to gather information from sensing devices and send them to the main computer using standard protocols, such as USB.

To conclude with hardware, Figure 2.12 shows the hardware components for the Oculus Rift DK2, from 2014. In the lower left corner, you can see a smartphone screen that serves as the display. Above that is a circuit board that contains the IMU, display interface chip, a USB driver chip, a set of chips for driving LEDs on the headset for tracking, and a programmable microcontroller. The lenses, shown in the lower right, are placed so that the smartphone screen appears to be "infinitely far" away but nevertheless fills most of the field of view of the user. The upper right shows flexible circuits that deliver power to IR LEDs embedded in the headset. (They are hidden behind IR-transparent plastic.) A camera is used for tracking, and its parts are shown in the center.

2.2 Software

From a developer's standpoint, it would be ideal to program the VR system by providing high-level descriptions and having the software determine automatically all of the low-level details. In a perfect world, there would be a *VR engine*, which serves a purpose similar to the game engines available today for creating video games. If the developer follows patterns that many before her have implemented already, then many complicated details can be avoided by simply calling functions from a well-designed software library. However, if the developer wants to try something original, then she would have to design the functions from scratch. This requires a deeper understanding of the VR fundamentals, as well as familiarity with lower-level system operations.

Unfortunately, we are still a long way from having fully functional, general-purpose VR engines. As applications of VR broaden, specialized VR engines are also likely to emerge. For example, one might be targeted for immersive cinematography, while another is geared toward engineering design. Which components will become more like part of a VR "operating system" and which will become higher-level "engine" components? In many situations, developers will likely be implementing much of the functionality of their VR systems from scratch. This may involve utilizing a *software development kit (SDK)* for particular headsets that handles the lowest-level operations, such as device drivers, head tracking, and display output. Alternatively, they might find themselves using a game engine that has been adapted for VR, even though it was fundamentally designed for video games on a fixed screen. This can avoid substantial effort at first, but then may be cumbersome when someone wants to implement ideas that are not part of standard video games.

What software components are needed to produce a VR experience? Figure 2.13 presents a high-level view that highlights the central role of the Virtual World Generator (VWG). The VWG receives inputs from low-level systems that indicate what the user is doing in the real world. A head tracker provides timely estimates of the user's head position and orientation. Keyboard, mouse, and game controller events arrive in a queue that are ready to be processed. The key role of the VWG is to maintain enough of an internal "reality" so that renderers can extract the information they need to calculate outputs for their displays.

Virtual World: Real versus Synthetic

At one extreme, the virtual world could be completely synthetic. In this case, numerous triangles are defined in a 3D space, along with material properties that indicate how they interact with light, sound, forces, and so on. The field of *computer graphics* addresses computer-generated images from synthetic models, and it remains important for VR; see Chapter 7. At the other extreme, the virtual world might be a recorded physical world that was captured using modern cameras, computer vision, and Simultaneous Localization and Mapping (SLAM) techniques; see Figure 2.14.

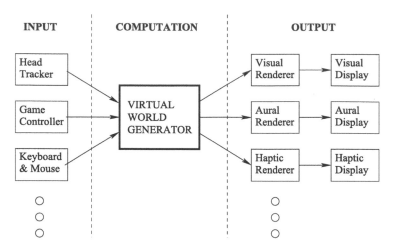

Figure 2.13 The Virtual World Generator (VWG) maintains another world, which could be synthetic, real, or some combination. From a computational perspective, the inputs are received from the user and his surroundings, and appropriate views of the world are rendered to displays.

Many possibilities exist between the extremes. For example, camera images may be taken of a real object and then mapped onto a synthetic object in the virtual world. This is called *texture mapping*, a common operation in computer graphics; see Section 7.2.

Matched Motion

The most basic operation of the VWG is to maintain a correspondence between user motions in the real world and the virtual world; see Figure 2.15. In the real world, the user's motions are confined to a safe region, which we will call the *matched zone*. Imagine the matched zone as a place where the real and virtual worlds perfectly align. One of the greatest challenges is the mismatch of obstacles: what if the user is blocked in the virtual world but not in the real world? The reverse is also possible. In a seated experience, the user sits in a chair while wearing a headset. The matched zone in this case is a small region, such as one cubic meter, in which users can move their heads. Head motions should be matched between the two worlds. If the user is not constrained to a seat, then the matched zone could be an entire room or an outdoor field. Note that safety becomes an issue because the user might spill a drink, hit walls, or fall into pits that exist only in the real world, but are not visible in the virtual world. Larger matched zones tend to lead to greater safety issues. Users must make sure that the matched zone is cleared of dangers in the real world, or the developer should make them visible in the virtual world.

Which motions from the real world should be reflected in the virtual world? This varies among VR experiences. In a VR headset that displays images to the eyes, head motions must be matched so that the visual renderer uses the correct viewpoint in the virtual world. Other parts of the body are less critical but may become important if the user needs to perform hand-eye coordination or looks at other parts of her body and expects them to move naturally.

Figure 2.14 Using both color and depth information from cameras, a 3D model of the world can be extracted automatically using Simultaneous Localization and Mapping (SLAM) techniques [130].

User Locomotion

In many VR experiences, users want to move well outside the matched zone. This motivates *locomotion*, which means moving oneself in the virtual world, while this motion is not matched in the real world. Imagine you want to explore a virtual city while remaining seated in the real world. How should this be achieved? You could pull up a map and point to where you want to go, with a quick teleportation operation sending you to the destination. A popular option is to move oneself in the virtual world by operating a game controller, mouse, or keyboard. By pressing buttons or moving knobs, your self in the virtual world could be walking, running, jumping, swimming, flying, and so on. You could also climb aboard a vehicle in the virtual world and operate its controls to move yourself. These operations are certainly convenient but often lead to sickness because of a mismatch between your balance and visual senses. See Sections 2.3, 10.2, and 12.3.

Physics

The VWG handles the *geometric* aspects of motion by applying the appropriate mathematical transformations. In addition, the VWG usually implements some *physics* so that as time progresses, the virtual world behaves like the real world. In most cases, the basic laws of mechanics should govern how objects move in the virtual world. For example, if you drop an object, then it should accelerate

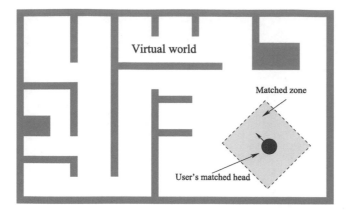

Virtual world

Matched zone

User's matched head

Real world

Figure 2.15 A matched zone is maintained between the user in their real world and his representation in the virtual world. The matched zone could be moved in the virtual world by using an interface, such as a game controller, while the user does not correspondingly move in the real world.

to the ground due to gravitational force acting on it. One important component is a *collision detection* algorithm, which determines whether two or more bodies are intersecting in the virtual world. If a new collision occurs, then an appropriate response is needed. For example, suppose the user pokes his head through a wall in the virtual world. Should the head in the virtual world be stopped, even though it continues to move in the real world? To make it more complex, what should happen if you unload a dump truck full of basketballs into a busy street in the virtual world? Simulated physics can become quite challenging, and is a discipline in itself. There is no limit to the complexity. See Section 8.3 for more about virtual-world physics.

In addition to handling the motions of moving objects, the physics must also take into account how potential stimuli for the displays are created and propagate through the virtual world. How does light propagate through the environment? How does light interact with the surfaces in the virtual world? What are the sources of light? How do sound and smells propagate? These correspond to rendering problems, which are covered in Chapters 7 and 11 for visual and audio cases, respectively.

Networked Experiences

In the case of a networked VR experience, a shared virtual world is maintained by a server. Each user has a distinct matched zone. Their matched zones might overlap in a real world, but one must then be careful so that they avoid unwanted collisions. Most often, these zones are disjoint and distributed around the Earth. Within the virtual world, user interactions, including collisions, must be managed by the VWG. If multiple users are interacting in a social setting, then the burdens of matched motions may increase. As users meet each other, they could expect to see eye motions, facial expressions, and body language; see Section 10.4.

Developer Choices for VWGs

To summarize, a developer could start with a basic Software Development Kit (SDK) from a VR headset vendor and then build her own VWG from scratch.

The SDK should provide the basic drivers and an interface to access tracking data and make calls to the graphical rendering libraries. In this case, the developer must build the physics of the virtual world from scratch, handling problems such as avatar movement, collision detection, lighting models, and audio. This gives the developer the greatest amount of control and ability to optimize performance; however, it may come in exchange for a difficult implementation burden. In some special cases, it might not be too difficult. For example, in the case of the Google Street viewer (recall Figure 1.10), the "physics" is simple: the viewing location needs to jump between panoramic images in a comfortable way while maintaining a sense of location on the Earth. In the case of telepresence using a robot, the VWG would have to take into account movements in the physical world. Failure to handle collision detection could result in a broken robot (or human!).

At the other extreme, a developer may use a ready-made VWG that is customized to make a particular VR experience by choosing menu options and writing high-level scripts. Examples available today are OpenSimulator, Vizard by WorldViz, CryEngine by Crytek, Unity 3D, and Unreal Engine by Epic Games. The latter two are game engines that were adapted to work for VR, and are by far the most popular among current VR developers. The first one, OpenSimulator, was designed as an open-source alternative to Second Life for building a virtual society of avatars. As already stated, using such higher-level engines makes it easy for developers to make a VR experience in little time; however, the drawback is that it is harder to make highly original experiences that were not imagined by the engine builders.

2.3 Human Physiology and Perception

Our bodies were not designed for VR. By applying artificial stimulation to the senses, we are disrupting the operation of biological mechanisms that have taken hundreds of millions of years to evolve in a natural environment. We are also providing input to the brain that is not exactly consistent with all of our other life experiences. In some instances, our bodies may adapt to the new stimuli. This could cause us to become unaware of flaws in the VR system. In other cases, we might develop heightened awareness or the ability to interpret 3D scenes that were once difficult or ambiguous. Unfortunately, there are also many cases where our bodies react by increased fatigue or headaches, partly because the brain is working harder than usual to interpret the stimuli. Finally, the worst case is the onset of VR sickness, which typically involves symptoms of dizziness and nausea.

Perceptual psychology is the science of understanding how the brain converts sensory stimulation into perceived phenomena. Here are some typical questions that arise in VR and fall under this umbrella:

- How far away does some object appear to be?
- How much video resolution is needed to avoid seeing pixels?
- How many frames per second are enough to perceive motion as continuous?
- Is the user's head appearing at the proper height in the virtual world?
- Where is some virtual sound coming from?
- Why am I feeling nauseated?
- Why is one experience more tiring than another?
- What is presence?

To answer these questions and more, we must understand several things: (1) basic physiology of the human body, including sense organs and neural pathways, (2) the key theories and insights of experimental perceptual psychology, and (3) the interference of the engineered VR system with our common perceptual processes and the resulting implications or side effects.

The perceptual side of VR often attracts far too little attention among developers. In the real world, perceptual processes are mostly invisible to us. Think about how much effort it requires to recognize a family member. When you see someone you know well, the process starts automatically, finishes immediately, and seems to require no effort. Scientists have conducted experiments that reveal how much work actually occurs in this and other perceptual processes. Through brain lesion studies, they are able to see the effects when a small part of the brain is not functioning correctly. Some people suffer from *prosopagnosia*, which makes them unable to recognize the faces of familiar people, including themselves in a mirror, even though nearly everything else functions normally. Scientists are also able to perform *single-unit recordings*, mostly on animals, which reveal the firings of a single neuron in response to sensory stimuli. Imagine, for example, a single neuron that fires whenever you see a sphere.

Optical Illusions

One of the most popular ways to appreciate the complexity of our perceptual processing is to view optical illusions. These yield surprising results and are completely unobtrusive. Each one is designed to reveal some shortcoming of our visual system by providing a stimulus that is not quite consistent with ordinary stimuli in our everyday lives. Figure 2.16 shows two. These should motivate you to appreciate the amount of work that our sense organs and neural structures are doing to fill in missing details and make interpretations based on the context of our life experiences and existing biological structures. Interfering with these without understanding them is not wise!

Classification of Senses

Perception and illusions are not limited to our eyes. Figure 2.17 shows a classification of our basic senses. Recall that a sensor converts an energy source into signals in a circuit. In the case of our bodies, this means that a stimulus is converted into neural impulses. For each sense, Figure 2.17 indicates the type of energy for the stimulus and the *receptor* that converts the stimulus into neural impulses. Think of each receptor as a sensor that targets a particular kind of stimulus. This is referred to as *sensory system selectivity*. In each eye, over 100 million photoreceptors target electromagnetic energy precisely in the frequency range of visible light. Different kinds even target various colors and light levels; see Section 5.1. The auditory, touch, and balance senses involve motion, vibration, or gravitational force; these are sensed by mechanoreceptors. The physiology and perception of hearing are covered in Sections 11.2 and 11.3, respectively. The sense of touch additionally involves thermoreceptors to detect change in temperature. Touch is covered in Section 13.1. Our *balance sense* helps us to know which way our head is oriented, including sensing the direction of "up"; this is covered in Section 8.2. Finally, our sense of taste and smell is grouped

(a)   (b)

Figure 2.16 Optical illusions present an unusual stimulus that highlights limitations of our vision system. (a) The *Ponzo illusion* causes the upper line segment to appear larger than the lower one, even though they are the same length. (b) The *checker shadow illusion* causes the B tile to appear lighter than the A tile, even though they are exactly the same shade of gray.

Sense	Stimulus	Receptor	Sense Organ
Vision	Electromagnetic energy	Photoreceptors	Eye
Auditory	Air pressure waves	Mechanoreceptors	Ear
Touch	Tissue distortion	Mechanoreceptors	Skin, muscles
		Thermoreceptors	Skin
Balance	Gravity, acceleration	Mechanoreceptors	Vestibular organs
Taste/smell	Chemical composition	Chemoreceptors	Mouth, nose

Figure 2.17 A classification of the human body senses.

into one category, called the *chemical senses*, that relies on chemoreceptors; these provide signals based on chemical composition of matter appearing on our tongue or in our nasal passages; see Section 13.2.

Note that senses have engineering equivalents, most of which appear in VR systems. Imagine you are designing a humanoid telepresence robot, which you expect to interface with through a VR headset. You could then experience life through your surrogate robotic self. Digital cameras would serve as its eyes, and microphones would be the ears. Pressure sensors and thermometers could be installed to give a sense of touch. For balance, we can install an IMU. In fact, the human *vestibular organs* and modern IMUs bear a striking resemblance in terms of the signals they produce; see Section 8.2. We could even install chemical sensors, such as a pH meter, to measure aspects of chemical composition to provide taste and smell.

Big Brains

Perception happens after the sense organs convert the stimuli into neural impulses. According to the latest estimates [15], human bodies contain around 86 billion neurons. Around 20 billion are devoted to the part of the brain called the *cerebral cortex*, which handles perception and many other high-level functions such as attention, memory, language, and consciousness. It is a large sheet of neurons around three

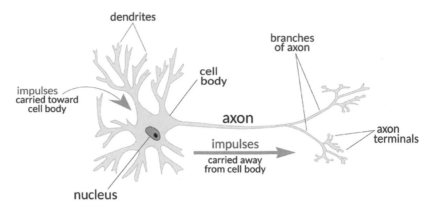

Figure 2.18 A typical neuron receives signals through dendrites, which interface to other neurons. It outputs a signal to other neurons through axons.

millimeters thick and is heavily folded so that it fits into our skulls. In case you are wondering where we lie among other animals, a roundworm, fruit fly, and rat have 302, 100 thousand, and 200 million neurons, respectively. An elephant has over 250 billion neurons, which is more than we have!

Only mammals have a cerebral cortex. The cerebral cortex of a rat has around 20 million neurons. Cats and dogs are at 300 and 160 million, respectively. A gorilla has around 4 billion. A type of dolphin called the long-finned pilot whale has an estimated 37 billion neurons in its cerebral cortex, making it roughly twice as many as in the human cerebral cortex; however, scientists claim this does not imply superior cognitive abilities [225, 278].

Another important factor in perception and overall cognitive ability is the interconnection between neurons. Imagine an enormous directed graph, with the usual nodes and directed edges. The nucleus or cell body of each neuron is a node that does some kind of "processing." Figure 2.18 shows a neuron. The *dendrites* are essentially input edges to the neuron, whereas the *axons* are output edges. Through a network of dendrites, the neuron can aggregate information from numerous other neurons, which themselves may have aggregated information from others. The result is sent to one or more neurons through the axon. For a connected axon-dendrite pair, communication occurs in a gap called the *synapse*, where electrical or chemical signals are passed along. Each neuron in the human brain has on average about 7,000 synaptic connections to other neurons, which results in about 10^{15} edges in our enormous brain graph!

Hierarchical Processing

Upon leaving the sense-organ receptors, signals propagate among the neurons to eventually reach the cerebral cortex. Along the way, *hierarchical processing* is performed; see Figure 2.19. Through selectivity, each receptor responds to a narrow range of stimuli, across time, space, frequency, and so on. After passing through several neurons, signals from numerous receptors are simultaneously taken into account. This allows increasingly complex patterns to be detected in the stimulus. In the case of vision, feature detectors appear in the early hierarchical stages,

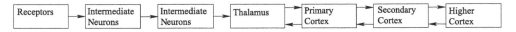

Figure 2.19 The stimulus captured by receptors works its way through a hierarchical network of neurons. In the early stages, signals are combined from multiple receptors and propagated upward. At later stages, information flows bidirectionally.

enabling us to detect features such as edges, corners, and motion. Once in the cerebral cortex, the signals from sensors are combined with anything else from our life experiences that may become relevant for making an interpretation of the stimuli. Various *perceptual phenomena* occur, such as recognizing a face or identifying a song. Information or concepts that appear in the cerebral cortex tend to represent a global picture of the world around us. Surprisingly, *topographic mapping* methods reveal that spatial relationships among receptors are maintained in some cases among the distribution of neurons. Also, recall from Section 1.1 that place cells and grid cells encode spatial maps of familiar environments.

Proprioception

In addition to information from senses and memory, we also use *proprioception*, which is the ability to sense the relative positions of parts of our bodies and the amount of muscular effort being involved in moving them. Close your eyes and move your arms around in an open area. You should have an idea of where your arms are located, although you might not be able to precisely reach out and touch your fingertips together without using your eyes. This information is so important to our brains that the *motor cortex*, which controls body motion, sends signals called *efference copies* to other parts of the brain to communicate what motions have been executed. Proprioception is effectively another kind of sense. Continuing our comparison with robots, it corresponds to having *encoders* on joints or wheels to indicate how far they have moved. One interesting implication of proprioception is that you cannot tickle yourself because you know where your fingers are moving; however, if someone else tickles you, then you do not have access to their efference copies. The lack of this information is crucial to the tickling sensation.

Fusion of Senses

Signals from multiple senses and proprioception are being processed and combined with our experiences by our neural structures throughout our lives. In ordinary life, without VR or drugs, our brains interpret these combinations of inputs in coherent, consistent, and familiar ways. Any attempt to interfere with these operations is likely to cause a mismatch among the data from our senses. The brain may react in a variety of ways. It could be the case that we are not consciously aware of the conflict, but we may become fatigued or develop a headache. Even worse, we could develop symptoms of dizziness or nausea. In other cases, the brain might react by making us so consciously aware of the conflict that we immediately understand that the experience is implausible. This would correspond to a case in which the VR experience is failing to convince people that they are present in a virtual world. To make an effective and comfortable VR experience, trials with human subjects are essential to understand how the brain reacts. It is practically impossible to predict what would

ILLUSION PRODUCED BY A RIDE IN THE SWING.

Figure 2.20 A virtual swinging experience was made by spinning the surrounding room instead of the swing. This is known as the *haunted swing illusion*. People who tried it were entertained, but they became nauseated from an extreme version of vection.

happen in an unknown scenario, unless it is almost identical to other well-studied scenarios.

One of the most important examples of bad sensory conflict in the context of VR is *vection*, which is the illusion of self motion. The conflict arises when your vision sense reports to your brain that you are accelerating, but your balance sense reports that you are motionless. As people walk down the street, their balance and vision senses are in harmony. You might have experienced vection before, even without VR. If you have ever been stuck in traffic or stopped on a train, you might have felt as if you were moving backwards while seeing a vehicle in your periphery that is moving forward. In the 1890s, Amariah Lake constructed an amusement park ride that consisted of a swing that remains at rest while the entire room surrounding the swing rocks back-and-forth (Figure 2.20). In VR, vection is caused by the loco-motion operation described in Section 2.2. For example, if you accelerate yourself forward using a controller, rather than moving forward in the real world, then you perceive acceleration with your eyes but not your vestibular organ. For strategies to alleviate this problem, see Section 10.2.

Adaptation

A universal feature of our sensory systems is *adaptation*, which means that the per-ceived effect of stimuli changes over time. This may happen with any of our senses and over a wide spectrum of time intervals. For example, the perceived loudness of motor noise in an aircraft or car decreases within minutes. In the case of vision, the optical system of our eyes and the photoreceptor sensitivities adapt to change perceived brightness. Over long periods of time, *perceptual training* can lead to adap-tation; see Section 12.1. In military training simulations, sickness experienced by soldiers appears to be less than expected, perhaps due to regular exposure [174]. Anecdotally, the same seems to be true of experienced video game players. Those who have spent many hours and days in front of large screens playing first-person shooter games apparently experience less vection when locomoting themselves in VR.

Adaptation therefore becomes a crucial factor for VR. Through repeated expo-sure, developers may become comfortable with an experience that is nauseating to a newcomer. This gives them a terrible bias while developing an experience; recall from Section 1.1 the problem of confusing the scientist with the lab subject in the VR experiment. On the other hand, through repeated, targeted training, developers may be able to improve their debugging skills by noticing flaws in the system that an "untrained eye" would easily miss. Common examples include:

- A large amount of tracking latency has appeared, which interferes with the *perception of stationarity*.
- The left- and right-eye views are swapped.
- Objects appear to one eye but not the other.
- One eye view has significantly more latency than the other.
- Straight lines are slightly curved due to uncorrected warping in the optical system.

This disconnect between the actual stimulus and one's perception of the stimulus leads to the next topic.

Psychophysics

Psychophysics is the quantitative study of perceptual phenomena that are produced by physical stimuli. For example, under what conditions would someone call an

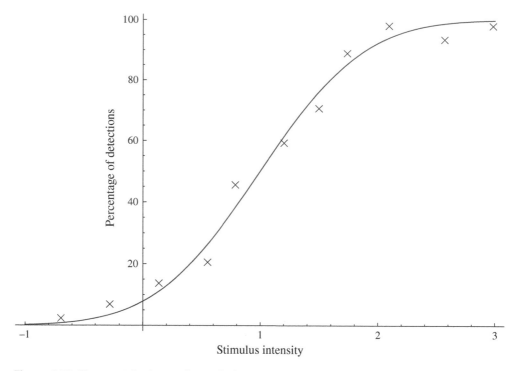

Figure 2.21 The most basic *psychometric function*. For this example, as the stimulus intensity is increased, the percentage of people detecting the phenomenon increases. The point along the curve that corresponds to 50 percent indicates a critical threshold or boundary in the stimulus intensity. The curve here corresponds to the cumulative distribution function of the error model (often assumed to be Gaussian).

object "red?" The stimulus corresponds to light entering the eye, and the perceptual phenomenon is the concept of "red" forming in the brain. Other examples of perceptual phenomena are "straight," "larger," "louder," "tickles," and "sour." Figure 2.21 shows a typical scenario in a psychophysical experiment. As one parameter is varied, such as the frequency of a light, there is usually a range of values for which subjects cannot reliably classify the phenomenon. For example, there may be a region where they are not sure whether the light is red. At one extreme, they may consistently classify it as "red" and at the other extreme, they may consistently classify it as "not red." For the region in between, the *probability of detection* is recorded, which corresponds to the frequency with which it is classified as "red." Section 12.4 will discuss how such experiments are designed and conducted.

Stevens' Power Law

One of the best known results from psychophysics is *Stevens' power law*, which characterizes the relationship between the magnitude of a physical stimulus and its *perceived* magnitude [317]. The hypothesis is that an exponential relationship occurs over a wide range of sensory systems and stimuli:

$$p = cm^x, \tag{2.1}$$

in which

- m is the magnitude or intensity of the stimulus,
- p is the perceived magnitude,
- x relates the actual magnitude to the perceived magnitude, and is the most important part of the equation, and
- c is an uninteresting constant that depends on units.

Note that for $x = 1$, (2.1) is a linear relationship, $p = cm$; see Figure 2.22. An example of this is our perception of the length of an isolated line segment directly in front of our eyes. The length we perceive is proportional to its actual length. The more interesting cases are when $x \neq 1$. For the case of perceiving the brightness of a target in the dark, $x = 0.33$, which implies that a large increase in brightness is perceived as a smaller increase. In the other direction, our perception of electric shock as current flows through the fingers yields $x = 3.5$. A little more shock is a lot more uncomfortable!

Just Noticeable Difference
Another key psychophysical concept is the *just noticeable difference* (*JND*). This is the amount that the stimulus needs to be changed so that subjects would perceive it to have changed in at least 50 percent of trials. For a large change, all or nearly all subjects would report a change. If the change is too small, then none or nearly none of the subjects would notice. The experimental challenge is to vary the amount of change until the chance of someone reporting a change is 50 percent.

Consider the JND for a stimulus with varying magnitude, such as brightness. How does the JND itself vary as the magnitude varies? This relationship is captured by *Weber's law*:

$$\frac{\Delta m}{m} = c, \tag{2.2}$$

in which Δm is the JND, m is the magnitude of the stimulus, and c is a constant.

Design of Experiments
VR disrupts the ordinary perceptual processes of its users. It should be clear from this section that proposed VR systems and experiences need to be evaluated on users to understand whether they are yielding the desired effect while also avoiding unwanted side effects. This amounts to applying the scientific method to make observations, formulate hypotheses, and design experiments that determine their validity. When human subjects are involved, this becomes extremely challenging. How many subjects are enough? What happens if they adapt to the experiment? How does their prior world experience affect the experiment? What if they are slightly sick the day that they try the experiment? What did they eat for breakfast? The answers to these questions could dramatically affect the outcome.

It gets worse. Suppose they already know your hypothesis going into the experiment. This will most likely bias their responses. Also, what will the data from the experiment look like? Will you ask them to fill out a questionnaire, or will you make inferences about their experience from measured data such as head motions, heart rate, and skin conductance? These choices are also critical. See Section 12.4 for more on this topic.

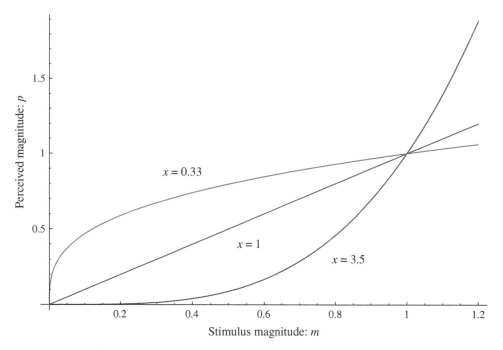

Figure 2.22 Steven's power law (2.1) captures the relationship between the magnitude of a stimulus and its perceived magnitude. The model is an exponential curve, and the exponent depends on the stimulus type.

Further Reading

The particular software and hardware technologies described in this chapter are rapidly evolving. A quick search of the Internet at any given time should reveal the latest headsets and associated tools for developers. The core concepts, however, remain largely unchanged and are covered in the coming chapters. For broader coverage of human physiology and perception, see [207] and numerous other books with "Sensation and Perception" in the title.

CHAPTER THREE

The Geometry of Virtual Worlds

Section 2.2 introduced the Virtual World Generator (VWG), which maintains the geometry and physics of the virtual world. This chapter covers the *geometry* part, which is needed to make models and move them around. The models could include the walls of a building, furniture, clouds in the sky, the user's avatar, and so on. Section 3.1 covers the basics of how to define consistent, useful models. Section 3.2 explains how to apply mathematical transforms that move them around in the virtual world. This involves two components: translation (changing position) and rotation (changing orientation). Section 3.3 presents the best ways to express and manipulate 3D rotations, which are the most complicated part of moving models. Section 3.4 then covers how the virtual world appears if we try to "look" at it from a particular perspective. This is the geometric component of visual rendering, which is covered in Chapter 7. Finally, Section 3.5 puts all of the transformations together, so that you can see how to go from defining a model to having it appear in the correct place on the display.

If you work with high-level engines to build a VR experience, then most of the concepts from this chapter might not seem necessary. You might need only to select options from menus and write simple scripts. However, an understanding of the basic transformations, such as how to express 3D rotations or move a camera viewpoint, is essential to making the software do what you want. Furthermore, if you want to build virtual worlds from scratch, or at least to *understand* what is going on under the hood of a software engine, then this chapter is critical.

3.1 Geometric Models

We first need a virtual world to contain the geometric models. For our purposes, it is enough to have a 3D Euclidean space with Cartesian coordinates. Therefore, let $\mathbb{R}^3$ denote the virtual world, in which every point is represented as a triple of real-valued coordinates: (x, y, z). The coordinate axes of our virtual world are shown in Figure 3.1. We will consistently use right-handed coordinate systems in this book because they represent the predominant choice throughout physics and engineering; however, left-handed systems appear in some places, with the most notable being Microsoft's DirectX graphical rendering library. In these cases, one of the three axes points in the opposite direction in comparison to its direction in a right-handed system. This inconsistency can lead to hours of madness when writing software;

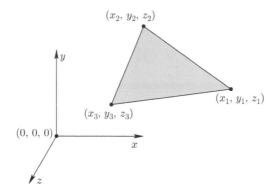

Figure 3.1 Points in the virtual world are given coordinates in a right-handed coordinate system in which the y-axis is pointing upward. The origin $(0, 0, 0)$ lies at the point where axes intersect. Also shown is a 3D triangle defined by its three vertices, each of which is a point in $\mathbb{R}^3$.

therefore, be aware of the differences and their required conversions if you mix software or models that use both. If possible, avoid mixing right-handed and left-handed systems altogether.

Geometric models are made of surfaces or solid regions in $\mathbb{R}^3$ and represent an infinite number of points. Because representations in a computer must be finite, models are defined in terms of *primitives* in which each represents an infinite set of points. The simplest and most useful primitive is a *3D triangle*, as shown in Figure 3.1. A planar surface patch that corresponds to all points "inside" and on the boundary of the triangle is fully specified by the coordinates of the triangle *vertices*:

$$((x_1, y_1, z_1), (x_2, y_2, z_2), (x_3, y_3, z_3)). \tag{3.1}$$

To model a complicated object or body in the virtual world, numerous triangles can be arranged into a *mesh*, as shown in Figure 3.2. This inspires many important questions:

1. How do we specify how each triangle "looks" whenever viewed by a user in VR?
2. How do we make the object "move?"
3. If the object surface is sharply curved, then should we use curved primitives, rather than trying to approximate the curved object with tiny triangular patches?
4. Is the interior of the object part of the model, or does the object consist only of its surface?
5. Is there an efficient algorithm for determining which triangles are adjacent to a given triangle along the surface?
6. Should we avoid duplicating vertex coordinates that are common to many neighboring triangles?

We address these questions in reverse order.

Data Structures

Consider listing all of the triangles in a file or memory array. If the triangles form a mesh, then most or all vertices will be shared among multiple triangles. This is clearly a waste of space. Another issue is that we will frequently want to perform operations

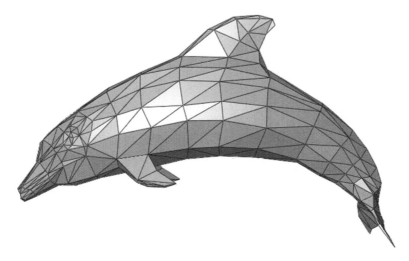

Figure 3.2 A geometric model of a dolphin, formed from a mesh of 3D triangles.

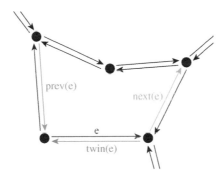

Figure 3.3 Part of a doubly connected edge list is shown here for a face that has five edges on its boundary. Each half-edge structure *e* stores pointers to the next and previous edges along the face boundary. It also stores a pointer to its twin half-edge, which is part of the boundary of the adjacent face.

on the model. For example, after moving an object, can we determine whether it is in collision with another object (covered in Section 8.3)? A typical low-level task might be to determine which triangles share a common vertex or edge with a given triangle. This might require linearly searching through the triangle list to determine whether they share a vertex or two. If there are millions of triangles, which is not uncommon, then it would cost too much to perform this operation repeatedly.

For these reasons and more, geometric models are usually encoded in clever data structures. The choice of the data structure should depend on which operations will be performed on the model. One of the most useful and common is the *doubly connected edge list*, also known as *half-edge data structure* [55, 229]. See Figure 3.3. In this and similar data structures, there are three kinds of data elements: *faces*, *edges*, and *vertices*. These represent two, one, and zero-dimensional parts, respectively, of the model. In our case, every face element represents a triangle. Each edge represents the border of one or two triangles, without duplication. Each vertex is shared between one or more triangles, again without duplication. The data structure contains pointers between adjacent faces, edges, and vertices so that algorithms can quickly traverse the model components in a way that corresponds to how they are connected together.

Inside versus Outside

Now consider the question of whether the object interior is part of the model (recall Figure 3.2). Suppose the mesh triangles fit together perfectly so that every edge borders exactly two triangles and no triangles intersect unless they are adjacent along the surface. In this case, the model forms a complete barrier between the *inside* and *outside* of the object. If we were to hypothetically fill the inside with a gas, then it could not leak to the outside. This is an example of a *coherent model*. Such models are required if the notion of inside or outside is critical to the VWG. For example, a penny could be inside of the dolphin, but not intersecting with any of its boundary triangles. Would this ever need to be detected? If we remove a single triangle, then the hypothetical gas would leak out. There would no longer be a clear distinction between the inside and outside of the object, making it difficult to answer the question about the penny and the dolphin. In the simplest case, we could have a single triangle in space. There is clearly no natural inside or outside. At an extreme, the model could be as bad as *polygon soup*, which is a jumble of triangles that do not fit together nicely and could even have intersecting interiors. In conclusion, be careful when constructing models so that the operations you want to perform later will be logically clear. If you are using a high-level design tool, such as Blender or Maya, to make your models, then coherent models will be automatically built.

Why Triangles?

Continuing upward through the preceding questions, triangles are used because they are the simplest for algorithms to handle, especially if implemented in hardware. Implementations of GPUs tend to be biased toward smaller representations so that a compact list of instructions can be applied to numerous model parts in parallel. It is certainly possible to use more complicated primitives, such as quadrilaterals, splines, and semialgebraic surfaces [89, 125, 226]. This could lead to smaller model sizes but often comes at the expense of greater computational cost for handling each primitive. For example, it is much harder to determine whether two spline surfaces are colliding than it is to do so for two 3D triangles.

Stationary versus Movable Models

There will be two kinds of models in the virtual world, which is embedded in $\mathbb{R}^3$:

- *Stationary models*, which keep the same coordinates forever. Typical examples are streets, floors, and buildings.
- *Movable models*, which can be *transformed* into various positions and orientations. Examples include vehicles, avatars, and small furniture.

Motion can be caused in a number of ways. Using a tracking system (Chapter 9), the model might move to match the user's motions. Alternatively, users might operate a controller to move objects in the virtual world, including a representation of themselves. Finally, objects might move on their own according to the laws of physics in the virtual world. Section 3.2 will cover the mathematical operations that move models to the desired places, and Chapter 8 will describe velocities, accelerations, and other physical aspects of motion.

Choosing Coordinate Axes

One often neglected point is the choice of coordinates for the models in terms of their placement and scale. If these are defined cleverly at the outset, then many tedious complications can be avoided. If the virtual world is supposed to correspond to familiar environments from the real world, then the axis scaling should match common units. For example, $(1, 0, 0)$ should mean *one meter* to the right of $(0, 0, 0)$. It is also wise to put the origin $(0, 0, 0)$ in a convenient location. Commonly, $y = 0$ corresponds to the floor of a building or sea level of a terrain. The location of $x = 0$ and $z = 0$ could be in the center of the virtual world so that it nicely divides into quadrants based on sign. Another common choice is to place it in the upper left when viewing the world from above so that all x and z coordinates are nonnegative. For movable models, the location of the origin and the axis directions become extremely important because they affect how the model is rotated. This should become clear in Sections 3.2 and 3.3 as we present rotations.

Viewing the Models

Of course, one of the most important aspects of VR is how the models are going to look when viewed on a display. This problem is divided into two parts. The first part involves determining where the points in the virtual world should appear on the display. This is accomplished by viewing transformations in Section 3.4, which are combined with other transformations in Section 3.5 to produce the final result. The second part involves how each part of the model should appear after taking into account lighting sources and surface properties that are defined in the virtual world. This is the rendering problem, which is covered in Chapter 7.

3.2 Changing Position and Orientation

Suppose that a movable model has been defined as a mesh of triangles. To move it, we apply a single transformation to every vertex of every triangle. This section first considers the simple case of *translation*, followed by the considerably more complicated case of *rotations*. By combining translation and rotation, the model can be placed anywhere, and at any orientation in the virtual world $\mathbb{R}^3$.

Translations

Consider the following 3D triangle,

$$((x_1, y_1, z_1), (x_2, y_2, z_2), (x_3, y_3, z_3)), \tag{3.2}$$

in which the vertex coordinates are expressed as generic constants.

Let x_t, y_t, and z_t be the amount we would like to change the triangle's position along the x-, y-, and z-axes, respectively. The operation of changing position is called *translation*, and it is given by

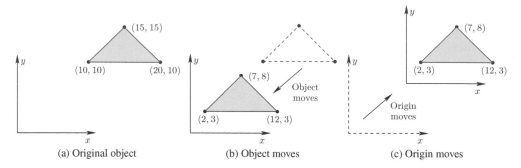

(a) Original object　　　　　(b) Object moves　　　　　(c) Origin moves

Figure 3.4 Every transformation has two possible interpretations, even though the math is the same. Here is a 2D example, in which a triangle is defined in (a). We could translate the triangle by $x_t = -8$ and $y_t = -7$ to obtain the result in (b). If we instead wanted to hold the triangle fixed but move the origin up by eight in the x direction and seven in the y direction, then the coordinates of the triangle vertices change the exact same way, as shown in (c).

$$(x_1, y_1, z_1) \mapsto (x_1 + x_t, y_1 + y_t, z_1 + z_t)$$
$$(x_2, y_2, z_2) \mapsto (x_2 + x_t, y_2 + y_t, z_2 + z_t) \qquad (3.3)$$
$$(x_3, y_3, z_3) \mapsto (x_3 + x_t, y_3 + y_t, z_3 + z_t),$$

in which $a \mapsto b$ denotes that a becomes replaced by b after the transformation is applied. Applying (3.3) to every triangle in a model will translate all of it to the desired location. If the triangles are arranged in a mesh, then it is sufficient to apply the transformation to the vertices alone. All of the triangles will retain their size and shape.

Relativity

Before the transformations become too complicated, we want to caution you about the importance of interpreting them correctly. Figures 3.4(a) and 3.4(b) show an example in which a triangle is translated by $x_t = -8$ and $y_t = -7$. The vertex coordinates are the same in Figures 3.4(b) and 3.4(c). Figure 3.4(b) shows the case we are intending to cover so far: the triangle is interpreted as having moved in the virtual world. However, Figure 3.4(c) shows another possibility: the coordinates of the virtual world have been reassigned so that the triangle is closer to the origin. This is equivalent to having moved the entire world, with the triangle being the only part that does not move. In this case, the translation is applied to the coordinate axes, but the amounts are negated. When we apply more general transformations, this extends so that transforming the coordinate axes results in an *inverse* of the transformation that would correspondingly move the model. Negation is simply the inverse in the case of translation.

Thus, we have a kind of "relativity": did the object move, or did the whole world move around it? This idea will become important in Section 3.4 when we want to change viewpoints. If we were standing at the origin, looking at the triangle, then the result would appear the same in either case; however, if the origin moves, then we would move with it. A deep perceptual problem lies here as well. If we perceive ourselves as having moved, then VR sickness might increase, even though it was the object that moved. In other words, our brains make their best guess as to which type of motion occurred, and sometimes they get it wrong.

Getting Ready for Rotations
How do we make the wheels roll on a car? Or turn a table over onto its side? To accomplish these, we need to change the model's *orientation* in the virtual world. The operation that changes the orientation is called *rotation*. Unfortunately, rotations in three dimensions are much more complicated than translations, leading to countless frustrations for engineers and developers. To improve the clarity of 3D rotation concepts, we first start with a simpler problem: 2D linear transformations.

Consider a 2D virtual world, in which points have coordinates (x, y). You can imagine this as a vertical plane in our original, 3D virtual world. Now consider a generic two-by-two matrix,

$$M = \begin{bmatrix} m_{11} & m_{12} \\ m_{21} & m_{22} \end{bmatrix}, \tag{3.4}$$

in which each of the four entries could be any real number. We will look at what happens when this matrix is multiplied by the point (x, y), when it is written as a column vector.

Performing the multiplication, we obtain

$$\begin{bmatrix} m_{11} & m_{12} \\ m_{21} & m_{22} \end{bmatrix} \begin{bmatrix} x \\ y \end{bmatrix} = \begin{bmatrix} x' \\ y' \end{bmatrix}, \tag{3.5}$$

in which (x', y') is the transformed point. Using simple algebra, the matrix multiplication yields

$$\begin{aligned} x' &= m_{11}x + m_{12}y \\ y' &= m_{21}x + m_{22}y. \end{aligned} \tag{3.6}$$

Using notation as in (3.3), M is a transformation for which $(x, y) \mapsto (x', y')$.

Applying the 2D Matrix to Points
Suppose we place two points $(1, 0)$ and $(0, 1)$ in the plane. They lie on the x- and y-axes, respectively, at one unit of distance from the origin $(0, 0)$. Using vector spaces, these two points would be the standard unit basis vectors (sometimes written as $\hat{\imath}$ and $\hat{\jmath}$). Watch what happens if we substitute them into (3.5):

$$\begin{bmatrix} m_{11} & m_{12} \\ m_{21} & m_{22} \end{bmatrix} \begin{bmatrix} 1 \\ 0 \end{bmatrix} = \begin{bmatrix} m_{11} \\ m_{21} \end{bmatrix} \tag{3.7}$$

and

$$\begin{bmatrix} m_{11} & m_{12} \\ m_{21} & m_{22} \end{bmatrix} \begin{bmatrix} 0 \\ 1 \end{bmatrix} = \begin{bmatrix} m_{12} \\ m_{22} \end{bmatrix}. \tag{3.8}$$

These special points simply select the column vectors on M. What does this mean? If M is applied to transform a model, then each column of M indicates precisely how each coordinate axis is changed.

Figure 3.5 illustrates the effect of applying various matrices M to a model. Starting with Figure 3.5(a), the identity matrix does not cause the coordinates to change: $(x, y) \mapsto (x, y)$. The second example (Figure 3.5(b) causes a flip as if a mirror were placed at the y-axis. In this case, $(x, y) \mapsto (-x, y)$. The second row (Figure 3.5(c) and 3.5(d)) shows examples of scaling. The matrix in Figure 3.5(c) produces $(x, y) \mapsto (2x, 2y)$, which doubles the size. The matrix in Figure 3.5(d) only stretches the model in the y direction, causing an *aspect ratio* distortion. In the third row (Figure 3.5(e) and 3.5(f)), it might seem that the matrix shown in Figure 3.5(e) produces a mirror image with respect to both x- and y-axes. This is true, except that the mirror

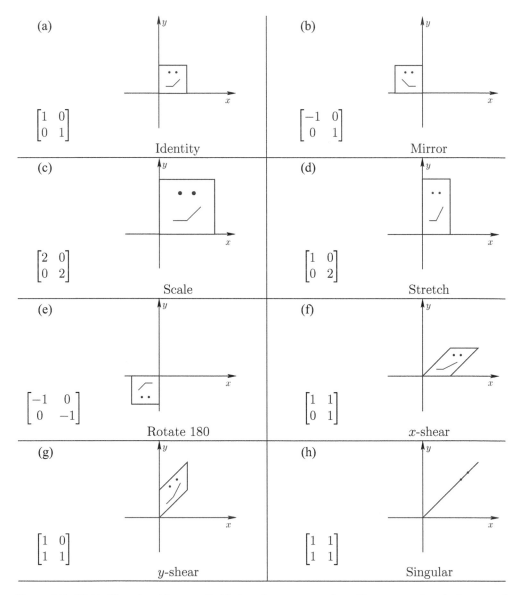

Figure 3.5 Eight different matrices applied to transform a square face. These examples nicely cover all of the possible cases, in a qualitative sense.

image of a mirror image restores the original. Thus, this corresponds to the case of a 180-degree (π radians) rotation rather than a mirror image. The matrix shown in Figure 3.5(f) produces a shear along the x direction: $(x, y) \mapsto (x+y, y)$. The amount of displacement is proportional to y. In the bottom row (Figure 3.5(g) and 3.5(h)), the matrix in Figure 3.5(g) shows a skew in the y direction. The final matrix, shown in Figure 3.5(h), might at first appear to cause more skewing, but it is degenerate. The two-dimensional shape collapses into a single dimension when M is applied: $(x, y) \mapsto (x + y, x + y)$. This corresponds to the case of a *singular* matrix, which means that its columns are not linearly independent. (They are in fact identical.) A matrix is singular if and only if its determinant is zero.

Only Some Matrices Produce Rotations

The examples in Figure 3.5 span the main qualitative differences between various two-by-two matrices M. Two of them were rotation matrices: the identity matrix, which is zero degrees of rotation, and the 180-degree rotation matrix. Among the set of all possible M, which ones are valid rotations? We must ensure that the model does not become distorted. This is achieved by ensuring that M satisfies the following rules:

1. No stretching of axes.
2. No shearing.
3. No mirror images.

If none of these rules is violated, then the result is a rotation.

To satisfy the first rule, the columns of M must have unit length:

$$m_{11}^2 + m_{21}^2 = 1 \text{ and } m_{12}^2 + m_{22}^2 = 1. \tag{3.9}$$

The scaling and shearing transformations in Figure 3.5 violate this.

To satisfy the second rule, the coordinate axes must remain perpendicular. Otherwise, shearing occurs. Since the columns of M indicate how axes are transformed, the rule implies that their inner (dot) product is zero:

$$m_{11}m_{12} + m_{21}m_{22} = 0. \tag{3.10}$$

The shearing transformations in Figure 3.5 violate this rule, which clearly causes right angles in the model to be distorted.

Satisfying the third rule requires that the determinant of M is positive. After satisfying the first two rules, the only possible remaining determinants are 1 (the normal case) and -1 (the mirror-image case). Thus, the rule implies that

$$\det \begin{bmatrix} m_{11} & m_{12} \\ m_{21} & m_{22} \end{bmatrix} = m_{11}m_{22} - m_{12}m_{21} = 1. \tag{3.11}$$

The mirror image example in Figure 3.5 results in $\det M = -1$.

The first constraint (3.9) indicates that each column must be chosen so that its components lie on a unit circle, centered at the origin. In standard planar coordinates, we commonly write the equation of this circle as $x^2 + y^2 = 1$. Recall the common parameterization of the unit circle in terms of an angle θ that ranges from 0 to 2π radians (see Figure 3.6):

$$x = \cos\theta \text{ and } y = \sin\theta. \tag{3.12}$$

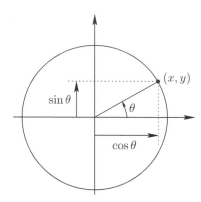

Figure 3.6 For a circle with unit radius, centered at the origin, a single parameter θ reaches all *xy* points along the circle as it ranges from $\theta = 0$ to $\theta = 2\pi$.

Instead of x and y, we use the notation of the matrix components. Let $m_{11} = \cos\theta$ and $m_{21} = \sin\theta$. Substituting this into M from (3.4) yields

$$\begin{bmatrix} \cos\theta & -\sin\theta \\ \sin\theta & \cos\theta \end{bmatrix},$$
(3.13)

in which m_{12} and m_{22} were uniquely determined by applying (3.10) and (3.11). By allowing θ to range from 0 to 2π, the full range of all allowable rotations is generated.

Think about degrees of freedom. Originally, we could choose all four components of M independently, resulting in four DOFs. The constraints in (3.9) each removed a DOF. Another DOF was removed by (3.10). Note that (3.11) does not reduce the DOFs; it instead eliminates exactly half of the possible transformations: the ones that are mirror flips and rotations together. The result is one DOF, which was nicely parameterized by the angle θ. Furthermore, we were lucky, because the set of all possible 2D rotations can be nicely interpreted as points along a unit circle.

The 3D Case
Now we try to describe the set of all 3D rotations by following the same general template as the 2D case. The matrix from (3.4) is extended from 2D to 3D, resulting in nine components:

$$M = \begin{bmatrix} m_{11} & m_{12} & m_{13} \\ m_{21} & m_{22} & m_{23} \\ m_{31} & m_{32} & m_{33} \end{bmatrix}.$$
(3.14)

Thus, we start with nine DOFs and want to determine what matrices remain as valid rotations. Follow the same three rules from the 2D case. The columns must have unit length. For example, $m_{11}^2 + m_{21}^2 + m_{31}^2 = 1$. This means that the components of each column must lie on a unit sphere. Thus, the unit-length rule reduces the DOFs from nine to six. By following the second rule to ensure that perpendicular axes result, the pairwise inner products of the columns must be zero. For example, by choosing the first two columns, the constraint is

$$m_{11}m_{12} + m_{21}m_{22} + m_{31}m_{32} = 0.$$
(3.15)

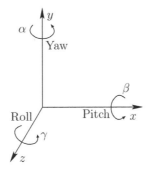

Figure 3.7 Any three-dimensional rotation can be described as a sequence of yaw, pitch, and roll rotations.

We must also apply the rule to the remaining pairs: the second and third columns, and then the first and third columns. Each of these cases eliminates a DOF, resulting in only the remaining DOFs. To avoid mirror images, the constraint $\det M = 1$ is applied, which does not reduce the DOFs.

Finally, we arrive at a set of matrices that must satisfy the algebraic constraints; however, they unfortunately do not fall onto a nice circle or sphere. We only know that there are three degrees of rotational freedom, which implies that it should be possible to pick three independent parameters for a 3D rotation and then derive all nine elements of (3.14) from them.

Yaw, Pitch, and Roll

One of the simplest ways to parameterize 3D rotations is to construct them from "2D-like" transformations, as shown in Figure 3.7. First consider a rotation about the z-axis. Let *roll* be a counterclockwise rotation of γ about the z-axis. The rotation matrix is given by

$$R_z(\gamma) = \begin{bmatrix} \cos\gamma & -\sin\gamma & 0 \\ \sin\gamma & \cos\gamma & 0 \\ 0 & 0 & 1 \end{bmatrix}. \tag{3.16}$$

The sine and cosine terms of the matrix look exactly like those of the 2D rotation matrix (3.13), except that θ is replaced by γ. This causes yaw to behave exactly like 2D rotation in the xy plane. The remainder of $R_z(\gamma)$ looks like the identity matrix, which causes z to remain unchanged after a roll.

Similarly, let *pitch* be a counterclockwise rotation of β about the x-axis:

$$R_x(\beta) = \begin{bmatrix} 1 & 0 & 0 \\ 0 & \cos\beta & -\sin\beta \\ 0 & \sin\beta & \cos\beta \end{bmatrix}. \tag{3.17}$$

In this case, points are rotated with respect to y and z, while the x coordinate is left unchanged.

Finally, let *yaw* be a counterclockwise rotation of α about the *y*-axis:

$$R_y(\alpha) = \begin{bmatrix} \cos\alpha & 0 & \sin\alpha \\ 0 & 1 & 0 \\ -\sin\alpha & 0 & \cos\alpha \end{bmatrix}. \tag{3.18}$$

In this case, rotation occurs with respect to x and z while leaving y unchanged.

Combining Rotations

Each of (3.16), (3.17), and (3.18) provides a single DOF of rotations. The yaw, pitch, and roll rotations can be combined sequentially to attain any possible 3D rotation:

$$R(\alpha, \beta, \gamma) = R_y(\alpha)R_x(\beta)R_z(\gamma). \tag{3.19}$$

In this case, the ranges of α and γ are from 0 to 2π; however, the pitch β need only range from $-\pi/2$ to $\pi/2$ while nevertheless reaching all possible 3D rotations.

Be extra careful when combining rotations in a sequence because the operations are not commutative. For example, a yaw by $\pi/2$ followed by a pitch by $\pi/2$ does not produce the same result as the pitch followed by the yaw. You can easily check this by substituting $\pi/2$ into (3.17) and (3.18), and observing how the result depends on the order of matrix multiplication. The 2D case is commutative because the rotation axis is always the same, allowing the rotation angles to additively combine. Having the wrong matrix ordering is one of the most frustrating problems when writing software for VR.

Matrix Multiplications Seem "Backwards"

Which operation is getting applied to the model first when we apply a product of matrices? Consider rotating a point $p = (x, y, z)$. We have two rotation matrices R and Q. If we rotate p using R, we obtain $p' = Rp$. If we then apply Q, we get $p'' = Qp'$. Now suppose that we instead want to first combine the two rotations and then apply them to p to get p''. Programmers are often tempted to combine them as RQ because we read from left to right and also write sequences in this way. However, it is backwards for linear algebra because Rp is already acting from the left side. Thus, it reads from right to left.[1] We therefore must combine the rotations as QR to obtain $p'' = QRp$. Later in this chapter, we will be chaining together several matrix transforms. Read them from right to left to understand what they are doing!

Translation and Rotation in One Matrix

It would be convenient to apply both rotation and translation together in a single operation. Suppose we want to apply a rotation matrix R and follow it with a translation by (x_t, y_t, z_t). Algebraically, this is

$$\begin{bmatrix} x' \\ y' \\ z' \end{bmatrix} = R \begin{bmatrix} x \\ y \\ z \end{bmatrix} + \begin{bmatrix} x_t \\ y_t \\ z_t \end{bmatrix}. \tag{3.20}$$

---

[1] Perhaps coders who speak Arabic, Farsi, or Hebrew are not confused about this.

Although there is no way to form a single three-by-three matrix to accomplish both operations, it can be done by increasing the matrix dimensions by one. Consider the following four-by-four *homogeneous transformation matrix*:

$$
T_{rb} = \left[\begin{array}{ccc|c} & & & x_t \\ & R & & y_t \\ & & & z_t \\ \hline 0 & 0 & 0 & 1 \end{array} \right],
\tag{3.21}
$$

in which R fills the upper left three rows and columns. The notation T_{rb} is used to denote that the matrix is a *rigid body transform*, meaning that it does not distort objects. A homogeneous transform matrix could include other kinds of transforms, which will appear in Section 3.5.

The same result as in (3.20) can be obtained by performing multiplication with (3.21) as follows:

$$
\left[\begin{array}{ccc|c} & & & x_t \\ & R & & y_t \\ & & & z_t \\ \hline 0 & 0 & 0 & 1 \end{array} \right]
\left[\begin{array}{c} x \\ y \\ z \\ 1 \end{array} \right]
=
\left[\begin{array}{c} x' \\ y' \\ z' \\ 1 \end{array} \right].
\tag{3.22}
$$

Because of the extra dimension, we extended the point (x, y, z) by one dimension to obtain $(x, y, z, 1)$. Note that (3.21) represents rotation *followed by* translation, not the other way around. Translation and rotation do not commute; therefore, this is an important point.

Inverting Transforms
We frequently want to invert (or undo) transformations. For a translation (x_t, y_t, z_t), we simply apply the negation $(-x_t, -y_t, -z_t)$. For a general matrix transform M, we apply the matrix inverse M^{-1} (if it exists). This is often complicated to calculate. Fortunately, inverses are much simpler for our cases of interest. In the case of a rotation matrix R, the inverse is equal to the transpose $R^{-1} = R^T$.[2] To invert the homogeneous transform matrix (3.21), it is tempting to write

$$
\left[\begin{array}{ccc|c} & & & -x_t \\ & R^T & & -y_t \\ & & & -z_t \\ \hline 0 & 0 & 0 & 1 \end{array} \right].
\tag{3.23}
$$

This will undo both the translation and the rotation; however, the order is wrong. Remember that these operations are not commutative, which implies that order must be correctly handled. See Figure 3.8. The algebra for very general matrices (part of noncommutative group theory) works out so that the inverse of a product of matrices reverses their order:

$$
(ABC)^{-1} = C^{-1}B^{-1}A^{-1}.
\tag{3.24}
$$

---

[2] Recall that to transpose a square matrix, we simply swap the i and j indices, which turns columns into rows.

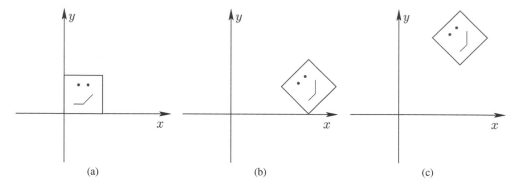

Figure 3.8 (a) A rigid model that is contained in a one-by-one square. (b) The result after rotation by $\pi/4$ (45 degrees), followed with translation by $x_t = 2$. (c) The result after reversing the order: translation by $x_t = 2$, followed with rotation by $\pi/4$.

This can be seen by putting the inverse next to the original product:

$$ABCC^{-1}B^{-1}A^{-1}. \tag{3.25}$$

In this way, C cancels with its inverse, followed by B and its inverse, and finally A and its inverse. If the order were wrong, then these cancellations would not occur.

The matrix T_{rb} (from 3.21) applies the rotation first, followed by translation. Applying (3.23) undoes the rotation first and then the translation, without reversing the order. Thus, the inverse of T_{rb} is

$$\left[\begin{array}{ccc|c} & & & 0 \\ & R^T & & 0 \\ & & & 0 \\ \hline 0 & 0 & 0 & 1 \end{array}\right] \left[\begin{array}{cccc} 1 & 0 & 0 & -x_t \\ 0 & 1 & 0 & -y_t \\ 0 & 0 & 1 & -z_t \\ 0 & 0 & 0 & 1 \end{array}\right]. \tag{3.26}$$

The matrix on the right first undoes the translation (with no rotation). After that, the matrix on the left undoes the rotation (with no translation).

3.3 Axis-Angle Representations of Rotation

As observed in Section 3.2, 3D rotation is complicated for several reasons: (1) nine matrix entries are specified in terms of only three independent parameters, and with no simple parameterization; (2) the axis of rotation is not the same every time; and (3) the operations are noncommutative, implying that the order of matrices is crucial. None of these problems existed for the 2D case.

Kinematic Singularities

An even worse problem arises when using yaw, pitch, and roll angles (and related Euler-angle variants). Even though they start off being intuitively pleasing, the representation becomes degenerate, leading to *kinematic singularities* that are nearly impossible to visualize. An example will be presented shortly. To prepare for this, recall how we represent locations on the Earth. These are points in $\mathbb{R}^3$ but are represented with longitude and latitude coordinates. Just like the limits of yaw and pitch, longitude ranges from 0 to 2π and latitude only ranges from $-\pi/2$ to $\pi/2$. (Longitude is usually expressed as 0 to 180 degrees west or east, which is equivalent.) As we travel anywhere on the Earth, the latitude and longitude coordinates behave very much like xy coordinates; however, we tend to stay away from the poles. Near the North Pole, the latitude behaves normally, but the longitude could vary a large amount while corresponding to a tiny distance traveled. Recall how a wall map of the world looks near the poles: Greenland is enormous, and Antarctica wraps across the entire bottom (assuming it uses a projection that keeps longitude lines straight). The poles themselves are the kinematic singularities: at these special points, you can vary longitude, but the location on the Earth is not changing. One of two DOFs seems to be lost.

The same problem occurs with 3D rotations, but it is harder to visualize due to the extra dimension. If the pitch angle is held at $\beta = \pi/2$, then a kind of "North Pole" is reached in which α and γ vary independently but cause only one DOF. (In the case of latitude and longitude, it was one parameter varying but causing zero DOFs.) Here is how it looks when combining the yaw, pitch, and roll matrices:

$$
\begin{bmatrix} \cos\alpha & 0 & \sin\alpha \\ 0 & 1 & 0 \\ -\sin\alpha & 0 & \cos\alpha \end{bmatrix} \begin{bmatrix} 1 & 0 & 0 \\ 0 & 0 & -1 \\ 0 & 1 & 0 \end{bmatrix} \begin{bmatrix} \cos\gamma & -\sin\gamma & 0 \\ \sin\gamma & \cos\gamma & 0 \\ 0 & 0 & 1 \end{bmatrix}
$$
$$
= \begin{bmatrix} \cos(\alpha-\gamma) & \sin(\alpha-\gamma) & 0 \\ 0 & 0 & -1 \\ -\sin(\alpha-\gamma) & \cos(\alpha-\gamma) & 0 \end{bmatrix}. \tag{3.27}
$$

The second matrix corresponds to pitch (3.17) with $\beta = \pi/2$. The result on the bottom is obtained by performing matrix multiplication and applying a subtraction trigonometric identity. You should observe that the resulting matrix is a function of both α and γ, but there is one DOF because only the difference $\alpha - \gamma$ affects the resulting rotation. In the video game industry there have been some back-and-forth battles about whether this problem is crucial. In an FPS game, the avatar is usually not allowed to pitch his head all the way to $\pm\pi/2$, thereby avoiding this problem. In VR, it happens all the time that a user could pitch her head straight up or down. The kinematic singularity often causes the viewpoint to spin uncontrollably. This phenomenon also occurs when sensing and controlling a spacecraft's orientation using mechanical gimbals; the result is called *gimbal lock*.

The problems can be easily solved with *axis-angle* representations of rotation. They are harder to learn than yaw, pitch, and roll; however, it is a worthwhile investment because it avoids these problems. Furthermore, many well-written software libraries and game engines work directly with these representations. Thus, to use them effectively, you should understand what they are doing.

The most important insight to solving the kinematic singularity problems is Euler's rotation theorem (1775), shown in Figure 3.9. Even though the rotation axis may change after rotations are combined, Euler showed that *any* 3D rotation can be expressed as a rotation θ about some axis that pokes through the origin. This

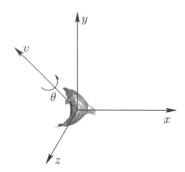

Figure 3.9 Euler's rotation theorem states that every 3D rotation can be considered as a rotation by an angle θ about an axis through the origin, given by the unit direction vector $v = (v_1, v_2, v_3)$.

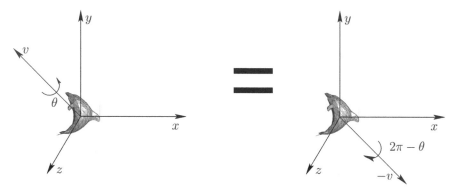

Figure 3.10 There are two ways to encode the same rotation in terms of axis and angle, using either v or $-v$.

matches the three DOFs for rotation: it takes two parameters to specify the direction of an axis and one parameter for θ. The only trouble is that conversions back and forth between rotation matrices and the axis-angle representation are somewhat inconvenient. This motivates the introduction of a mathematical object that is close to the axis-angle representation, closely mimics the algebra of 3D rotations, and can even be applied directly to rotate models. The perfect representation: *quaternions*.

Two-to-One Problem
Before getting to quaternions, it is important point out one annoying problem with Euler's rotation theorem. As shown in Figure 3.10, it does not claim that the axis-angle representation is unique. In fact, for every 3D rotation, there are exactly two representations. This is due to the fact that the axis could "point" in either direction. We could insist that the axis always point in one direction, such as positive y, but this does not fully solve the problem because of the boundary cases (horizontal axes). Quaternions, which are coming next, nicely handle all problems with 3D rotations except this one, which is unavoidable.

Quaternions were introduced in 1843 by William Rowan Hamilton. When seeing them the first time, most people have difficulty understanding their peculiar algebra. Therefore, we will instead focus on precisely which quaternions correspond to

Table 3.1 For these cases, you should be able to look at the quaternion and quickly picture the axis and angle of the corresponding 3D rotation.

Quaternion	Axis-Angle	Description
$(1, 0, 0, 0)$	(undefined, 0)	Identity rotation
$(0, 1, 0, 0)$	$((1, 0, 0), \pi)$	Pitch by π
$(0, 0, 1, 0)$	$((0, 1, 0), \pi)$	Yaw by π
$(0, 0, 0, 1)$	$((0, 0, 1), \pi)$	Roll by π
$(\frac{1}{\sqrt{2}}, \frac{1}{\sqrt{2}}, 0, 0)$	$((1, 0, 0), \pi/2)$	Pitch by $\pi/2$
$(\frac{1}{\sqrt{2}}, 0, \frac{1}{\sqrt{2}}, 0)$	$((0, 1, 0), \pi/2)$	Yaw by $\pi/2$
$(\frac{1}{\sqrt{2}}, 0, 0, \frac{1}{\sqrt{2}})$	$((0, 0, 1), \pi/2)$	Roll by $\pi/2$

which rotations. After that, we will introduce some limited quaternion algebra. The algebra is much less important for developing VR systems, unless you want to implement your own 3D rotation library. The correspondence between quaternions and 3D rotations, however, is crucial.

A quaternion q is a 4D vector:

$$q = (a, b, c, d), \tag{3.28}$$

in which a, b, c, and d can take on real values. Thus, q can be considered as a point in $\mathbb{R}^4$. It turns out that we will only use *unit quaternions*, which means that

$$a^2 + b^2 + c^2 + d^2 = 1 \tag{3.29}$$

must always hold. This should remind you of the equation of a unit sphere ($x^2 + y^2 + z^2 = 1$), but it is one dimension higher. A sphere is a 2D surface, whereas the set of all unit quaternions is a 3D hypersurface, more formally known as a *manifold* [27, 154]. We will use the space of unit quaternions to represent the space of all 3D rotations. Both have 3 DOFs, which seems reasonable.

Let (v, θ) be an axis-angle representation of a 3D rotation, as depicted in Figure 3.9. Let this be represented by the following quaternion:

$$q = \left(\cos \frac{\theta}{2}, \ v_1 \sin \frac{\theta}{2}, \ v_2 \sin \frac{\theta}{2}, \ v_3 \sin \frac{\theta}{2} \right). \tag{3.30}$$

Think of q as a data structure that encodes the 3D rotation. It is easy to recover (v, θ) from q:

$$\theta = 2 \cos^{-1} a \text{ and } v = \frac{1}{\sqrt{1 - a^2}}(b, c, d). \tag{3.31}$$

If $a = \pm 1$, then (3.31) breaks; however, this corresponds to the case of the identity rotation.

You now have the mappings $(v, \theta) \mapsto q$ and $q \mapsto (v, \theta)$. To test your understanding, Table 3.1 shows some simple examples that commonly occur in practice. Furthermore, Figure 3.11 shows some simple relationships between quaternions

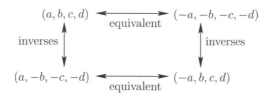

Figure 3.11   Simple relationships between equivalent quaternions and their inverses.

and their corresponding rotations. The horizontal arrows indicate that q and $-q$ represent the same rotation. This is true because of the double representation issue shown in Figure 3.10. Applying (3.30) to both cases establishes their equivalence. The vertical arrows correspond to inverse rotations. These hold because reversing the direction of the axis causes the rotation to be reversed (rotation by θ becomes rotation by $2\pi - \theta$).

How do we apply the quaternion $q = (a, b, c, d)$ to rotate the model? One way is to use the following conversion into a 3D rotation matrix:

$$R(q) = \begin{bmatrix} 2(a^2 + b^2) - 1 & 2(bc - ad) & 2(bd + ac) \\ 2(bc + ad) & 2(a^2 + c^2) - 1 & 2(cd - ab) \\ 2(bd - ac) & 2(cd + ab) & 2(a^2 + d^2) - 1 \end{bmatrix}. \qquad (3.32)$$

A more efficient way exists that avoids converting h into a rotation matrix. To accomplish this, we need to define quaternion multiplication. For any two quaternions, q_1 and q_2, let $q_1 * q_2$ denote the product, which is defined as

$$\begin{aligned} a_3 &= a_1 a_2 - b_1 b_2 - c_1 c_2 - d_1 d_2, \\ b_3 &= a_1 b_2 + a_2 b_1 + c_1 d_2 - c_2 d_1, \\ c_3 &= a_1 c_2 + a_2 c_1 + b_2 d_1 - b_1 d_2, \\ d_3 &= a_1 d_2 + a_2 d_1 + b_1 c_2 - b_2 c_1. \end{aligned} \qquad (3.33)$$

In other words, $q_3 = q_1 * q_2$ as defined in (3.33).

Here is a way to rotate the point (x, y, z) using the rotation represented by q. Let $p = (0, x, y, z)$, which is done to give the point the same dimensions as a quaternion. Perhaps surprisingly, the point is rotated by applying quaternion multiplication as

$$p' = q * p * q^{-1}, \qquad (3.34)$$

in which $q^{-1} = (a, -b, -c, -d)$ (recall from Figure 3.11). The rotated point is (x', y', z'), which is taken from the result $p' = (0, x', y', z')$.

Here is a simple example for the point $(1, 0, 0)$. Let $p = (0, 1, 0, 0)$ and consider executing a yaw rotation by π. According to Table 3.1, the corresponding quaternion is $\left(\frac{1}{\sqrt{2}}, 0, \frac{1}{\sqrt{2}}, 0\right)$. The inverse is $q^{-1} = \left(\frac{1}{\sqrt{2}}, 0, -\frac{1}{\sqrt{2}}, 0\right)$. After tediously applying (3.33) to calculate (3.34), the result is $p' = (0, 0, 1, 0)$. Thus, the rotated point is $(0, 1, 0)$, which is a correct yaw by $\pi/2$.

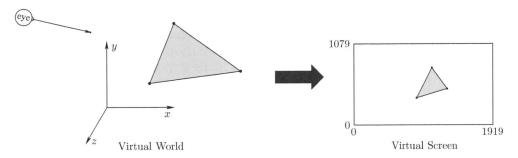

Figure 3.12 If we placed a virtual eye or camera into the virtual world, what would it see? Section 3.4 provides transformations that place objects from the virtual world onto a virtual screen, based on the particular viewpoint of a virtual eye. A flat rectangular shape is chosen for engineering and historical reasons, even though it does not match the shape of our retinas.

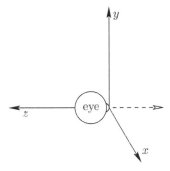

Figure 3.13 Consider an eye that is looking down the z-axis in the negative direction. The origin of the model is the point at which light enters the eye.

3.4 Viewing Transformations

This section describes how to transform the models in the virtual world so that they appear on a virtual screen. The main purpose is to set the foundation for graphical rendering, which adds effects due to lighting, material properties, and quantization. Ultimately, the result appears on the physical display. These transforms also explain how cameras form images, at least as idealized mathematics of the process. Think of this section as describing a virtual camera that is placed in the virtual world. What should the virtual picture, taken by that camera, look like? To make VR work correctly, the "camera" should actually be one of two virtual human eyes that are placed into the virtual world. Thus, what should a virtual eye see, based on its position and orientation in the virtual world? Rather than determine precisely what would appear on the retina, which should become clear after Section 4.4, here we merely calculate where the model vertices would appear on a flat, rectangular screen in the virtual world. See Figure 3.12.

An Eye's View
Figure 3.13 shows a virtual eye that is looking down the negative z-axis. It is placed in this way so that from the eye's perspective, x increases to the right and y is upward.

This corresponds to familiar Cartesian coordinates. The alternatives would be (1) to face the eye in the positive z direction, which makes the xy coordinates appear backwards, or (2) reverse the z-axis, which would unfortunately lead to a left-handed coordinate system. Thus, we have made an odd choice to avoid worse complications.

Suppose that the eye is an object model that we want to place into the virtual world $\mathbb{R}^3$ at some position $e = (e_1, e_2, e_3)$ and orientation given by the matrix

$$R_{eye} = \begin{bmatrix} \hat{x}_1 & \hat{y}_1 & \hat{z}_1 \\ \hat{x}_2 & \hat{y}_2 & \hat{z}_2 \\ \hat{x}_3 & \hat{y}_3 & \hat{z}_3 \end{bmatrix}. \tag{3.35}$$

If the eyeball in Figure 3.13 were made of triangles, then rotation by R_{eye} and translation by e would be applied to all vertices to place it in $\mathbb{R}^3$.

This does not, however, solve the problem of how the virtual world should appear to the eye. Rather than moving the eye in the virtual world, we need to move all of the models in the virtual world to the eye's frame of reference. This means that we need to apply the *inverse* transformation. The inverse rotation is R_{eye}^T, the transpose of R_{eye}. The inverse of e is $-e$. Applying (3.26) results in the appropriate transform:

$$T_{eye} = \begin{bmatrix} \hat{x}_1 & \hat{x}_2 & \hat{x}_3 & 0 \\ \hat{y}_1 & \hat{y}_2 & \hat{y}_3 & 0 \\ \hat{z}_1 & \hat{z}_2 & \hat{z}_3 & 0 \\ 0 & 0 & 0 & 1 \end{bmatrix} \begin{bmatrix} 1 & 0 & 0 & -e_1 \\ 0 & 1 & 0 & -e_2 \\ 0 & 0 & 1 & -e_3 \\ 0 & 0 & 0 & 1 \end{bmatrix}. \tag{3.36}$$

Note that R_{eye}, as shown in (3.35), has been transposed and placed into the left matrix in (3.36). Also, the order of translation and rotation has been swapped, which is required for the inverse, as mentioned in Section 3.2.

Following Figure 3.4, there are two possible interpretations of (3.36). As stated, this could correspond to moving all of the virtual world models (corresponding to Figure 3.4(b)). A more appropriate interpretation in the current setting is that the virtual world's coordinate frame is being moved so that it matches the eye's frame from Figure 3.13. This corresponds to the case of Figure 3.4(c), which was not the appropriate interpretation in Section 3.2.

Starting from a Look-at

For VR, the position and orientation of the eye in the virtual world are given by a tracking system and possibly controller inputs. By contrast, in computer graphics, it is common to start with a description of where the eye is located and which way it is looking. This is called a *look-at*, and has the following components:

1. Position of the eye: e
2. Central looking direction of the eye: $\hat{c}$
3. Up direction: $\hat{u}$.

Both $\hat{c}$ and $\hat{u}$ are unit vectors. The first direction $\hat{c}$ corresponds to the center of the view. Whatever $\hat{c}$ is pointing at should end up in the center of the display. If we want this to be a particular point p in $\mathbb{R}^3$ (see Figure 3.14), then $\hat{c}$ can be calculated as

$$\hat{c} = \frac{p - e}{\|p - e\|}, \tag{3.37}$$

Figure 3.14 The vector from the eye position e to a point p that it is looking at is normalized to form $\hat{c}$ in (3.37).

in which $\| \cdot \|$ denotes the length of a vector. The result is just the vector from e to p, but normalized.

The second direction $\hat{u}$ indicates which way is up. Imagine holding a camera out as if you are about to take a photo and then performing a roll rotation. You can make level ground appear to be slanted or even upside down in the picture. Thus, $\hat{u}$ indicates the up direction for the virtual camera or eye.

We now construct the resulting transform T_{eye} from (3.36). The translation components are already determined by e, which was given in the look-at. We need only to determine the rotation R_{eye}, as expressed in (3.35). Recall from Section 3.2 that the matrix columns indicate how the coordinate axes are transformed by the matrix (refer to (3.7) and (3.8)). This simplifies the problem of determining R_{eye}. Each column vector is calculated as

$$\hat{z} = -\hat{c},$$
$$\hat{x} = \hat{u} \times \hat{z}, \tag{3.38}$$
$$\hat{y} = \hat{z} \times \hat{x}.$$

The minus sign appears for calculating $\hat{z}$ because the eye is looking down the negative z-axis. The $\hat{x}$ direction is calculated using the standard cross product $\hat{z}$. For the third equation, we could use $\hat{y} = \hat{u}$; however, $\hat{z} \times \hat{x}$ will cleverly correct cases in which $\hat{u}$ generally points upward but is not perpendicular to $\hat{c}$. The unit vectors from (3.38) are substituted into (3.35) to obtain R_{eye}. Thus, we have all the required information to construct T_{eye}.

Orthographic Projection

Let (x, y, z) denote the coordinates of any point, after T_{eye} has been applied. What would happen if we took all points and directly projected them into the vertical xy plane by forcing each z coordinate to be 0? In other words, $(x, y, z) \mapsto (x, y, 0)$, which is called *orthographic projection*. If we imagine the xy plane as a virtual display of the models, then there would be several problems:

1. A jumble of objects would be superimposed, rather than hiding parts of a model that are in front of another.
2. The display would extend infinitely in all directions (except z). If the display is a small rectangle in the xy plane, then the model parts that are outside of its range can be eliminated.
3. Objects that are closer should appear larger than those further away. This happens in the real world. Recall from Section 1.3 (Figure 1.23(c)) paintings that correctly handle perspective.

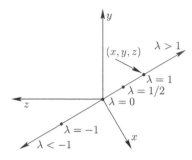

Figure 3.15 Starting with any point (x, y, z), a line through the origin can be formed using a parameter λ. It is the set of all points of the form $(\lambda x, \lambda y, \lambda z)$ for any real value λ. For example, $\lambda = 1/2$ corresponds to the midpoint between (x, y, z) and $(0, 0, 0)$ along the line.

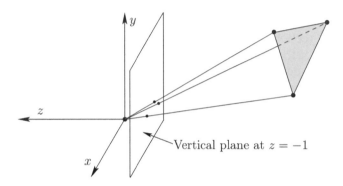

Figure 3.16 An illustration of perspective projection. The model vertices are projected onto a virtual screen by drawing lines through them and the origin $(0, 0, 0)$. The "image" of the points on the virtual screen corresponds to the intersections of the line with the screen.

The first two problems are important graphics operations that are deferred until Chapter 7. The third problem is addressed next.

Perspective Projection

Instead of using orthographic projection, we define a *perspective projection*. For each point (x, y, z), consider a line through the origin. This is the set of all points with coordinates

$$(\lambda x, \lambda y, \lambda z), \qquad (3.39)$$

in which λ can be any real number. In other words λ is a parameter that reaches all points on the line that contains both (x, y, z) and $(0, 0, 0)$. See Figure 3.15.

Now we can place a planar "movie screen" anywhere in the virtual world and see where all of the lines pierce it. To keep the math simple, we pick the $z = -1$ plane to place our virtual screen directly in front of the eye; see Figure 3.16. Using the third component of (3.39), we have $\lambda z = -1$, implying that $\lambda = -1/z$. Using the first two components of (3.39), the coordinates for the points on the screen are calculated as $x' = -x/z$ and $y' = -y/z$. Note that because x and y are scaled by the same amount z for each axis, their aspect ratio is preserved on the screen.

More generally, suppose the vertical screen is placed at some location d along the z-axis. In this case, we obtain more general expressions for the location of a point on the screen:

$$x' = dx/z$$
$$y' = dy/z. \tag{3.40}$$

This was obtained by solving $d = \lambda z$ for λ and substituting it into (3.39).

This is all we need to project the points onto a virtual screen, while respecting the scaling properties of objects at various distances. Getting this right in VR helps in the perception of depth and scale, which are covered in Section 6.1. In Section 3.5, we will adapt (3.40) using transformation matrices. Furthermore, only points that lie within a zone in front of the eye will be projected onto the virtual screen. Points that are too close, too far, or outside the normal field of view will not be rendered on the virtual screen; this is addressed in Section 3.5 and Chapter 7.

3.5 Chaining the Transformations

This section links all of the transformations of this chapter together while also slightly adjusting their form to match what is currently used in the VR and computer graphics industries. Some of the matrices appearing in this section may seem unnecessarily complicated. The reason is that the expressions are motivated by algorithm and hardware issues, rather than mathematical simplicity. In particular, there is a bias toward putting every transformation into a four-by-four homogeneous transform matrix, even in the case of perspective projection, which is not even linear (recall (3.40)). In this way, an efficient matrix multiplication algorithm can be iterated over the chain of matrices to produce the result.

The chain generally appears as follows:

$$T = T_{vp} T_{can} T_{eye} T_{rb}. \tag{3.41}$$

When T is applied to a point $(x, y, z, 1)$, the location of the point on the screen is produced. Remember that these matrix multiplications are not commutative, and the operations are applied from right to left. The first matrix T_{rb} is the rigid body transform (3.21) applied to points on a movable model. For each rigid object in the model, T_{rb} remains the same; however, different objects will generally be placed in various positions and orientations. For example, the wheel of a virtual car will move differently than the avatar's head. After T_{rb} is applied, T_{eye} transforms the virtual world into the coordinate frame of the eye, according to (3.36). At a fixed instant in time, this and all remaining transformation matrices are the same for all points in the virtual world. Here we assume that the eye is positioned at the midpoint between the two virtual human eyes, leading to a *cyclopean viewpoint*. Later in this section, we will extend it to the case of left and right eyes so that stereo viewpoints can be constructed.

Canonical View Transform

The next transformation, T_{can} performs the perspective projection as described in Section 3.4; however, we must explain how it is unnaturally forced into a four-by-four matrix. We also want the result to be in a canonical form that appears to be

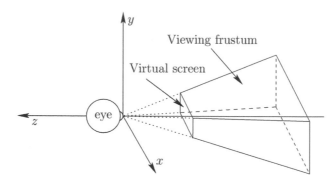

Figure 3.17 The viewing frustum.

unitless, which is again motivated by industrial needs. Therefore, T_{can} is called the *canonical view transform*. Figure 3.17 shows a *viewing frustum*, which is based on the four corners of a rectangular *virtual screen*. At $z = n$ and $z = f$ lie a *near plane* and *far plane*, respectively. Note that $z < 0$ for these cases because the z-axis points in the opposite direction. The virtual screen is contained in the near plane. The perspective projection should place all of the points inside the frustum onto a virtual screen that is centered in the near plane. This implies $d = n$ using (3.40).

We now want to reproduce (3.40) using a matrix. Consider the result of applying the following matrix multiplication:

$$\begin{bmatrix} n & 0 & 0 & 0 \\ 0 & n & 0 & 0 \\ 0 & 0 & n & 0 \\ 0 & 0 & 1 & 0 \end{bmatrix} \begin{bmatrix} x \\ y \\ z \\ 1 \end{bmatrix} = \begin{bmatrix} nx \\ ny \\ nz \\ z \end{bmatrix}. \tag{3.42}$$

In the first two coordinates, we obtain the numerator of (3.40). The nonlinear part of (3.40) is the $1/z$ factor. To handle this, the fourth coordinate is used to represent z, rather than 1 as in the case of T_{rb}. From this point onward, the resulting 4D vector is interpreted as a 3D vector that is scaled by dividing out its fourth component. For example, (v_1, v_2, v_3, v_4) is interpreted as

$$(v_1/v_4, v_2/v_4, v_3/v_4). \tag{3.43}$$

Thus, the result from (3.42) is interpreted as

$$(nx/z, ny/z, n), \tag{3.44}$$

in which the first two coordinates match (3.42) with $d = n$, and the third coordinate is the location of the virtual screen along the z-axis.

Keeping Track of Depth for Later Use
The following matrix is commonly used in computer graphics and will be used here in our chain:

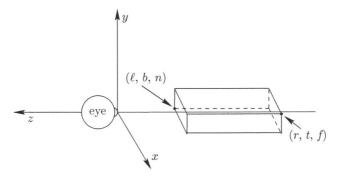

Figure 3.18 The rectangular region formed by the corners of the viewing frustum, after they are transformed by T_p. The coordinates of the selected opposite corners provide the six parameters, ℓ, r, b, t, n, and f, which are used in T_{st}.

$$T_p = \begin{bmatrix} n & 0 & 0 & 0 \\ 0 & n & 0 & 0 \\ 0 & 0 & n+f & -fn \\ 0 & 0 & 1 & 0 \end{bmatrix}. \tag{3.45}$$

It is identical to the matrix in (3.42) except in how it transforms the z coordinate. For purposes of placing points on the virtual screen, it is unnecessary because we already know they are all placed at $z = n$. The z coordinate is therefore co-opted for another purpose: keeping track of the distance of each point from the eye so that graphics algorithms can determine which objects are in front of other objects. The matrix T_p calculates the third coordinate as

$$(n+f)z - fn. \tag{3.46}$$

When divided by z, (3.46) does not preserve the exact distance, but the graphics methods (some of which are covered in Chapter 7) require only that the distance *ordering* is preserved. In other words, if point p is farther from the eye than point q, then it remains farther after the transformation, even if the distances are distorted. It does, however, preserve the distance in two special cases: $z = n$ and $z = f$. This can be seen by substituting these into (3.46) and dividing by z.

Additional Translation and Scaling
After T_p is applied, the eight corners of the frustum are transformed into the corners of a rectangular box, shown in Figure 3.18. The following performs a simple translation of the box along the z-axis and some rescaling so that it is centered at the origin, and the coordinates of its corners are $(\pm 1, \pm 1, \pm 1)$:

$$T_{st} = \begin{bmatrix} \frac{2}{r-\ell} & 0 & 0 & -\frac{r+\ell}{r-\ell} \\ 0 & \frac{2}{t-b} & 0 & -\frac{t+b}{t-b} \\ 0 & 0 & \frac{2}{n-f} & -\frac{n+f}{n-f} \\ 0 & 0 & 0 & 1 \end{bmatrix}. \tag{3.47}$$

If the frustum is perfectly centered in the xy plane, then the first two components of the last column become zero. Finally, we define the canonical view transform T_{can} from (3.41) as

$$T_{can} = T_{st} T_p. \tag{3.48}$$

Viewport Transform

The last transform to be applied in the chain (3.41) is the *viewport transform* T_{vp}. After T_{can} has been applied, the x and y coordinates each range from -1 to 1. One last step is required to bring the projected points to the coordinates used to index pixels on a physical display. Let m be the number of horizontal pixels and n be the number of vertical pixels. For example, $n = 1,080$ and $m = 1,920$ for a 1080p display. Suppose that the display is indexed with rows running from 0 to $n - 1$ and columns from 0 to $m - 1$. Furthermore, $(0, 0)$ is in the lower left corner. In this case, the viewport transform is

$$T_{vp} = \begin{bmatrix} \frac{m}{2} & 0 & 0 & \frac{m-1}{2} \\ 0 & \frac{n}{2} & 0 & \frac{n-1}{2} \\ 0 & 0 & 1 & 0 \\ 0 & 0 & 0 & 1 \end{bmatrix}. \tag{3.49}$$

Left and Right Eyes

We now address how the transformation chain (3.41) is altered for stereoscopic viewing. Let t denote the distance between the left and right eyes. Its value in the real world varies across people, and its average is around $t = 0.064$ meters. To handle the left eye view, we need to simply shift the cyclopean (center) eye horizontally to the left. Recall from Section 3.4 that the inverse actually gets applied. The models need to be shifted to the right. Therefore, let

$$T_{left} = \begin{bmatrix} 1 & 0 & 0 & \frac{t}{2} \\ 0 & 1 & 0 & 0 \\ 0 & 0 & 1 & 0 \\ 0 & 0 & 0 & 1 \end{bmatrix}, \tag{3.50}$$

which corresponds to a right shift of the models, when viewed from the eye. This transform is placed after T_{eye} to adjust its output. The appropriate modification to (3.41) is

$$T = T_{vp} T_{can} T_{left} T_{eye} T_{rb}. \tag{3.51}$$

By symmetry, the right eye is similarly handled by replacing T_{left} in (3.51) with

$$T_{right} = \begin{bmatrix} 1 & 0 & 0 & -\frac{t}{2} \\ 0 & 1 & 0 & 0 \\ 0 & 0 & 1 & 0 \\ 0 & 0 & 0 & 1 \end{bmatrix}. \tag{3.52}$$

This concludes the explanation of the entire chain of transformations to place and move models in the virtual world and then have them appear in the right place on a display. After reading Chapter 4, it will become clear that one final transformation may be needed after the entire chain has been applied. This is done to compensate for nonlinear optical distortions that occur due to wide-angle lenses in many VR headsets.

Further Reading

Most of the matrix transforms appear in standard computer graphics texts. The presentation in this chapter closely follows [205]. For more details on quaternions and their associated algebraic properties, see [160]. Robotics texts usually cover 3D transformations for both rigid bodies and chains of bodies, and also consider kinematic singularities; see [166, 309].

CHAPTER FOUR
Light and Optics

Knowing how light propagates in the physical world is crucial to understanding VR. One reason is the interface between visual displays and our eyes. Light is emitted from displays and arrives on our retinas in a way that convincingly reproduces how light arrives through normal vision in the physical world. In the current generation of VR headsets, a system of both engineered and natural lenses (parts of our eyes) guides the light. Another reason to study light propagation is the construction of virtual worlds. Chapter 3 covered purely *geometric* aspects of modeling. The next logical step is to model the *physics* of light propagation through virtual worlds; this will be continued in Chapter 7, which describes what should be rendered on the visual display. Finally, light propagation is also helpful to understanding how cameras work, which provides another way to present a virtual world: through panoramic videos. Cameras are also important for tracking, which will be discussed in Section 9.3.

Section 4.1 covers basic physical properties of light, including its interaction with materials and its spectral properties. Section 4.2 provides idealized models of how lenses work. Section 4.3 then shows many ways that lens behavior deviates from the ideal model, thereby degrading VR experiences. Section 4.4 introduces the human eye as an optical system of lenses, before eyes and human vision are covered in much more detail in Chapter 5. Cameras, which can be considered as engineered eyes, are introduced in Section 4.5. Finally, Section 4.6 briefly covers visual display technologies, which emit light that is intended for consumption by the human eyes.

4.1 Basic Behavior of Light

Light can be described in three ways that appear to be mutually incompatible:

1. Photons: Tiny particles of energy moving through space at high speeds (no need for quantum mechanics in this book!). This interpretation is helpful when considering the amount of light received by a sensor or receptor.
2. Waves: Ripples through space that are similar to waves propagating on the surface of water, but are 3D. The *wavelength* is the distance between peaks. This interpretation is helpful when considering the spectrum of colors.

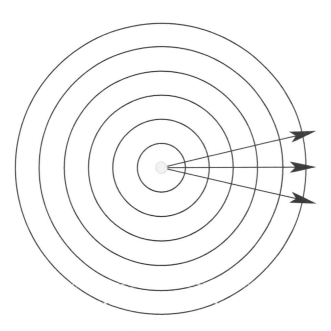

Figure 4.1 Waves and visibility rays emanating from a point light source.

3. Rays: A ray traces the motion of a single hypothetical photon. The direction is perpendicular to the wavefronts (see Figure 4.1). This interpretation is helpful when explaining lenses and defining the concept of visibility.

Fortunately, modern physics has explained how these interpretations are in fact compatible; each is useful in this book.

Spreading Waves

Figure 4.1 shows how waves would propagate from a hypothetical point light source. The density would be the same in all directions (radial symmetry), but would decrease as the light source becomes more distant. Recall that the surface area of a sphere with radius r is $4\pi r^2$. Consider centering a spherical screen around the light source. The total number of photons per second hitting a screen of radius 1 should be the same as for a screen of radius 2; however, the density (photons per second per area) should decrease by a factor of 1/4 because they are distributed over four times the area. Thus, photon density decreases quadratically as a function of distance from a point light source.

The curvature of the wavefronts also decreases as the point light source becomes further away. If the waves were to propagate infinitely far away, then they would completely flatten, as shown in Figure 4.2. This results in the important case of *parallel wavefronts*. Without the help of lenses or mirrors, it is impossible to actually obtain this case from a tiny light source in the physical world because it cannot be so far away; however, it serves as both a useful approximation for distant light sources and as an ideal way to describe lenses mathematically. Keep in mind that at any finite distance from a point light source, the rays of light always diverge; it is impossible to make them converge without the help of lenses or mirrors.

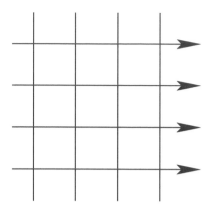

Figure 4.2 If the point light source were infinitely far away, then parallel wavefronts would be obtained. Other names for this setting are collimated light, parallel rays, rays from infinity, rays to infinity, and zero vergence.

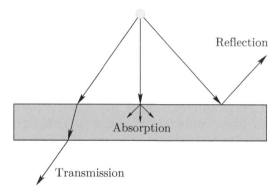

Figure 4.3 As light energy hits the boundary of a different medium, there are three possibilities: transmission, absorption, and reflection.

Interactions with Materials

As light strikes the surface of a material, one of three behaviors might occur, as shown in Figure 4.3. In the case of *transmission*, the energy travels through the material and exits the other side. For a transparent material, such as glass, the transmitted light rays alter their speed and bend according to Snell's law, which will be covered in Section 4.2. For a translucent material that is not transparent, the rays scatter into various directions before exiting. In the case of *absorption*, energy is absorbed by the material as the light becomes trapped. The third case is *reflection*, in which the light is deflected from the surface. Along a perfectly smooth or polished surface, the rays reflect in the same way: the exit angle is equal to the entry angle. See Figure 4.4. This case is called *specular reflection*, in contrast to *diffuse reflection*, in which the reflected rays scatter in arbitrary directions. Usually, all three cases of transmission, absorption, and reflection occur simultaneously. The amount of energy divided between the cases depends on many factors, such as the angle of approach, the wavelength, and differences between the two adjacent materials or media.

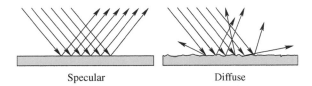

Specular   Diffuse

Figure 4.4 Two extreme modes of reflection are shown. Specular reflection means that all rays reflect at the same angle at which they approached. Diffuse reflection means that the rays scatter in a way that could be independent of their approach angle. Specular reflection is common for a polished surface, such as a mirror, whereas diffuse reflection corresponds to a rough surface.

Figure 4.5 Visible light spectrum corresponds to the range of electromagnetic waves that have wavelengths between 400 nm and 700 nm.

A Jumble of Wavelengths

Figure 4.1 presents an oversimplified view that will make it easy to understand idealized lenses in Section 4.2. Unfortunately, it misses many details that become important in other settings, such as understanding lens aberrations (Section 4.3) or how light interacts with materials in the physical world. The remainder of this section therefore considers various realistic complications that arise.

Coherent versus Jumbled Light

The first complication is that light sources usually do not emit *coherent light*, a term that means the wavefronts are perfectly aligned in time and space. A laser is an exceptional case that indeed produces coherent light. It emits parallel waves of a constant wavelength that are also synchronized in time so that their peaks align as they propagate. Common light sources, such as light bulbs and the sun, instead emit a jumble of waves that have various wavelengths and do not have their peaks aligned.

Wavelengths and Colors

To make sense out of the jumble of waves, we will describe how they are distributed in terms of wavelengths. Figure 4.5 shows the range of wavelengths that are visible to humans. Each wavelength corresponds to a *spectral color*, which is what we would perceive with a coherent light source fixed at that wavelength alone. Wavelengths between 700 and 1000 nm are called *infrared*, which are not visible to us, but some cameras can sense them (see Section 9.3). Wavelengths between 100 and 400 nm are called *ultraviolet*; they are not part of our visible spectrum, but some birds, insects, and fish can perceive ultraviolet wavelengths over 300 nm. Thus, our notion of visible light is already tied to *human* perception.

Spectral Power

Figure 4.6 shows how the wavelengths are distributed for common light sources. An ideal light source would have all visible wavelengths represented with equal energy, leading to idealized *white* light. The opposite is total darkness, which is *black*. We

LIGHT AND OPTICS

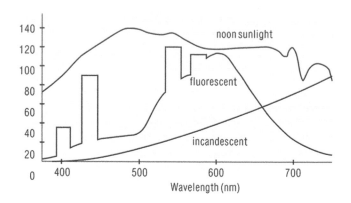

Figure 4.6 The *spectral power distribution* for some common light sources [298].

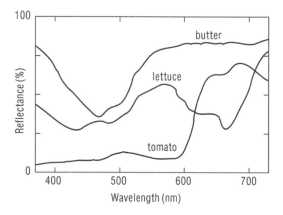

Figure 4.7 The *spectral reflection function* of some common familiar materials [298].

usually do not allow a light source to propagate light directly onto our retinas. (Don't stare at the sun!) Instead, we observe light that is reflected from objects all around us, causing us to perceive their color. Each surface has its own distribution of wavelengths that it *reflects*. The fraction of light energy that is reflected back depends on the wavelength, leading to the plots shown in Figure 4.7. For us to perceive an object surface as red, the red wavelengths must be included in the light source *and* the surface must strongly reflect red wavelengths. Other wavelengths must also be suppressed. For example, the light source could be white (containing all wavelengths) and the object could strongly reflect all wavelengths, causing the surface to appear white, not red. Section 6.3 will provide more details on color perception.

Frequency
Often, it is useful to talk about frequency instead of wavelength. The *frequency* is the number of times per second that wave peaks pass through a fixed location. Using both the wavelength λ and the speed s, the frequency f is calculated as

$$f = \frac{s}{\lambda}.$$

(4.1)

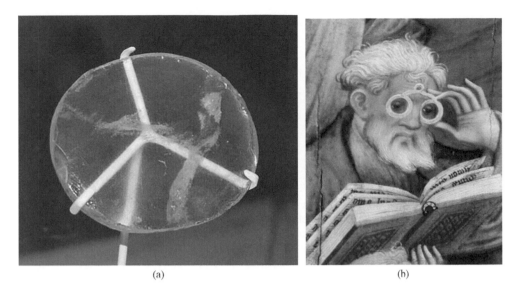

Figure 4.8 (a) The earliest known artificially constructed lens, which was made between 750 and 710 BC in the ancient Assyrian city of Nimrud. It is not known whether this artifact was purely ornamental or used to produce focused images. (b) A painting by Conrad con Soest from 1403, which shows the use of reading glasses for an elderly male.

The speed of light in a vacuum is a universal constant c with value approximately equal to 3×10^8 m/s. In this case, $s = c$ in (4.1). Light propagates roughly 0.03 percent faster in a vacuum than in air, causing the difference to be neglected in most engineering calculations. Visible light in air has a frequency range of roughly 400 to 800 terahertz, which is obtained by applying (4.1). As light propagates through denser media, such as water or lenses, s is significantly smaller; that difference is the basis of optical systems, which are covered next.

4.2 Lenses

Lenses have been made for thousands of years, with the oldest known artifact shown in Figure 4.8(a). It was constructed before 700 BC in the ancient Assyrian city of Nimrud. Whether constructed from transparent materials or from polished surfaces that act as mirrors, lenses bend rays of light so that a focused image is formed. Over the centuries, their uses have given rise to several well-known devices, such as eyeglasses (Figure 4.8(b)), telescopes, magnifying glasses, binoculars, cameras, and microscopes. Optical engineering is therefore filled with design patterns that indicate how to optimize the designs of these well-understood devices. Virtual reality headsets are unlike classical optical devices, leading to many new challenges that are outside of the standard patterns that have existed for centuries. Thus, the lens design patterns for VR are still being written. The first step toward addressing the current challenges is to understand how simple lenses work.

Snell's Law
Lenses work because of *Snell's law*, which expresses how much rays of light bend when entering or exiting a transparent material. Recall that the speed of light in a

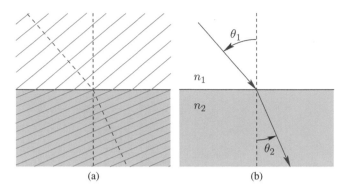

Figure 4.9 Propagating wavefronts from a medium with low refractive index (such as air) to one with a higher index (such as glass). (a) The effect of slower propagation on the wavefronts is shown as they enter the lower medium. (b) This shows the resulting bending of a light ray, which is always perpendicular to the wavefronts. Snell's law relates the refractive indices and angles as $n_1 \sin \theta_1 = n_2 \sin \theta_2$.

medium is less than the speed c in an vacuum. For a given material, let its *refractive index* be defined as

$$n = \frac{c}{s}, \tag{4.2}$$

in which s is the speed of light in the medium. For example, $n = 2$ means that light takes twice as long to traverse the medium than through a vacuum. For some common examples, $n = 1.000293$ for air, $n = 1.33$ for water, and $n = 1.523$ for crown glass.

Figure 4.9 shows what happens to incoming light waves and rays. Suppose in this example that the light is traveling from air into glass, so that $n_1 < n_2$. Let θ_1 represent the incoming angle with respect to the surface normal, and let θ_2 represent the resulting angle as it passes through the material. Snell's law relates the four quantities as

$$n_1 \sin \theta_1 = n_2 \sin \theta_2. \tag{4.3}$$

Typically, n_1/n_2 and θ_1 are given, so that (4.3) is solved for θ_2 to obtain

$$\theta_2 = \sin^{-1}\left(\frac{n_1 \sin \theta_1}{n_2}\right). \tag{4.4}$$

If $n_1 < n_2$, then θ_2 is closer to perpendicular than θ_1. If $n_1 > n_2$, then θ_2 is further from perpendicular. The case of $n_1 > n_2$ is also interesting in that light may not penetrate the surface if the incoming angle θ_1 is too large. The range of $\sin^{-1}$ is 0 to 1, which implies that (4.4) provides a solution for θ_2 only if

$$(n_1/n_2)\sin \theta_1 \leq 1. \tag{4.5}$$

If the preceding condition does not hold, then the light rays reflect from the surface. This situation occurs while one is underwater and looking up at the surface. Rather than being able to see the world above, a swimmer, for example, might instead see a reflection, depending on the viewing angle.

Prisms
Imagine shining a laser beam through a prism, as shown in Figure 4.10. Snell's law can be applied to calculate how the light ray bends after it enters and exits

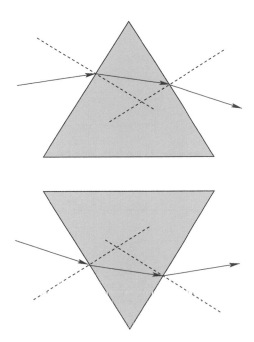

Figure 4.10 The upper part shows how a simple prism bends ascending rays into descending rays, provided that the incoming ray slope is not too high. This was achieved by applying Snell's law at the incoming and outgoing boundaries. Placing the prism upside down causes descending rays to become ascending. Pulling both of these together, we will see that a lens is like a stack of prisms that force diverging rays to converge through the power of refraction.

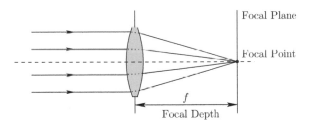

Figure 4.11 A simple convex lens causes parallel rays to converge at the focal point. The dashed line is the *optical axis*, which is perpendicular to the lens and pokes through its center.

the prism. Note that for the upright prism, a ray pointing slightly upward becomes bent downward. Recall that a larger refractive index inside the prism would cause greater bending. By placing the prism upside down, rays pointing slightly downward are bent upward. Once the refractive index is fixed, the bending depends only on the angles at which the rays enter and exit the surface, rather than on the thickness of the prism. To construct a lens, we will exploit this principle and construct a kind of curved version of Figure 4.10.

Simple Convex Lens

Figure 4.11 shows a simple convex lens, which should remind you of the prisms in Figure 4.10. Instead of making a diamond shape, the lens surface is spherically

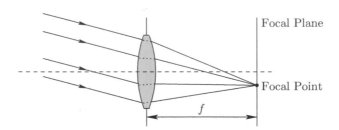

Figure 4.12 If the rays are not perpendicular to the lens, then the focal point is shifted away from the optical axis.

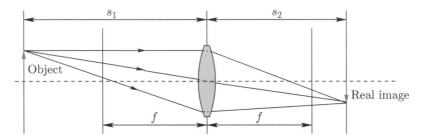

Figure 4.13 In the real world, an object is not infinitely far away. When placed at distance s_1 from the lens, a real image forms in a focal plane at distance $s_2 > f$ behind the lens, as calculated using (4.6).

curved so that incoming, parallel, horizontal rays of light converge to a point on the other side of the lens. This special place of convergence is called the *focal point*. Its distance from the lens center is called the *focal depth* or *focal length*.

The incoming rays in Figure 4.11 are special in two ways: (1) they are parallel, thereby corresponding to a source that is infinitely far away, and (2) they are perpendicular to the plane in which the lens is centered. If the rays are parallel but not perpendicular to the lens plane, then the focal point shifts accordingly, as shown in Figure 4.12. In this case, the focal point is not on the optical axis. There are two DOFs of incoming ray directions, leading to a *focal plane* that contains all of the focal points. Unfortunately, this planarity is just an approximation; Section 4.3 explains what really happens. In this idealized setting, a *real image* is formed in the image plane, as if it were a projection screen that is showing how the world looks in front of the lens (assuming everything in the world is very far away).

If the rays are not parallel, then it may still be possible to focus them into a real image, as shown in Figure 4.13. Suppose that a lens is given that has focal length f. If the light source is placed at distance s_1 from the lens, then the rays from that will be in focus if and only if the following equation is satisfied (which is derived from Snell's law):

$$\frac{1}{s_1} + \frac{1}{s_2} = \frac{1}{f}. \tag{4.6}$$

Figure 4.11 corresponds to the idealized case in which $s_1 = \infty$, for which solving (4.6) yields $s_2 = f$. What if the object being viewed is not completely flat and lying in a plane perpendicular to the lens? In this case, there does not exist a single plane behind the lens that would bring the entire object into focus. We must tolerate the fact that most of it will be approximately in focus. Unfortunately, this is the situation

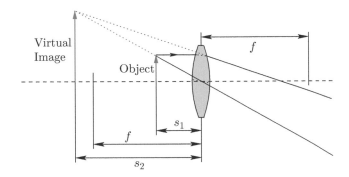

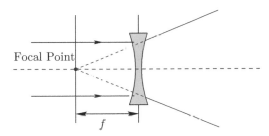

Figure 4.14 If the object is very close to the lens, then the lens cannot force its outgoing light rays to converge to a focal point. In this case, however, a virtual image appears and the lens works as a magnifying glass. This is the way lenses are commonly used for VR headsets.

Figure 4.15 In the case of a concave lens, parallel rays are forced to diverge. The rays can be extended backward through the lens to arrive at a focal point on the left side. The usual sign convention is that $f < 0$ for concave lenses.

almost always encountered in the real world, including the focus provided by our own eyes (see Section 4.4).

If the light source is placed too close to the lens, then the outgoing rays might be diverging so much that the lens cannot force them to converge. If $s_1 = f$, then the outgoing rays would be parallel ($s_2 = \infty$). If $s_1 < f$, then (4.6) yields $s_2 < 0$. In this case, a real image is not formed; however, something interesting happens: the phenomenon of *magnification*. A *virtual image* appears when looking into the lens, as shown in Figure 4.14. This is exactly what happens in the case of the View-Master and the VR headsets that were shown in Figure 2.11. The screen is placed so that it appears magnified. To the user viewing looking through the lenses, it appears as if the screen is infinitely far away (and quite enormous!).

Lensmaker's Equation

For a given simple lens, the focal length f can be calculated using the Lensmaker's Equation (also derived from Snell's law):

$$(n_2 - n_1)\left(\frac{1}{r_1} + \frac{1}{r_2}\right) = \frac{1}{f}. \tag{4.7}$$

The parameters r_1 and r_2 represent the radius of curvature of each of the two lens surfaces (front and back). This version assumes a *thin lens approximation*, which

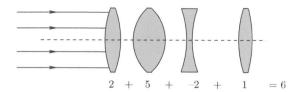

Figure 4.16 To calculate the combined optical power of a chain of lenses, the algebra is simple: add their diopters. This arrangement of four lenses is equivalent to a six-diopter lens, which has a focal length of 0.1667 m.

means that the lens thickness is small relative to r_1 and r_2. Also, it is typically assumed that $n_1 = 1$, which is approximately true for air.

Concave Lenses

For the sake of completeness, we include the case of a *concave* simple lens, shown in Figure 4.15. Parallel rays are forced to diverge rather than converge; however, a meaningful notion of negative focal length exists by tracing the diverging rays backwards through the lens. The Lensmaker's Equation (4.7) can be slightly adapted to calculate negative f in this case [105].

Diopters

For some optical systems used in VR, several lenses will be combined in succession. What is the effect of the combination? A convenient method to answer this question with simple arithmetic was invented by ophthalmologists. The idea is to define a *diopter*, which is $D = 1/f$. Thus, it is the reciprocal of the focal length. If a lens focuses parallel rays at a distance of 0.2 m in behind the lens, then $D = 5$. A larger diopter D means greater converging power. Likewise, a concave lens yields $D < 0$, with a lower number implying greater divergence. To combine several nearby lenses in succession, we simply add their diopters to determine their equivalent power as a single, simple lens. Figure 4.16 shows an example.

4.3 Optical Aberrations

If lenses in the real world behaved *exactly* as described in Section 4.2, then VR systems would be much simpler and more impressive than they typically are. Unfortunately, numerous imperfections, called *aberrations*, degrade the images formed by lenses. Because these problems are perceptible in everyday uses, such as viewing content through VR headsets or images from cameras, they are important to understand so that some compensation for them can be designed into the VR system.

Chromatic Aberration

Recall from Section 4.1 that light energy is usually a jumble of waves with a spectrum of wavelengths. You have probably seen that the colors of the entire visible spectrum nicely separate when white light is shined through a prism. This is a beautiful phenomenon, but for lenses is a terrible annoyance because it separates the focused image based on color. This problem is called *chromatic aberration*.

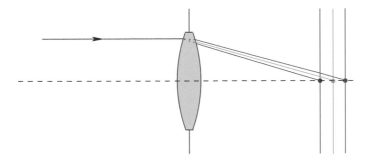

Figure 4.17 Chromatic aberration is caused by longer wavelengths traveling more quickly through the lens. The unfortunate result is a different focal plane for each wavelength or color.

Figure 4.18 The upper image is properly focused whereas the lower image suffers from chromatic aberration.

The problem is that the speed of light through a medium depends on the wavelength. We should therefore write a material's refractive index as $n(\lambda)$ to indicate that it is a function of λ. Figure 4.17 shows the effect on a simple convex lens. The focal depth becomes a function of wavelength. If we shine red, green, and blue lasers directly into the lens along the same ray, then each color would cross the optical axis in a different place, resulting in red, green, and blue focal points. Recall the spectral power distribution and reflection functions from Section 4.1. For common light sources and materials, the light passing through a lens results in a whole continuum of focal points. Figure 4.18 shows an image with chromatic aberration artifacts. Chromatic aberration can be reduced at greater expense by combining convex and concave lenses of different materials so that the spreading rays are partly coerced into converging [304].

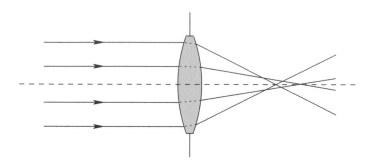

Figure 4.19 Spherical aberration causes imperfect focus because rays away from the optical axis are refracted more than those at the periphery.

Spherical Aberration

Figure 4.19 shows *spherical aberration*, which is caused by rays further away from the lens center being refracted more than rays near the center. The result is similar to that of chromatic aberration, but this phenomenon is a *monochromatic* aberration because it is independent of the light wavelength. Incoming parallel rays are focused at varying depths, rather then being concentrated at a single point. The result is some blur that cannot be compensated for by moving the object, lens, or image plane. Alternatively, the image might instead focus onto a curved surface, called the *Petzval surface*, rather then the image plane. This aberration arises due to the spherical shape of the lens. An *aspheric lens* is more complex and has nonspherical surfaces that are designed to specifically eliminate the spherical aberration and reduce other aberrations.

Optical Distortion

Even if the image itself projects onto the image plane, it might be distorted at the periphery. Assuming that the lens is radially symmetric, the distortion can be described as a stretching or compression of the image that becomes increasingly severe away from the optical axis. Figure 4.20 shows how this affects the image for two opposite cases: *barrel distortion* and *pincushion distortion*. For lenses that have a wide field of view, the distortion is stronger, especially in the extreme case of a *fish-eyed lens*. Figure 4.21 shows an image that has strong barrel distortion. Correcting this distortion is crucial for VR headsets that have a wide field of view; otherwise, the virtual world would appear to be warped.

Astigmatism

Figure 4.22 depicts *astigmatism*, which is a lens aberration that occurs for incoming rays that are not perpendicular to the lens. Up until now, our lens drawings have been 2D; however, a third dimension is needed to understand this new aberration. The rays can be off-axis in one dimension, but aligned in another. By moving the image plane along the optical axis, it becomes impossible to bring the image into focus. Instead, horizontal and vertical focal depths appear, as shown in Figure 4.23.

Coma and Flare

Finally, *coma* is yet another aberration. In this case, the image magnification varies dramatically as the rays are far from perpendicular to the lens. The result is a

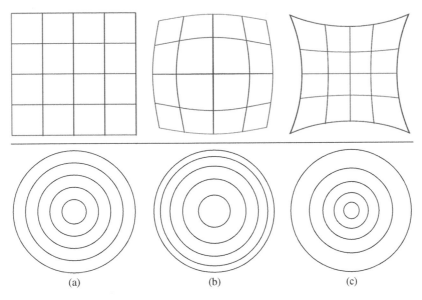

Figure 4.20 Common optical distortions. (a) Original images. (b) Barrel distortion. (c) Pincushion distortion. For the upper row, the grid becomes nonlinearly distorted. The lower row illustrates how circular symmetry is nevertheless maintained.

Figure 4.21 An image with barrel distortion, taken by a fish-eyed lens.

"comet" pattern in the image plane. Another phenomenon is *lens flare*, in which rays from very bright light scatter through the lens and often show circular patterns. This is often seen in movies as the viewpoint passes by the sun or stars, and is sometimes added artificially.

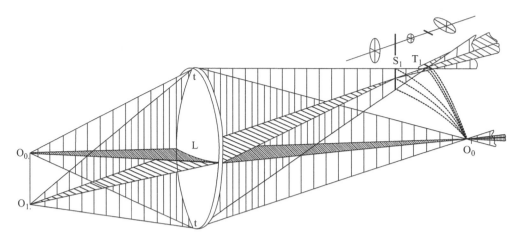

Figure 4.22 Astigmatism is primarily caused by incoming rays being off-axis in one plane, but close to perpendicular in another [362].

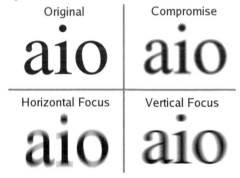

Figure 4.23 Due to astigmatism, it becomes impossible to bring the image perfectly into focus. At one depth, it might be focused horizontally, while at another it is focused vertically. We are forced to choose a compromise.

All of the aberrations of this section complicate the system or degrade the experience in a typical VR headset; therefore, substantial engineering effort is spent on mitigating these problems.

4.4 The Human Eye

We have covered enough concepts in this chapter to describe the basic operation of the human eye, which is clearly an important component in any VR system. Here it will be considered as part of an optical system of lenses and images. The physiological and perceptual parts of human vision are deferred until Chapter 5.

Figure 4.24 shows a cross section of the human eye facing left. Parallel light rays are shown entering from the left; compare to Figure 4.11, which shows a similar situation for an engineered convex lens. Although the eye operation is similar to the engineered setting, several important differences arise at this stage. The focal plane is replaced by a spherically curved surface called the *retina*. The retina contains *photoreceptors* that convert the light into neural pulses; this is covered in Sections 5.1 and 5.2. The interior of the eyeball is actually liquid, as opposed to air. The refractive

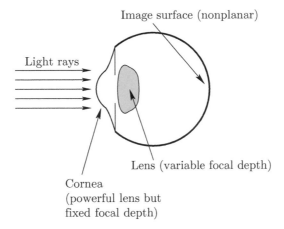

Figure 4.24 A simplified view of the human eye as an optical system.

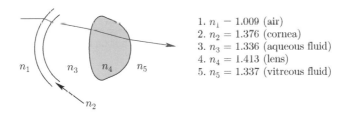

1. $n_1 - 1.009$ (air)
2. $n_2 = 1.376$ (cornea)
3. $n_3 = 1.336$ (aqueous fluid)
4. $n_4 = 1.413$ (lens)
5. $n_5 = 1.337$ (vitreous fluid)

Figure 4.25 A ray of light travels through five media before hitting the retina. The indices of refraction are indicated. Considering Snell's law, the greatest bending occurs due to the transition from air to the cornea. Note that once the ray enters the eye, it passes through only liquid or solid materials.

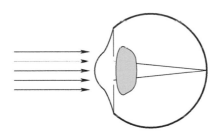

Figure 4.26 Normal eye operation, with relaxed lens.

indices of materials along the path from the outside air to the retina are shown in Figure 4.25.

The Optical Power of the Eye

The outer diameter of the eyeball is roughly 24 mm, which implies that a lens of at least 40D would be required to cause convergence of parallel rays onto the retina center inside of the eye (recall diopters from Section 4.2). There are effectively two convex lenses: the *cornea* and the *lens*. The cornea is the outermost part of the eye where the light first enters and has the greatest optical power, approximately 40D.

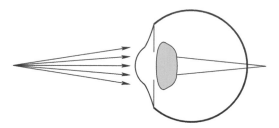

Figure 4.27 A closer object yields diverging rays, but with a relaxed lens the image is blurry on the retina.

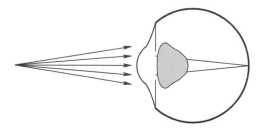

Figure 4.28 The process of accommodation: the eye muscles pull on the lens, causing it to increase the total optical power and focus the image on the retina.

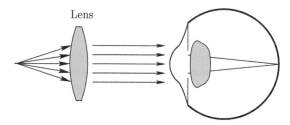

Figure 4.29 Placing a convex lens in front of the eye is another way to increase the optical power so that nearby objects can be brought into focus by the eye. This is the principle of reading glasses.

The eye lens is less powerful and provides an additional 20D. By adding diopters, the combined power of the cornea and lens is 60D, which means that parallel rays are focused onto the retina at a distance of roughly 17 mm from the outer cornea. Figure 4.26 shows how this system acts on parallel rays for a human with normal vision. Images of faraway objects are thereby focused onto the retina.

Accommodation

What happens when we want to focus on a nearby object, rather than one "infinitely far" away? Without any changes to the optical system, the image would be blurry on the retina, as shown in Figure 4.27. Fortunately, and miraculously, the lens changes its diopter to accommodate the closer distance. This process is appropriately called *accommodation*, as is depicted in Figure 4.28. The diopter change is effected through muscles that pull on the lens to change its shape. In young children, the lens can increase its power by an additional 15 to 20D, which explains why a child might hold something right in front of your face and expect you to focus on it; they can! At 20D, this corresponds to focusing on an object that is only 5 cm from the cornea.

Young adults already lose this ability and can accommodate up to about 10D. Thus, with normal vision they can read a book down to a distance of about 10 cm (with some eyestrain). Once adults reach 50 years old, little or no accommodation ability remains. This condition is called *presbyopia*. Figure 4.29 shows the most common treatment, which is to place reading glasses in front of the eye.

Vision Abnormalities

The situations presented so far represent normal vision throughout a person's lifetime. One problem could be that the optical system simply does not have enough optical power to converge parallel rays onto the retina. This condition is called *hyperopia* or *farsightedness*. Eyeglasses come to the rescue. The simple fix is to place a convex lens (positive diopter) in front of the eye, as in the case of reading glasses. In the opposite direction, some eyes have too much optical power. This case is called *myopia* or *nearsightedness*, and a concave lens (negative diopter) is placed in front of the eye to reduce the optical power appropriately. Recall that we have two eyes, not one. This allows the possibility for each eye to have a different problem, resulting in different lens diopters per eye. Other vision problems may exist beyond optical power. The most common is astigmatism, which was covered in Section 4.3. In human eyes this is caused by the cornea having an excessively elliptical shape, rather than being radially symmetric. Special, nonsimple lenses are needed to correct this condition. You might also wonder whether the aberrations from Section 4.3, such as chromatic aberration, occur in the human eye. They do; however, they are corrected automatically by our brains because we have learned to interpret such flawed images our entire lives!

A Simple VR Headset

Now suppose we are constructing a VR headset by placing a screen very close to the eyes. Young adults would already be unable to bring it into focus if it were closer than 10 cm. We want to bring it close so that it fills the view of the user. Therefore, the optical power is increased by using a convex lens, functioning in the same way as reading glasses. See Figure 4.30. This is also the process of magnification, from Section 4.2. Each lens is usually placed at the distance of its focal depth. Using (4.6), this implies that $s_2 = -f$, resulting in $s_1 = \infty$. The screen appears as an enormous virtual image that is infinitely far away. Note, however, that a real image is nevertheless projected onto the retina. We do not perceive the world around us unless real images are formed on our retinas.

To account for people with vision problems, a focusing knob may appear on the headset, which varies the distance between the lens and the screen. This adjusts the optical power so that the rays between the lens and the cornea are no longer parallel. They can be made to converge, which helps people with hyperopia. Alternatively, they can be made to diverge, which helps people with myopia. Thus, they can focus sharply on the screen without placing their eyeglasses in front of the lens. However, if each eye requires a different diopter, then a focusing knob would be required for *each* eye. Furthermore, if they have astigmatism, then it cannot be corrected. Placing eyeglasses inside the headset may be the only remaining solution, but it may be uncomfortable and could reduce the field of view.

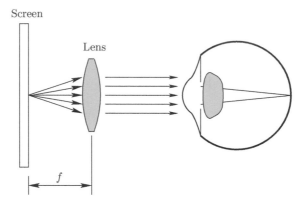

Figure 4.30 In VR headsets, the lens is typically placed so that the screen appears to be infinitely far away.

Many details have been skipped or dramatically simplified in this section. One important detail for a VR headset is that each lens should be centered perfectly in front of the cornea. If the distance between the two lenses is permanently fixed, then this is impossible to achieve for everyone who uses the headset. The *interpupillary distance*, or IPD, is the distance between human eye centers. The average among humans is around 64 mm, but it varies greatly by race, gender, and age (in the case of children). To be able to center the lenses for everyone, the distance between lens centers should be adjustable from around 55 to 75 mm. This is a common range for binoculars. Unfortunately, the situation is not even this simple because our eyes also rotate within their sockets, which changes the position and orientation of the cornea with respect to the lens. This amplifies optical aberration problems that were covered in Section 4.3. Eye movements will be covered in Section 5.3. Another important detail is the fidelity of our vision: what pixel density is needed for the screen that is placed in front of our eyes so that we do not notice the pixels? A similar question is how many dots per inch (DPI) are needed on a printed piece of paper so that we do not see the dots, even when viewed under a magnifying glass? We return to this question in Section 5.1.

4.5 Cameras

Now that we have covered the human eye, it seems natural to describe an engineered eye, otherwise known as a camera. People have built and used cameras for hundreds of years, starting with a *camera obscura* that allows light to pass through a *pinhole* and onto a surface that contains the real image. Figure 4.31 shows an example that you might have constructed to view a solar eclipse. (Recall the perspective transformation math from Section 3.4.) Eighteenth-century artists incorporated a mirror and tracing paper to un-invert the image and allow it to be perfectly copied. Across the nineteenth century, various chemically based technologies were developed to etch the image automatically from the photons hitting the imaging surface. Across the twentieth century, film was in widespread use, until *digital cameras* avoided the etching process altogether by electronically capturing the image using a sensor. Two

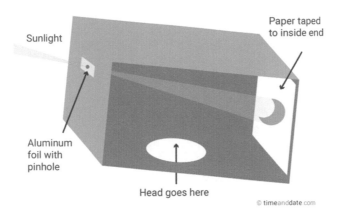

Figure 4.31 A pinhole camera that is recommended for viewing a solar eclipse.

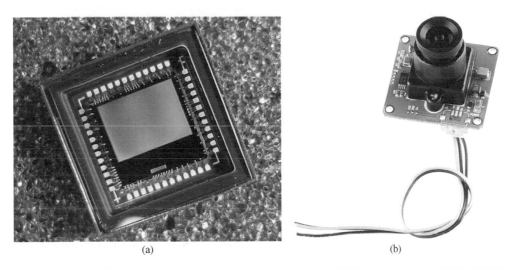

(a)   (b)

Figure 4.32 (a) A CMOS active-pixel image sensor. (b) A low-cost CMOS camera module (SEN-11745), ready for hobbyist projects.

popular technologies have been a *Charge-Coupled Device* (*CCD*) array and a *CMOS active-pixel image sensor*, which is shown in Figure 4.32(a). Such digital technologies record the amount of light hitting each pixel location along the image, which directly produces a captured image. The costs of these devices continue to plummet, allowing typical hobbyists to buy low cost camera modules for their projects.

Shutters
Several practical issues arise when capturing digital images. The image is an 2D array of *pixels*, each of which having red (R), green (G), and blue (B) values that typically range from 0 to 255. Consider the total amount of light energy that hits the image plane. For a higher-resolution camera, there will generally be less photons per pixel because the pixels are smaller. Each sensing element (one per color per pixel) can be imagined as a bucket that collects photons, much like drops of rain. To control

Figure 4.33 The wings of a flying helicopter are apparently bent backwards due to the rolling shutter effect.

the amount of photons, a *shutter* blocks all the light, opens for a fixed interval of time, and then closes again. For a long interval (low *shutter speed*), more light is collected; however, the drawbacks are that moving objects in the scene will become blurry and that the sensing elements could become saturated with too much light. Photographers must strike a balance when determining the shutter speed to account for the amount of light in the scene, the sensitivity of the sensing elements, and the motion of the camera and objects in the scene.

Also relating to shutters, CMOS sensors unfortunately work by sending out the image information sequentially, line-by-line. The sensor is therefore coupled with a *rolling shutter*, which allows light to enter for each line, just before the information is sent. This means that the capture is not synchronized over the entire image, which leads to odd artifacts, such as the one shown in Figure 4.33. Image processing algorithms that work with rolling shutters and motion typically transform the image to correct for this problem. CCD sensors grab and send the entire image at once, resulting in a *global shutter*. CCDs have historically been more expensive than CMOS sensors, which resulted in widespread appearance of rolling shutter cameras in smartphones; however, the cost of global shutter cameras has rapidly decreased.

Aperture

The optical system also impacts the amount of light that arrives to the sensor. Using a pinhole, as shown in Figure 4.31, light would fall onto the image sensor, but it would not be bright enough for most purposes (other than viewing a solar eclipse). Therefore, a convex lens is used instead so that multiple rays are converged to the same point in the image plane; recall Figure 4.11. This generates more photons per sensing element. The main drawback is that the lens sharply focuses objects at a

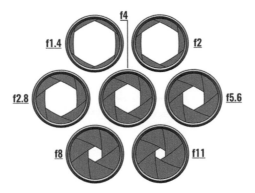

Figure 4.34 A spectrum of aperture settings, which control the amount of light that enters the lens. The values shown are called the *focal ratio* or *f-stop*.

single depth, while blurring others; recall (4.6). In the pinhole case, all depths are essentially "in focus," but there might not be enough light. Photographers therefore want to tune the optical system to behave more like a pinhole or more like a full lens, depending on the desired outcome. The result is a controllable *aperture* (Figure 4.34), which appears behind the lens and sets the size of the hole through which the light rays enter. A small radius mimics a pinhole by blocking all but the center of the lens. A large radius allows light to pass through the entire lens. Our eyes control the light levels in a similar manner by contracting or dilating our pupils. Finally, note that the larger the aperture, the more that the aberrations covered in Section 4.3 interfere with the imaging process.

4.6 Displays

Section 2.1 introduced displays as devices that stimulate a sense organ, which in this chapter is the human eye. What should we consider to be the first visual displays? The paintings shown in Section 1.3 are early instances of displays, but they have the unfortunate limitation that they display a single image in their lifetime. The ability to change images, ultimately leading to motion pictures, was first enabled by projection technologies. The camera obscura principle was refined into a *magic lantern*, which was invented in the seventeenth century by Christiaan Huygens. Popular until the nineteenth century, it allowed small, painted images to be projected onto a wall through the use of lenses and a bright light source. By the end of the nineteenth century, motion pictures could be shown on a large screen by a mechanical projector that cycled quickly through the frames.

Cathode Ray Tubes
The most important technological leap was the *cathode ray tube* or *CRT*, which gave birth to electronic displays, launched the era of television broadcasting, and helped

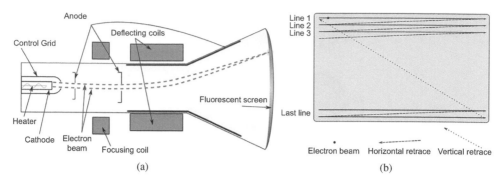

(a)   (b)

Figure 4.35 (a) In a cathode ray tube (CRT), an electron gun emits a beam of electrons, which are deflected in both X and Y directions according to an analog signal. When the beam hits the screen, an element of phosphor briefly lights up. (b) A special scanning pattern is used to draw out each video frame, line by line.

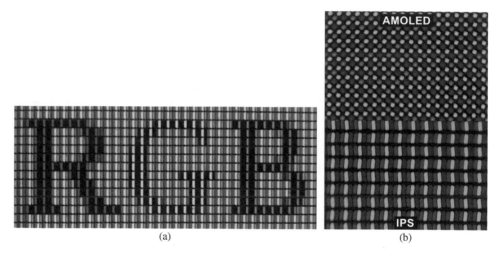

(a)   (b)

Figure 4.36 In displays, the pixels break into subpixels, much in the same way that photoreceptors break into red, blue, and green components. (a) An LCD display. (b) An AMOLED PenTile display from the Nexus One smartphone.

shape many concepts and terms that persist in modern displays today. Figure 4.35 shows the basic principles. The CRT enabled videos to be rendered to a screen, frame by frame. Each frame was scanned out line by line due to the physical limitations of the hardware. The scanning needed to repeat frequently, known as refreshing the phosphor elements. Each light in each position would persist for less than a millisecond. The scanout behavior and timing remains today for modern smartphone displays because of memory and computation architectures, but it is not ideal for VR usage. Section 6.2.2 will explain how motion is perceived when a sequence of frames is rendered to a display, and what goes wrong with VR systems.

The next major advance was to enable each picture element, or pixel, to be directly and persistently lit. Various technologies have been used to produce *flat-panel displays*, the output of which is illustrated in Figure 4.36. *Liquid crystal displays* (*LCD* displays) became widely available in calculators in the 1970s and progressed into larger, colorful screens by the 1990s. The liquid crystals themselves do not emit light, but most commonly a *backlight* shines from behind to illuminate the whole screen. Currently, the vast majority of flat-panel displays are on either LCDs or light emitting diodes (LEDs). In the case of LEDs, each pixel is directly lit. The consumer market for flat-panel displays was first driven by the need for flat, big-screen televisions and computer monitors. With the advancement of smartphones, miniaturized versions of these displays have been available with low cost, low power, and extremely high resolution. This enabled low-cost VR headset solutions by putting a lens in front of a smartphone screen, as shown in Figure 4.30.

Toward Custom VR Displays

The first step toward thinking about displays for VR is to consider the distance from the eyes. If it is meant to be viewed from far away, then it is called a *naked-eye display*. For a person with normal vision (or while wearing prescription glasses), the display should appear sharp without any additional help. If it is close enough so that lenses are needed to bring it into focus, then it is called a *near-eye display*. This is the common case in current VR headsets because the display needs to be placed very close to the eyes. It remains an active area of research to develop better near-eye display technologies, with a key challenge being whether the solutions are manufacturable on a large scale.

An important family of near-eye displays is based on a *microdisplay* and *waveguide*. The microdisplay is typically based on *liquid crystal on silicon* (or *LCoS*), which is a critical component in overhead projectors; microdisplays based on organic LEDs (*OLEDs*) are also gaining popularity. The size of the microdisplay is typically a few millimeters, and its emitted light is transported to the eyes through the use of reflective structures called a *waveguide*; see Figure 4.37. The Microsoft Hololens, Google Glass, and Magic Leap One are some well-known devices that were based on waveguides. The current engineering challenges are limited field of view, overall weight, difficult or costly manufacturing, and power loss and picture degradation as the waves travel through the waveguide.

A growing VR display technology is the *virtual retinal display* [341]. It works by a scanning beam principle similar to the CRT, but instead draws the image directly onto the human retina. A low-power laser can be pointed into a micromirror that can be rapidly rotated so that full images are quickly drawn onto the retina. Current engineering challenges are eye safety (do not shine an ordinary laser into your eyes!), mirror rotation frequency, and expanding the so-called *eye box* so that the images are drawn onto the retina regardless of where the eye is rotated.

To maximize human comfort, a display should ideally reproduce the conditions that occur from the propagation of light in a natural environment, which would allow the eyes to focus on objects at various distances in the usual way. The previously mentioned displays are known to cause vergence-accommodation mismatch (see Section 5.4), which causes discomfort to human viewers. For this reason, researchers have created displays that overcome this limitation. Two categories of research are *light-field displays* [75, 164, 201] and *varifocal displays* [4, 50, 129, 190, 209].

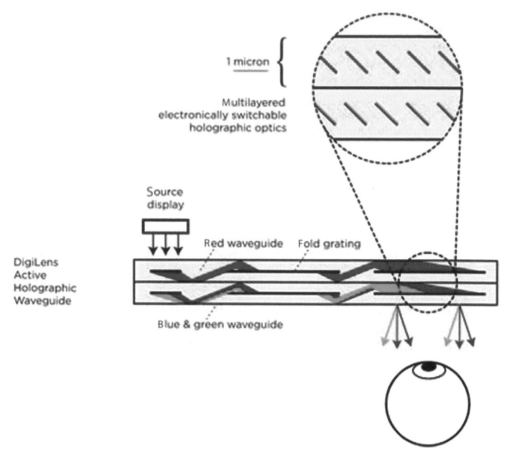

1 micron

Multilayered
electronically switchable
holographic optics

Source
display

Red waveguide   Fold grating

DigiLens
Active
Holographic
Waveguide

Blue & green waveguide

Figure 4.37 An illustration of how a DigiLens waveguide operates, as light is propagated from a small source display to the human eye.

Further Reading

Most of the basic lens and optical system concepts are covered in introductory university physics texts. For more advanced coverage, especially lens aberrations, see the classic optical engineering text: [304]. A convenient guide that quickly covers the geometry of optics is [105]. Thorough coverage of optical systems that utilize electronics, lasers, and MEMS is given in [159]. This provides a basis for understanding next-generation visual display technologies. An excellent book that considers the human eye in combination with engineered optical components is [302]. Cameras are covered from many different perspectives, including computer vision [113, 324], camera engineering [128], and photography [303]. Mathematical foundations of imaging are thoroughly covered in [19].

CHAPTER FIVE

The Physiology of Human Vision

What you perceive about the world around you is "all in your head." After reading Chapter 4, especially Section 4.4, you should understand that the light around us forms images on our retinas that capture colors, motions, and spatial relationships in the physical world. For someone with normal vision, these captured images may appear to have perfect clarity, speed, accuracy, and resolution, while being distributed over a large field of view. However, we are being fooled. We will see in this chapter that this apparent perfection of our vision is mostly an illusion because neural structures are filling in plausible details to generate a coherent picture in our heads that is consistent with our life experiences. When building VR technology that disrupts these processes, it is important to understand how they work. They were designed to do more with less, and fooling these processes with VR produces many unexpected side effects because the displayed stimuli are not a perfect replica of the surrounding world.

Section 5.1 continues where Section 4.4 left off by adding some anatomy of the human eye to the optical system. Most of the section is on photoreceptors, which are the "input pixels" that get paired with the "output pixels" of a digital display for VR. Section 5.2 offers a taste of neuroscience by explaining what is known about the visual information that hierarchically propagates from the photoreceptors up to the visual cortex. Section 5.3 explains how our eyes move, which serves a good purpose, but incessantly interferes with the images in our retinas. Section 5.4 concludes the chapter by applying the knowledge gained about visual physiology to determine VR display requirements, such as the screen resolution.

5.1 From the Cornea to Photoreceptors

Parts of the Eye

Figure 5.1 shows the physiology of a human eye. The shape is approximately spherical, with a diameter of around 24 mm and only slight variation among people. The *cornea* is a hard, transparent surface through which light enters and provides the greatest optical power (recall from Section 4.4). The rest of the outer surface of the eye is protected by a hard, white layer called the *sclera*. Most of the eye interior consists of *vitreous humor*, which is a transparent, gelatinous mass that allows light rays to penetrate with little distortion or attenuation.

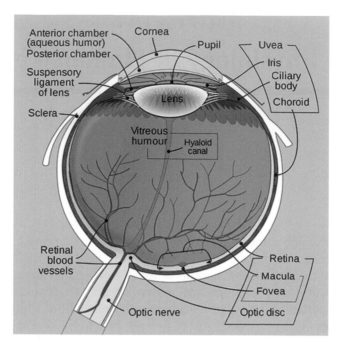

Figure 5.1 Physiology of the human eye. This viewpoint shows how the right eye would appear if sliced horizontally. (The nose would be to the left.)

As light rays cross the cornea, they pass through a small chamber containing *aqueous humor*, which is another transparent, gelatinous mass. After crossing this, rays enter the *lens* by passing through the *pupil*. The size of the pupil is controlled by a disc-shaped structure called the *iris*, which provides an aperture that regulates the amount of light that is allowed to pass. The optical power of the lens is altered by *ciliary muscles*. After passing through the lens, rays pass through the vitreous humor and strike the *retina*, which lines more than 180° of the inner eye boundary. Since Figure 5.1 shows a 2D cross section, the retina is shaped like an arc; however, keep in mind that it is a 2D surface. Imagine it as a curved counterpart to a visual display. To catch the light from the output pixels, it is lined with *photoreceptors*, which behave like "input pixels." The most important part of the retina is the *fovea*; the highest *visual acuity*, which is a measure of the sharpness or clarity of vision, is provided for rays that land on it. The *optic disc* is a small hole in the retina through which neural pulses are transmitted outside of the eye through the *optic nerve*. It is on the same side of the fovea as the nose.

Photoreceptors
The retina contains two kinds of photoreceptors for vision: (1) *rods*, which are triggered by very low levels of light, and (2) *cones*, which require more light and are designed to distinguish between colors. See Figure 5.2. To understand the scale, the width of the smallest cones is around 1000 nm. This is quite close to the wavelength of visible light, implying that photoreceptors could not be much smaller. Each human retina contains about 120 million rods and 6 million cones that are densely

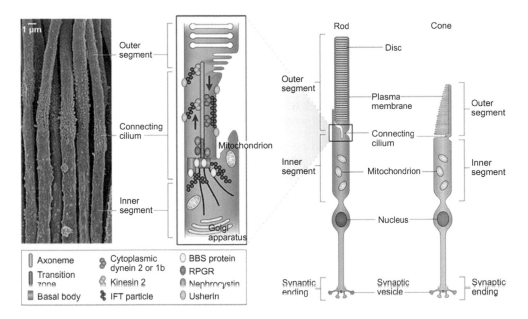

Figure 5.2 On the left is an electron micrograph image of photoreceptors. The right shows the structure and components of rods and cones. The outer segments contain photopigments that electrochemically respond when bombarded by photons [361]. Reprinted by permission of Springer Nature.

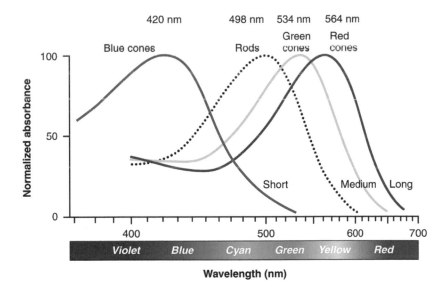

Figure 5.3 The sensitivity of rods and cones as a function of wavelength [29].

packed along the retina. Figure 5.3 shows the detection capabilities of each photoreceptor type. Rod sensitivity peaks at 498 nm, between blue and green in the spectrum. Three categories of cones exist, based on whether they are designed to sense blue, green, or red light.

Light source	Luminance (cd/m^2)	Photons per receptor
Paper in starlight	0.0003	0.01
Paper in moonlight	0.2	1
Computer monitor	63	100
Room light	316	1,000
Blue sky	2,500	10,000
Paper in sunlight	40,000	100,000

Figure 5.4 Several familiar settings and the approximate number of photons per second hitting a photoreceptor. (Figure adapted from [163, 207].)

Photoreceptors respond to light levels over a large dynamic range. Figure 5.4 shows several familiar examples. The luminance is measured in SI units of candelas per square meter, which corresponds directly to the amount of light power per area. The range spans seven orders of magnitude, from one photon hitting a photoreceptor every 100 seconds up to 100,000 photons per receptor per second. At low light levels, only rods are triggered. Our inability to distinguish colors at night is caused by the inability of rods to distinguish colors. Our eyes may take up to 35 minutes to fully adapt to low light, resulting in a monochromatic mode called *scotopic vision*. By contrast, our cones become active in brighter light. Adaptation to this trichromatic mode, called *photopic vision*, may take up to ten minutes. (You have undoubtedly noticed the adjustment period when someone unexpectedly turns on lights while you are lying in bed at night.)

Photoreceptor Density

The density of photoreceptors across the retina varies greatly, as plotted in Figure 5.5. The most interesting region is the *fovea*, which has the greatest concentration of photoreceptors. The innermost part of the fovea has a diameter of only 0.5 mm or an angular range of ±0.85°, and contains almost entirely cones. This implies that the eye must be pointed straight at a target to perceive a sharp, colored image. The entire fovea has diameter 1.5 mm (±2.6° angular range), with the outer ring having a dominant concentration of rods. Rays that enter the cornea from the sides land on parts of the retina with lower rod density and very low cone density. This corresponds to the case of *peripheral vision*. We are much better at detecting movement in our periphery, but cannot distinguish colors effectively. Peripheral movement detection may have helped our ancestors avoid being eaten by predators. Finally, the most intriguing part of the plot is the *blind spot*, where there are no photoreceptors. This is due to our retinas being inside-out and having no other way to route the neural signals to the brain; see Section 5.2.

The photoreceptor densities shown in Figure 5.5 leave us with a conundrum. With 20/20 vision, we perceive the world as if our eyes are capturing a sharp, colorful image over a huge angular range. This seems impossible, however, because we can only sense sharp, colored images in a narrow range. Furthermore, the blind spot should place a black hole in our image. Surprisingly, our *perceptual* processes produce an illusion that a complete image is being captured. This is accomplished by filling in the missing details using contextual information, which is described in Section 5.2, and by frequent eye movements, the subject of Section 5.3. If you are still

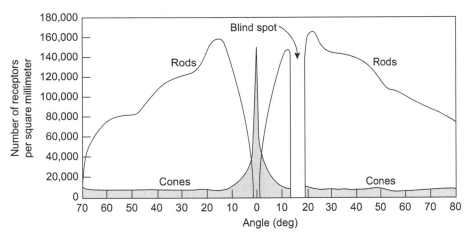

Figure 5.5 Photoreceptor density as a function of angle. The right of the plot is the nasal side (which corresponds to rays entering from the opposite, temporal side). An early version of this figure appeared in [245].

Figure 5.6 An experiment that reveals your blind spot. Close your right eye and look directly at the "X." Vary the distance of the paper (or screen) from your eye. Over some range, the dot should appear to vanish. You can carry this experiment one step further by writing an "X" and a dot on a textured surface, such as graph paper. In that case, the dot disappears and you might notice the surface texture perfectly repeating in the place where the dot once existed. This is caused by your brain filling in the expected texture over the blind spot!

not convinced that your brain is fooling you into seeing a complete image, then try the blind spot experiment shown in Figure 5.6.

5.2 From Photoreceptors to the Visual Cortex

Photoreceptors are transducers that convert the light-energy stimulus into an electrical signal called a neural impulse, thereby inserting information about the outside world into our neural structures. Recall from Section 2.3 that signals are propagated upward in a hierarchical manner, from photoreceptors to the visual cortex (Figure 2.19). Think about the influence that each photoreceptor has on the network of neurons. Figure 5.7 shows a simplified model. As the levels increase, the number of influenced neurons grows rapidly. Figure 5.8 shows the same diagram, but highlighted in a different way by showing how the number of photoreceptors that influence a single neuron increases with level. Neurons at the lowest levels are able to make simple comparisons of signals from neighboring photoreceptors. As the levels increase, the neurons may respond to a larger patch of the retinal image. This principle will become clear when seeing more neural structures in this section. Eventually, when signals reach the highest levels (beyond these figures), information from the memory of a lifetime of experiences is fused with the information that propagated

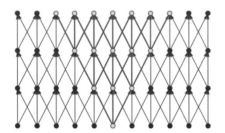

Level 3: Neural Cells

Level 2: Neural Cells

Level 1: Neural Cells

Level 0: Photoreceptors

Figure 5.7 Four levels in a simple hierarchy are shown. Each disk corresponds to a neural cell or photoreceptor, and the arrows indicate the flow of information. Photoreceptors generate information at Level 0. In this extremely simplified and idealized view, each photoreceptor and neuron connects to exactly three others at the next level. The red and gold part highlights the growing zone of influence that a single photoreceptor can have as the levels increase.

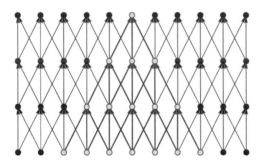

Level 3: Neural Cells

Level 2: Neural Cells

Level 1: Neural Cells

Level 0: Photoreceptors

Figure 5.8 This diagram is the same as Figure 5.7 except that the information feeding into a single neuron is highlighted. Consider the set of photoreceptors involved in the reaction of a single neural cell. This is called the *receptive field*. As the level increases, the receptive field size grows dramatically. Due to the spatial arrangement of the photoreceptors, this will imply that each neuron responds to a growing patch in the image on the retina. The patch increases in size at higher levels.

up from photoreceptors. As the brain performs significant processing, a perceptual phenomenon results, such as recognizing a face or judging the size of a tree. It takes the brain over 100 ms to produce a result that enters our consciousness.

Now consider the first layers of neurons in more detail, as shown in Figure 5.9. The information is sent from right to left, passing from the rods and cones to the bipolar, amacrine, and horizontal cells. These three types of cells are in the *inner nuclear layer*. From there, the signals reach the ganglion cells, which form the *ganglion cell layer*. Note that the light appears to be entering from the wrong direction: it passes over these neural cells before reaching the photoreceptors. This is due to the fact that the human retina is inside-out, as shown in Figure 5.10. Evolution got it right with octopuses and other cephalopods, for which the light directly reaches the photoreceptors. One consequence of an inside-out retina is that the axons of the ganglion cells cannot be directly connected to the *optic nerve* (item 3 in Figure 5.10), which sends the signals outside of the eye. Therefore, a hole has been punctured in our retinas so that the "cables" from the ganglion cells can be routed outside of the eye (item 4 in Figure 5.10). This causes the blind spot that was illustrated in Figure 5.6.

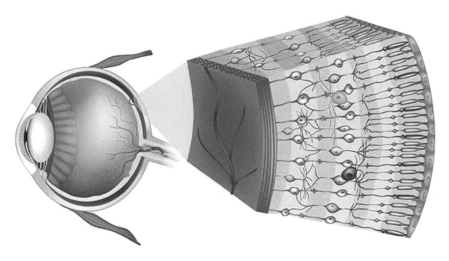

Figure 5.9 Light passes through a few neural layers before hitting the rods and cones.

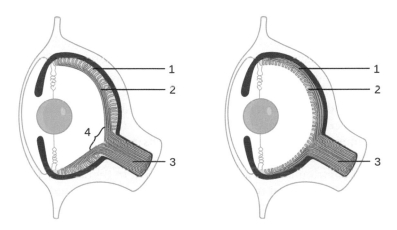

Figure 5.10 Vertebrates (including humans) have inside-out retinas, which lead to a blind spot and photoreceptors aimed away from the incoming light. The left shows a vertebrate eye, and the right shows a cephalopod eye, for which nature got it right: the photoreceptors face the light and there is no blind spot.

Upon studying Figure 5.9 closely, it becomes clear that the neural cells are not arranged in the ideal way of Figure 5.8. The *bipolar cells* transmit signals from the photoreceptors to the ganglion cells. Some bipolars connect only to cones, with the number being between 1 and 10 cones per bipolar. Others connect only to rods, with about 30 to 50 rods per bipolar. There are two types of bipolar cells based on their function. An *ON bipolar* activates when the rate of photon absorption in its connected photoreceptors *increases*. An *OFF bipolar* activates for *decreasing* photon absorption. The bipolars connected to cones have both kinds; however, the bipolars for rods have only ON bipolars. The bipolar connections are considered to be *vertical* because they connect directly from photoreceptors to the ganglion cells. This is in contrast to the remaining two cell types in the inner nuclear layer. The *horizontal cells* are connected by inputs (dendrites) to photoreceptors and bipolar cells within a radius of up to 1 mm. Their output (axon) is fed into photoreceptors, causing *lateral*

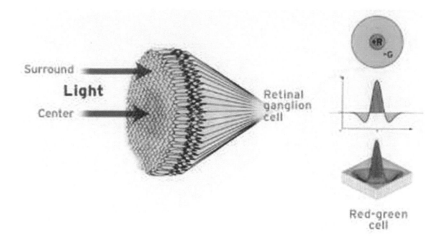

Figure 5.11 The receptive field of an ON-center ganglion cell.

inhibition, which means that the activation of one photoreceptor tends to decrease the activation of its neighbors. Finally, *amacrine cells* connect horizontally between bipolar cells, other amacrine cells, and vertically to ganglion cells. There are dozens of types, and their function is not well understood. Thus, scientists do not have a complete understanding of human vision, even at the lowest layers. Nevertheless, the well-understood parts contribute greatly to our ability to design effective VR systems and predict other human responses to visual stimuli.

At the ganglion cell layer, several kinds of cells process portions of the retinal image. Each ganglion cell has a large receptive field, which corresponds to the photoreceptors that contribute to its activation, as shown in Figure 5.8. The three most common and well-understood types of ganglion cells are called *midget*, *parasol*, and *bistratified*. They perform simple filtering operations over their receptive fields based on spatial, temporal, and spectral (color) variations in the stimulus across the photoreceptors. Figure 5.11 shows one example. In this case, a ganglion cell is triggered when red is detected in the center but not green in the surrounding area. This condition is an example of *spatial opponency*, for which neural structures are designed to detect local image variations. Thus, consider ganglion cells as tiny image processing units that can pick out local changes in time, space, and/or color. They can detect and emphasize simple image features such as edges. Once the ganglion axons leave the eye through the optic nerve, a significant amount of image processing has already been performed to aid in visual perception. The raw image based purely on photons hitting the photoreceptor never leaves the eye.

The optic nerve connects to a part of the *thalamus* called the *lateral geniculate nucleus* (*LGN*); see Figure 5.12. The LGN mainly serves as a router that sends signals from the senses to the brain, but also performs some processing. The LGN sends image information to the *primary visual cortex* (V1), which is located at the back of the brain. The *visual cortex*, highlighted in Figure 5.13, contains several interconnected areas that each perform specialized functions. Figure 5.14 shows one well-studied operation performed by the visual cortex. Chapter 6 will describe

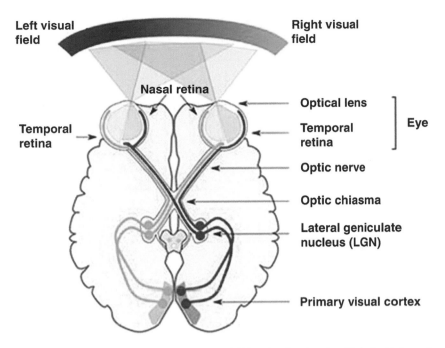

Figure 5.12 The visual pathway from the eyes to the LGN to the visual cortex. Note that information from the right and left sides of the visual field becomes swapped in the cortex.

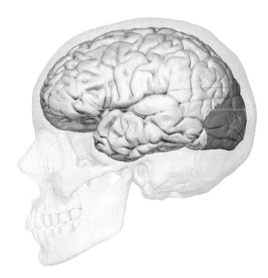

Figure 5.13 The visual cortex is located in the back of the head.

visual perception, which is the conscious result of processing in the visual cortex, based on neural circuitry, stimulation of the retinas, information from other senses, and expectations based on prior experiences. Characterizing how all of these processes function and integrate together remains an active field of research.

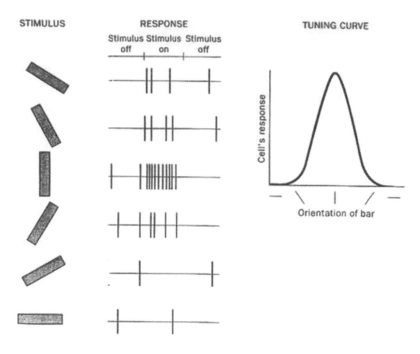

Figure 5.14 A popular example of visual cortex function is *orientation tuning*, in which a single-unit recording is made of a single neuron in the cortex. As the bar is rotated in front of the eye, the response of the neuron varies. It strongly favors one particular orientation.

5.3 Eye Movements

Eye rotations are a complicated and integral part of human vision. They occur both voluntarily and involuntarily, and allow a person to fixate on features in the world, even as her head or target features are moving. One of the main reasons for eye movement is to position the feature of interest on the fovea. Recall from Section 5.2 that only the fovea can sense dense color images, and it unfortunately spans a very narrow field of view. To gain a coherent, detailed view of a large object, the eyes rapidly scan over it while fixating on points of interest. Figure 5.15 shows an example. Another reason for eye movement is that our photoreceptors are slow to respond to stimuli due to their chemical nature. They take up to 10 ms to fully respond to stimuli and produce a response for up to 100 ms. Eye movements help keep the image fixed on the same set of photoreceptors so that they can fully charge. This is similar to the image blurring problem that occurs in cameras at low light levels and slow shutter speeds. Additional reasons for eye movement are to maintain a stereoscopic view and to prevent adaptation to a constant stimulation. To support the last claim, it has been shown experimentally that when eye motions are completely suppressed, visual perception disappears completely [118]. As movements combine to build a coherent view, it is difficult for scientists to predict and explain how people interpret some stimuli. For example, the optical illusion in Figure 5.16 appears to be moving when our eyes scan over it.

Figure 5.15 The trace of scanning a face using saccades.

Figure 5.16 The fractal appears to be moving until you carefully fixate on a single part to verify that it is not.

Eye Muscles

The rotation of each eye is controlled by six muscles that are each attached to the sclera (outer eyeball surface) by a tendon. Figures 5.17 and 5.18 show their names and arrangement. The tendons pull on the eye in opposite pairs. For example, to perform a yaw (side-to-side) rotation, the tensions on the medial rectus and lateral rectus are varied while the other muscles are largely unaffected. To cause a pitch

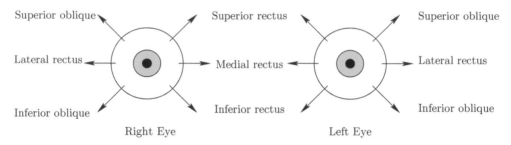

Figure 5.17 There are six muscles per eye, each of which is capable of pulling the pupil toward its location.

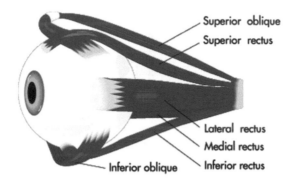

Figure 5.18 The six muscle tendons attach to the eye so that yaw, pitch, and a small amount of roll become possible.

motion, four muscles per eye become involved. All six are involved to perform both a pitch and yaw, for example, looking upward and to the right. A small amount of roll can be generated; however, our eyes are generally not designed for much roll motion. Imagine if you could turn your eyeballs upside-down inside of their sockets! Thus, it is reasonable in most cases to approximate eye rotations as a 2D set that includes only yaw and pitch, rather than the full three DOF obtained for rigid body rotations in Section 3.2.

Types of Movements

We now consider movements based on their purpose, resulting in six categories: (1) saccades, (2) smooth pursuit, (3) vestibulo-ocular reflex, (4) optokinetic reflex, (5) vergence, and (6) microsaccades. All of these motions cause both eyes to rotate approximately the same way, except for vergence, which causes the eyes to rotate in opposite directions. We will skip a seventh category of motion, called *rapid eye movements* (REMs), because they only occur while we are sleeping and therefore do not contribute to a VR experience. The remaining six categories will now be discussed in detail.

Saccades

The eye can move in a rapid motion called a *saccade*, which lasts less than 45 ms with rotations of about 900° per second. The purpose is to quickly relocate the fovea so that important features in a scene are sensed with highest visual acuity. Figure 5.15 showed an example in which a face is scanned by *fixating* on various features in rapid succession. Each transition between features is accomplished by a saccade. Interestingly, our brains use *saccadic masking* to hide the intervals of time over which saccades occur from our memory. This results in distorted time perception, as in the case when second hands click into position on an analog clock. The result of saccades is that we obtain the illusion of high acuity over a large angular range. Although saccades frequently occur while we have little or no awareness of them, we have the ability to consciously control them as we choose features for fixation.

Smooth Pursuit

In the case of *smooth pursuit*, the eye slowly rotates to track a moving target feature. Examples are a car, a tennis ball, or a person walking by. The rate of rotation is usually less than 30° per second, which is much slower than for saccades. The main function of smooth pursuit is to reduce motion blur on the retina; this is also known as *image stabilization*. The blur is due to the slow response time of photoreceptors, as discussed in Section 5.1. If the target is moving too fast, then saccades may be intermittently inserted into the pursuit motions to catch up to it.

Vestibulo-Ocular Reflex

One of the most important motions to understand for VR is the *vestibulo-ocular reflex* or *VOR*. Hold your finger at a comfortable distance in front of your face and fixate on it. Next, yaw your head back and forth (like you are nodding "no"), turning about 20° or 30° degrees to the left and right sides each time. You may notice that your eyes are effortlessly rotating to counteract the rotation of your head so that your finger remains in view. The eye motion is involuntary. If you do not believe it, then try to avoid rotating your eyes while paying attention to your finger and rotating your head. It is called a reflex because the motion control bypasses higher brain functions. Figure 5.19 shows how this circuitry works. Based on angular accelerations sensed by vestibular organs, signals are sent to the eye muscles to provide the appropriate counter motion. The main purpose of the VOR is to provide image stabilization, as in the case of smooth pursuit. For more details about the vestibular organ, see Section 8.2.

Optokinetic Reflex

The next category is called the *optokinetic reflex*, which occurs when a fast object speeds along. This occurs when watching a fast-moving train while standing nearby on fixed ground. The eyes rapidly and involuntarily choose features for tracking on the object, while alternating between smooth pursuit and saccade motions.

Vergence

Stereopsis refers to the case in which both eyes are fixated on the same object, resulting in a single perceived image. Two kinds of *vergence* motions occur to align the eyes with an object. See Figure 5.20. If the object is closer than a previous fixation, then a *convergence* motion occurs. This means that the eyes are rotating so that the

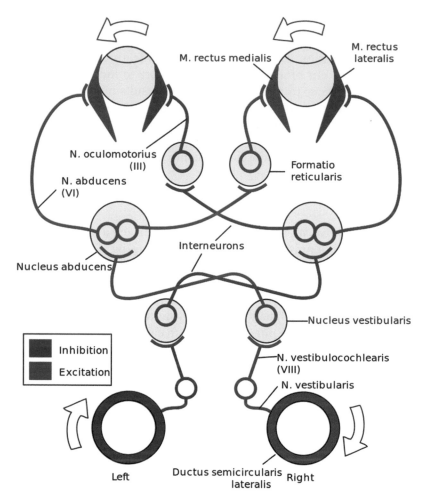

Figure 5.19 The vestibulo-ocular reflex (VOR). The eye muscles are wired to angular accelerometers in the vestibular organ to counter head movement with the opposite eye movement with less than 10 ms of latency. The connection between the eyes and the vestibular organ is provided by specialized vestibular and extraocular motor nuclei, thereby bypassing higher brain functions.

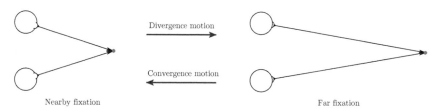

Figure 5.20 In the process of stereopsis, both eyes are fixated on the same feature in the world. To transition from a close to a far feature, a divergence motion occurs. A convergence motion happens for the opposite transition.

pupils are becoming closer. If the object is further, then *divergence* motion occurs, which causes the pupils to move further apart. The eye orientations resulting from vergence motions provide important information about the distance of objects.

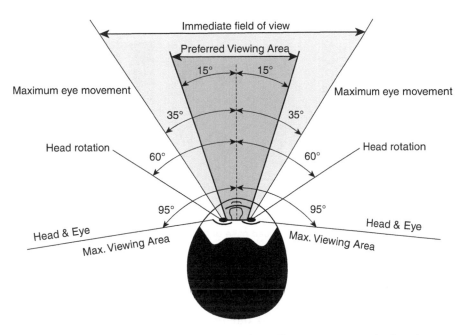

Figure 5.21 The head and eyes rotate together to fixate on new or moving targets.

Microsaccades

The sixth category of movements is called *microsaccades*, which are small, involuntary jerks of less than one degree that trace out an erratic path. They are believed to augment many other processes, including control of fixations, reduction of perceptual fading due to adaptation, improvement of visual acuity, and resolving perceptual ambiguities [274]. Although these motions have been known since the eighteenth century [54], their behavior is extremely complex and not fully understood. Microsaccades are an active topic of research in perceptual psychology, biology, and neuroscience.

Eye and Head Movements Together

Although this section has focused on eye movement, it is important to understand that most of the time the eyes and head are moving together. Figure 5.21 shows the angular range for yaw rotations of the head and eyes. Although eye yaw is symmetric by allowing 35° to the left or right, pitching of the eyes is not. Human eyes can pitch 20° upward and 25° downward, which suggests that it might be optimal to center a VR display slightly below the pupils when the eyes are looking directly forward. In the case of VOR, eye rotation is controlled to counteract head motion. In the case of smooth pursuit, the head and eyes may move together to keep a moving target in the preferred viewing area.

5.4 Implications for VR

This chapter has so far covered the human hardware for vision. Basic physiological properties, such as photoreceptor density or VOR circuitry, directly impact the

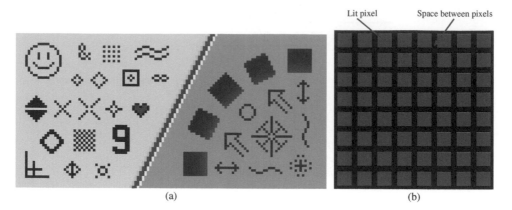

Figure 5.22 (a) Due to pixels, we obtain a bad case of the *jaggies* (more formally known as *aliasing*) instead of sharp, straight lines. (b) In the *screen-door effect*, a black grid is visible around the pixels.

engineering requirements for visual display hardware. The engineered systems must be good enough to adequately fool our senses, but they need not have levels of quality that are well beyond the limits of our receptors. Thus, the VR display should ideally be designed to perfectly match the performance of the sense it is trying to fool.

How Good Does the VR Visual Display Need to Be?
Three crucial factors for the display are:

1. *Spatial resolution:* How many pixels per square area are needed?
2. *Intensity resolution and range:* How many intensity values can be produced, and what are the minimum and maximum intensity values?
3. *Temporal resolution:* How fast do displays need to change their pixels?

The spatial resolution factor will be addressed in the next paragraph. The second factor could also be called *color resolution and range* because the intensity values of each red, green, or blue subpixel produce points in the space of colors; see Section 6.3. Recall the range of intensities from Figure 5.4 that trigger photoreceptors. Photoreceptors can span seven orders of magnitude of light intensity. However, most displays have only 256 intensity levels per color to cover this range. Entering scotopic vision mode does not even seem possible using most display technology because of the high intensity resolution needed at extremely low light levels. Temporal resolution is extremely important but is deferred until Section 6.2, in the context of motion perception.

How Much Pixel Density Is Enough?
We now address the spatial resolution. Insights into the required spatial resolution are obtained from the photoreceptor densities. As was shown in Figure 4.36, we see individual lights when a display is highly magnified. As it is zoomed out, we may still perceive sharp diagonal lines as being jagged, as shown in Figure 5.22(a); this phenomenon is known as *aliasing*. Another artifact is the *screen-door effect*, shown

Figure 5.23 Red, green, and blue cone photoreceptors are distributed in a complicated mosaic in the center of the fovea.

in Figure 5.22(b); this is commonly noticed in an image produced by a digital LCD projector. What does the display pixel density need to be so that we do not perceive individual pixels? In 2010, Steve Jobs of Apple Inc. claimed that 326 pixels per linear inch (*PPI*) is enough, achieving what they called a *retina display*.[1] Is this reasonable, and how does it relate to VR?

Assume that the fovea is pointed directly at the display to provide the best sensing possible. The first issue is that red, green, and blue cones are arranged in a mosaic, as shown in Figure 5.23. The patterns are more erratic than the engineered versions in Figure 4.36. Vision scientists and neurobiologists have studied the effective or perceived input resolution through measures of *visual acuity* [142]. Subjects in a study are usually asked to indicate whether they can *detect* or *recognize* a particular target. In the case of detection, for example, scientists might like to know the smallest dot that can be perceived when printed onto a surface. In terms of displays, a similar question is: How small do pixels need to be so that a single white pixel against a black background is not detectable? In the case of recognition, a familiar example is attempting to read an eye chart, which displays arbitrary letters of various sizes. In terms of displays, this could correspond to trying to read text under various sizes, resolutions, and fonts. Many factors contribute to acuity tasks, such as brightness, contrast, eye movements, time exposure, and the part of the retina that is stimulated.

One of the most widely used concepts is *cycles per degree*, which roughly corresponds to the number of stripes (or sinusoidal peaks) that can be seen as separate along a viewing arc; see Figure 5.24. The *Snellen eye chart*, which is widely used by optometrists, is designed so that patients attempt to recognize printed letters from 20 feet away (or 6 meters). A person with "normal" 20/20 (or 6/6 in metric) vision is

---

[1] This is equivalent to a density of 165 pixels per mm^2, but we will use linear inches because it is the international standard for display comparisons.

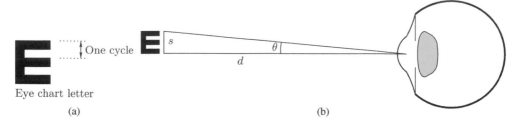

Figure 5.24 (a) A single letter on an eye chart. (b) The size s of the letter (or other feature of interest), the distance d of the viewer, and the viewing angle θ are related as $s = d \tan \theta$.

expected to barely make out the horizontal stripes in the letter "E" shown in Figure 5.24. This assumes he is looking directly at the letters, using the photoreceptors in the central fovea. The 20/20 line on the chart is designed so that letter height corresponds to 30 cycles per degree when the eye is 20 feet away. The total height of the "E" is 1/12 of a degree. Note that each stripe is half of a cycle. What happens if the subject stands only 10 feet away from the eye chart? The letters should roughly appear to twice as large.

Using simple trigonometry,

$$s = d \tan \theta, \tag{5.1}$$

we can determine what the size s of some feature should be for a viewing angle θ at a distance d from the eye. For very small θ, $\tan \theta \approx \theta$ (in radians). For the example of the eye chart, s could correspond to the height of a letter. Doubling the distance d and the size s should keep θ roughly fixed, which corresponds to the size of the image on the retina.

We now return to the retina display concept. Suppose that a person with 20/20 vision is viewing a large screen that is 20 feet (6.096 m) away. To generate 30 cycles per degree, it must have at least 60 pixels per degree. Using (5.1), the size would be $s = 20 * \tan 1° = 0.349$ ft, which is equivalent to 4.189 in. Thus, only $60/4.189 = 14.32$ PPI would be sufficient. Now suppose that a smartphone screen is placed 12 inches from the user's eye. In this case, $s = 12 * \tan 1° = 0.209$ in. This requires that the screen have at least $60/0.209 = 286.4$ PPI, which was satisfied by the 326 PPI originally claimed by Apple.

In the case of VR, the user is not looking directly at the screen as in the case of smartphones. By inserting a lens for magnification, the display can be brought even closer to the eye. This is commonly done for VR headsets, as was shown in Figure 4.30. Suppose that the lens is positioned at its focal distance away from the screen, which for the sake of example is only 1.5 in. (This is comparable to many VR headsets.) In this case, $s = 1 * \tan 1° = 0.0261$ in, and the display must have at least 2291.6 PPI to achieve 60 cycles per degree! One of the highest-density smartphone displays available in 2015 was in the Sony Xperia Z5 Premium. It has only 801 PPI, which means that the PPI needs to increase by roughly a factor of three to obtain retina display resolution for VR headsets.

This is not the complete story because some people, particularly youths, have better than 20/20 vision. The limits of visual acuity have been established to be around 60 to 77 cycles per degree, based on photoreceptor density and neural processes

[38, 52]; however, this is based on shining a laser directly onto the retina, which bypasses many optical aberration problems, as the light passes through the eye. A small number of people (perhaps 1 percent) have acuity up to 60 cycles per degree. In this extreme case, the display density would need to be 4, 583 PPI. Thus, many factors are involved in determining a sufficient resolution for VR. It suffices to say that the resolutions that exist in typical consumer VR headsets are inadequate, and retinal display resolution will not be achieved until the PPI is several times higher.

How Much Field of View Is Enough?
What if the screen is brought even closer to the eye to fill more of the field of view? Based on the photoreceptor density plot in Figure 5.5 and the limits of eye rotations shown in Figure 5.21, the maximum field of view seems to be around 270°, which is larger than what could be provided by a flat screen (less than 180°). Increasing the field of view by bringing the screen closer would require even higher pixel density, but lens aberrations (Section 4.3) at the periphery may limit the effective field of view. Furthermore, if the lens is too thick and too close to the eye, then the eyelashes may scrape it; Fresnel lenses may provide a thin alternative, but introduce artifacts. Thus, the quest for a VR retina display may end with a balance between optical system quality and limitations of the human eye. Curved screens may help alleviate some of the problems.

Foveated Rendering
One of the frustrations with this analysis is that we have not been able to exploit the fact that photoreceptor density decreases away from the fovea. We had to keep the pixel density high everywhere because we have no control over which part of the display the user will look at. If we could track where the eye is looking and have a tiny, movable display that is always positioned in front of the pupil, with zero delay, then much fewer pixels would be needed. This would greatly decrease computational burdens on graphical rendering systems (covered in Chapter 7). Instead of moving a tiny screen, the process can be simulated by keeping the fixed display but focusing the graphical rendering only in the spot where the eye is looking. This is called *foveated rendering*, which has been shown to work well [106], and is implemented along with eye tracking in some headsets such as the Varjo Aero, Vive Pro Eye, and PlayStation VR 2.

VOR Gain Adaptation
The *VOR gain* is a ratio that compares the eye rotation rate (numerator) to counter the rotation and translation rate of the head (denominator). Because head motion has six DOF, it is appropriate to break the gain into six components. In the case of head pitch and yaw, the VOR gain is close to 1.0. For example, if you yaw your head to the left at 10° per second, then your eyes yaw at 10° per second in the opposite direction. The VOR roll gain is very small because the eyes have a tiny roll range. The VOR translational gain depends on the distance to the features.

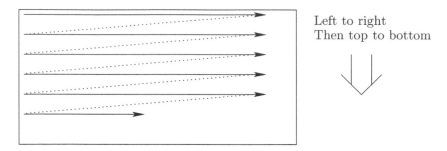

Left to right
Then top to bottom

Figure 5.25 Most displays still work in the same way as old TV sets and CRT monitors: by updating pixels line by line. For a display that has 60 FPS (frames per second), this could take up to 16.67 ms.

Recall from Section 2.3 that adaptation is a universal feature of our sensory systems. VOR gain is no exception. For those who wear eyeglasses, the VOR gain must adapt due to the optical transformations described in Section 4.2. Lenses affect the field of view and perceived size and distance of objects. The VOR comfortably adapts to this problem by changing the gain. Now suppose that you are wearing a VR headset that may suffer from flaws such as an imperfect optical system, tracking latency, and incorrectly rendered objects on the screen. In this case, adaptation may occur as the brain attempts to adapt its perception of stationarity to compensate for the flaws. In this case, your visual system could convince your brain that the headset is functioning correctly, and then your perception of stationarity in the real world would become distorted until you readapt. For example, after a flawed VR experience, you might yaw your head in the real world and have the sensation that truly stationary objects are sliding back and forth![2]

Display Scanout
Recall from Section 4.5 that cameras have either a rolling or global shutter based on whether the sensing elements are scanned line by line or in parallel. Displays work the same way, but whereas cameras are an *input* device, displays are the *output* equivalent. Most displays today have a *rolling scanout* (called *raster scan*) rather than *global scanout*. This implies that the pixels are updated line by line, as shown in Figure 5.25. This procedure is an artifact of old TV sets and monitors, each of which had a cathode ray tube (CRT) with phosphor elements on the screen. An electron beam was bent by electromagnets so that it would repeatedly strike and refresh the glowing phosphors.

Due to the slow charge and response time of photoreceptors, we do not perceive the scanout pattern during normal use. However, when our eyes, features in the scene, or both are moving, then side effects of the rolling scanout may become perceptible. Think about the operation of a line-by-line printer, as in the case of a receipt printer on a cash register. If we pull on the tape while it is printing, then the lines become stretched apart. If it is unable to print a single line at once, then the lines themselves become slanted. If we could pull the tape to the side while it is printing, then the entire page would become slanted. You can also achieve this effect by repeatedly drawing a horizontal line with a pencil while using the other hand to

[2] This frequently happened to the author while developing and testing the Oculus Rift.

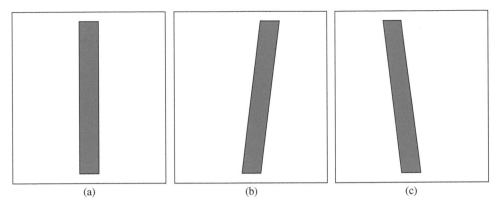

(a)   (b)   (c)

Figure 5.26 Artifacts due to display scanout. (a) A vertical rectangle in the scene. (b) How it may distort during smooth pursuit while the rectangle moves to the right in the virtual world. (c) How a stationary rectangle may distort when rotating the head to the right while using the VOR to compensate. The cases of (b) and (c) are swapped if the direction of motion is reversed in each case.

gently pull the paper in a particular direction. The paper in this analogy is the retina and the pencil corresponds to light rays attempting to charge photoreceptors. Figure 5.26 shows how a rectangle would distort under cases of smooth pursuit and VOR. One possibility is to fix this by rendering a distorted image that will be corrected by the distortion due to the line-by-line, scanout [217]. (This was later suggested in [1].) Constructing these images requires precise calculations of the scanout timings. Yet another problem with displays is that the pixels could take so long to switch (up to a few ms) that sharp edges appear to be blurred. We will continue discussing these problems in Section 6.2 in the context of motion perception, and Section 7.4 in the context of rendering.

Retinal Image Slip

Recall that eye movements contribute both to maintaining a target in a fixed location on the retina (smooth pursuit, VOR) and also to changing its location slightly to reduce perceptual fading (microsaccades). During ordinary activities (not VR), the eyes move and the image of a feature may move slightly on the retina due to motions and optical distortions. This is called *retinal image slip*. Once a VR headset is used, the motions of image features on the retina might not match what would happen in the real world. This is due to many factors already mentioned, such as optical distortions, tracking latency, and display scanout. Thus, the retinal image slip due to VR artifacts does not match the retinal image slip encountered in the real world. The consequences of this have barely been identified, much less characterized scientifically. They are likely to contribute to fatigue, and possibly VR sickness. As an example of the problem, there is evidence that microsaccades are triggered by the lack of retinal image slip [72]. This implies that differences in retinal image slip due to VR usage could interfere with microsaccade motions, which themselves are not fully understood.

Vergence-Accommodation Mismatch

Recall from Section 4.4 that accommodation is the process of changing the eye lens' optical power so that close objects can be brought into focus. This normally occurs with both eyes fixated on the same object, resulting in a stereoscopic view that is brought into focus. In the real world, the vergence motion of the eyes and the accommodation of the lens are tightly coupled. For example, if you place your finger 10 cm in front of your face, then your eyes will try to increase the lens power while the eyes are strongly converging. If a lens is placed at a distance of its focal length from a screen, then with normal eyes it will always be in focus while the eye is relaxed (recall Figure 4.30). What if an object is rendered to the screen so that it appears to be only 10 cm away? In this case, the eyes strongly converge, but they do not need to change the optical power of the eye lens. The eyes may nevertheless try to accommodate, which would have the effect of blurring the perceived image. The result is called *vergence-accommodation mismatch* because the stimulus provided by VR is inconsistent with the real world. Even if the eyes become accustomed to the mismatch, the user may feel extra strain or fatigue after prolonged use [251, 295]. The eyes are essentially being trained to allow a new degree of freedom: separating vergence from accommodation rather than coupling them. New display technologies may provide some relief from this problem, but they may be too costly and imprecise. For example, the mismatch can be greatly reduced by using eye tracking to estimate the amount of vergence and then altering the power of the optical system [4, 190].

Further Reading

Most of the concepts from Sections 5.1 to 5.1 appear in standard textbooks on sensation and perception [98, 207, 359]. Chapter 7 of [207] contains substantially more neuroscience than covered in this chapter. More details on photoreceptor structure appear in [52, 230, 346]. The interface between eyes and engineered optical systems is covered in [302]; digital optical systems are also related [159].

Sweeping coverage of eye movements is provided in [187]. For eye movements from a neuroscience perspective, see [180]. VOR gain adaptation is studied in [59, 92, 290]. Theories of microsaccade function are discussed in [274]. Coordination between smooth pursuit and saccades is explained in [74]. Coordination of head and eye movements is studied in [165, 252]. See [17, 251, 295] regarding comfort issues with vergence-accommodation mismatch.

CHAPTER SIX

Visual Perception

This chapter continues where Chapter 5 left off by transitioning from the *physiology* of human vision to *perception*. If we were computers, then this transition might seem like going from low-level hardware to higher-level software and algorithms. How do our brains interpret the world around us so effectively in spite of our limited biological hardware? To understand how we may be fooled by visual stimuli presented by a display, you must first understand how we perceive or interpret the real world under normal circumstances. It is not always clear what we will perceive. We have already seen several optical illusions. VR itself can be considered as a grand optical illusion. Under what conditions will it succeed or fail?

Section 6.1 covers perception of the *distance* of objects from our eyes, which is also related to the perception of object *scale*. Section 6.2 explains how we perceive motion. An important part of this is the illusion of motion that we perceive from videos, which are merely a sequence of pictures. Section 6.3 covers the perception of color, which may help explain why displays use only three colors (red, green, and blue) to simulate the entire spectral power distribution of light (recall from Section 4.1). Finally, Section 6.4 presents a statistically based model of how information is combined from multiple sources to produce a perceptual experience.

6.1 Perception of Depth

This section explains how humans judge the distance from their eyes to objects in the real world using vision. The perceived distance could be *metric*, which means that an estimate of the absolute distance is obtained. For example, a house may appear to be about 100 meters away. Alternatively, the distance information could be *ordinal*, which means that the relative arrangement of visible objects can be inferred. For example, one house appears to be closer than another if it is partially blocking the view of the further one.

Monocular versus Stereo Cues
A piece of information that is derived from sensory stimulation and is relevant for perception is called a *sensory cue* or simply a *cue*. In this section, we consider only *depth cues*, which contribute toward depth perception. If a depth cue is derived from the photoreceptors or movements of a single eye, then it is called a *monocular depth*

VISUAL PERCEPTION

Figure 6.1 This 1877 painting by Gustave Caillebotte uses a monocular depth cue called a *texture gradient* to enhance depth perception: the bricks become smaller and thinner as the depth increases. Other cues arise from perspective projection, including height in the visual field and retinal image size.

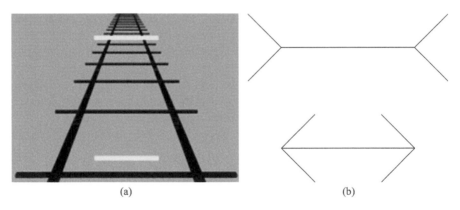

(a)   (b)

Figure 6.2 Even simple line drawings provide significant cues. (a) The Ponzo illusion: the upper yellow bar appears to be longer, but both are the same length. (b) The Müller–Lyer illusion: the lower horizontal segment appears to be shorter than the one above, but they are the same length.

cue. If both eyes are required, then it is a *stereo depth cue.* There are many more monocular depth cues than stereo, which explains why we are able to infer so much depth information from a single photograph. Figure 6.1 shows an example. The illusions in Figure 6.2 show that even simple line drawings are enough to provide strong cues. Interestingly, the cues used by humans also work in computer vision algorithms to extract depth information from images [324].

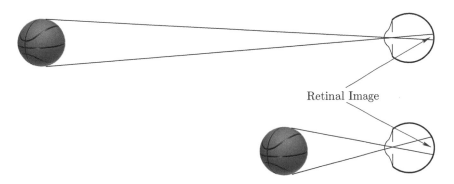

Figure 6.3 The retinal image size of a familiar object is a strong monocular depth cue. The closer object projects onto a larger number of photoreceptors, which cover a larger portion of the retina.

6.1.1 Monocular Depth Cues

Retinal Image Size

Many cues result from the geometric distortions caused by perspective projection; recall the 3D appearance of Figure 1.23(c). For a familiar object, such as a human, coin, or basketball, we often judge its distance by how "large" it appears to be. Recalling the perspective projection math from Section 3.4, the size of the image on the retina is proportional to $1/z$, in which z is the distance from the eye (or the common convergence point for all projection lines). See Figure 6.3. The same thing happens when taking a picture with a camera: A picture of a basketball would occupy the larger part of the image, covering more pixels as it becomes closer to the camera. This cue is called *retinal image size* and was studied in [97].

Two important factors exist. First, the viewer must be familiar with the object to the point of comfortably knowing its true size. For familiar objects, such as people or cars, our brains perform *size constancy scaling* by assuming that the distance, rather than the size, of the person is changing if they come closer. Size constancy falls under the general heading of *subjective constancy*, which appears through many aspects of perception, including shape, size, and color. The second factor is that the object must appear naturally so that it does not conflict with other depth cues.

If there is significant uncertainty about the size of an object, then knowledge of its distance should contribute to estimating its size. This falls under *size perception*, which is closely coupled to depth perception. Cues for each influence the other, in a way discussed in Section 6.4.

One controversial theory is that our *perceived visual angle* differs from the actual visual angle. The visual angle is proportional to the retinal image size. This theory is used to explain the illusion that the moon appears to be larger when it is near the horizon. For another example, see Figure 6.4.

Height in the Visual Field

Figure 6.5(a) illustrates another important cue, which is the height of the object in the visual field. The Ponzo illusion in Figure 6.2(a) exploits this cue. Suppose that we can see over a long distance without obstructions. Due to perspective projection, the horizon is a line that divides the view in half. The upper half is perceived as

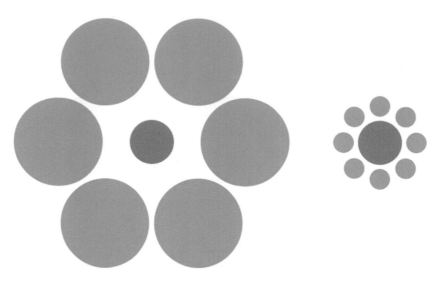

Figure 6.4 For the Ebbinghaus illusion, the inner disc appears larger when surrounded by smaller discs. The inner disc is the same size in either case. This may be evidence of discrepancy between the true visual angle (or retinal image size) and the *perceived* visual angle.

(a)   (b)

Figure 6.5 Height in visual field. (a) Trees closer to the horizon appear to be further away, even though all yield the same retinal image size. (b) Incorrect placement of people (the author and his son, Ethan) in the visual field illustrates *size constancy scaling*, which is closely coupled with depth cues. Photo printed by permission of Nadia Inturias, Uyuni, Bolivia.

the sky, and the lower half is the ground. The distance of objects from the horizon line corresponds directly to their distance due to perspective projection: the closer to the horizon, the further the perceived distance. Size constancy scaling, if available, combines with the height in the visual field, as shown in Figure 6.5(b).

Accommodation
Recall from Section 4.4 that the human eye lens can change its optical power through the process of accommodation. For young adults, the amount of change is around

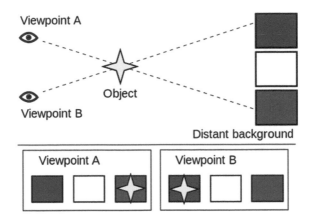

Figure 6.6 Motion parallax: as the perspective changes laterally, closer objects have larger image displacements than further objects.

10D (diopters), but it decreases to less than 1D for adults over 50 years old. The ciliary muscles control the lens and their tension level is reported to the brain through efference copies of the motor control signal. This is the first depth cue that does not depend on signals generated by the photoreceptors.

Motion Parallax

Up until now, the depth cues have not exploited motions. If you have ever looked out of the side window of a fast-moving vehicle, you might have noticed that the nearby objects race by much faster than farther objects. The relative difference in speeds is called *parallax* and is an important depth cue; see Figure 6.6. Even two images, from varying viewpoints within a short amount of time, provide strong depth information. Imagine trying to simulate a *stereo rig* of cameras by snapping one photo and quickly moving the camera sideways to snap another. If the rest of the world is stationary, then the result is roughly equivalent to having two side-by-side cameras. Pigeons frequently bob their heads back and forth to obtain stronger depth information than is provided by their pair of eyes. Finally, closely related to motion parallax is *optical flow*, which is a characterization of the rates at which features move across the retina. This will be revisited in Sections 6.2 and 8.4.

Other Monocular Cues

Figure 6.7 shows several other monocular cues. As shown in Figure 6.7(a), shadows that are cast by a light source encountering an object provide an important cue. Figure 6.7(b) shows a simple drawing that provides an ordinal depth cue called *interposition* by indicating which objects are in front of others. Figure 6.7(c) illustrates the *image blur* cue, where levels are depths are inferred from the varying sharpness of focus. Figure 6.7(d) shows an *atmospheric cue* in which air humidity causes faraway scenery to have lower contrast, thereby appearing to be farther away.

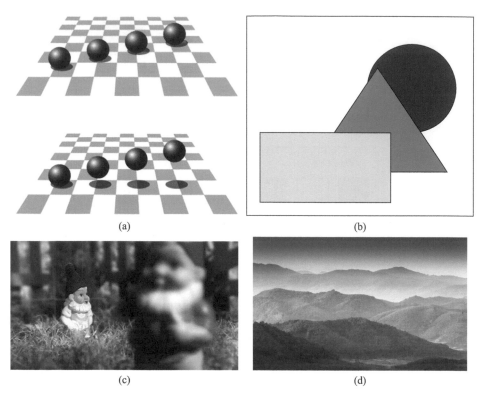

Figure 6.7 Several more monocular depth cues. (a) *Shadows* resolve ambiguous depth in the *ball and shadow illusion*. (b) The *interposition* of objects provides an ordinal depth cue. (c) Due to *image blur*, one gnome appears to be much closer than the others. (d) This scene provides an *atmospheric cue*: Some scenery is perceived to be further away because it has lower contrast.

6.1.2 Stereo Depth Cues

As you may expect, focusing both eyes on the same object enhances depth perception. Humans perceive a single focused image over a surface in space called the *horopter*; see Figure 6.8. Recall the vergence motions from Section 5.3. Similar to the accommodation cue case, motor control of the eye muscles for vergence motions provides information to the brain about the amount of convergence, thereby providing a direct estimate of distance. Each eye provides a different viewpoint, which results in different images on the retina. This phenomenon is called *binocular disparity*. Recall from (3.50) in Section 3.5 that the viewpoint is shifted to the right or left to provide a lateral offset for each of the eyes. The transform essentially shifts the virtual world to either side. The same shift would happen for a stereo rig of side-by-side cameras in the real world. However, the binocular disparity for humans is different because the eyes can rotate to converge, in addition to having a lateral offset. Thus, when fixating on an object, the retinal images between the left and right eyes may vary only slightly, but this nevertheless provides a powerful cue used by the brain.

Furthermore, when converging on an object at one depth, we perceive double images of objects at other depths (although we usually pay no attention to it). This double-image effect is called *diplopia*. You can perceive it by placing your finger

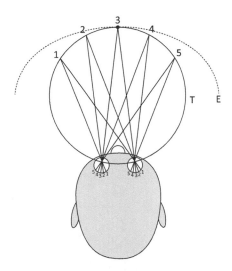

Figure 6.8 The *horopter* is the loci of points over which the eyes can converge and focus on a single depth. The T curve shows the theoretical horopter based on simple geometry. The E curve shows the empirical horopter, which is much larger and corresponds to the region over which a single focused image is perceived.

about 20 cm in front of your face and converging on it. While fixating on your finger, you should perceive double images of other objects around the periphery. You can also stare into the distance while keeping your finger in the same place. You should see a double image of your finger. If you additionally roll your head back and forth, it should appear as if the left and right versions of your finger are moving up and down with respect to each other. These correspond to dramatic differences in the retinal image, but we are usually not aware of them because we perceive both retinal images as a single image.

6.1.3 Implications for VR

Incorrect Scale Perception
A virtual world may be filled with objects that are not familiar to us in the real world. In many cases, they might resemble familiar objects, but their precise scale might be difficult to determine. Consider the Tuscany demo world from Oculus VR, shown in Figure 6.9. The virtual villa is designed to be inhabited with humans, but it is difficult to judge the relative sizes and distances of objects because there are not enough familiar objects. Further complicating the problem is that the user's height in VR might not match her height in the virtual world. Is the user too short, or is the world too big? A common and confusing occurrence is that the user might be sitting down in the real world, but standing in the virtual world. An additional complication occurs if the interpupillary distance (see Section 4.4) is not matched with the real world. For example, if the user's pupils are 64 mm apart in the real world but only 50 mm apart in the virtual world, then the virtual world will seem much larger, which dramatically affects depth perception. Likewise, if the pupils are very far apart, the user could either feel enormous or the virtual world might seem

Figure 6.9 In the Tuscany demo from Oculus VR, there are not enough familiar objects to precisely resolve depth and size. Have you ever been to a villa like this? Are the floor tiles a familiar size? Is the desk too low?

small. Imagine simulating a Godzilla experience, where the user is 200 meters tall and the entire city appears to be a model. It is fine to experiment with such scale and depth distortions in VR, but it is important to understand their implications on the user's perception.

Mismatches

In the real world, all of the depth cues work together in harmony. We are sometimes fooled by optical illusions that are designed to intentionally cause inconsistencies among cues. Sometimes a simple drawing is sufficient. Figure 6.10 shows an elaborate illusion that requires building a distorted room in the real world. It is perfectly designed so that when viewed under perspective projection from one location, it appears to be a rectangular box. Once our brains accept this, we unexpectedly perceive the size of people changing as they walk across the room! This is because all of the cues based on perspective appear to be functioning correctly. Section 6.4 may help you to understand how multiple cues are resolved, even in the case of inconsistencies.

In a VR system, it is easy to cause mismatches, and in many cases they are unavoidable. Recall from Section 5.4 that vergence-accommodation mismatch occurs in VR headsets. Another source of mismatch may occur from imperfect head tracking. If there is significant latency, then the visual stimuli will not appear in the correct place at the expected time. Furthermore, many tracking systems track the head orientation only. This makes it impossible to use motion parallax as a depth cue if the user moves from side to side without any rotation. To preserve most depth cues based on motion, it is important to track head *position*, in addition to orientation; see Section 9.3. Optical distortions may cause even more mismatch.

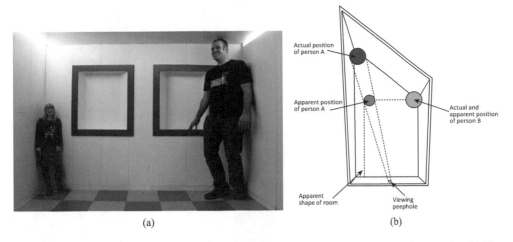

Figure 6.10 The Ames room. (a) Due to incorrect depth cues, incorrect size perception results. (b) The room is designed so that it only appears to be rectangular after perspective projection is applied. One person is actually much further away than the other.

Monocular Cues Are Powerful!

A common misunderstanding among the general public is that depth perception is enabled by stereo cues alone. We are bombarded with marketing of 3D movies and *stereo displays*. The most common instance has been the use of circularly polarized *3D glasses* in movie theaters so that each eye receives a different image when looking at the screen. VR is no exception to this common misunderstanding. CAVE systems provided 3D glasses with an active shutter inside so that alternating left and right frames can be presented to the eyes. Note that this cuts the frame rate in half. Now that we have comfortable headsets, presenting separate visual stimuli to each eye is much simpler. One drawback is that the rendering effort (the subject of Chapter 7) is doubled, although this can be improved through some context-specific tricks.

As you have seen in this section, there are many more monocular depth cues than stereo cues. Therefore, it is wrong to assume that the world is perceived as "3D" *only if* there are stereo images. This insight is particularly valuable for leveraging captured data from the real world. Recall from Section 1.1 that the virtual world may be synthetic or captured. It is generally more costly to create synthetic worlds, but it is then simple to generate stereo viewpoints (at a higher rendering cost). On the other hand, capturing panoramic, monoscopic images and movies is fast and inexpensive. (Examples were shown in Figure 1.9.) There are already smartphone apps that stitch pictures together to make a panoramic photo, and direct capture of panoramic video is available in consumer devices. By recognizing that this content is sufficiently "3D" due to the wide field of view and monocular depth cues, it becomes a powerful way to create VR experiences. There are already hundreds of millions of images in Google Street View, shown in Figure 6.11, which can be easily viewed using existing VR headsets. They provide a highly immersive experience with substantial depth perception, even though there is no stereo. There is even strong evidence that stereo displays cause significant fatigue and discomfort, especially for objects at a close depth [250, 251]. Therefore, one should think very carefully about the use of stereo. In many cases, it might be more time, cost, and trouble than it is worth to

Figure 6.11 In VR headsets, hundreds of millions of panoramic Google Street View images can be viewed. There is significant depth perception, even when the same image is presented to both eyes, because of monoscopic depth cues.

obtain the stereo cues when there may already be sufficient monocular cues for the VR task or experience.

6.2 Perception of Motion

We rely on our vision to perceive motion for many crucial activities. One use is to separate a moving figure from a stationary background. For example, a camouflaged animal in the forest might only become noticeable when moving. This is clearly useful whether humans are the hunter or the hunted. Motion also helps people to assess the 3D structure of an object. Imagine assessing the value of a piece of fruit in the market by rotating it around. Another use is to visually guide actions, such as walking down the street or hammering a nail. VR systems have the tall order of replicating these uses in a virtual world in spite of limited technology. Just as important as the perception of motion is the perception of non-motion, which we called *perception of stationarity* in Section 2.3. For example, if we apply the VOR by turning our heads, then do the virtual world objects move correctly on the display so that they appear to be stationary? Slight errors in time or image position might inadvertently trigger the perception of motion.

6.2.1 Detection Mechanisms

Reichardt Detector
Figure 6.12 shows a neural circuitry model, called a *Reichardt detector*, which responds to directional motion in the human vision system. Neurons in the ganglion layer and LGN detect simple features in different spots in the retinal image. At

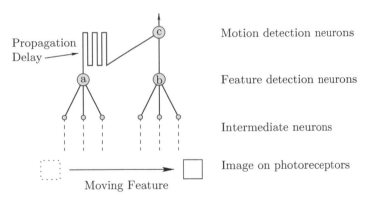

Figure 6.12 The neural circuitry directly supports motion detection. As the image feature moves across the retina, nearby feature detection neurons (labeled *a* and *b*) activate in succession. Their outputs connect to motion detection neurons (labeled *c*). Due to different path lengths from *a* and *b* to *c*, the activation signal arrives at different times. Thus, *c* activates when the feature was detected by *a* slightly before being detected by *b*.

higher levels, motion detection neurons exist that respond when the feature moves from one spot on the retina to another nearby spot. The motion detection neuron activates for a feature speed that depends on the difference in path lengths from its input neurons. It is also sensitive to a particular direction of motion based on the relative locations of the receptive fields of the input neurons. Due to the simplicity of the motion detector, it can be easily fooled. Figure 6.12 shows a feature moving from left to right. Suppose that a train of features moves from right to left. Based on the speed of the features and the spacing between them, the detector may inadvertently fire, causing motion to be perceived in the opposite direction. This is the basis of the *wagon-wheel effect*, for which a wheel with spokes or a propeller may appear to be rotating in the opposite direction, depending on the speed. The process can be further disrupted by causing eye vibrations from humming [281]. This simulates stroboscopic conditions, which is discussed in Section 6.2.2. Another point is that the motion detectors are subject to adaptation. Therefore, several illusions exist, such as the *waterfall illusion* [18] and the *spiral aftereffect*, in which incorrect motions are perceived due to aftereffects from sustained fixation [18, 208].

From Local Data to Global Conclusions
Motion detectors are *local* in the sense that a tiny portion of the visual field causes each to activate. In most cases, data from detectors across large patches of the visual field are *integrated* to indicate coherent motions of rigid bodies. (An exception would be staring at pure analog TV static.) All pieces of a rigid body move through space according to the equations from Section 3.2. This coordinated motion is anticipated by our visual system to match common expectations. If too much of the moving body is blocked, then the *aperture problem* results, which is shown in Figure 6.13. A clean mathematical way to describe the global motions across the retina is by a *vector field*, which assigns a velocity vector at every position. The global result is called the *optical flow*, which provides powerful cues for both object motion and self

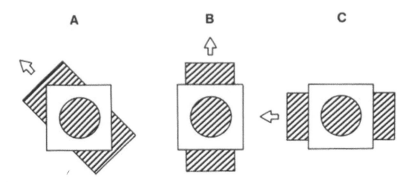

Figure 6.13 Due to local nature of motion detectors, the *aperture problem* results. The motion of the larger body is ambiguous when perceived through a small hole because a wide range of possible body motions could produce the same effect inside of the hole. An incorrect motion inference usually results.

motion. The latter case results in *vection*, which is a leading cause of VR sickness; see Sections 8.4 and 10.2 for details.

Distinguishing Object Motion from Observer Motion
Figure 6.14 shows two cases that produce the same images across the retina over time. In Figure 6.14(a), the eye is fixed while the object moves by. In Figure 6.14(b), the situation is reversed: the object is fixed, but the eye moves. The brain uses several cues to differentiate between these cases. Saccadic suppression, which was mentioned in Section 5.3, hides vision signals during movements; this may suppress motion detectors in the second case. Another cue is provided by proprioception, which is the body's ability to estimate its own motions due to motor commands. This includes the use of eye muscles in the second case. Finally, information is provided by large-scale motion. If it appears that the entire scene is moving, then the brain assumes the most likely interpretation, which is that the user must be moving. This is why the haunted swing illusion, shown in Figure 2.20, is so effective.

6.2.2 Stroboscopic Apparent Motion

Nearly everyone on Earth has seen a motion picture, whether through a TV, smartphone, or movie screen. The motions we see are an illusion because a sequence of still pictures is being flashed onto the screen. This phenomenon is called *stroboscopic apparent motion*; it was discovered and refined across the nineteenth century. The *zoetrope*, shown in Figure 6.15, was developed around 1834. It consists of a rotating drum with slits that allow each frame to be visible for an instant while the drum rotates. In Section 1.3, Figure 1.24 showed the Horse in Motion film from 1878.

Why does this illusion of motion work? An early theory, which has largely been refuted in recent years, is called *persistence of vision*. The theory states that images persist in the vision system during the intervals in between frames, thereby causing them to be perceived as continuous. One piece of evidence against this theory is that images persist in the visual cortex for around 100 ms, which implies that 10 FPS is the slowest speed at which stroboscopic apparent motion would work; however, it is also perceived down to 2 FPS [313]. Another piece of evidence against the persistence of vision is the existence of stroboscopic apparent motions that cannot be accounted for by it. The *phi phenomenon* and *beta movement* are examples of motion perceived

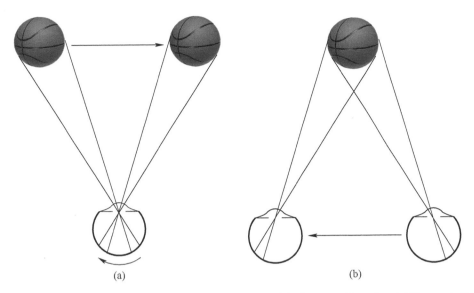

Figure 6.14 Two motions that cause equivalent movement of the image on the retina. (a) The eye is fixed and the object moves. (b) The eye moves while the object is fixed. Both of these are hard to achieve in practice due to eye rotations (smooth pursuit and VOR).

Figure 6.15 The *zoetrope* was developed in the 1830s and provided stroboscopic apparent motion as images became visible through slits in a rotating disc.

in a sequence of blinking lights, rather than flashing frames (see Figure 6.16). The most likely reason that stroboscopic apparent motion works is that it triggers the neural motion detection circuitry illustrated in Figure 6.12 [207, 215].

Frame Rates

How many frames per second are appropriate for a motion picture? The answer depends on the intended use. Figure 6.17 shows a table of significant frame rates from 2 to 5,000. Stroboscopic apparent motion begins at 2 FPS. Imagine watching a security video at this rate. It is easy to distinguish individual frames, but the motion of a person would also be perceived. Once 10 FPS is reached, the motion is obviously more smooth and we start to lose the ability to distinguish individual frames.

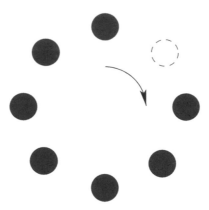

Figure 6.16 The *phi phenomenon* and *beta movement* are physiologically distinct effects in which motion is perceived [356, 313]. In the sequence of dots, one is turned *off* at any given time. A different dot is turned *off* in each frame, following a clockwise pattern. At a very low speed (2 FPS, or Frames Per Second), beta movement triggers a motion perception of each *on* dot directly behind the *off* dot. The *on* dot appears to jump to the position of the *off* dot. At a higher rate, such as 15 FPS, there instead appears to be a moving hole; this corresponds to the phi phenomenon.

FPS	Occurrence
2	Stroboscopic apparent motion starts
10	Ability to distinguish individual frames is lost
16	Old home movies; early silent films
24	Hollywood classic standard
25	PAL television before interlacing
30	NTSC television before interlacing
48	Two-blade shutter; proposed new Hollywood standard
50	Interlaced PAL television
60	Interlaced NTSC television; perceived flicker in some displays
72	Three-blade shutter; minimum CRT refresh rate for comfort
90	Modern VR headsets; no more discomfort from flicker
1,000	Ability to see zipper effect for fast, blinking LED
5,000	Cannot perceive zipper effect

Figure 6.17 Various frame rates and comments on the corresponding stroboscopic apparent motion. Units are in frames per second (FPS).

Early silent films ranged from 16 to 24 FPS. The frame rates were often fluctuating and were played at a faster speed than they were filmed. Once sound was added to film, incorrect speeds and fluctuations in the speed were no longer tolerated because both sound and video needed to be synchronized. This motivated playback at the fixed rate of 24 FPS, which is still used today by the movie industry. Personal video cameras remained at 16 or 18 FPS into the 1970s. The famous Zapruder film of the Kennedy assassination in 1963 was taken at 18.3 FPS. Although 24 FPS may be enough to perceive motions smoothly, a large part of cinematography is devoted to ensuring that motions are not so fast that jumps are visible due to the low frame rate.

Such low frame rates unfortunately lead to perceptible *flicker* as the images rapidly flash on the screen with black in between. This motivated several workarounds.

In the case of movie projectors, two-blade and three-blade shutters were invented so that they would show each frame two or three times, respectively. This enabled movies to be shown at 48 FPS and 72 FPS, thereby reducing discomfort from flickering. Analog television broadcasts in the 20th century were at 25 (*PAL standard*) or 30 FPS (*NTSC standard*), depending on the country. To double the frame rate and reduce perceived flicker, they used *interlacing* to draw half the image in one frame time, and then half in the other. Every other horizontal line is drawn in the first half, and the remaining lines are drawn in the second. This increased the frame rates on television screens to 50 and 60 FPS. The game industry has used the 60 FPS standard target for smooth game play.

As people started sitting close to giant CRT monitors in the early 1990s, the flicker problem became problematic again because sensitivity to flicker is stronger at the periphery. Furthermore, even when flicker cannot be directly perceived, it may still contribute to fatigue or headaches. Therefore, frame rates were increased to even higher levels. A minimum acceptable ergonomic standard for large CRT monitors was 72 FPS, with 85 to 90 FPS being widely considered as sufficiently high to eliminate most flicker problems. The problem has been carefully studied by psychologists under the heading of *flicker fusion threshold*; the precise rates at which flicker is perceptible or causes fatigue depends on many factors in addition to FPS, such as position on retina, age, color, and light intensity. Thus, the actual limit depends on the kind of display, its size, specifications, how it is used, and who is using it. Modern LCD and LED displays, used as televisions, computer screens, and smartphone screens, have 60, 120, and even 240 FPS.

The story does not end there. If you connect an LED to a pulse generator (put a resistor in series), then flicker can be perceived at much higher rates. Set the pulse generator to produce a square wave at several hundred hertz. Go to a dark room and hold the LED in your hand. If you wave it around so fast that your eyes cannot track it, then the flicker becomes perceptible as a zipper pattern. Let this be called the *zipper effect*. This happens because each time the LED pulses on, it is imaged in a different place on the retina. Without image stabilization, it appears as an array of lights. The faster the motion, the further apart the images will appear. The higher the pulse rate (or FPS), the closer together the images will appear. Therefore, to see the zipper effect at very high speeds, you need to move the LED very quickly. It is possible to see the effect for a few thousand FPS.

6.2.3 Implications for VR

Unfortunately, VR systems require much higher display performance than usual. We have already seen in Section 5.4 that much higher resolution is needed so that pixels and aliasing artifacts are not visible. The next problem is that higher frame rates are needed in comparison to ordinary television or movie standards of 24 FPS or even 60 FPS. To understand why, see Figure 6.18. The problem is easiest to understand in terms of the *perception of stationarity*, which was mentioned in Section 2.3. Fixate on a nearby object and yaw your head to the left. Your eyes should then rotate to the right to maintain the object in a fixed location on the retina, due to the VOR (Section 5.3). If you do the same while wearing a VR headset and fixating on an object in the virtual world, then the image of the object needs to shift across the

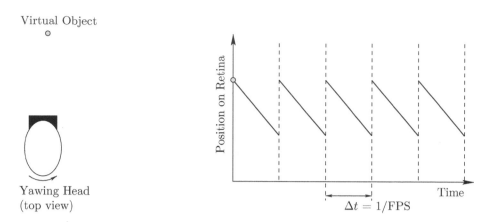

Figure 6.18 A problem with *perception of stationarity* under stroboscopic apparent motion. The image of a feature slips across the retina in a repeating pattern as the VOR is performed.

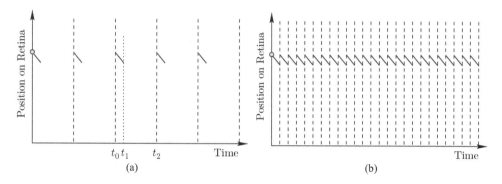

Figure 6.19 An engineering solution to reduce retinal image slip. (a) Using *low persistence*, the display is lit for a short enough time to trigger photoreceptors ($t_1 - t_0$) and then blanked for the remaining time ($t_2 - t_1$). Typically, $t_1 - t_0$ is around one to two milliseconds. (b) If the frame rate were extremely fast (at least 500 FPS), then the blank interval would not be needed.

screen while you turn your head. Assuming that the pixels instantaneously change at each new frame time, the image of the virtual object will slip across the retina as shown in Figure 6.18. The result is a kind of *judder* in which the object appears to be wobbling from side to side with high frequency but small amplitude.

The problem is that each feature is fixed on the screen for too long when ideally it should be moving continuously across the screen. At 60 FPS, it is fixed for 16.67 ms during each frame (in an idealized setting, which ignores scanout issues from Section 5.4). If the screen is instead turned on for only one or two milliseconds for each frame, and then made black during the remaining times, then the amount of retinal image slip is greatly reduced. This display mode is called *low persistence*, and is shown in Figure 6.19(a). The short amount of time that the display is illuminated is sufficient for the photoreceptors to collect enough photons to cause the image to be perceived. The problem is that at 60 FPS in low-persistence mode, flicker is perceived, which can lead to fatigue or headaches. This was easily perceived at the periphery in a bright scene in the Samsung Gear VR headset. If the frame rate is increased to 90 FPS or above, then the adverse side effects of flicker subside for nearly everyone. If the frame rate is increased to 500 FPS or beyond, then it would not even need to flicker, as depicted in Figure 6.19(b).

One final point is that fast pixel switching speed is implied in Figure 6.19. In a modern OLED display panel, the pixels can reach their target intensity values in less than 0.1 ms. However, older LCD displays changed pixel values much more slowly. The delay to reach the target intensity was as long as 20 ms, depending on the amount and direction of intensity change. In this case, a fixed virtual object appeared to smear or blur in the direction of motion. This was easily observable in the Oculus Rift DK1, which used an LCD display panel. More recently, last LCD technology switches pixels within a few milliseconds.

6.3 Perception of Color

What makes an object "purple," "pink," or "gray?" Color perception is unusual because it is purely the result of our visual physiology and neural structures, rather than something that can be measured in the physical world. In other words, "It's all in your head." If two people have comparable color perception systems, then they can discuss colors using commonly agreed-upon names while they perceive an object as having the same color. This contrasts other perception topics such as motion, depth, and scale, all of which correspond to measurable quantities in the surrounding world. The size of an object or the speed of its motion relative to some frame could be determined by instrumentation. Humans would be forced to agree on the numerical outcomes regardless of how their individual perceptual systems are functioning.

The Dress

The *dress color illusion* became a viral Internet phenomenon when millions of people quickly began to argue about the color of a dress. It was worn by Cecilia Bleasdale in a photograph shared on Facebook in 2015.[1] Based on the precise combination of colors and lighting conditions, its appearance fell on the boundary of what human color perceptual systems can handle. About 57 percent perceive it as blue and black (correct), 30 percent perceive it as white and gold, 10 percent perceive blue and brown, and 10 percent could switch between perceiving any of the color combinations [162].

Dimensionality Reduction

Recall from Section 4.1 that light energy is a jumble of wavelengths and magnitudes that form the spectral power distribution. Figure 4.6 provided an illustration. As we see objects, the light in the environment is reflected off of surfaces in a wavelength-dependent way according to the spectral distribution function (Figure 4.7). As the light passes through our eyes and is focused onto the retina, each photoreceptor receives a jumble of light energy that contains many wavelengths. Since the power distribution is a function of wavelength, the set of all possible distributions is a *function space*, which is generally infinite-dimensional. Our limited hardware cannot

[1] The image could not be reproduced here for copyright reasons, but can easily be found on the Internet.

possibly sense the entire function. Instead, the rod and cone photoreceptors sample it with a bias toward certain target wavelengths, as was shown in Figure 5.3 of Section 5.1. The result is a well-studied principle in engineering called *dimensionality reduction*. Here, the infinite-dimensional space of power distributions collapses down to a 3D *color space*. It is no coincidence that human eyes have precisely three types of cones, and that our RGB displays target the same colors as the photoreceptors.

Yellow = Green + Red

To help understand this reduction, consider the perception of "yellow". According to the visible light spectrum (Figure 4.5), yellow has a wavelength of about 580 nm. Suppose we had a pure light source that shines light of exactly 580 nm wavelength onto our retinas with no other wavelengths. The spectral distribution function would have a spike at 580 nm and be zero everywhere else. If we had a cone with peak detection at 580 nm and no sensitivity to other wavelengths, then it would perfectly detect yellow. Instead, we perceive yellow by activation of both green and red cones because their sensitivity regions (Figure 5.3) include 580 nm. It should then be possible to generate the same photoreceptor response by sending a jumble of light that contains precisely two wavelengths: (1) some "green" at 533 nm, and (2) some "red" at 564 nm. If the magnitudes of green and red are tuned so that the green and red cones activate in the same way as they did for pure yellow, then it becomes impossible for our visual system to distinguish the green/red mixture from pure yellow. Both are perceived as "yellow." This matching of colors from red, green, and blue components is called *metamerism*. Such a blending is precisely what is done on a RGB display to produce yellow. Suppose the intensity of each color ranges from 0 (dark) to 255 (bright). Red is produced by RGB = $(255, 0, 0)$, and green is RGB $= (0, 255, 0)$. These each activate one LED (or LCD) color, thereby producing a pure red or green. If both are turned on, then yellow is perceived. Thus, yellow is RGB $= (255, 255, 0)$.

Color Spaces

For convenience, a parameterized *color space* is often defined. One of the most common in computer graphics is called *HSV*, which has the following three components (Figure 6.20):

- The hue, which corresponds directly to the perceived color, such as "red" or "green."
- The saturation, which is the purity of the color. In other words, how much energy is coming from wavelengths other than the wavelength of the hue?
- The *value*, which corresponds to the brightness.

There are many methods to scale the HSV coordinates, which distort the color space in various ways. The RGB values could alternatively be used, but are sometimes more difficult for people to interpret.

It would be ideal to have a representation in which the distance between two points corresponds to the amount of perceptual difference. In other words, as two points are further apart, our ability to distinguish them is increased. The distance should correspond directly to the amount of distinguishability. Vision scientists designed

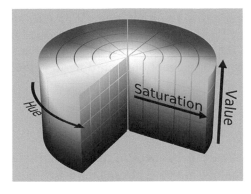

Figure 6.20 One representation of the HSV color space, which involves three parameters: hue, saturation, and value (brightness).

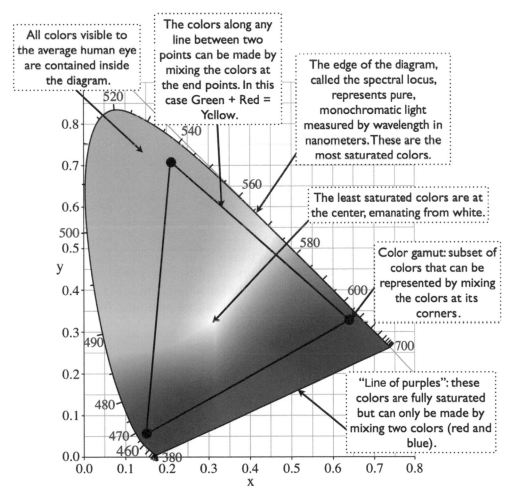

Anatomy of a CIE Chromaticity Diagram

Figure 6.21 1931 CIE color standard with RGB triangle. This representation attempts to preserve distances between perceived colors.

a representation to achieve this, resulting in the 1931 *CIE color standard* shown in Figure 6.21. Thus, the CIE is considered to be undistorted from a perceptual perspective. It is only two-dimensional because it disregards the brightness component, which is independent of color perception according to color matching experiments [207].

Mixing Colors

Suppose that we have three pure sources of light, as in that produced by an LED, in red, blue, and green colors. We have already discussed how to produce yellow by blending red and green. In general, most perceptible colors can be matched by a mixture of three. This is called *trichromatic theory* (or *Young–Helmholtz theory*). A set of colors that achieves this is called *primary colors*. Mixing all three evenly produces perceived *white light*, which on a display is achieved as RGB = (255, 255, 255). Black is the opposite: RGB = (0, 0, 0). Such light mixtures follow a linearity property. Suppose primary colors are used to perceptually match power distributions of two different light sources. If the light sources are combined, then their intensities of the primary colors need only to be added to obtain the perceptual match for the combination. Furthermore, the overall intensity can be scaled by multiplying the red, green, and blue components without affecting the perceived color. Only the perceived brightness may be changed.

The discussion so far has focused on *additive mixtures*. When mixing paints or printing books, colors mix subtractively because the spectral reflectance function is being altered. When starting with a white canvass or sheet of paper, virtually all wavelengths are reflected. Painting a green line on the page prevents all wavelengths other than green from being reflected at that spot. Removing all wavelengths results in black. Rather than using RGB components, printing presses are based on CMYK, which correspond to cyan, magenta, yellow, and black. The first three are pairwise mixes of the primary colors. A black component is included to reduce the amount of ink wasted by using the other three colors to subtractively produce black. Note that the targeted colors are observed only if the incoming light contains the targeted wavelengths. The green line would appear green under pure, matching green light, but might appear black under pure blue light.

Constancy

In spite of the dress color illusion, human color perception is surprisingly robust to the source of color. A red shirt appears to be red whether illuminated under indoor lights at night or in direct sunlight. These correspond to vastly different cases in terms of the spectral power distribution that reaches the retina. Our ability to perceive an object as having the same color over a wide variety of lighting conditions is called *color constancy*. Several perceptual mechanisms allow this to happen. One of them is *chromatic adaptation*, which results in a shift in perceived colors due to prolonged exposure to specific colors. Another factor in the perceived color is the expectation from the colors of surrounding objects. Furthermore, memory about how objects are usually colored in the environment biases our interpretation.

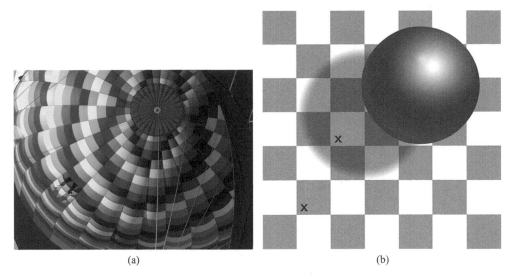

(a)   (b)

Figure 6.22 (a) The perceived hot air balloon colors are perceived the same regardless of the portions that are in direct sunlight or in a shadow. (b) The *checker shadow illusion* from Section 2.3 is explained by the *lightness constancy* principle, as the shadows prompt compensation of the perceived lightness.

The constancy principle also appears without regard to particular colors. Our perceptual system also maintains *lightness constancy* so that the overall brightness levels appear to be unchanged, even after lighting conditions are dramatically altered; see Figure 6.22(a). Under the *ratio principle* theory, only the ratio of reflectances between objects in a scene are perceptually maintained, whereas the overall amount of reflected intensity is not perceived. Further complicating matters, our perception of object lightness and color are maintained as the scene contains uneven illumination. A clear example is provided from shadows cast by one object onto another. Our perceptual system accounts for the shadow and adjusts our perception of the object shade or color. The checker shadow illusion shown in Figure 6.22(b) is caused by this compensation due to shadows.

Display Issues

Displays generally use RGB lights to generate the palette of colors and brightness. Recall Figure 4.36, which showed the subpixel mosaic of individual component colors for some common displays. Usually, the intensity of each R, G, and B value is set by selecting an integer from 0 to 255. This is a severe limitation on the number of brightness levels, as stated in Section 5.4. One cannot hope to densely cover all seven orders of magnitude of perceptible light intensity. One way to enhance the amount of contrast over the entire range is to perform *gamma correction*; see Figure 6.23. In most displays, images are encoded with a gamma of about 0.45 and decoded with a gamma of 2.2.

Another issue is that the set of all available colors lies inside of the triangle formed by R, G, and B vertices. This limitation is shown for the case of the *sRGB* standard in Figure 6.21. Most the CIE is covered, but many colors that humans are capable of perceiving cannot be generated on the display.

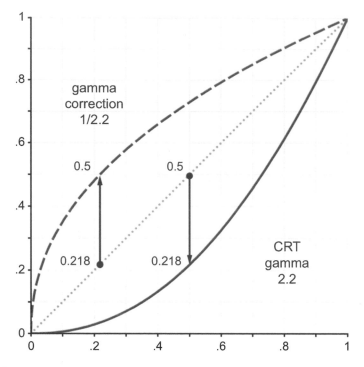

Figure 6.23 Gamma correction is used to span more orders of magnitude in spite of a limited number of bits. The transformation is $v' = cv^\gamma$, in which c is constant (usually $c = 1$) and γ controls the nonlinearity of the correction or distortion.

6.4 Combining Sources of Information

Throughout this chapter, we have seen perceptual processes that combine information from multiple sources. These could be cues from the same sense, as in the numerous monocular cues used to judge depth. Perception may also combine information from two or more senses. For example, people typically combine both visual and auditory cues when speaking face to face. Information from both sources makes it easier to understand someone, especially if there is significant background noise. We have also seen that information is integrated over time, as in the case of saccades being employed to fixate on several object features. Finally, our memories and general expectations about the behavior of the surrounding world bias our conclusions. Thus, information is integrated from prior expectations and the reception of many cues, which may come from different senses at different times.

Statistical decision theory provides a useful and straightforward mathematical model for making choices that incorporate prior biases and sources of relevant, observed data. It has been applied in many fields, including economics, psychology, signal processing, and computer science. One key component is *Bayes' rule*, which specifies how the *prior* beliefs should be updated in light of new observations, to obtain *posterior* beliefs. More formally, the "beliefs" are referred to as *probabilities*. If the probability takes into account information from previous information, it is called a *conditional probability*. There is no room to properly introduce *probability theory* here; only the basic ideas are given to provide some intuition without the rigor. For further study, find an online course or classic textbook (for example, [277]).

Let

$$H = \{h_1, h_2, \ldots, h_n\} \tag{6.1}$$

be a set of alternative *hypotheses* (or interpretations). Similarly, let

$$C = \{c_1, c_2, \ldots, c_m\} \tag{6.2}$$

be a set of possible outputs of a *cue detector*. For example, the cue detector might output the eye color of a face that is currently visible. In this case C is the set of possible colors:

$$C = \{\text{BROWN}, \text{BLUE}, \text{GREEN}, \text{HAZEL}\}. \tag{6.3}$$

Modeling a face recognizer, H would correspond to the set of people familiar to the person.

We want to calculate probability values for each of the hypotheses in H. Each probability value must lie between 0 and 1, and the probability values for every hypothesis in H must sum to one. Before any cues, we start with an assignment of values called the *prior distribution*, which is written as $P(h)$. The "P" denotes that it is a probability function or assignment; $P(h)$ means that an assignment has been applied to every h in H. The assignment must be made so that

$$P(h_1) + P(h_2) + \cdots + P(h_n) = 1, \tag{6.4}$$

and $0 \leq P(h_i) \leq 1$ for each i from 1 to n.

The prior probabilities are generally distributed across the hypotheses in a diffuse way; an example is shown in Figure 6.24(a). The likelihood of any hypothesis being true before any cues is proportional to its frequency of occurring naturally, based on evolution and the lifetime of experiences of the person. For example, if you open your eyes at a random time in your life, what is the likelihood of seeing a human being versus a wild boar?

Under normal circumstances (not VR!), we expect that the probability for the correct interpretation will rise as cues arrive. The probability of the correct hypothesis should pull upward toward one, effectively stealing probability mass from the other hypotheses, which pushes their values toward zero; see Figure 6.24(b). A "strong" cue should lift the correct hypothesis upward more quickly than a "weak" cue. If a single hypothesis has a probability value close to one, then the distribution is considered *peaked*, which implies high confidence; see Figure 6.24(c). In the other direction, inconsistent or incorrect cues have the effect of diffusing the probability across two or more hypotheses. Thus, the probability of the correct hypothesis may be lowered as other hypotheses are considered plausible and receive higher values. It may also be possible that two alternative hypotheses remain strong due to ambiguity that cannot be solved from the given cues; see Figure 6.24(d).

To take into account information from a cue, a *conditional distribution* is defined, which is written as $P(h \mid c)$. This is spoken as "the probability of h given c." This corresponds to a probability assignment for all possible combinations of hypotheses and cues. For example, it would include $P(h_2 \mid c_5)$, if there are at least two hypotheses and five cues. Continuing our face recognizer, this

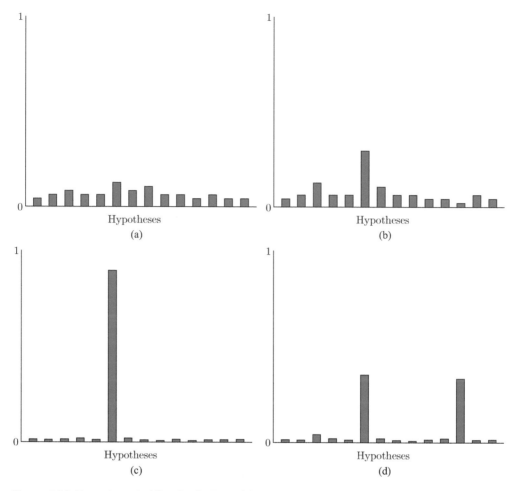

Figure 6.24 Example probability distributions. (a) A possible prior distribution. (b) Preference for one hypothesis starts to emerge after a cue. (c) A peaked distribution, which results from strong, consistent cues. (d) Ambiguity may result in two (or more) hypotheses that are strongly favored over others; this is the basis of multistable perception.

would look like $P(\textsc{Barack Obama} \mid \textsc{brown})$, which should be larger than $P(\textsc{Barack Obama} \mid \textsc{blue})$ (he has brown eyes).

We now arrive at the fundamental problem, which is to calculate $P(h \mid c)$ after the cue arrives. This is accomplished by *Bayes' rule*:

$$P(h \mid c) = \frac{P(c \mid h)P(h)}{P(c)}. \tag{6.5}$$

The denominator can be expressed as

$$P(c) = P(c \mid h_1)P(h_1) + P(c \mid h_2)P(h_2) + \cdots + P(c \mid h_n)P(h_n), \tag{6.6}$$

or it can be ignored it as a normalization constant, at which point only relative likelihoods are calculated instead of proper probabilities.

The only thing accomplished by Bayes' rule was to express $P(h \mid c)$ in terms of the prior distribution $P(h)$ and a new conditional distribution $P(c \mid h)$. The new

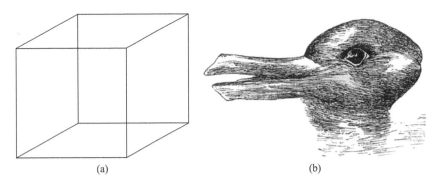

Figure 6.25 (a) The Necker cube, studied in 1832 by Swiss crystallographer Louis Albert Necker. (b) The *rabbit duck illusion*, from the October 23, 1892, issue of Fliegende Blätter.

conditional distribution is easy to work with in terms of modeling. It characterizes the likelihood that each specific cue will appear given that the hypothesis is true.

What if information arrives from a second cue detector? In this case, (6.5) is applied again, but $P(h \mid c)$ is now considered the prior distribution with respect to the new information. Let $D = \{d_1, d_2, \ldots, d_k\}$ represent the possible outputs of the new cue detector. Bayes' rule becomes

$$P(h \mid c, d) = \frac{P(d \mid h)P(h \mid c)}{P(d|c)}. \tag{6.7}$$

Here, $P(d \mid h)$ makes what is called a *conditional independence* assumption: $P(d \mid h)$ = $P(d \mid h, c)$. This is simpler from a modeling perspective. More generally, all four conditional parts of (6.7) should contain c because it is given before d arrives. As information from even more cues becomes available, Bayes' rule is applied again as many times as needed. One difficulty that occurs in practice and is modeled here is *cognitive bias*, which corresponds to numerous ways in which humans make irrational judgments in spite of the probabilistic implications of the data.

Multistable Perception
In some cases, our perceptual system may alternate between two or more conclusions. This is called *multistable perception*, for which the special case of two conclusions is called *bistable perception*. Figure 6.25(a) shows two well-known examples. For the *Necker cube*, it is ambiguous which cube face that is parallel to the viewing plane is in the foreground. It is possible to switch between both interpretations, resulting in bistable perception. Figure 6.25(b) shows another example, in which people may see a rabbit or a duck at various times. Another well-known example is called the *spinning dancer illusion* by Nobuyuki Kayahara. In that case, the silhouette of a rotating dancer is shown and it is possible to interpret the motion as clockwise or counterclockwise.

McGurk Effect
The *McGurk effect* is an experiment that clearly indicates the power of integration by mixing visual and auditory cues [211]. A video of a person speaking is shown

with the audio track dubbed so that the spoken sounds do not match the video. Two types of illusions were then observed. If "ba" is heard and "ga" is shown, then most subjects perceive "da" being said. This corresponds to a plausible fusion of sounds that explains the mismatch, but does not correspond to either original cue. Alternatively, the sounds may combine to produce a perceived "bga" in the case of "ga" on the sound track and "ba" on the visual track.

Implications for VR

Not all senses are taken over by VR. Thus, conflict will arise because of mismatch between the real and virtual worlds. As stated several times, the most problematic case of this is vection, which is a sickness-causing conflict between visual and vestibular cues arising from apparent self motion in VR while remaining stationary in the real world; see Section 8.4. As another example of mismatch, the user's body may sense that it is sitting in a chair, but the VR experience may involve walking. There would then be a height mismatch between the real and virtual worlds, in addition to mismatches based on proprioception and touch. In addition to mismatches among the senses, imperfections in the VR hardware, software, content, and interfaces cause inconsistencies in comparison with real-world experiences. The result is that incorrect or untended interpretations may arise. Even worse, such inconsistencies may increase fatigue as human neural structures use more energy to interpret the confusing combination. In light of the McGurk effect, it is easy to believe that many unintended interpretations or perceptions may arise from a VR system that does not provide perfectly consistent cues.

VR is also quite capable of generating new multistable perceptions. One example, which actually occurred in the VR industry, involved designing a pop-up menu. Suppose that users are placed into a dark environment and a large menu comes rushing up to them. A user may perceive one of two cases: (1) the menu approaches the user, or (2) the user is rushing up to the menu. The vestibular sense should be enough to resolve whether the user is moving, but the visual sense is overpowering. Prior knowledge about which is happening helps yield the correct perception. Unfortunately, if the wrong interpretation is made, then VR sickness in increased due to the sensory conflict. This, our perceptual system could be tricked into an interpretation that is worse for our health! Knowledge is one of many VR sickness factors discussed in Section 12.3.

Further Reading

As with Chapter 5, much of the material from this chapter appears in textbooks on sensation and perception [98, 207, 359] For a collection of optical illusions and their explanations, see [238]. For more on motion detection, see chapter 7 of [207]. Related to this is the history of motion pictures [28, 32].

To better understand the mathematical foundations of combining cues from multiple sources, look for books on Bayesian analysis and statistical decision theory. For example, see [272] and chapter 9 of [166]. An important issue is adaptation to VR system flaws through repeated use [288, 354]. This dramatically affects the perceptual results and fatigue from mismatches, and is a form of perceptual learning, which will be discussed in Section 12.1.

CHAPTER SEVEN

Visual Rendering

This chapter addresses visual rendering, which specifies what the visual display should show through an interface to the virtual world generator (VWG). Chapter 3 already provided the mathematical parts, which express *where* the objects in the virtual world should appear on the screen. This was based on geometric models, rigid body transformations, and viewpoint transformations. We next need to determine *how* these objects should appear, based on knowledge about light propagation, visual physiology, and visual perception. These were the topics of Chapters 4, 5, and 6, respectively. Thus, visual rendering is a culmination of everything covered so far.

Sections 7.1 and 7.2 cover the basic concepts; these are considered the core of computer graphics, but VR-specific issues also arise. They mainly address the case of rendering for virtual worlds that are formed synthetically. Section 7.1 explains how to determine the light that should appear at a pixel based on light sources and the reflectance properties of materials that exist purely in the virtual world. Section 7.2 explains rasterization methods, which efficiently solve the rendering problem and are widely used in specialized graphics hardware, called GPUs. Section 7.3 addresses VR-specific problems that arise from imperfections in the optical system. Section 7.4 focuses on latency reduction, which is critical to VR, so that virtual objects appear in the right place at the right time. Otherwise, many side effects could arise, such as VR sickness, fatigue, adaptation to the flaws, or simply having an unconvincing experience. Finally, Section 7.5 explains rendering for captured, rather than synthetic, virtual worlds. This covers VR experiences that are formed from panoramic photos and videos.

7.1 Ray Tracing and Shading Models

Suppose that a virtual world has been defined in terms of triangular primitives. Furthermore, a virtual eye has been placed in the world to view it from some particular position and orientation. Using the full chain of transformations from Chapter 3, the location of every triangle is correctly positioned onto a virtual screen (this was depicted in Figure 3.13). The next steps are to determine which screen pixels are covered by the transformed triangle and then illuminate them according to the physics of the virtual world.

An important condition must also be checked: for each pixel, is the triangle even *visible* to the eye, or will it be blocked by part of another triangle? This classic *visibility computation* problem dramatically complicates the rendering process. The general problem is to determine, for any pair of points in the virtual world, whether the line segment that connects them intersects with any objects (triangles). If an intersection occurs, then the line-of-sight visibility between the two points is blocked. The main difference between the two major families of rendering methods is how visibility is handled.

Object-Order versus Image-Order Rendering

For rendering, we need to consider all combinations of objects and pixels. This suggests a nested loop. One way to resolve the visibility is to iterate over the list of all triangles and attempt to render each one to the screen. This is called *object-order rendering*, and is the main topic of Section 7.2. For each triangle that falls into the field of view of the screen, the pixels are updated *only if* the corresponding part of the triangle is closer to the eye than any triangles that have been rendered so far. In this case, the outer loop iterates over triangles, whereas the inner loop iterates over pixels. The other family of methods is called *image-order rendering*, and it reverses the order of the loops: iterate over the image pixels and, for each one, determine which triangle should influence its RGB values. To accomplish this, the path of light waves that would enter each pixel is traced out through the virtual environment. This method will be covered first, and many of its components apply to object-order rendering as well.

Ray Tracing

To calculate the RGB values at a pixel, a *viewing ray* is drawn from the focal point through the center of the pixel on a virtual screen that is placed in the virtual world; see Figure 7.1. The process is divided into two phases:

1. *Ray casting*, in which the viewing ray is defined and its nearest point of intersection among all triangles in the virtual world is calculated.
2. *Shading*, in which the pixel RGB values are calculated based on lighting conditions and material properties at the intersection point.

The first step is based entirely on the virtual world geometry. The second step uses simulated physics of the virtual world. Both the material properties of objects and the lighting conditions are artificial and are chosen to produce the desired effect, whether realism or fantasy. Remember that the ultimate judge is the user, who interprets the image through perceptual processes.

Ray Casting

Calculating the first triangle hit by the viewing ray after it leaves the image pixel (Figure 7.1) is straightforward if we neglect the computational performance. Starting with the triangle coordinates, focal point, and the ray direction (vector), the closed-form solution involves basic operations from analytic geometry, including dot products, cross products, and the plane equation [327]. For each triangle, it must be determined whether the ray intersects it. If not, then the next triangle is considered. If it does, then the intersection is recorded as the candidate solution only if it is

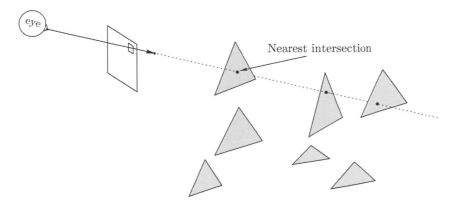

Figure 7.1 The first step in a ray tracing approach is called *ray casting*, which extends a viewing ray that corresponds to a particular pixel on the image. The ray starts at the focal point, which is the origin after the eye transform T_{eye} has been applied. The task is to determine what part of the virtual world model is visible. This is the closest intersection point between the viewing ray and the set of all triangles.

closer than the closest intersection encountered so far. After all triangles have been considered, the closest intersection point will be found. Although this is simple, it is far more efficient to arrange the triangles into a 3D data structure. Such structures are usually hierarchical so that many triangles can be eliminated from consideration by quick coordinate tests. Popular examples include BSP-trees and Bounding Volume Hierarchies [42, 86]. Algorithms that sort geometric information to obtain greater efficiently generally fall under *computational geometry* [55]. In addition to eliminating many triangles from quick tests, many methods of calculating the ray-triangle intersection have been developed to reduce the number of operations. One of the most popular is the *Möller–Trumbore intersection algorithm* [222].

Lambertian Shading

Now consider lighting each pixel and recall the basic behavior of light from Section 4.1. The virtual world simulates the real-world physics, which includes the spectral power distribution and spectral reflection function. Suppose that a point-sized light source is placed in the virtual world. Using the trichromatic theory from Section 6.3, its spectral power distribution is sufficiently represented by R, G, and B values. If the viewing ray hits the surface as shown in Figure 7.2, then how should the object appear? Assumptions about the spectral reflection function are taken into account by a *shading model*. The simplest case is *Lambertian shading*, for which the angle that the viewing ray strikes the surface is independent of the resulting pixel R, G, and B values. This corresponds to the case of diffuse reflection, which is suitable for a "rough" surface (recall Figure 4.4). All that matters is the angle that the surface makes with respect to the light source.

Let n be the outward surface normal and let ℓ be a vector from the surface intersection point to the light source. Assume both n and ℓ are unit vectors, and let θ denote the angle between them. The dot product $n \cdot \ell = \cos \theta$ yields the amount of attenuation (between 0 and 1) due to the tilting of the surface relative to the light source. Think about how the effective area of the triangle is reduced due to its tilt. A pixel under the *Lambertian shading* model is illuminated as

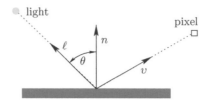

Figure 7.2 In the *Lambertian shading* model, the light reaching the pixel depends on the angle θ between the incoming light and the surface normal, but is independent of the viewing angle.

$$R = d_R I_R \max(0, n \cdot \ell),$$
$$G = d_G I_G \max(0, n \cdot \ell), \qquad (7.1)$$
$$B = d_B I_B \max(0, n \cdot \ell),$$

in which (d_R, d_G, d_B) represents the spectral reflectance property of the material (triangle) and (I_r, I_G, I_R) is represents the spectral power distribution of the light source. Under the typical case of white light, $I_R = I_G = I_B$. For a white or gray material, we would also have $d_R = d_G = d_B$.

Using vector notation, (7.1) can be compressed into

$$L = dI \max(0, n \cdot \ell), \qquad (7.2)$$

in which $L = (R, G, B)$, $d = (d_R, d_G, d_B)$, and $I = (I_R, I_G, I_B)$. Each triangle is assumed to be on the surface of an object, rather than the object itself. Therefore, if the light source is behind the triangle, then the triangle should not be illuminated because it is facing away from the light. (It cannot be lit from behind.) To handle this case, the max function appears in (7.2) to avoid $n \cdot \ell < 0$.

Blinn–Phong Shading
Now suppose that the object is shiny. If it were a perfect mirror, then all of the light from the source would be reflected to the pixel only if they are perfectly aligned; otherwise, no light would reflect at all. Such full reflection would occur if v and ℓ form the same angle with respect to n. What if the two angles are close, but do not quite match? The *Blinn–Phong shading* model proposes that some amount of light is reflected, depending on the amount of surface shininess and the difference between v and ℓ [24]. See Figure 7.3. The *bisector b* is the vector obtained by averaging ℓ and v:

$$b = \frac{\ell + v}{\|\ell + v\|}. \qquad (7.3)$$

Using the compressed vector notation, the *Blinn–Phong shading* model sets the RGB pixel values as

$$L = dI \max(0, n \cdot \ell) + sI \max(0, n \cdot b)^x. \qquad (7.4)$$

This additively takes into account shading due to both diffuse and specular components. The first term is just the Lambertian shading model, (7.2). The second component causes increasing amounts of light to be reflected as b becomes closer to n. The exponent x is a material property that expresses the amount of surface shininess. A lower value, such as $x = 100$, results in a mild amount of shininess,

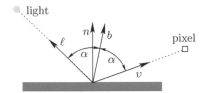

Figure 7.3 In the *Blinn–Phong shading* model, the light reaching the pixel depends on the angle between the normal n and the bisector b of the ℓ and v. If $n = b$, then ideal reflection is obtained, as in the case of a mirror.

whereas $x = 10,000$ would make the surface almost like a mirror. This shading model does not correspond directly to the physics of the interaction between light and surfaces. It is merely a convenient and efficient heuristic, but widely used in computer graphics.

Ambient Shading

Another heuristic is *ambient shading*, which causes an object to glow without being illuminated by a light source. This lights surfaces that fall into the shadows of all lights; otherwise, they would be completely black. In the real world this does not happen because light interreflects between objects to illuminate an entire environment. Such propagation has not been taken into account in the shading model so far, thereby requiring a hack to fix it. Adding ambient shading yields

$$L = dI \max(0, n \cdot \ell) + sI \max(0, n \cdot b)^x + L_a, \tag{7.5}$$

in which L_a is the ambient light component.

Multiple Light Sources

Typically, the virtual world contains multiple light sources. In this case, the light from each is combined additively at the pixel. The result for N light sources is

$$L = L_a + \sum_{i=1}^{N} dI_i \max(0, n \cdot \ell_i) + sI_i \max(0, n \cdot b_i)^x, \tag{7.6}$$

in which I_i, ℓ_i, and b_i correspond to each source.

BRDFs

The shading models presented so far are in widespread use due to their simplicity and efficiency, even though they neglect most of the physics. To account for shading in a more precise and general way, a *bidirectional reflectance distribution function* (*BRDF*) is constructed [236]; see Figure 7.4. The θ_i and θ_r parameters represent the angles of light source and viewing ray, respectively, with respect to the surface. The ϕ_i and ϕ_r parameters range from 0 to 2π and represent the angles made by the light and viewing vectors when looking straight down on the surface. (The vector n would point at your eye.)

The BRDF is a function of the form

$$f(\theta_i, \phi_i, \theta_r, \theta_i) = \frac{\text{radiance}}{\text{irradiance}}, \tag{7.7}$$

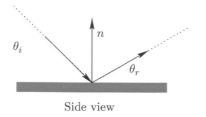 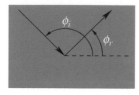

Side view   Top view

Figure 7.4 A *bidirectional reflectance distribution function (BRDF)* meticulously specifies the ratio of incoming and outgoing light energy for all possible perspectives.

in which *radiance* is the light energy reflected from the surface in directions θ_r and ϕ_r, and *irradiance* is the light energy arriving at the surface from directions θ_i and ϕ_i. These are expressed at a differential level, roughly corresponding to an infinitesimal surface patch. Informally, it is the ratio of the amount of outgoing light to the amount of incoming light at one point on the surface. The previous shading models can be expressed in terms of a simple BRDF. For Lambertian shading, the BRDF is constant because the surface reflects equally in all directions. The BRDF and its extensions can account for much more complex and physically correct lighting effects, with a wide variety of surface textures. See chapter 7 of [5] for extensive coverage.

Global Illumination

Recall that the ambient shading term (7.5) was introduced to prevent surfaces in the shadows of the light source from appearing black. The computationally intensive but proper way to fix this problem is to calculate how light reflects from object to object in the virtual world. In this way, objects are illuminated *indirectly* from the light that reflects from others, as in the real world. Unfortunately, this effectively turns all object surfaces into potential sources of light. This means that ray tracing must account for multiple reflections. This requires considering piecewise linear paths from the light source to the viewpoint, in which each bend corresponds to a reflection. An upper limit is usually set on the number of bounces to consider. The simple Lambertian and Blinn–Phong models are often used, but more general BDRFs are also common. Increasing levels of realism can be calculated, but with corresponding increases in computation time.

VR-Specific Issues

VR inherits all of the common issues from computer graphics, but also contains unique challenges. Chapters 5 and 6 mentioned the increased resolution and frame rate requirements. This provides strong pressure to reduce rendering complexity. Furthermore, many heuristics that worked well for graphics on a screen may be perceptibly wrong in VR. The combination of high field-of-view, resolution, varying viewpoints, and stereo images may bring out new problems. For example, Figure 7.5 illustrates how differing viewpoints from stereopsis could affect the appearance of shiny surfaces. In general, some rendering artifacts could even contribute to VR sickness. Throughout the remainder of this chapter, complications that are unique to VR will be increasingly discussed.

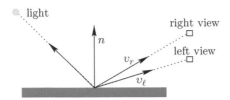

Figure 7.5 Complications emerge with shiny surfaces because the viewpoints are different for the right and left eyes. Using the Blinn–Phong shading model, a specular reflection should have different brightness levels for each eye. It may be difficult to match the effect so that it is consistent with real-world behavior.

7.2 Rasterization

The ray casting operation quickly becomes a bottleneck. For a 1080p image at 90 Hz, it would need to be performed over 180 million times per second, and the ray-triangle intersection test would be performed for every triangle (although data structures such as a BSP would quickly eliminate many from consideration). In most common cases, it is much more efficient to switch from such image-order rendering to object-order rendering. The objects in our case are triangles and the resulting process is called *rasterization*, which is the main function of modern graphical processing units (GPUs). In this case, an image is rendered by iterating over every triangle and attempting to color the pixels where the triangle lands on the image. The main difficulty is that the method must solve the unavoidable problem of determining which part, if any, of the triangle is the closest to the focal point (roughly, the location of the virtual eye).

One way to solve it is to sort the triangles in *depth order* so that the closest triangle is last. This enables the triangles to be drawn on the screen in back-to-front order. If they are properly sorted, then any later triangle to be rendered will rightfully clobber the image of previously rendered triangles at the same pixels. The triangles can be drawn one-by-one while totally neglecting the problem of determining which is nearest. This is known as the *Painter's algorithm*. The main flaw, however, is the potential existence of *depth cycles*, shown in Figure 7.6, in which three or more triangles cannot be rendered correctly in any order by the Painter's algorithm. One possible fix is to detect such cases and split the triangles.

Depth Buffer

A simple and efficient method to resolve this problem is to manage the depth problem on a pixel-by-pixel basis by maintaining a *depth buffer* (also called *z-buffer*), which for every pixel records the distance of the triangle from the focal point to the intersection point of the ray that intersects the triangle at that pixel. In other words, if this were the ray casting approach, it would be distance along the ray from the focal point to the intersection point. Using this method, the triangles can be rendered in arbitrary order. The method is also commonly applied to compute the effect of shadows by determining depth order from a light source, rather than the viewpoint. Objects that are closer to the light cast a shadow on further objects.

The depth buffer stores a positive real number (floating point number in practice) at every pixel location. Before any triangles have been rendered, a maximum value

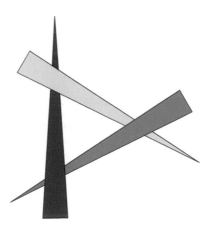

Figure 7.6 Due to the possibility of *depth cycles*, objects cannot be sorted in three dimensions with respect to distance from the observer. Each object is partially in front of one and partially behind another.

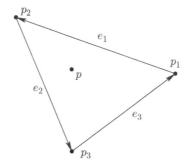

Figure 7.7 If p is inside the triangle, then it must be to the right of each of the edge vectors, e_1, e_2 and e_3. Barycentric coordinates specify the location of every point p in a triangle as a weighted average of its vertices p_1, p_2, and p_3.

(floating-point infinity) is stored at every location to reflect that no surface has yet been encountered at each pixel. At any time in the rendering process, each value in the depth buffer records the distance of the point on the most recently rendered triangle to the focal point, for the corresponding pixel in the image. Initially, all depths are at maximum to reflect that no triangles were rendered yet.

Each triangle is rendered by calculating a rectangular part of the image that fully contains it. This is called a *bounding box*. The box is quickly determined by transforming all three of the triangle vertices to determine the minimum and maximum values for i and j (the row and column indices). An iteration is then performed over all pixels inside the bounding box to determine which ones lie inside the triangle and should therefore be rendered. This can be quickly determined by forming the three edge vectors shown in Figure 7.7 as

$$
\begin{aligned}
e_1 &= p_2 - p_1, \\
e_2 &= p_3 - p_2, \\
e_3 &= p_1 - p_3.
\end{aligned}
\tag{7.8}
$$

The point p lies inside the triangle if and only if

$$
(p - p_1) \times e_1 < 0 \,, (p - p_2) \times e_2 < 0 \,, (p - p_3) \times e_3 < 0,
\tag{7.9}
$$

in which $\times$ denotes the standard vector cross product. These three conditions ensure that p is "to the left" of each edge vector.

Barycentric Coordinates
As each triangle is rendered, information from it is mapped from the virtual world onto the screen. This is usually accomplished using *barycentric coordinates* (see Figure 7.7), which express each point in the triangle interior as a weighted average of the three vertices:

$$p = \alpha_1 p_1 + \alpha_2 p_2 + \alpha_3 p_3, \qquad (7.10)$$

for which $0 \le \alpha_1, \alpha_2, \alpha_3 \le 1$ and $\alpha_1 + \alpha_2 + \alpha_3 = 1$. The closer p is to a vertex p_i, the larger the weight α_i. If p is at the centroid of the triangle, then $\alpha_1 = \alpha_2 = \alpha_3 = 1/3$. If p lies on an edge, then the opposing vertex weight is zero. For example, if p lies on the edge between p_1 and p_2, then $\alpha_3 = 0$. If p lies on a vertex, p_i, then $\alpha_i = 1$, and the other two barycentric coordinates are zero.

The coordinates are calculated using Cramer's rule to solve a resulting linear system of equations. In particular, let $d_{ij} = e_i \cdot e_j$ for all combinations of i and j. Furthermore, let

$$s = 1/(d_{11}d_{22} - d_{12}d_{12}). \qquad (7.11)$$

The coordinates are then given by

$$\begin{aligned}
\alpha_1 &= s(d_{22}d_{31} - d_{12}d_{32}), \\
\alpha_2 &= s(d_{11}d_{32} - d_{12}d_{31}), \\
\alpha_3 &= 1 - \alpha_1 - \alpha_2.
\end{aligned} \qquad (7.12)$$

The same barycentric coordinates may be applied to the points on the model in $\mathbb{R}^3$, or on the resulting 2D projected points (with i and j coordinates) in the image plane. In other words, α_1, α_2, and α_3 refer to the same point on the model both before, during, and after the entire chain of transformations from Section 3.5.

Furthermore, given the barycentric coordinates, the test in (7.9) can be replaced by simply determining whether $\alpha_1 \ge 0$, $\alpha_2 \ge 0$, and $\alpha_3 \ge 0$. If any barycentric coordinate is less than zero, then p must lie outside the triangle.

Mapping the Surface
Barycentric coordinates provide a simple and efficient method for linearly interpolating values across a triangle. The simplest case is the propagation of RGB values. Suppose RGB values are calculated at the three triangle vertices using the shading methods of Section 7.1. This results in values (R_i, G_i, B_i) for each i from 1 to 3. For a point p in the triangle with barycentric coordinates $(\alpha_1, \alpha_2, \alpha_3)$, the RGB values for the interior points are calculated as

$$\begin{aligned}
R &= \alpha_1 R_1 + \alpha_2 R_2 + \alpha_3 R_3, \\
G &= \alpha_1 G_1 + \alpha_2 G_2 + \alpha_3 G_3, \\
B &= \alpha_1 B_1 + \alpha_2 B_2 + \alpha_3 B_3.
\end{aligned} \qquad (7.13)$$

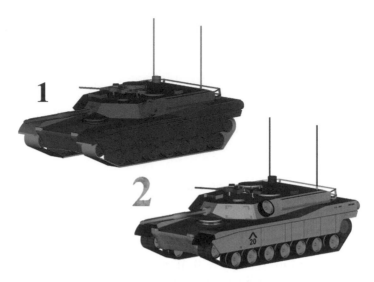

Figure 7.8 Texture mapping: a simple pattern or an entire image can be mapped across the triangles and then rendered in the image to provide much more detail than provided by the triangles in the model.

Figure 7.9 Bump mapping: by artificially altering the surface normals, the shading algorithms produce an effect that looks like a rough surface.

The object need not maintain the same properties over an entire triangular patch. With *texture mapping*, a repeating pattern, such as tiles or stripes, can be propagated over the surface [41]; see Figure 7.8. More generally, any digital picture can be mapped onto the patch. The barycentric coordinates reference a point inside the image to be used to influence a pixel. The picture or "texture" is treated as if it were painted onto the triangle; the lighting and reflectance properties are additionally taken into account for shading the object.

Another possibility is *normal mapping*, which alters the shading process by allowing the surface normal to be artificially varied over the triangle, even though geometrically it is impossible. Recall from Section 7.1 that the normal is used in the shading models. By allowing it to vary, simulated curvature can be given to an object. An important case of mapping the normals is called *bump mapping*, which makes a flat surface look rough by irregularly perturbing the normals. If the normals appear to have texture, then the surface will look rough after shading is computed.

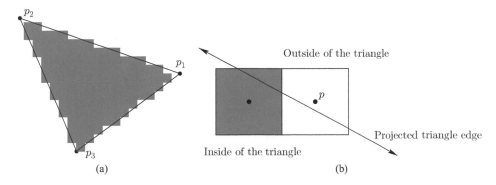

Figure 7.10 (a) The rasterization stage results in aliasing; straight edges appear to be staircases. (b) Pixels are selected for inclusion based on whether their center point p lies inside the triangle.

Aliasing

Several artifacts arise due to discretization. Aliasing problems were mentioned in Section 5.4, which result in perceptible staircases in the place of straight lines, due to insufficient pixel density. Figure 7.10(a) shows the pixels selected inside a small triangle by using (7.9). The point p usually corresponds to the center of the pixel, as shown in Figure 7.10(b). Note that the point may be inside the triangle while the entire pixel is not. Likewise, part of the pixel might be inside the triangle while the center is not. You may notice that Figure 7.10 is not entirely accurate due to the subpixel mosaics used in displays (recall Figure 4.36). To be more precise, aliasing analysis should take this into account as well.

By deciding to fully include or exclude the triangle based on the coordinates of p alone, the staircasing effect is unavoidable. A better way is to render the pixel according to the fraction of the pixel region that is covered by the triangle. This way, its values could be blended from multiple triangles that are visible within the pixel region. Unfortunately, this requires *supersampling*, which means casting rays at a much higher density than the pixel density so that the triangle coverage fraction can be estimated. This dramatically increases cost. Commonly, a compromise is reached in a method called *multisample anti-aliasing* (or *MSAA*), in which only some values are calculated at the higher density. Typically, depth values are calculated for each sample, but shading is not.

A *spatial aliasing* problem results from texture mapping. The viewing transformation may dramatically reduce the size and aspect ratio of the original texture as it is mapped from the virtual world onto the screen. This may leave insufficient resolution to properly represent a repeating pattern in the texture; see Figure 7.12. This problem is often addressed in practice by precalculating and storing a *mipmap* for each texture; see Figure 7.11. The texture is calculated at various resolutions by performing high-density sampling and storing the rasterized result in images. Based on the size and viewpoint of the triangle on the screen, the appropriately scaled texture image is selected and mapped onto the triangle to reduce the aliasing artifacts.

Culling

In practice, many triangles can be quickly eliminated before attempting to render them. This results in a preprocessing phase of the rendering approach called *culling*,

Figure 7.11 A mipmap stores the texture at multiple resolutions so that it can be appropriately scaled without causing significant aliasing. The overhead for storing the extra image is typically only 1/3 the size of the original (largest) image.

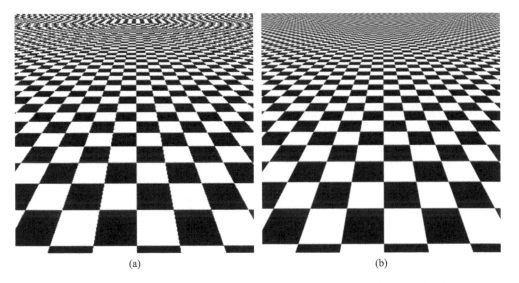

(a)   (b)

Figure 7.12 (a) Due to the perspective transformation, the tiled texture suffers from *spatial aliasing* as the depth increases. (b) The problem can be fixed by performing supersampling.

which dramatically improves performance and enables faster frame rates. The efficiency of this operation depends heavily on the data structure used to represent the triangles. Thousands of triangles could be eliminated with a single comparison of coordinates if they are all arranged in a hierarchical structure. The most basic form of culling is called *view volume culling*, which eliminates all triangles that are wholly outside of the viewing frustum (recall Figure 3.17). For a VR headset, the frustum may have a curved cross section due to the limits of the optical system (see Figure 7.13). In this case, the frustum must be replaced with a region that has the appropriate shape. In the case of a truncated cone, a simple geometric test can quickly eliminate all objects outside the view. For example, if

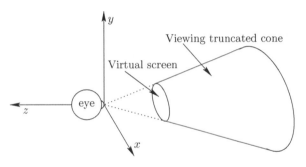

Stencil buffer pattern

Figure 7.13 Due to the optical system in front of the screen, the viewing frustum is replaced by a truncated cone in the case of a circularly symmetric view. Other cross-sectional shapes may be possible to account for the asymmetry of each eye view. (For example, the nose is obstructing part of the view.)

$$\frac{\sqrt{x^2 + y^2}}{-z} > \tan\theta, \tag{7.14}$$

in which 2θ is the angular field of view, then the point (x, y, z) is outside of the cone. Alternatively, the *stencil buffer* can be used in a GPU to mark all pixels that would be outside the lens view. These are quickly eliminated from consideration by a simple test as each frame is rendered.

Another form is called *backface culling*, which removes triangles that have outward surface normals that point away from the focal point. These should not be rendered "from behind" if the model is consistently formed. Additionally, *occlusion culling* may be used to eliminate parts of the model that might be hidden from view by a closer object. This can get complicated because it once again considers the depth ordering problem. For complete details, see [5].

VR-Specific Rasterization Problems

The staircasing problem due to aliasing is expected to be worse for VR because resolutions are often well below the required retina display limit calculated in Section 5.4. The problem is made significantly worse by the continuously changing viewpoint due to head motion. Even as the user attempts to stare at an edge, the "stairs" appear to be more like an "escalator" because the exact choice of pixels to include in a triangle depends on subtle variations in the viewpoint. As part of our normal perceptual processes, our eyes are drawn toward this distracting motion. With stereo viewpoints, the situation is worse: The "escalators" from the right and left images will usually not match. As the brain attempts to fuse the two images into one coherent view, the aliasing artifacts provide a strong, moving mismatch. Reducing contrast at edges and using anti-aliasing techniques help alleviate the problem, but aliasing is likely to remain a significant problem unless the display reaches the required retina display density for VR.

A more serious difficulty is caused by the enhanced depth perception afforded by a VR system. Both head motions and stereo views enable users to perceive small differences in depth across surfaces. This should be a positive outcome; however, many tricks developed in computer graphics over the decades rely on the fact that people cannot perceive these differences when a virtual world is rendered onto a fixed

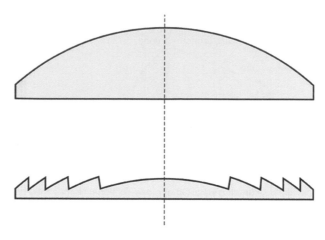

Figure 7.14 A Fresnel lens (pronounced like "frenelle") simulates a simple lens by making a corrugated surface. The convex surface on the top lens is implemented in the Fresnel lens shown on the bottom.

screen that is viewed from a significant distance. The result for VR is that texture maps may look fake. For example, texture mapping a picture of a carpet onto the floor might inadvertently cause the floor to look as if it were simply painted. In the real world we would certainly be able to distinguish painted carpet from real carpet. The same problem occurs with normal mapping. A surface that might look rough in a single static image due to bump mapping could look completely flat in VR as both eyes converge onto the surface. Thus, as the quality of VR systems improves, we should expect the rendering quality requirements to increase, causing many old tricks to be modified or abandoned.

7.3 Correcting Optical Distortions

Recall from Section 4.3 that barrel and pincushion distortions are common for an optical system with a high field of view (Figure 4.20). When looking through the lens of a VR headset, a pincushion distortion typically results. If the images are drawn on the screen without any correction, then the virtual world appears to be incorrectly warped. If the user yaws her head back and forth, then fixed lines in the world, such as walls, appear to dynamically change their curvature because the distortion in the periphery is much stronger than in the center. If it is not corrected, then the perception of stationarity will fail because static objects should not appear to be warping dynamically. Furthermore, contributions may be made to VR sickness because incorrect accelerations are being visually perceived near the periphery.

How can this problem be solved? Significant research is being done in this area, and the possible solutions involve different optical systems and display technologies. For example, *digital light processing* (*DLP*) technology directly projects light into the eye without using lenses. Another way to greatly reduce this problem is to use a *Fresnel lens* (see Figure 7.14), which more accurately controls the bending of light rays by using a corrugated or sawtooth surface over a larger area; an aspheric design can be implemented as well. A Fresnel lens was used, for example, in the HTC Vive VR headset. One unfortunate side effect of Fresnel lenses is that glaring can be frequently observed as light scatters across the ridges along the surface.

Whether small or large, the distortion can also be corrected in software. One assumption is that the distortion is circularly symmetric. This means that the amount of distortion depends only on the distance from the lens center, and not the particular direction from the center. Even if the lens distortion is perfectly circularly symmetric, it must also be placed so that it is centered over the eye. Some headsets offer IPD adjustment, which allows the distance between the lenses to be altered so that they are matched to the user's eyes. If the eye is not centered on the lens, then asymmetric distortion arises. The situation is not perfect because as the eye rotates, the pupil moves along a spherical arc. As the position of the pupil over the lens changes laterally, the distortion varies and becomes asymmetric. This motivates making the lens as large as possible so that this problem is reduced. Another factor is that the distortion will change as the distance between the lens and the screen is altered. This adjustment may be useful to accommodate users with nearsightedness or farsightedness, as was done in the Samsung Gear VR headset. The adjustment is also common in binoculars, which explains why many people do not need their glasses to use them. To handle distortion correctly, the headset should ideally sense the adjustment setting and take it into account.

To fix radially symmetric distortion, suppose that the transformation chain $T_{can} T_{eye} T_{rb}$ has been applied to the geometry, resulting in the canonical view volume, as covered in Section 3.5. All points that were inside the viewing frustum now have x and y coordinates ranging from -1 to 1. Consider referring to these points using polar coordinates (r, θ):

$$r = \sqrt{x^2 + y^2},$$
$$\theta = \text{atan2}(y, x),$$

$$(7.15)$$

in which atan2 represents the inverse tangent of y/x. This function is commonly used in programming languages to return an angle θ over the entire range from 0 to 2π. (The arctangent alone cannot do this because the quadrant that (x, y) came from is needed.)

We now express the lens distortion in terms of transforming the radius r, without affecting the direction θ (because of symmetry). Let f denote a function that applies to positive real numbers and distorts the radius. Let r_u denote the undistorted radius, and let r_d denote the distorted radius. Both pincushion and barrel distortion are commonly approximated using polynomials with odd powers, resulting in f being defined as

$$r_d = f(r_u) = r_u + c_1 r_u^3 + c_2 r_u^5,$$

$$(7.16)$$

in which c_1 and c_2 are suitably chosen constants. If $c_1 < 0$, then barrel distortion occurs. If $c_1 > 0$, then pincushion distortion results. Higher-order polynomials could also be used, such as adding a term $c_3 r_u^7$ on the right side of Eq. (7.16); however, in practice this is often considered unnecessary.

Correcting the distortion involves two phases:

1. Determine the radial distortion function f for a particular headset, which involves a particular lens placed at a fixed distance from the screen. This is a regression or curve-fitting problem that involves an experimental setup that measures the distortion of many points and selects the coefficients c_1, c_2, and so on, that provide the best fit.

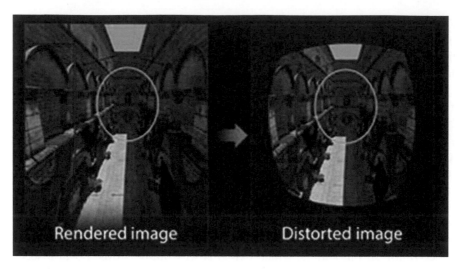

Figure 7.15 The rendered image appears to have a barrel distortion. Note that the resolution is effectively dropped near the periphery.

2. Determine the inverse of f so that it be applied to the rendered image before the lens causes its distortion. The composition of the inverse with f should cancel out the distortion function.

Unfortunately, polynomial functions generally do not have inverses that can be determined or even expressed in a closed form. Therefore, approximations are used. One commonly used approximation is [120]:

$$f^{-1}(r_d) \approx \frac{c_1 r_d^2 + c_2 r_d^4 + c_1^2 r_d^4 + c_2^2 r_d^8 + 2c_1 c_2 r_d^6}{1 + 4c_1 r_d^2 + 6c_2 r_d^4}. \tag{7.17}$$

Alternatively, the inverse can be calculated very accurately off-line and then stored in an array for fast access. It needs to be done only once per headset design. Linear interpolation can be used for improved accuracy. The inverse values can be accurately calculated using Newton's method, with initial guesses provided by simply plotting $f(r_u)$ against r_u and swapping the axes.

The transformation f^{-1} could be worked directly into the perspective transformation, thereby replacing T_p and T_{can} with a nonlinear operation. By leveraging the existing graphics rendering pipeline, it is instead handled as a post-processing step. The process of transforming the image is sometimes called *distortion shading* because it can be implemented as a shading operation in the GPU; it has nothing to do with "shading" as defined in Section 7.1. The rasterized image that was calculated using methods in Section 7.2 can be converted into a transformed image using (7.17), or another representation of f^{-1}, on a pixel-by-pixel basis. If compensating for a pincushion distortion, the resulting image will appear to have a barrel distortion; see Figure 7.15. To improve VR performance, *multiresolution shading* was used in Nvidia GTX 1080 GPUs. One problem is that the resolution is effectively dropped near the periphery because of the transformed image (Figure 7.15). This results in wasted shading calculations in the original image. Instead, the image can be rendered before the transformation by taking into account the final resulting resolutions after the transformation. A lower-resolution image is rendered in a region that will become compressed by the transformation.

The methods described in this section may also be used for other optical distortions that are radially symmetric. For example, chromatic aberration can be partially corrected by transforming the red, green, and blue subpixels differently. Each color is displaced radially by a different amount to compensate for the radial distortion that occurs based on its wavelength. If chromatic aberration correction is being used, then if the lenses are removed from the VR headset, it would become clear that the colors are not perfectly aligned in the images being rendered to the display. The rendering system must create a distortion of pixel placements on the basis of color so that they will be moved closer to the correct places after they pass through the lens.

7.4 Improving Latency and Frame Rates

The *motion-to-photons* latency in a VR headset is the amount of time it takes to update the display in response to a change in head orientation and position. For example, suppose the user is fixating on a stationary feature in the virtual world. As the head yaws to the right, the image of the feature on the display must immediately shift to the left. Otherwise, the feature will appear to move if the eyes remain fixated on it. This breaks the perception of stationarity.

A Simple Example

Consider the following example to get a feeling for the latency problem. Let d be the density of the display in pixels per degree. Let ω be the angular velocity of the head in degrees per second. Let ℓ be the latency in seconds. Due to latency ℓ and angular velocity ω, the image is shifted by $d\omega\ell$ pixels. For example, if $d = 40$ pixels per degree, $\omega = 50$ degrees per second, and $\ell = 0.02$ seconds, then the image is incorrectly displaced by $d\omega\ell = 4$ pixels. An extremely fast head turn might be at 300 degrees per second, which would result in a 24-pixel error.

The Perfect System

As a thought experiment, imagine the perfect VR system. As the head moves, the viewpoint must accordingly change for visual rendering. A magic oracle perfectly indicates the head position and orientation at any time. The VWG continuously maintains the positions and orientations of all objects in the virtual world. The visual rendering system maintains all perspective and viewport transformations, and the entire rasterization process continuously sets the RGB values on the display according to the shading models. Progressing with this fantasy, the display itself continuously updates, taking no time to switch the pixels. The display has retina-level resolution, as described in Section 5.4, and a dynamic range of light output over seven orders of magnitude to match human perception. In this case, visual stimulation provided by the virtual world should match what would occur in a similar physical world in terms of the geometry. There would be no errors in time and space (although the physics might not match anyway due to assumptions about lighting, shading, material properties, color spaces, and so on).

Historical Problems

In practice, the perfect system is not realizable. All of these operations require time to propagate information and perform computations. In early VR systems, the total motion-to-photons latency was often over 100 ms. In the 1990s, 60 ms was considered an acceptable amount. Latency has been stated as one of the greatest causes of VR sickness, and therefore one of the main obstructions to widespread adoption over the past decades. People generally adapt to a fixed latency, which somewhat mitigates the problem but then causes problems when they have to readjust to the real world. Variable latencies are even worse due to the inability to adapt [69]. Fortunately, latency is no longer the main problem in most VR systems because of the latest-generation tracking, GPU, and display technology. The latency may be around 15 to 25 ms, which is even compensated for by predictive methods in the tracking system. The result is that the *effective* latency is very close to zero. Thus, other factors are now contributing more strongly to VR sickness and fatigue, such as vection and optical aberrations.

Overview of Latency Reduction Methods

The following strategies are used together to both reduce the latency and to minimize the side effects of any remaining latency:

1. Lower the complexity of the virtual world.
2. Improve rendering pipeline performance.
3. Remove delays along the path from the rendered image to switching pixels.
4. Use prediction to estimate future viewpoints and world states.
5. Shift or distort the rendered image to compensate for last-moment viewpoint errors and missing frames.

Each of these will be described in succession.

Simplifying the Virtual World

Recall from Section 3.1 that the virtual world is composed of geometric primitives, which are usually 3D triangles arranged in a mesh. The chain of transformations and rasterization process must be applied for each triangle, resulting in a computational cost that is directly proportional to the number of triangles. Thus, a model that contains tens of millions of triangles will take orders of magnitude longer to render than one made of a few thousand. In many cases, we obtain models that are much larger than necessary. They can often be made much smaller (fewer triangles) with no perceptible difference, much in the same way that image, video, and audio compression works. Why are they too big in the first place? If the model was captured from a 3D scan of the real world, then it is likely to contain highly dense data. Capture systems such as the FARO Focus3D X Series capture large worlds while facing outside. Others, such as the Matter and Form MFSV1, capture a small object by rotating it on a turntable. As with cameras, systems that construct 3D models automatically are focused on producing highly accurate and dense representations, which maximize the model size. Even in the case of purely synthetic worlds, a modeling tool such as Maya or Blender will automatically construct a highly accurate mesh of triangles over a curved surface. Without taking specific care of later rendering burdens, the model could quickly become unwieldy. Fortunately, it is possible

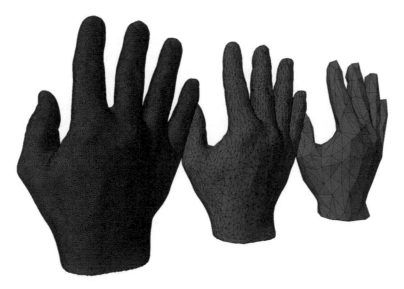

Figure 7.16 A variety of mesh simplification algorithms can be used to reduce the model complexity while retaining the most important structures. Shown here is a simplification of a hand model made by the open-source library CGAL.

to reduce the model size by using *mesh simplification* algorithms; see Figure 7.16. In this case, one must be careful to make sure that the simplified model will have sufficient quality from all viewpoints that might arise in the targeted VR system. In some game engines, such as Unity 3D, reducing the number of different material properties across the model will also improve performance.

In addition to reducing the rendering time, a simplified model will also lower computational demands on the Virtual World Generator (VWG). For a *static world*, the VWG does not need to perform any updates after initialization. The user simply views the fixed world. For *dynamic worlds*, the VWG maintains a simulation of the virtual world that moves all geometric bodies while satisfying physical laws that mimic the real world. It must handle the motions of any avatars, falling objects, moving vehicles, swaying trees, and so on. Collision detection methods are needed to make bodies react appropriately when in contact. Differential equations that model motion laws may be integrated to place bodies correctly over time. These issues will be explained in Chapter 8, but for now it is sufficient to understand that the VWG must maintain a coherent snapshot of the virtual world each time a rendering request is made. Thus, the VWG has a frame rate in the same way as a display or visual rendering system. Each VWG frame corresponds to the placement of all geometric bodies for a common time instant. How many times per second can the VWG be updated? Can a high, constant rate of VWG frames be maintained? What happens when a rendering request is made while the VWG is in the middle of updating the world? If the rendering module does not wait for the VWG update to be completed, then some objects could be incorrectly placed because some are updated while others are not. Thus, the system should ideally wait until a complete VWG frame is finished before rendering. This suggests that the VWG update should be at least as fast as the rendering process, and the two should be carefully synchronized so that a complete, fresh VWG frame is always ready for rendering.

Improving Rendering Performance

Any techniques that improve rendering performance in the broad field of computer graphics apply here; however, one must avoid cases in which side effects that were imperceptible on a computer display become noticeable in VR. It was already mentioned in Section 7.2 that texture and normal mapping methods are less effective in VR for this reason; many more discrepancies are likely to be revealed in coming years. Regarding improvements that are unique to VR, it was mentioned in Sections 7.2 and 7.3 that the stencil buffer and multiresolution shading can be used to improve rendering performance by exploiting the shape and distortion due to the lens in a VR headset. A further improvement is to perform rasterization for the left and right eyes in parallel in the GPU, using one processor for each. The two processes are completely independent. This represents an important first step, among many that are likely to come, in design of GPUs that are targeted specifically for VR.

From Rendered Image to Switching Pixels

The problem of waiting for coherent VWG frames also arises in the process of rendering frames to the display: When it is time to scan out the rendered image to the display, it might not be finished yet. Recall from Section 5.4 that most displays have a rolling scanout that draws the rows of the rasterized image, which sits in the *video memory*, onto the screen one-by-one. This was motivated by the motion of the electron beam that lit phosphors on analog TV screens. The motion is left to right, and top to bottom, much in the same way we would write out a page of English text with a pencil and paper. Due to inductive inertia in the magnetic coils that bent the beam, there was a period of several milliseconds called VBLANK (*vertical blanking interval*) in which the beam moves from the lower right back to the upper left of the screen to start the next frame. During this time, the beam was turned off to avoid drawing a diagonal streak across the frame, hence, the name "blanking." Short blanking intervals also occurred at each horizontal line to bring the beam back from the right to the left.

In the era of digital displays, the scanning process is unnecessary, but it nevertheless persists and causes some trouble. Suppose that a display runs at 100 FPS. In this case, a request to draw a new rendered image is made every 10 ms. Suppose that VBLANK occurs for 2 ms and the remaining 8 ms is spent drawing lines on the display. If the new rasterized image is written to the video memory during the 2 ms of VBLANK, then it will be correctly drawn in the remaining 8 ms. It is also possible to earn extra time through beam tracing [25, 217]. However, if a new image is being written and passes where the beam is scanning it out, then tearing occurs because it appears as if is screen is torn into pieces; see Figure 7.17. If the VWG and rendering system produce frames at 300 FPS, then parts of three or four images could appear on the display because the image changes several times while the lines are being scanned out. One solution to this problem is to use VSYNC (pronounced "vee sink"), which is a flag that prevents the video memory from being written outside the VBLANK interval.

Another strategy to avoid tearing is *buffering*, which is shown in Figure 7.18. The approach is simple for programmers because it allows the frames to be written in memory that is not being scanned for output to the display. The unfortunate side

Figure 7.17 If a new frame is written to the video memory while a display scanout occurs, then *tearing* arises, in which parts of two or more frames become visible at the same time.

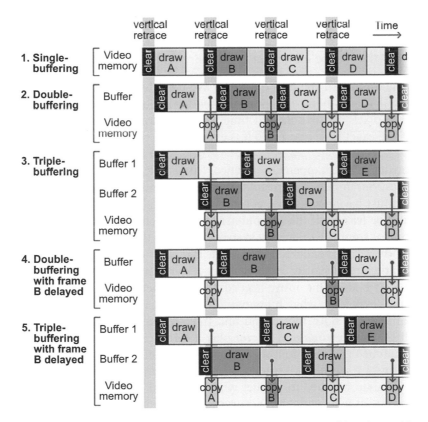

Figure 7.18 Buffering is commonly used in visual rendering pipelines to avoid tearing and lost frames; however, it introduces more latency, which is detrimental to VR.

175

---

effect is that it increases the latency. For *double buffering*, a new frame is first drawn into the buffer and then transferred to the video memory during VBLANK. It is often difficult to control the rate at which frames are produced because the operating system may temporarily interrupt the process or alter its priority. In this case, *triple buffering* is an improvement that allows more time to render each frame. For avoiding tearing and providing smooth video game performance, buffering has been useful; however, it is detrimental to VR because of the increased latency.

Ideally, the displays should have a global scanout, in which all pixels are switched at the same time. This allows a much longer interval to write to the video memory and avoids tearing. It would also reduce the latency in the time it takes to scan the first pixel to the last pixel. In our example, this was an 8 ms interval. Finally, displays should reduce the pixel switching time as much as possible.

The Power of Prediction

For the rest of this section, we consider how to live with whatever latency remains. As another thought experiment, imagine that a fortune teller is able to accurately predict the future. With such a device, it should be possible to eliminate all latency problems. We would want to ask the fortune teller the following:

1. At what future time will the pixels be switching?
2. What will be the positions and orientations of all virtual world models at that time?
3. Where will the user be looking at that time?

Let t_s be the answer to the first question. We need to ask the VWG to produce a frame for time t_s and then perform visual rendering for the user's viewpoint at time t_s. When the pixels are switched at time t_s, then the stimulus will be presented to the user at the exact time and place it is expected. In this case, there is *zero effective latency*.

Now consider what happens in practice. First, note that using information from all three questions implies significant time synchronization across the VR system: all operations must have access to a common clock. For the first question, determining t_s should be feasible if the computer is powerful enough and the VR system has enough control from the operating system to ensure that VWG frames will be consistently produced and rendered at the frame rate. The second question is easy for the case of a static virtual world. In the case of a dynamic world, it might be straightforward for all bodies that move according to predictable physical laws. However, it is difficult to predict what humans will do in the virtual world. This complicates the answers to both the second and third questions. Fortunately, the latency is so small that *momentum* and *inertia* play a significant role; see Chapter 8. Bodies in the matched zone are following physical laws of motion from the real world. These motions are sensed and tracked according to methods covered in Chapter 9. Although it might be hard to predict where you will be looking in 5 seconds, it is possible to predict with very high accuracy where your head will be positioned and oriented in 20 ms. You have no free will on the scale of 20 ms! Instead, momentum dominates and the head motion can be accurately predicted. Some body parts, especially fingers, have much less inertia, and therefore become more difficult to predict; however, these are not as important as predicting head motion. The viewpoint

Perturbation	Image effect
$\Delta\alpha$ (yaw)	Horizontal shift
$\Delta\beta$ (pitch)	Vertical shift
$\Delta\gamma$ (roll)	Rotation about image center
Δx	Horizontal shift
Δy	Vertical shift
Δz	Contraction or expansion

Figure 7.19 Six cases of post-rendering image warp based on the degrees of freedom for a change in viewpoint. The first three correspond to an orientation change. The remaining three correspond to a position change. These operations can be visualized by turning on a digital camera and observing how the image changes under each of these perturbations.

depends only on the head motion, and latency reduction is most critical in this case to avoid perceptual problems that lead to fatigue and VR sickness.

Post-rendering Image Warp

Due to both latency and imperfections in the prediction process, a last-moment adjustment might be needed before the frame is scanned out to the display. This is called *post-rendering image warp* [204]. (It has also been rediscovered and called *time warp* and *asynchronous reprojection* in the VR industry.) At this stage, there is no time to perform complicated shading operations; therefore, a simple transformation is made to the image.

Suppose that an image has been rasterized for a particular viewpoint, expressed by position (x, y, z) and orientation given by yaw, pitch, and roll (α, β, γ). What would be different about the image if it were rasterized for a nearby viewpoint? Based on the degrees of freedom for viewpoints, there are six types of adjustments; see Figure 7.19. Each of these has a direction that is not specified in the figure. For example, if $\Delta\alpha$ is positive, which corresponds to a small, counterclockwise yaw of the viewpoint, then the image is shifted horizontally *to the right*.

Figure 7.20 shows some examples of the image warp. Most cases require the rendered image to be larger than the targeted display; otherwise, there will be no data to shift into the warped image; see Figure 7.20(d). If this ever happens, then it is perhaps best to repeat pixels from the rendered image edge rather than turning them black [204].

Flaws in the Warped Image

Image warping due to orientation changes produces a correct image in the sense that it should be exactly what would have been rendered from scratch for that orientation (without taking aliasing issues into account). However, positional changes are incorrect! Perturbations in x and y do not account for motion parallax (recall from Section 6.1), which would require knowing the depths of the objects. Changes in z produce similarly incorrect images because nearby objects should expand or contract by a larger amount than further ones. To make matters worse, changes in viewpoint position might lead to a *visibility event*, in which part of an object may become visible only in the new viewpoint; see Figure 7.21. Data structures such as an *aspect graph* [255] and *visibility complex* [257] are designed to maintain such events,

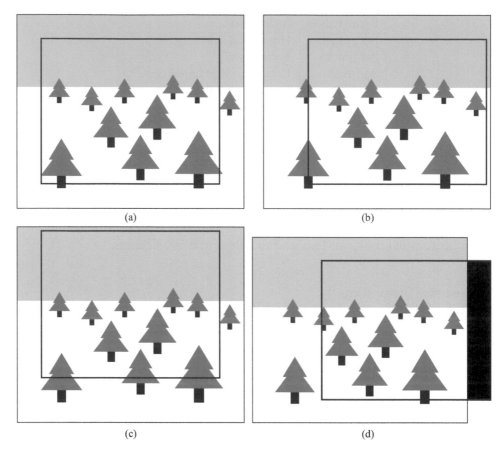

Figure 7.20 Several examples of post-rendering image warp. (a) Before warping, a larger image is rasterized. The red box shows the part that is intended to be sent to the display based on the viewpoint that was used at the time of rasterization. (b) A negative yaw (turning the head to the right) causes the red box to shift to the right. The image appears to shift to the left. (c) A positive pitch (looking upward) causes the box to shift upward. (d) In this case, the yaw is too large and there is no rasterized data to use for part of the image. (This region is shown as a black rectangle.)

but are usually not included in the rendering process. As latencies become shorter and prediction becomes better, the amount of perturbation is reduced. Careful perceptual studies are needed to evaluate conditions under which image warping errors are perceptible or cause discomfort. An alternative to image warping is to use parallel processing to sample several future viewpoints and render images for all of them. The most correct image can then be selected, to greatly reduce the image warping artifacts.

Increasing the Frame Rate
Post-rendering image warp can also be used to artificially increase the frame rate. For example, suppose that only one rasterized image is produced every 100 milliseconds by a weak computer or GPU. This would result in poor performance at 10 FPS. Suppose we would like to increase this to 100 FPS. In this case, a single rasterized image can be warped to produce frames every 10 ms until the next rasterized

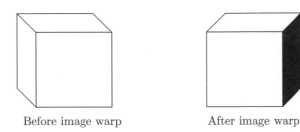

Before image warp   After image warp

Figure 7.21 If the viewing position changes, then a *visibility event* might be encountered. This means that part of the object might suddenly become visible from the new perspective. In this sample, a horizontal shift in the viewpoint reveals a side of the cube that was originally hidden. Furthermore, the top of the cube changes its shape.

image is computed. In this case, nine warped frames are inserted for every raster-ized image that is properly rendered. This process is called *inbetweening* or *tweening* and has been used for over a century. (One of the earliest examples is the making of Fantasmagorie, which was depicted in Figure 1.26(a).)

7.5 Immersive Photos and Videos

Up until now, this chapter has focused on rendering a virtual world that was con-structed synthetically from geometric models. The methods developed over decades of computer graphics research have targeted this case. The trend has changed, though, toward capturing real-world images and video, which are then easily embed-ded into VR experiences. This change is mostly due to the smartphone industry, which has led to hundreds of millions of people carrying high-resolution cameras with them everywhere. Furthermore, 3D camera technology continues to advance, which provides distance information in addition to color and light intensity. All of this technology is quickly expanding to the case of *panoramas*, which contain cap-tured image data from all possible viewing directions. A substantial challenge is to also capture data within a region of all possible viewing *positions and orientations*.

Texture Mapping onto a Virtual Screen
Putting a photo or video into a virtual world is an extension of texture mapping. Fig-ure 7.22 shows a commercial use in which a company offers online movie streaming through the a VR headset. The virtual screen is a single rectangle, which may be viewed as a simple mesh consisting of two triangles. A photo can be mapped across any triangular mesh in the virtual world. In the case of a movie, each frame is treated as a photo that is texture-mapped to the mesh. The movie frame rate is usually much lower than that of the VR headset (recall Figure 6.17). As an example, suppose the movie was recorded at 24 FPS and the headset runs at 96 FPS. In this case, each movie frame is rendered for four frames on the headset display. Most often, the frame rates are not perfectly divisible, which causes the number of repeated frames to alternate in a pattern. An old example of this is called *3:2 pull down*, in which 24 FPS movies were converted to NTSC TV format at 30 FPS. Interestingly, a 3D movie (stereoscopic) experience can even be simulated. For the left eye on the head-set display, the left-eye movie frame is rendered to the virtual screen. Likewise, the right-eye movie frame is rendered to the right-eyed portion of the headset display.

Figure 7.22 Bigscreen offers online movie streaming onto a large virtual TV screen while the users sit as avatars in a living room. The content is texture-mapped onto the TV screen, frame by frame.

The result is that the user perceives it as a 3D movie, without wearing the special glasses! Of course, she would still be wearing a VR headset.

Capturing a Wider Field of View

Mapping onto a rectangle makes it easy to bring pictures or movies that were captured with ordinary cameras into VR; however, the VR medium itself allows great opportunities to expand the experience. Unlike life in the real world, the size of the virtual screen can be expanded without any significant cost. To fill the field of view of the user, it makes sense to curve the virtual screen and put the user at the center. Such curving already exists in the real world; examples are the 1950's Cinerama experience, which was shown in Figure 1.29(d), and modern curved displays. In the limiting case, we obtain a panoramic photo, sometimes called a *photosphere*. Displaying many photospheres per second leads to a panoramic movie, which we may call a *moviesphere*.

Recalling the way cameras work from Section 4.5, it is impossible to capture a photosphere from a single camera in a single instant of time. Two obvious choices exist:

1. Take multiple images with one camera by pointing it in different directions each time, until the entire sphere of all viewing directions is covered.
2. Use multiple cameras, pointing in various viewing directions, so that all directions are covered by taking synchronized pictures.

The first case leads to a well-studied problem in computer vision and computational photography called *image stitching*. A hard version of the problem can be made by stitching together an arbitrary collection of images, from various cameras and times. This might be appropriate, for example, to build a photosphere of a popular tourist

(a)   (b)

Figure 7.23 (a) The 360Heros Pro10 HD is a rig that mounts ten GoPro cameras in opposing directions to capture panoramic images. (b) The GoPro Max 360 Action Camera creates panoramic photos and videos using only two cameras, each with a lens that provides a field of view larger than 180 degrees.

site from online photo collections. More commonly, a smartphone user may capture a photosphere by pointing the outward-facing camera in enough directions. In this case, a software app builds the photosphere dynamically while images are taken in rapid succession. For the hard version, a difficult optimization problem arises in which features need to be identified and matched across overlapping parts of multiple images while unknown, intrinsic camera parameters are taken into account. Differences in perspective, optical aberrations, lighting conditions, exposure time, and changes in the scene over different times must be taken into account. In the case of using a smartphone app, the same camera is being used and the relative time between images is short; therefore, the task is much easier. Furthermore, by taking rapid images in succession and using internal smartphone sensors, it is much easier to match the overlapping image parts. Most flaws in such hand-generated photospheres are due to the user inadvertently changing the position of the camera while pointing it in various directions.

For the second case, a rig of identical cameras can be carefully designed so that all viewing directions are covered; see Figure 7.23(a). Once the rig is calibrated so that the relative positions and orientations of the cameras are precisely known, stitching the images together becomes straightforward. Corrections may nevertheless be applied to account for variations in lighting or calibration; otherwise, the seams in the stitching may become perceptible. A trade-off exists in terms of the number of cameras. By using many cameras, very-high-resolution captures can be made with relatively little optical distortion because each camera contributes a narrow field-of-view image to the photosphere. At the other extreme, as few as two cameras are sufficient, as shown in Figure 7.23(b). The cameras are pointed 180 degrees apart, and a fish-eyed lens is able to capture a view that is larger than 180 degrees.

181

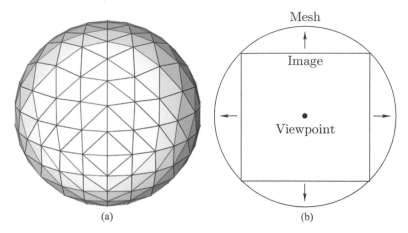

(a)   (b)

Figure 7.24 (a) The photosphere is texture-mapped onto the interior of a sphere that is modeled as a triangular mesh. (b) A photosphere stored as a cube of six images can be quickly mapped to the sphere with relatively small loss of resolution; a cross section is shown here.

This design dramatically reduces costs but requires significant unwarping of the two captured images.

Mapping onto a Sphere

The well-known *map projection* problem from cartography would be confronted to map the photosphere onto a screen; however, this does not arise when rendering a photosphere in VR because it is mapped directly onto a sphere in the virtual world. The sphere of all possible viewing directions maps to the virtual-world sphere without distortions. To directly use texture mapping techniques, the virtual-world sphere can be approximated by uniform triangles, as shown in Figure 7.24(a). The photosphere itself should be stored in a way that does not degrade its resolution in some places. We cannot simply use latitude and longitude coordinates to index the pixels because the difference in resolution between the poles and the equator would be too large. We could use coordinates that are similar to the way quaternions cover the sphere by using indices (a, b, c) and requiring that $a^2 + b^2 + c^2 = 1$; however, the structure of neighboring pixels (up, down, left, and right) is not clear. A simple and efficient compromise is to represent the photosphere as six square images, each corresponding to the face of a cube. This is like a virtual version of a six-sided CAVE projection system. Each image can then be easily mapped onto the mesh with little loss in resolution, as shown in Figure 7.24(b).

Once the photosphere (or moviesphere) is rendered onto the virtual sphere, the rendering process is very similar to post-rendering image warp. The image presented to the user is shifted for the rotational cases that were described in Figure 7.19. In fact, the entire rasterization process could be performed only once, for the entire sphere, while the image rendered to the display is adjusted based on the viewing direction. Further optimizations could be made by even bypassing the mesh and directly forming the rasterized image from the captured images.

Perceptual Issues

Does the virtual world appear to be 3D when viewing a photosphere or moviesphere? Recall from Section 6.1 that there are many more monocular depth cues than stereo cues. Due to the high field-of-view of modern VR headsets and monocular depth cues, a surprisingly immersive experience is obtained. Thus, it may feel more 3D than people expect, even if the same part of the panoramic image is presented to both eyes. Many interesting questions remain for future research regarding the perception of panoramas. If different viewpoints are presented to the left and right eyes, then what should the radius of the virtual sphere be for comfortable and realistic viewing? Continuing further, suppose positional head tracking is used. This might improve viewing comfort, but the virtual world will appear more flat because parallax is not functioning. For example, closer objects will not move more quickly as the head moves from side to side. Can simple transformations be performed to the images so that depth perception is enhanced? Can limited depth data, which could even be extracted automatically from the images, greatly improve parallax and depth perception? Another issue is designing interfaces inside photospheres. Suppose we would like to have a shared experience with other users inside the sphere. In this case, how do we perceive virtual objects inserted into the sphere, such as menus or avatars? How well would a virtual laser pointer work well to select objects?

Panoramic Light Fields

Panoramic images are simple to construct but are clearly flawed because they do not account for how the surround world would appear from any viewpoint that could be obtained by user movement. To accurately determine this, the ideal situation would be to capture the entire *light field* of energy inside whatever viewing volume that user is allowed to move. A light field provides both the spectral power and direction of light propagation at every point in space. If the user is able to walk around in the physical world while wearing a VR headset, then this seems to be an impossible task. How can a rig of cameras capture the light energy in all possible locations at the same instant in an entire room? If the user is constrained to a small area, then the light field can be approximately captured by a rig of cameras arranged on a sphere. In this case, dozens of cameras may be necessary, and image warping techniques are used to approximate viewpoints between the cameras or from the interior of the spherical rig. To further improve the experience, *light-field cameras* (also called *plenoptic cameras*) offer the ability to capture both the intensity of light rays and the direction that they are traveling through space. This offers many advantages, such as refocusing images to different depths, after the light field has already been captured.

Further Reading

Close connections exist between VR and computer graphics because both are required to push visual information onto a display; however, many subtle differences arise and VR is much less developed. For basic computer graphics, many texts provide additional coverage on the topics of this chapter; see, for example [205]. For much more detail on high-performance, high-resolution rendering for computer graphics, see [5]. Comprehensive coverage of BRDFs appears in [22], in addition to [5].

Ray tracing paradigms may need to be redesigned for VR. Useful algorithmic background from a computational geometry perspective can be found in [42, 345]. For optical distortion and correction background, see [46, 119, 132, 202, 334, 338]. Chromatic aberration correction appears in [235]. Automatic stitching of panoramas is covered in [33, 305, 323].

CHAPTER EIGHT

Motion in Real and Virtual Worlds

Up to this point, the discussion of movement has been confined to specialized top-ics. Section 5.3 covered eye movements, and Section 6.2 covered the perception of motion. The transformations from Chapter 3 indicate how to place bodies and change viewpoints, but precise mathematical descriptions of motions have not yet been necessary. We now want to model motions more accurately because the physics of both real and virtual worlds impact VR experiences. The accelerations and veloc-ities of moving bodies impact simulations in the VWG and tracking methods used to capture user motions in the physical world. Therefore, this chapter provides foun-dations that will become useful for reading Chapter 9 on tracking and Chapter 10 on interfaces.

Section 8.1 introduces fundamental concepts from math and physics, including velocities, accelerations, and the movement of rigid bodies. Section 8.2 presents the physiology and perceptual issues from the human vestibular system, which senses velocities and accelerations. Section 8.3 then describes how motions are described and produced in a VWG. This includes numerical integration and collision detec-tion. Section 8.4 focuses on vection, which is a source of VR sickness that arises due to sensory conflict between the visual and vestibular systems: The eyes may per-ceive motion while the vestibular system is not fooled. This can be considered as competition between the physics of the real and virtual worlds.

8.1 Velocities and Accelerations

8.1.1 A One-Dimensional World

We start with the simplest case, which is shown in Figure 8.1. Imagine a 1D world in which motion is only possible in the vertical direction. Let y be the coordinate of a moving point. Its position at any time t is indicated by $y(t)$, meaning that y actually defines a function of time. It is now as if y were an animated point, with an infinite number of frames per second!

Velocity
How fast is the point moving? Using calculus, its *velocity*, v, is defined as the derivative of y with respect to time:

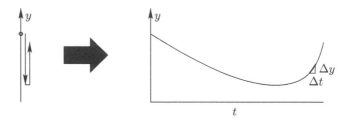

Figure 8.1 A point moving in a one-dimensional world.

$$v = \frac{dy(t)}{dt}. \tag{8.1}$$

Using numerical computations, v is approximately equal to $\Delta y/\Delta t$, in which Δt denotes a small change in time and

$$\Delta y = y(t + \Delta t) - y(t). \tag{8.2}$$

In other words, Δy is the change in y from the start to the end of the time change. The velocity v can be used to estimate the change in y over Δt as

$$\Delta y \approx v\Delta t. \tag{8.3}$$

The approximation quality improves as Δt becomes smaller and v itself varies less during the time from t to $t + \Delta t$.

We can write $v(t)$ to indicate that velocity may change over time. The position can be calculated for any time t from the velocity using integration as[1]

$$y(t) = y(0) + \int_0^t v(s)ds, \tag{8.4}$$

which assumes that y was known at the starting time $t = 0$. If $v(t)$ is constant for all time, represented as v, then $y(t) = y(0) + vt$. The integral in (8.4) accounts for $v(t)$ being allowed to vary.

Acceleration
The next step is to mathematically describe the change in velocity, which results in the *acceleration*, a; this is defined as

$$a = \frac{dv(t)}{dt}. \tag{8.5}$$

The form is the same as (8.1), except that y has been replaced by v. Approximations can similarly be made. For example, $\Delta v \approx a\Delta t$.

The acceleration itself can vary over time, resulting in $a(t)$. The following integral relates acceleration and velocity (compare to (8.4)):

$$v(t) = v(0) + \int_0^t a(s)ds. \tag{8.6}$$

---

[1] The parameter s is used instead of t to indicate that it is integrated away, much like the index in a summation.

Since acceleration may vary, you may wonder whether the naming process continues. It could, with the next derivative called *jerk*, followed by *snap*, *crackle*, and *pop*. In most cases, however, these higher-order derivatives are not necessary. One of the main reasons is that motions from classical physics are sufficiently characterized through forces and accelerations. For example, Newton's Second Law states that $F = ma$, in which F is the force acting on a point, m is its mass, and a is the acceleration.

For a simple example that should be familiar, consider acceleration due to gravity, $g = 9.8$ m/s^2. It is as if the ground were accelerating upward by g; hence, the point accelerates downward relative to the Earth. Using (8.6) to integrate the acceleration, the velocity over time is $v(t) = v(0) - gt$. Using (8.4) to integrate the velocity and supposing $v(0) = 0$, we obtain

$$y(t) = y(0) - \frac{1}{2}gt^2. \tag{8.7}$$

8.1.2 Motion in a 3D World

A Moving Point

Now consider the motion of a point in a 3D world $\mathbb{R}^3$. Imagine that a geometric model, as defined in Section 3.1, is moving over time. This causes each point (x, y, z) on the model to move, resulting in a function of time for each coordinate of each point:

$$(x(t), y(t), z(t)). \tag{8.8}$$

The velocity v and acceleration a from Section 8.1.1 must therefore expand to have three coordinates. The velocity v is replaced by (v_x, v_y, v_z) to indicate velocity with respect to the x, y, and z coordinates, respectively. The magnitude of v is called the *speed*:

$$\sqrt{v_x^2 + v_y^2 + v_z^2}. \tag{8.9}$$

Continuing further, the acceleration also expands to include three components: (a_x, a_y, a_z).

Rigid-Body Motion

Now suppose that a rigid body is moving through $\mathbb{R}^3$. In this case, all its points move together. How can we easily describe this motion? Recall from Section 3.2 that translations or rotations may be applied. First, consider a simple case. Suppose that rotations are prohibited, and the body is only allowed to translate through space. In this limited setting, knowing the position over time for one point on the body is sufficient for easily determining the positions of all points on the body over time. If one point has changed its position by some (x_t, y_t, z_t), then *all* points have changed by the same amount. More importantly, the velocity and acceleration of every point would be identical.

Once rotation is allowed, this simple behavior breaks. As a body rotates, the points no longer maintain the same velocities and accelerations. This becomes crucial to

(a)   (b)

Figure 8.2 (a) Consider a merry-go-round that rotates at constant angular velocity ω. (b) In a top-down view, the velocity vector, v, for a point on the merry-go-round is tangent to the circle that contains it; the circle is centered on the axis of rotation and the acceleration vector, a, points toward its center.

understanding VR sickness in Section 8.4 and how tracking methods estimate positions and orientations from sensors embedded in the world, which will be discussed in Chapter 9.

Angular Velocity

To understand the issues, consider the simple case of a spinning *merry-go-round*, as shown in Figure 8.2(a). Its orientation at every time can be described by $\theta(t)$; see Figure 8.2(b). Let ω denote its *angular velocity*:

$$\omega = \frac{d\theta(t)}{dt}. \tag{8.10}$$

By default, ω has units of radians per second. If $\omega = 2\pi$, then the rigid body returns to the same orientation after one second.

Assuming $\theta(0) = 0$ and ω is constant, the orientation at time t is given by $\theta = \omega t$. To describe the motion of a point on the body, it will be convenient to use polar coordinates r and θ:

$$x = r\cos\theta \text{ and } y = r\sin\theta. \tag{8.11}$$

Substituting $\theta = \omega t$ yields

$$x = r\cos\omega t \text{ and } y = r\sin\omega t. \tag{8.12}$$

Taking the derivative with respect to time yields[2]

$$v_x = -r\omega\sin\omega t \text{ and } v_y = r\omega\cos\omega t. \tag{8.13}$$

The velocity is a 2D vector that when placed at the point is tangent to the circle that contains the point (x, y); see Figure 8.2(b).

---

[2] If this is unfamiliar, then look up the derivatives of sines and cosines, and the chain rule, from standard calculus sources (for example, [327]).

This makes intuitive sense because the point is heading in that direction; however, the direction quickly changes because it must move along a circle. This change in velocity implies that a nonzero acceleration occurs. The acceleration of the point (x, y) is obtained by taking the derivative again:

$$a_x = -r\omega^2 \cos \omega t \text{ and } a_y = -r\omega^2 \sin \omega t. \tag{8.14}$$

The result is a 2D acceleration vector that is pointing toward the center (Figure 8.2(b)), which is the rotation axis. This is called *centripetal acceleration*. If you were standing at that point, then you would feel a pull in the opposite direction, as if nature were attempting to fling you away from the center. This is precisely how artificial gravity can be achieved in a rotating space station.

3D Angular Velocity
Now consider the rotation of a 3D rigid body. Recall from Section 3.3 that Euler's rotation theorem implies that every 3D rotation can be described as a rotation θ about an axis $v = (v_1, v_2, v_3)$ though the origin. As the orientation of the body changes over a short period of time Δt, imagine the axis that corresponds to the change in rotation. In the case of the merry-go-round, the axis would be $v = (0, 1, 0)$. More generally, v could be any unit vector.

The 3D angular velocity is therefore expressed as a 3D vector:

$$(\omega_x, \omega_y, \omega_z), \tag{8.15}$$

which can be imagined as taking the original ω from the 2D case and multiplying it by the vector v. This weights the components according to the coordinate axes. Thus, the components could be considered as $\omega_x = \omega v_1$, $\omega_y = \omega v_2$, and $\omega_z = \omega v_3$. The ω_x, ω_y, and ω_z components also correspond to the rotation rate in terms of pitch, roll, and yaw, respectively. We avoided these representations in Section 3.3 due to noncommutativity and kinematic singularities; however, it turns out that for velocities these problems do not exist [309]. Thus, we can avoid quaternions at this stage.

Angular Acceleration
If ω is allowed to vary over time, then we must consider *angular acceleration*. In the 2D case, this is defined as

$$\alpha = \frac{d\omega(t)}{dt}. \tag{8.16}$$

For the 3D case, there are three components, which results in

$$(\alpha_x, \alpha_y, \alpha_z). \tag{8.17}$$

These can be interpreted as accelerations of pitch, yaw, and roll angles, respectively.

8.2 The Vestibular System

As mentioned in Section 2.3, the *balance sense* (or *vestibular sense*) provides information to the brain about how the head is oriented or how it is moving in general.

This is accomplished through *vestibular organs* that measure both linear and angular accelerations of the head. These organs, together with their associated neural pathways, will be referred to as the *vestibular system*. This system plays a crucial role for bodily functions that involve motion, from ordinary activity such as walking or running, to activities that require substantial talent and training, such as gymnastics or ballet dancing. Recall from Section 5.3 that it also enables eye motions that counteract head movements via the VOR.

The vestibular system is important to VR because it is usually neglected, which leads to a mismatch of perceptual cues. (Recall this problem from Section 6.4.) In current VR systems, there is no engineered device that renders vestibular signals to a display that precisely stimulates the vestibular organs to values as desired. Some possibilities may exist in the future with *galvanic vestibular stimulation*, which provides electrical stimulation to the organ [80, 81]; however, it may take many years before such techniques are sufficiently accurate, comfortable, and generally approved for safe use by the masses. Another possibility is to stimulate the vestibular system through low-frequency vibrations, which at the very least provides some distraction.

Physiology

Figure 8.4 shows the location of the vestibular organs inside the human head. As in the cases of eyes and ears, there are two symmetric organs, corresponding to the right and left sides. Figure 8.3 shows the physiology of each vestibular organ. The *cochlea* handles hearing, which is covered in Section 11.2, and the remaining parts belong to the vestibular system. The *utricle* and *saccule* measure linear acceleration; together they form the *otolith system*, which is housed in the *vestibule* as shown in Figure 8.3. When the head is not tilted, the sensing surface of the utricle mostly lies in the horizontal plane (or xz plane in our common coordinate systems), whereas the corresponding surface of the saccule lies in a vertical plane that is aligned in the forward direction (called the *sagittal plane*, or yz plane). As will be explained shortly, the utricle senses acceleration components a_x and a_z, and the saccule senses a_y and a_z. (a_z is redundantly sensed.)

The *semicircular canals* measure angular acceleration. Each canal has a diameter of about 0.2 to 0.3 mm, and is bent along a circular arc with a diameter of about 2 to 3 mm. Amazingly, the three canals are roughly perpendicular so that they independently measure three components of angular velocity. The particular canal names are *anterior canal*, *posterior canal*, and *lateral canal*. They are not closely aligned with our usual 3D coordinate axes. Note from Figure 8.4 that each set of canals is rotated by 45 degrees with respect to the vertical axis. Thus, the anterior canal of the left ear aligns with the posterior canal of the right ear. Likewise, the posterior canal of the left ear aligns with the anterior canal of the right ear. Although not visible in the figure, the lateral canal is also tilted about 30° away from level. Nevertheless, all three components of angular acceleration are sensed because the canals are roughly perpendicular.

Sensing Linear Acceleration

To understand how accelerations are sensed, we start with the case of the otolith system. Figure 8.5 shows a schematic representation of an otolith organ, which may

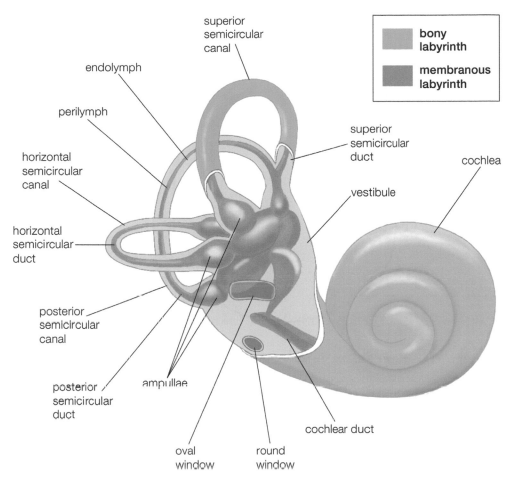

Figure 8.3 The vestibular organ.

be either the utricle or saccule. Mechanoreceptors, in the form of *hair cells*, convert acceleration into neural signals. Each hair cell has *cilia* that are embedded in a gelatinous matrix. Heavy weights lie on top of the matrix so that when acceleration occurs laterally, the shifting weight applies a shearing force that causes the cilia to bend. The higher the acceleration magnitude, the larger the bending, and neural impulses are transmitted at a higher rate. Two dimensions of lateral deflection are possible. For example, in the case of the utricle, linear acceleration in any direction in the xz plane would cause the cilia to bend. To distinguish between particular directions inside this plane, the cilia are *polarized* so that each cell is sensitive to one particular direction. This is accomplished by a thicker, lead hair called the *kinocilium*, to which all other hairs of the cell are attached by a ribbon across their tips so that they all bend together.

One major sensing limitation arises because of a fundamental law from physics: the *Einstein equivalence principle*. In addition to the vestibular system, it also impacts VR tracking systems (see Section 9.2). The problem is gravity. If we were deep in space, far away from any gravitational forces, then linear accelerations measured by

191

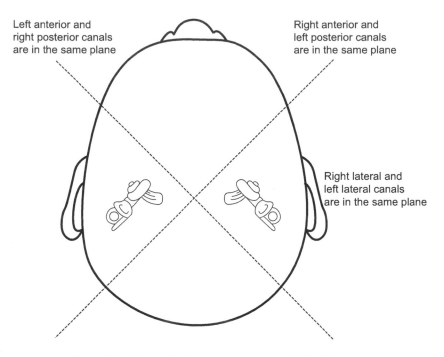

Left anterior and
right posterior canals
are in the same plane

Right anterior and
left posterior canals
are in the same plane

Right lateral and
left lateral canals
are in the same plane

Figure 8.4 The vestibular organs are located behind the ears.

a sensor would correspond to pure accelerations with respect to a fixed coordinate frame. On the Earth, we also experience force due to gravity, which feels as if we were on a rocket ship accelerating upward at roughly 9.8 m/s^2. The equivalence principle states that the effects of gravity and true linear accelerations on a body are indistinguishable. Figure 8.6 shows the result in terms of the otolith organs. The same signals are sent to the brain whether the head is tilted or it is linearly accelerating. If you close your eyes or wear a VR headset, then you should not be able to distinguish tilt from acceleration. In most settings, we are not confused because the vestibular signals are accompanied by other stimuli when accelerating, such as vision and a revving engine.

Sensing Angular Acceleration
The semicircular canals use the same principle as the otolith organs. They measure acceleration by bending cilia at the end of hair cells. A viscous fluid moves inside each canal. A flexible structure called the *cupula* blocks one small section of the canal and contains the hair cells; see Figure 8.7. Compare the rotation of a canal to the merry-go-round. If we were to place a liquid-filled tube around the periphery of the merry-go-round, then the fluid would remain fairly stable at a constant angular velocity. However, if angular acceleration is applied, then due to friction between the fluid and the tube (and also internal fluid viscosity), the fluid would start to travel inside the tube. In the semicircular canal, the moving fluid applies pressure to the cupula, causing it to deform and bend the cilia on hair cells inside it. Note that a constant angular velocity does not, in principle, cause pressure on the cupula; thus, the semicircular canals measure angular *acceleration* as opposed to velocity. Each canal is polarized in the sense that it responds mainly to rotations about an axis perpendicular to the plane that contains the entire canal.

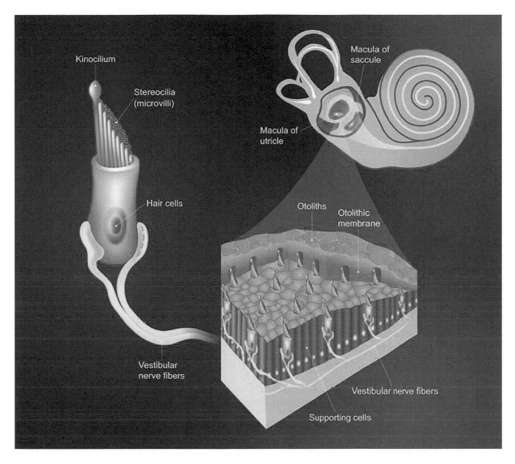

Figure 8.5 A depiction of an otolith organ (utricle or saccule), which senses linear acceleration.

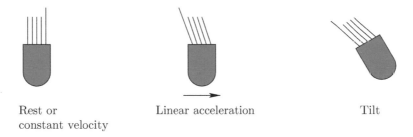

Rest or
constant velocity

Linear acceleration

Tilt

Figure 8.6 Because of the Einstein equivalence principle, the otolith organs cannot distinguish linear acceleration of the head from tilt with respect to gravity. In either case, the cilia deflect in the same way, sending equivalent signals to the neural structures.

Impact on Perception

Cues from the vestibular system are generally weak in comparison to other senses, especially vision. For example, a common danger for a skier buried in an avalanche is that he cannot easily determine which way is up without visual cues to accompany the perception of gravity from the vestibular system. Thus, the vestibular system functions well when providing consistent cues with other systems, including vision

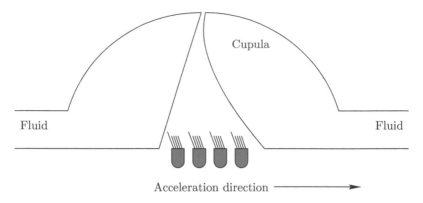

Figure 8.7 The cupula contains a center membrane that houses the cilia. If angular acceleration occurs that is aligned with the canal direction, then pressure is applied to the cupula, which causes the cilia to bend and send neural signals.

and proprioception. Mismatched cues are problematic. For example, some people may experience *vertigo* when the vestibular system is not functioning correctly. In this case, they feel as if the world around them is spinning or swaying. Common symptoms are nausea, vomiting, sweating, and difficulties walking. This may even impact eye movements because of the VOR. Section 8.4 explains a bad side effect that results from mismatched vestibular and visual cues in VR.

8.3 Physics in the Virtual World

8.3.1 Tailoring the Physics to the Experience

If we expect to fool our brains into believing that we inhabit the virtual world, then many of our expectations from the real world should be matched in the virtual world. We have already seen this in the case of the physics of light (Chapter 4) applying to visual rendering of virtual worlds (Chapter 7). Motions in the virtual world should also behave in a familiar way.

This implies that the VWG contains a *physics engine* that governs the motions of bodies in the virtual world by following principles from the physical world. Forces acting on bodies, gravity, fluid flows, and collisions between bodies should be handled in perceptually convincing ways. Physics engines arise throughout engineering and physics in the context of any simulation. In video games, computer graphics, and film, these engines perform operations that are very close to our needs for VR. This is why popular game engines such as Unity 3D and Unreal Engine have been adapted for use in VR. As stated in Section 2.2, we have not yet arrived at an era in which pure VR engines exist; therefore, game engines are worth understanding and utilizing at present.

To determine what kind of physics engine needs to be borrowed, adapted, or constructed from scratch, one should think about the desired VR experience and determine the kinds of motions that will arise. The following are some common, generic questions:

- Will the matched zone remain fixed, or will the user need to be moved by locomotion? If locomotion is needed, then will the user walk, run, swim, drive cars, or fly spaceships?

- Will the user interact with objects? If so, then what kind of interaction is needed? Possibilities include carrying weapons, opening doors, tossing objects, pouring drinks, operating machinery, drawing pictures, and assembling structures.
- Will multiple users be sharing the same virtual space? If so, then how will their motions be coordinated or constrained?
- Will the virtual world contain entities that appear to move autonomously, such as robots, animals, or humans?
- Will the user be immersed in a familiar or exotic setting? A familiar setting could be a home, classroom, park, or city streets. An exotic setting might be scuba diving, lunar exploration, or traveling through blood vessels.

In addition to the physics engine, these questions will also guide the design of the interface, which is addressed in Chapter 10.

Based on the answers to the preceding questions, the physics engine design may be simple and efficient, or completely overwhelming. As mentioned in Section 7.4, a key challenge is to keep the virtual world frequently updated so that interactions between users and objects are well synchronized and renderers provide a low-latency projection onto displays.

Note that the goal may not always be to perfectly match what would happen in the physical world. In a familiar setting, we might expect significant matching; however, in exotic settings, it often becomes more important to make a comfortable experience, rather than matching reality perfectly. Even in the case of simulating one-self walking around in the world, we often want to deviate from real-world physics because of vection, which causes VR sickness (see Section 8.4).

The remainder of this section covers some fundamental aspects that commonly arise: (1) numerical simulation of physical systems, (2) the control of systems using human input, and (3) collision detection, which determines whether bodies are interfering with each other.

8.3.2 Numerical Simulation

The State of the Virtual World

Imagine a virtual world that contains many moving rigid bodies. For each body, think about its degrees of freedom (*DOFs*), which corresponds to the number of independent parameters needed to uniquely determine its position and orientation. We would like to know the complete list of parameters needed to put every body in its proper place in a single time instant. A specification of values for all of these parameters is defined as the *state* of the virtual world.

The job of the physics engine can then be described as calculating the virtual world state for every time instant or "snapshot" of the virtual world that would be needed by a rendering system. Once the state is determined, the mathematical transforms of Chapter 3 are used to place the bodies correctly in the world and calculate how they should appear on displays.

Degrees of Freedom

How many parameters are there in a virtual world model? As discussed in Section 3.2, a free-floating body has six DOFs, which implies six parameters to place

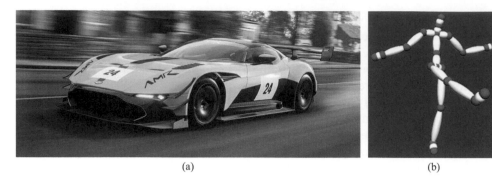

(a)   (b)

Figure 8.8 (a) The Aston Martin Vulcan Model from Forza Horizon 4 Series, XBox Games/ Microsoft; how many degrees of freedom should it have? (b) A human skeleton, with rigid bodies connected via joints, commonly underlies the motions of an avatar.

it anywhere. In many cases, DOFs are lost due to constraints. For example, a ball that rolls on the ground has only five DOFs because it can achieve any 2D position along the ground and also have any 3D orientation. It might be sufficient to describe a car with three DOFs by specifying the position along the ground (two parameters) and the direction it is facing (one parameter); see Figure 8.8(a). However, if the car is allowed to fly through the air while performing stunts or crashing, then all six DOFs are needed.

For many models, rigid bodies are attached together in a way that allows relative motions. This is called *multibody kinematics* [166, 309]. For example, a car usually has four wheels, which can roll to provide one rotational DOF per wheel. Furthermore, the front wheels can be steered to provide an additional DOF. Steering usually turns the front wheels in unison, which implies that one DOF is sufficient to describe both wheels. If the car has a complicated suspension system, then it cannot be treated as a single rigid body, which would add many more DOFs.

Similarly, an animated character can be made by attaching rigid bodies to form a skeleton; see Figure 8.8(b). Each rigid body in the skeleton is attached to one or more other bodies by a *joint*. For example, a simple human character can be formed by attaching arms, legs, and a neck to a rigid torso. The upper left arm is attached to the torso by a shoulder joint. The lower part of the arm is attached by an elbow joint, and so on. Some joints allow more DOFs than others. For example, the shoulder joint has three DOFs because it can yaw, pitch, and roll with respect to the torso, but an elbow joint has only one DOF.

To fully model the flexibility of the human body, 244 DOFs are needed, which are controlled by 630 muscles [375]. In many settings, this would be too much detail, which might lead to high computational complexity and difficult implementation. Furthermore, one should always beware of the uncanny valley (mentioned in Section 1.1), in which more realism might lead to increased perceived creepiness of the character. Thus, having more DOFs is not clearly better, and it is up to a VR content creator to determine how much mobility is needed to bring a character to life, in a way that is compelling for a targeted purpose.

In the extreme case, rigid bodies are not sufficient to model the world. We might want to see waves rippling realistically across a lake, or hair gently flowing in the breeze. In these general settings, *nonrigid models* are used, in which case the state can be considered as a continuous function. For example, a function of the form $y = f(x, z)$ could describe the surface of the water. Without making some limiting simplifications, the result could effectively be an infinite number of DOFs. Motions in this setting are typically described using *partial differential equations* (*PDEs*), which are integrated numerically to obtain the state at a desired time. Usually, the computational cost is high enough to prohibit their use in interactive VR experiences, unless shortcuts are taken by precomputing motions or dramatically simplifying the model.

Differential Equations

We now introduce some basic differential equations to model motions. The resulting description is often called a *dynamical system*. The first step is to describe rigid body velocities in terms of state. Returning to models that involve one or more rigid bodies, the state corresponds to a finite number of parameters. Let

$$x = (x_1, x_2, \ldots, x_n) \tag{8.18}$$

denote an n-dimensional *state vector*. If each x_i corresponds to a position or orientation parameter for a rigid body, then the state vector puts all bodies in their place. Let

$$\dot{x}_i = \frac{dx_i}{dt} \tag{8.19}$$

represent the time derivative, or velocity, for each parameter.

To obtain the state at any time t, the velocities need to be integrated over time. Following (8.4), the integration of each state variable determines the value at time t:

$$x_i(t) = x_i(0) + \int_0^t \dot{x}_i(s)ds, \tag{8.20}$$

in which $x_i(0)$ is the value of x_i at time $t = 0$.

Two main problems arise with (8.20):

1. The integral almost always must be evaluated numerically.
2. The velocity $\dot{x}_i(t)$ must be specified at each time t.

Sampling Rate

For the first problem, time is discretized into steps, in which Δt is the *step size* or *sampling rate*. For example, Δt might be 1 ms, in which case the state can be calculated for times $t = 0, 0.001, 0.002, \ldots$, in terms of seconds. This can be considered as a kind of frame rate for the physics engine. Each Δt corresponds to the production of a new frame.

As mentioned in Section 7.4, the VWG should synchronize the production of virtual world frames with rendering processes so that the world is not caught in an intermediate state with some variables updated to the new time and others stuck at the previous time. This is a kind of tearing in the virtual world. This does not, however, imply that the frame rates are the same between renderers and the physics engine. Typically, the frame rate for the physics engine is much higher to improve numerical accuracy.

Using the sampling rate Δt, (8.20) is approximated as

$$x_i((k+1)\Delta t) \approx x_i(0) + \sum_{j=1}^{k} \dot{x}_i(j\Delta t)\Delta t, \tag{8.21}$$

for each state variable x_i.

It is simpler to view (8.21) one step at a time. Let $x_i[k]$ denote $x_i(k\Delta t)$, which is the state at time $t = k\Delta t$. The following is an update law that expresses the new state $x_i[k+1]$ in terms of the old state $x_i[k]$:

$$x_i[k+1] \approx x_i[k] + \dot{x}_i(k\Delta t)\Delta t, \tag{8.22}$$

which starts with $x_i[0] = x_i(0)$.

Runge–Kutta Integration

The approximation used in (8.21) is known as Euler integration. It is the simplest approximation, but does not perform well enough in many practical settings. One of the most common improvements is the fourth-order *Runge–Kutta integration* method, which expresses the new state as

$$x_i[k+1] \approx x_i[k] + \frac{\Delta t}{6}(w_1 + 2w_2 + 2w_3 + w_4), \tag{8.23}$$

in which

$$
\begin{aligned}
w_1 &= f(\dot{x}_i(k\Delta t)), \\
w_2 &= f(\dot{x}_i(k\Delta t + \tfrac{1}{2}\Delta t) + \tfrac{1}{2}\Delta t\, w_1), \\
w_3 &= f(\dot{x}_i(k\Delta t + \tfrac{1}{2}\Delta t) + \tfrac{1}{2}\Delta t\, w_2), \\
w_4 &= f(\dot{x}_i(k\Delta t + \Delta t) + \Delta t\, w_3).
\end{aligned}
\tag{8.24}
$$

Although this is more expensive than Euler integration, the improved accuracy is usually worthwhile in practice. Many other methods exist, with varying performance depending on the particular ways in which $\dot{x}$ is expressed and varies over time [135].

Time-Invariant Dynamical Systems

The second problem from (8.20) is to determine an expression for $\dot{x}(t)$. This is where the laws of physics apply, such as the acceleration of rigid bodies due to applied forces and gravity. The most common case is *time-invariant dynamical systems*, in which $\dot{x}$ depends only on the current state and not the particular time. This means each component x_i is expressed as

$$\dot{x}_i = f_i(x_1, x_2, \ldots, x_n), \tag{8.25}$$

for some given vector-valued function $f = (f_1, \ldots, f_n)$. This can be written in compressed form by using x and $\dot{x}$ to represent n-dimensional vectors:

$$\dot{x} = f(x). \tag{8.26}$$

The preceding expression is often called the *state transition equation* because it indicates the state's rate of change.

Here is a simple, one-dimensional example of a state transition equation:

$$\dot{x} = 2x - 1. \tag{8.27}$$

This is called a *linear* differential equation. The velocity $\dot{x}$ roughly doubles with the value of x. Fortunately, linear problems can be fully solved "on paper." The solution to (8.27) is of the general form

$$x(t) = \frac{1}{2} + ce^{2t}, \tag{8.28}$$

in which c is a constant that depends on the given value for $x(0)$.

The Phase Space

Unfortunately, motions are usually described in terms of accelerations (and sometimes higher-order derivatives), which need to be integrated twice. This leads to higher-order differential equations, which are difficult to work with. For this reason, *phase space* representations were developed in physics and engineering. In this case, the velocities of the state variables are themselves treated as state variables. That way, the accelerations become the velocities of the velocity variables.

For example, suppose that a position x_1 is acted upon by gravity, which generates an acceleration $a = -9.8$ m/s^2. This leads to a second variable x_2, which is defined as the velocity of x_1. Thus, by definition, $\dot{x}_1 = x_2$. Furthermore, $\dot{x}_2 = a$ because the derivative of velocity is acceleration. Both of these equations fit the form of (8.25). Generally, the number of states increases to incorporate accelerations (or even higher-order derivatives), but the resulting dynamics are expressed in the form (8.25), which is easier to work with.

Handling User Input

Now consider the case in which a user commands an object to move. Examples include driving a car, flying a spaceship, or walking an avatar around. This introduces some new parameters, called the *controls*, actions, or inputs to the dynamical system. Differential equations that include these new parameters are called *control systems* [14].

Let $u = (u_1, u_2, \ldots, u_m)$ be a vector of controls. The state transition equation in (8.26) is simply extended to include u:

$$\dot{x} = f(x, u). \tag{8.29}$$

Figure 8.9 shows a useful example, which involves driving a car. The control u_s determines the speed of the car. For example, $u_s = 1$ drives forward, and $u_s = -1$ drives in reverse. Setting $u_s = 10$ drives forward at a much faster rate. The control u_ϕ determines how the front wheels are steered. The state vector is (x, z, θ), which corresponds to the position and orientation of the car in the horizontal, xz plane.

The state transition equation is

$$\begin{aligned} \dot{x} &= u_s \cos\theta, \\ \dot{z} &= u_s \sin\theta, \\ \dot{\theta} &= \frac{u_s}{L} \tan u_\phi. \end{aligned} \tag{8.30}$$

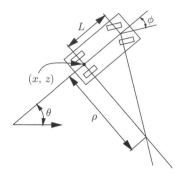

Figure 8.9 A top-down view of a simple, steerable car. Its position and orientation are given by (x, y, θ). The parameter ρ is the minimum turning radius, which depends on the maximum allowable steering angle ϕ. This model can also be used to "steer" human avatars by placing the viewpoint above the center of the rear axle.

Using Runge–Kutta integration or a similar numerical method, the future states can be calculated for the car, given that controls u_s and u_ϕ are applied over time.

This model can also be used to steer the virtual walking of a VR user from first-person perspective. The viewpoint then changes according to (x, z, θ), while the height y remains fixed. For the model in (8.30), the car must drive forward or backward to change its orientation. By changing the third component to $\theta = u_\omega$, the user could instead specify the angular velocity directly. This would cause the user to rotate in place, as if on a merry-go-round. Many more examples like these appear in Chapter 13 of [166], including bodies that are controlled via accelerations.

It is sometimes helpful conceptually to define the motions in terms of discrete points in time, called *stages*. Using numerical integration of (8.29), we can think about applying a control u over time Δt to obtain a new state $x[k + 1]$:

$$x[k + 1] = F(x[k], u[k]). \qquad (8.31)$$

The function F is obtained by integrating (8.29) over Δt. Thus, if the state is $x[k]$, and $u[k]$ is applied, then F calculates $x[k + 1]$ as the state at the next stage.

8.3.3 Collision Detection

One of the greatest challenges in building a physics engine is handling collisions between bodies. Standard laws of motion from physics or engineering usually do not take into account such interactions. Therefore, specialized algorithms are used to detect when such collisions occur and respond appropriately. Collision detection methods and corresponding software are plentiful because of widespread needs in computer graphics simulations and video games, and also for motion planning of robots.

Solid or Boundary Model?
Figure 8.10 shows one of the first difficulties with collision detection, in terms of two triangles in a 2D world. The first two cases (Figures 8.10(a) and 8.10(b)) show obvious cases; however, the third case, Figure 8.10(c), could be ambiguous. If one triangle is wholly inside of another, then is this a collision? If we interpret the outer

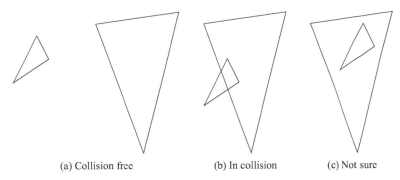

(a) Collision free   (b) In collision   (c) Not sure

Figure 8.10   Three interesting cases for collision detection. (These are 2D examples.) The last case may or may not cause collision, depending on the model.

triangle as a solid model, then YES. If the outer triangle is only the boundary edges and is meant to have an empty interior, then the answer is NO. This is why emphasis was placed on having a coherent model in Section 3.1; otherwise, the boundary might not be established well enough to distinguish the inside from the outside.

Distance Functions

Many collision detection methods benefit from maintaining a distance function, which keeps track of how far the bodies are from colliding. For example, let A and B denote the (closed) set of all points occupied in $\mathbb{R}^3$ by two different models. If they are in collision, then their intersection $A \cap B$ is not empty. If they are not in collision, then the *Hausdorff distance* between A and B is the Euclidean distance between the closest pair of points, taking one from A and one from B.[3] Let $d(A, B)$ denote this distance. If A and B intersect, then $d(A, B) = 0$ because any point in $A \cap B$ will yield zero distance. If A and B do not intersect, then $d(A, B) > 0$, which implies that they are not in collision (in other words, collision free).

If $d(A, B)$ is large, then A and B are mostly likely to be collision free in the near future, even if one or both are moving. This leads to a family of collision detection methods called *incremental distance computation*, which assumes that between successive calls to the algorithm, the bodies move only a small amount. Under this assumption the algorithm achieves "almost constant time" performance for the case of convex polyhedral bodies [184, 219]. Nonconvex bodies can be decomposed into convex components.

A concept related to distance is *penetration depth*, which indicates how far one model is poking into another [185]. This is useful for setting a threshold on how much interference between the two bodies is allowed. For example, the user might be able to poke his head two centimeters into a wall, but beyond that, an action should be taken.

Simple Collision Tests

At the lowest level, collision detection usually requires testing a pair of model primitives to determine whether they intersect. In the case of models formed from 3D

---

[3] This assumes models contain all of the points on their boundary and that they have finite extent; otherwise, topological difficulties arise [124, 166].

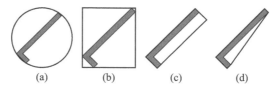

Figure 8.11 Four different kinds of bounding regions: (a) sphere, (b) axis-aligned bounding box (AABB), (c) oriented bounding box (OBB), and (d) convex hull. Each usually provides a tighter approximation than the previous one but is more expensive to test for intersection with others.

triangles, then we need a method that determines whether two triangles intersect. This is similar to the ray-triangle intersection test that was needed for visual rendering in Section 7.1, and involves basic tools from analytic geometry, such as cross products and plane equations. Efficient methods are given in [107, 221].

Broad and Narrow Phases

Suppose that a virtual world has been defined with millions of triangles. If two complicated, nonconvex bodies are to be checked for collision, then the computational cost may be high. For this complicated situation, collision detection often becomes a two-phase process:

1. **Broad Phase:** In the *broad phase*, the task is to avoid performing expensive computations for bodies that are far away from each other. Simple bounding boxes can be placed around each of the bodies, and simple tests can be performed to avoid costly collision checking unless the boxes intersect. Hashing schemes can be employed in some cases to greatly reduce the number of pairs of boxes that have to be tested for intersect [220].
2. **Narrow Phase:** In the *narrow phase* individual pairs of model parts are each checked carefully for collision. This involves the expensive tests, such as triangle-triangle intersection.

In the broad phase, *hierarchical methods* generally decompose each body into a tree. Each vertex in the tree represents a *bounding region* that contains some subset of the body. The bounding region of the root vertex contains the whole body. There are two opposing criteria that guide the selection of the type of bounding region:

1. The region should fit the intended model points as tightly as possible.
2. The intersection test for two regions should be as efficient as possible.

Several popular choices are shown in Figure 8.11, for the case of an L-shaped body. Hierarchical methods are also useful for quickly eliminating many triangles from consideration in visual rendering, as mentioned in Section 7.1.

The tree is constructed for a body, A (or alternatively, B) recursively as follows. For each vertex, consider the set X of all points in A that are contained in the bounding region. Two child vertices are constructed by defining two smaller bounding regions whose union covers X. The split is made so that the portion covered by each child is of similar size. If the geometric model consists of primitives such as triangles, then a split could be made to separate the triangles into two sets of roughly the same number of triangles. A bounding region is then computed for each of the children.

Figure 8.12 The large circle shows the bounding region for a vertex that covers an L-shaped body. After performing a split along the dashed line, two smaller circles are used to cover the two halves of the body. Each circle corresponds to a child vertex.

Figure 8.12 shows an example of a split for the case of an L-shaped body. Children are generated recursively by making splits until very small sets are obtained. For example, in the case of triangles in space, a split is made unless the vertex represents a single triangle. In this case, it is easy to test for the intersection of two triangles.

Consider the problem of determining whether bodies A and B are in collision. Suppose that the trees T_a and T_b have been constructed for A and B, respectively. If the bounding regions of the root vertices of T_a and T_b do not intersect, then it is known that T_a and T_b are not in collision without performing any additional computation. If the bounding regions do intersect, then the bounding regions of the children of T_a are compared to the bounding region of T_b. If either of these intersect, then the bounding region of T_b is replaced with the bounding regions of its children, and the process continues recursively. As long as the bounding regions intersect, lower levels of the trees are traversed, until eventually the leaves are reached. At the leaves the algorithm tests the individual triangles for collision, instead of bounding regions. Note that as the trees are traversed, if a bounding region from the vertex v_1 of T_a does not intersect the bounding region from a vertex, v_2, of T_b, then no children of v_1 have to be compared to children of v_2. Usually, this dramatically reduces the number of comparisons, relative to a naive approach that tests all pairs of triangles for intersection.

Mismatched Obstacles in VR
Although collision detection is a standard, well-solved problem, VR once again poses unusual challenges. One of the main difficulties is the matched zone, in which the real and virtual worlds share the same space. This leads to three interesting cases:

1. **Real obstacle only:** In this case, an obstacle exists in the real world, but not in the virtual world. This is potentially dangerous! For example, you could move your arm and knock over a real, hot cup of coffee that is not represented in the virtual world. If you were walking with a VR headset, then imagine what would happen if a set of real, downward stairs were not represented. At the very least, the boundary of the matched zone should be rendered if the user gets close to it. This mismatch motivated the introduction of the safety modes in many headsets, in which virtual safety walls appear if the user leaves a predetermined zone.

2. **Virtual obstacle only:** This case is not dangerous, but can be extremely frustrating. The user could poke her head through a wall in VR without feeling any response in the real world. This should not be allowed in most cases. The VWG could

simply stop moving the viewpoint in the virtual world as the virtual wall is contacted; however, this generates a mismatch between the real and virtual motions, which could be uncomfortable for the user. It remains a difficult challenge to keep users comfortable while trying to guide them away from interference with virtual obstacles.

3. **Real and virtual obstacle:** If obstacles are matched in both real and virtual worlds, then the effect is perceptually powerful. For example, you might stand on a slightly raised platform in the real world while the virtual world shows you standing on a building rooftop. If the roof and platform edges align perfectly, then you could feel the edge with your feet. Would you be afraid to step over the edge? A simpler case is to render a virtual chair that matches the real chair that a user might be sitting in.

8.4 Mismatched Motion and Vection

Vection was mentioned in Section 2.3 as an illusion of self motion that is caused by varying visual stimuli. In other words, the brain is tricked into believing that the head is moving based on what is seen, even though no motion actually occurs. Figure 2.20 showed the haunted swing illusion, which convinced people that they were swinging upside down; however, the room was moving while they were stationary. Vection is also commonly induced in VR by moving the user's viewpoint while there is no corresponding motion in the real world.

Vection is a prime example of mismatched cues, which were discussed in Section 6.4. Whereas the McGurk effect has no harmful side effects, vection unfortunately leads many people to experience sickness symptoms, such as dizziness, nausea, and occasionally even vomiting. Thus, it should be used very sparingly, if at all, for VR experiences. Furthermore, if it is used, attempts should be made to alter the content so that the side effects are minimized. Companies may proclaim that their VR headset has beaten the VR sickness problem; however, this neglects the following counterintuitive behavior:

> **If a headset is better in terms of spatial resolution, frame rate, tracking accuracy, field of view, and latency, then the potential is higher for making people sick through vection and other mismatched cues.**

Put simply and intuitively, if the headset more accurately mimics reality, then the sensory cues are stronger, and our perceptual systems become more confident about mismatched cues. It may even have the ability to emulate poorer headsets, resulting in a way to comparatively assess side effects of earlier VR systems. In some cases, the mismatch of cues may be harmless (although possibly leading to a decreased sense of presence). In other cases, the mismatches may lead to greater fatigue as the brain works harder to resolve minor conflicts. In the worst case, VR sickness emerges, with vection being the largest culprit based on VR experiences being made today. One of the worst cases is the straightforward adaptation of first-person shooter games to VR, in which the vection occurs almost all the time as the avatar explores the hostile environment.

Figure 8.13 The optical flow of features in an image due to motion in the world. These were computed automatically using image processing algorithms.

Optical Flow

Recall from Section 6.2 that the human visual system has neural structures dedicated to detecting the motion of visual features in the field of view, see Figure 8.13. It is actually the images of these features that move across the retina. It is therefore useful to have a mathematical concept that describes the velocities of moving points over a surface. We therefore define a *vector field*, which assigns a velocity vector at every point along a surface. If the surface is the xy plane, then a velocity vector,

$$(v_x, v_y) = \left(\frac{dx}{dt}, \frac{dy}{dt} \right),\qquad(8.32)$$

is assigned at every point (x, y). For example,

$$(x, y) \mapsto (-1, 0)\qquad(8.33)$$

is a *constant vector field*, which assigns $v_x = -1$ and $v_y = 0$ everywhere; see Figure 8.14(a). The vector field

$$(x, y) \mapsto (x + y, x + y)\qquad(8.34)$$

is nonconstant, and assigns $v_x = v_y = x + y$ at each point (x, y); see Figure 8.14(b). For this vector field, the velocity direction is always diagonal, but the length of the vector (speed) depends on $x + y$.

To more accurately describe the motion of features along the retina, the vector field should be defined over a spherical surface that corresponds to the locations of the photoreceptors. Instead, we will describe vector fields over a square region, with the understanding that it should be transformed onto a sphere for greater accuracy.

Types of Vection

Vection can be caused by any combination of angular and linear velocities of the viewpoint in the virtual world. To characterize the effects of different kinds of motions effectively, it is convenient to decompose the viewpoint velocities into the three linear components, v_x, v_y, and v_z, and three angular components, ω_x, ω_y, and ω_z. Therefore, we consider the optical flow for each of these six cases (see Figure 8.15):

205

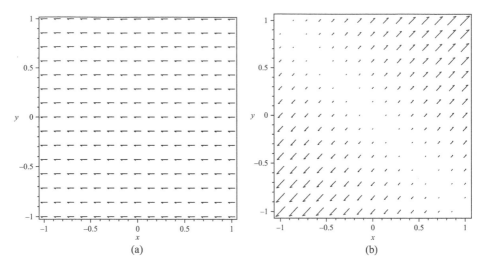

Figure 8.14 Example vector fields. (a) A constant vector field, for which every vector is $(-1, 0)$, regardless of the location. (b) In this vector field, $(x, y) \mapsto (x + y, x + y)$, the vectors point away from the diagonal line from $(-1, 1)$ to $(1, -1)$, and their length is proportional to the distance from it.

1. **Yaw vection:** If the viewpoint is rotated counterclockwise about the y-axis (positive ω_y), then all visual features move from right to left at the same velocity, as shown in Figure 8.15(a). Equivalently, the virtual world is rotating clockwise around the user; however, self motion in the opposite direction is perceived. This causes the user to feel as if she is riding a merry-go-round (recall Figure 8.2).

2. **Pitch vection:** By rotating the viewpoint counterclockwise about the x-axis (positive ω_x), all features move downward at the same velocity, as shown in Figure 8.15(b).

3. **Roll vection:** Rotating the viewpoint counterclockwise about z, the optical axis (positive ω_z), causes the features to rotate clockwise around the center of the image, as shown in Figure 8.15(c). The velocity of each feature is tangent to the circle that contains it, and the speed is proportional to the distance from the feature to the image center.

4. **Lateral vection:** In this case, the viewpoint is translated to the right, corresponding to positive v_x. As a result, the features move horizontally; however, there is an important distinction with respect to yaw vection: features that correspond to closer objects move more quickly than those from distant objects. Figure 8.15(d) depicts the field by assuming the vertical position of the feature corresponds to its depth (lower in the depth field is closer). This is a reappearance of *parallax*, which in this case gives the illusion of lateral motion and distinguishes it from yaw motion.

5. **Vertical vection:** The viewpoint is translated upward, corresponding to positive v_x, and resulting in downward flow as shown in Figure 8.15(e). Once again, parallax causes the speed of features to depend on the distance of the corresponding object. This enables vertical vection to be distinguished from pitch vection.

6. **Forward/backward vection:** If the viewpoint is translated along the optical axis away from the scene (positive v_z), then the features flow inward toward the image

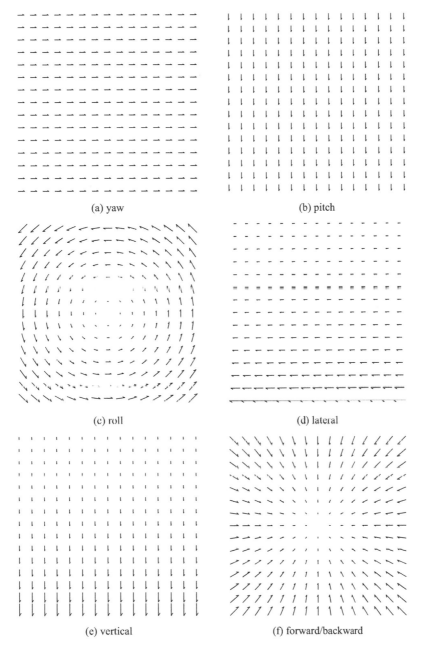

(a) yaw

(b) pitch

(c) roll

(d) lateral

(e) vertical

(f) forward/backward

Figure 8.15 Six different types of optical flows, based on six degrees of freedom for motion of a rigid body. Each of these is a contributing component of vection.

center, as shown in Figure 8.15(f). Their speed depends on *both* their distance from the image center and the distance of their corresponding objects in the virtual world. The resulting illusion is backward motion. Translation in the negative z direction results in perceived forward motion (as in the case of the Millennium Falcon spaceship after its jump to hyperspace in the *Star Wars* movies).

The first two are sometimes called *circular vection*, and the last three are known as *linear vection*. Since our eyes are drawn toward moving features, changing the viewpoint may trigger smooth pursuit eye movements (recall from Section 5.3). In this case, the optical flows shown in Figure 8.15 would not correspond to the motions of the features on the retina. Thus, our characterization so far ignores eye movements, which are often designed to counteract optical flow and provide stable images on the retina. Nevertheless, due to proprioception, the brain is aware of these eye rotations, which results in an equivalent perception of self motion.

All forms of vection cause perceived velocity, but the perception of acceleration is more complicated. First consider pure rotation of the viewpoint. Angular acceleration is perceived if the rotation rate of yaw, pitch, and roll vection are varied. Linear acceleration is also perceived, even in the case of yaw, pitch, or roll vection at constant angular velocity. This is due to the merry-go-round effect, which was shown in Figure 8.2(b).

Now consider pure linear vection (no rotation). Any linear acceleration of the viewpoint will be perceived as an acceleration. However, if the viewpoint moves at constant velocity, then this is the only form of vection in which there is no perceived acceleration. In a VR headset, the user may nevertheless perceive accelerations due to optical distortions or other imperfections in the rendering and display.

Vestibular Mismatch

We have not yet considered the effect of each of these six cases in terms of their mismatch with vestibular cues. If the user is not moving relative to the Earth, then only gravity should be sensed by the vestibular organ (in particular, the otolith organs). Suppose the user is facing forward without any tilt. In this case, any perceived acceleration from vection would cause a mismatch. For example, yaw vection should cause a perceived constant acceleration toward the rotation center (see Figure 8.2(b)), which mismatches the vestibular gravity cue. As another example, downward vertical vection should cause the user to feel like he is falling, but the vestibular cue would indicate otherwise.

For cases of yaw, pitch, and roll vection at constant angular velocity, there may not be a conflict with rotation sensed by the vestibular organ because the semicircular canals measure angular accelerations. Thus, the angular velocity of the viewpoint must change to cause mismatch with this part of the vestibular system. Sickness may nevertheless arise due to mismatch of perceived linear accelerations, as sensed by the otolith organs.

If the head is actually moving, then the vestibular organ is stimulated. This case is more complicated to understand because vestibular cues that correspond to linear and angular accelerations in the real world are combined with visual cues that indicate different accelerations. In some cases, these cues may be more consistent, and in other cases, they may diverge further.

Factors That Affect Sensitivity

The intensity of vection is affected by many factors:

- **Percentage of field of view:** If only a small part of the visual field is moving, then people tend to perceive that it is caused by a moving object. However, if most of the visual field is moving, then they perceive *themselves* as moving. The human visual system actually includes neurons with receptive fields that cover a large fraction of the retina for the purpose of detecting self motion [35]. As VR headsets have increased their field of view, they project onto a larger region of the retina, thereby strengthening vection cues.

- **Distance from center view:** Recall from Section 5.1 that the photoreceptors are not uniformly distributed, with the highest density being at the innermost part of the fovea. Thus, detection may seem stronger near the center. However, in the cases of yaw and forward/backward vection, the optical flow vectors are stronger at the periphery, which indicates that detection may be stronger at the periphery. Sensitivity to the optical flow may therefore be strongest somewhere between the center view and the periphery, depending on the viewpoint velocities, distances to objects, photoreceptor densities, and neural detection mechanisms.

- **Exposure time:** The perception of self motion due to vection increases with the time of exposure to the optical flow. If the period of exposure is very brief, such as a few milliseconds, then no vection may occur.

- **Spatial frequency:** If the virtual world is complicated, with many small structures or textures, then the number of visual features will be greatly increased and the optical flow becomes a stronger signal. As the VR headset display resolution increases, higher spatial frequencies can be generated.

- **Contrast:** With higher levels of contrast, the optical flow signal is stronger because the features are more readily detected. Therefore, vection typically occurs with greater intensity.

- **Other sensory cues:** Recall from Section 6.4 that a perceptual phenomenon depends on the combination of many cues. Vection can be enhanced by providing additional consistent cues. For example, forward vection could be accompanied by a fan blowing in the user's face, a rumbling engine, and the sounds of stationary objects in the virtual world racing by. Likewise, vection can be weakened by providing cues that are consistent with the real world, where no corresponding motion is occurring.

- **Prior knowledge:** Just by knowing beforehand what kind of motion should be perceived will affect the onset of vection. This induces a prior bias that might take longer to overcome if the bias is against self motion, but less time to overcome if it is consistent with self motion. The prior bias could be from someone telling the user what is going to happen, or it could simply be from an accumulation of similar visual experiences through the user's lifetime. Furthermore, the user might expect the motion as the result of an action taken, such as turning the steering wheel of a virtual car.

- **Attention:** If the user is distracted by another activity, such as aiming a virtual weapon or selecting a menu option, then vection and its side effects may be mitigated.

- **Prior training or adaptation:** With enough exposure, the body may learn to distinguish vection from true motion to the point that vection becomes comfortable. Thus, many users can be trained to overcome VR sickness through repeated, prolonged exposure.

Due to all of these factors, and the imperfections of VR headsets, it becomes extremely difficult to characterize the potency of vection and its resulting side effects on user comfort.

Further Reading

For basic concepts of vector fields, velocities, and dynamical systems, see [12]. Modeling and analysis of mechanical dynamical systems appears in [280]. The specific problem of human body movement is covered in [373, 374]. See [104] for an overview of game engines, including issues such as simulated physics and collision detection. For coverage of particular collision detection algorithms, see [101, 185].

A nice introduction to the vestibular system, including its response as a dynamical system, is [153]. Vection and visually induced motion sickness are thoroughly surveyed in [148], which includes an extensive collection of references for further reading. Some key articles that address sensitivities to vection include [6, 13, 70, 181, 182, 285, 349].

CHAPTER NINE

Tracking

Keeping track of motion in the physical world is a crucial part of any VR system. Tracking was one of the largest obstacles to bringing VR headsets into consumer electronics, and it will remain a major challenge due to our desire to expand and improve VR experiences. Highly accurate tracking methods have been mostly enabled by commodity hardware components, such as inertial measurement units (IMUs) and cameras, that have plummeted in size and cost due to the smartphone industry.

Three categories of tracking may appear in VR systems, based on what is being tracked:

1. **The user's sense organs:** Recall from Section 2.1 that sense organs, such as eyes and ears, have DOFs that are controlled by the body. If a display is attached to a sense organ, and it should be perceived in VR as being attached to the surrounding world, then the position and orientation of the organ needs to be tracked. The inverse of the tracked transformation is applied to the stimulus to correctly "undo" these DOFs. Most of the focus is on *head tracking*, which is sufficient for visual and aural components of VR; however, the visual system may further require *eye tracking* if the rendering and display technology requires accounting for the eye movements discussed in Section 5.3.

2. **The user's other body parts:** If the user would like to see a compelling representation of her body in the virtual world, then its motion should be tracked so that it can be reproduced in the matched zone. Perhaps facial expressions or hand gestures are needed for interaction. Although perfect matching is ideal for tracking sense organs, it is not required for tracking other body parts. Small movements in the real world could convert into larger virtual world motions so that the user exerts less energy. In the limiting case, the user could simply press a button to change the body configuration. For example, she might grasp an object in her virtual hand by making a single click.

3. **The rest of the environment:** In the real world that surrounds the user, physical objects may be tracked. For objects that exist in the physical world but not the virtual world, the system might alert the user to their presence for safety reasons. Imagine that the user is about to hit a wall, or trip over a toddler. In some VR applications, the tracked physical objects may be matched in VR so that the user receives touch feedback while interacting with them. In other applications, such

as telepresence, a large part of the physical world could be "brought into" the virtual world through live capture.

Section 9.1 covers the easy case of tracking rotations around a single axis to prepare for Section 9.2, which extends the framework to tracking the 3-DOF orientation of a 3D rigid body. This relies mainly on the angular velocity readings of an IMU. The most common use is to track the head that wears a VR headset, but it may apply to tracking handheld controllers or other devices. Section 9.3 addresses the tracking of position and orientation together, which in most systems requires line-of-sight visibility between a fixed part of the physical world and the object being tracked. Section 9.4 discusses the case of tracking multiple bodies that are attached together by joints. Finally, Section 9.5 covers the case of using sensors to build a representation of the physical world so that it can be brought into the virtual world.

9.1 Tracking 2D Orientation

This section explains how the orientation of a rigid body is estimated using an inertial measurement unit (IMU). The main application is determining the viewpoint orientation, R_{eye} from Section 3.4, while the user is wearing a VR headset. Another application is estimating the orientation of a hand-held controller. For example, suppose we would like to make a laser pointer that works in the virtual world, based on a direction indicated by the user. The location of a bright red dot in the scene would be determined by the estimated orientation of a controller. More generally, the orientation of any human body part or moving object in the physical world can be determined if it has an attached IMU.

To estimate orientation, we first consider the 2D case by closely following the merry-go-round model of Section 8.1.2. The technical issues are easy to visualize in this case, and extend to the more important case of 3D rotations. Thus, imagine that we mount a gyroscope on a spinning merry-go-round. Its job is to measure the angular velocity as the merry-go-round spins. It will be convenient throughout this chapter to distinguish a true parameter value from an estimate. To accomplish this, a "hat" will be placed over estimates. Thus, let $\hat{\omega}$ correspond to the estimated or measured angular velocity, which may not be the same as ω, the *true* value.

How are $\hat{\omega}$ and ω related? If the gyroscope were functioning perfectly, then $\hat{\omega}$ would equal ω; however, in the real world this cannot be achieved. The main contributor to the discrepancy between $\hat{\omega}$ and ω is *calibration error*. The quality of calibration is the largest differentiator between an expensive IMU (thousands of dollars) and a cheap one (a dollar).

We now define a simple model of calibration error. The following *sensor mapping* indicates how the sensor output is related to true angular velocity:

$$\hat{\omega} = a + b\,\omega. \tag{9.1}$$

Here, a and b are called the *offset* and *scale*, respectively. They are unknown constants that interfere with the measurement. If ω were perfectly measured, then we would have $a = 0$ and $b = 1$.

Consider the effect of calibration error. Comparing the measured and true angular velocities yields

$$\hat{\omega} - \omega = a + b\,\omega - \omega = a + \omega(b - 1). \tag{9.2}$$

Now imagine using the sensor to estimate the orientation of the merry-go-round. We would like to understand the difference between the true orientation θ and an estimate $\hat{\theta}$ computed using the sensor output. Let $d(t)$ denote a function of time called the *drift error*:

$$d(t) = \theta(t) - \hat{\theta}(t). \tag{9.3}$$

Note that $d(t)$ might be negative, which could be forced into being positive by applying the absolute value to obtain $|d(t)|$. This will be avoided to simplify the discussion.

Suppose it is initially given that $\theta(0) = 0$, and to keep it simple, the angular velocity ω is constant. By integrating (9.2) over time, drift error is

$$d(t) = (\hat{\omega} - \omega)t = (a + b\omega - \omega)t = (a + \omega(b - 1))t. \tag{9.4}$$

Of course, the drift error grows (positively or negatively) as a deviates from zero or as b deviates from one; however, note that the second component is proportional to ω. Ignoring a, this means that the drift error is proportional to the speed of the merry-go-round. In terms of tracking a VR headset using a gyroscope, this means that tracking error increases at a faster rate as the head rotates more quickly [171].

At this point, four general problems must be solved to make an effective tracking system, even for this simple case:

1. **Calibration:** If a better sensor is available, then the two can be closely paired so that the outputs of the worse sensor are transformed to behave as closely to the better sensor as possible.
2. **Integration:** The sensor provides measurements at discrete points in time, resulting in a *sampling rate*. The orientation is estimated by aggregating or integrating the measurements.
3. **Registration:** The initial orientation must somehow be determined, either by an additional sensor or a clever default assumption or start-up procedure.
4. **Drift error:** As the error grows over time, other sensors are needed to directly estimate it and reduce it.

All of these issues remain throughout this chapter for the more complicated settings. The process of combining information from multiple sensor readings is often called *sensor fusion* or *filtering*.

We discuss each of these for the 2D case, before extending the ideas to the 3D case in Section 9.2.

Calibration

You could buy a sensor and start using it with the assumption that it is already well calibrated. For a cheaper sensor, however, the calibration is often unreliable. Suppose we have one expensive, well-calibrated sensor that reports angular velocities with very little error. Let $\hat{\omega}'$ denote its output, to distinguish it from the unattainable true value ω. Now suppose that we want to calibrate a bunch of cheap sensors so that they behave as closely as possible to the expensive sensor. This could be accomplished by mounting them together on a movable surface and comparing their outputs. For greater accuracy and control, the most expensive sensor may be part of a complete mechanical system such as an expensive turntable, calibration rig, or robot. Let $\hat{\omega}$

denote the output of one cheap sensor to be calibrated; each cheap sensor must be calibrated separately.

Calibration involves taking many samples, sometimes thousands, and comparing $\hat{\omega}'$ to $\hat{\omega}$. A common criterion is the *sum of squares error*, which is given by

$$\sum_{i=1}^{n} (\hat{\omega}_i - \hat{\omega}'_i)^2 \tag{9.5}$$

for n samples of the angular velocity. The task is to determine a transformation to apply to the cheap sensor outputs $\hat{\omega}$ so that it behaves as closely as possible to the expensive sensor outputs $\hat{\omega}'$.

Using the error model from (9.1), we can select constants c_1 and c_2 that optimize the error:

$$\sum_{i=1}^{n} (c_1 + c_2 \hat{\omega}_i - \hat{\omega}')_i^2. \tag{9.6}$$

This is a classical regression problem referred to as *linear least-squares*. It is typically solved by calculating the Moore–Penrose pseudoinverse of a non-square matrix that contains the sampled data [350].

Once c_1 and c_2 are calculated, every future sensor reading is transformed as

$$\hat{\omega}_{cal} = c_1 + c_2 \hat{\omega}, \tag{9.7}$$

in which $\hat{\omega}$ is the original, raw sensor output, and $\hat{\omega}_{cal}$ is the calibrated output. Thus, the calibration produces a kind of invisible wrapper around the cheap sensor outputs so that the expensive sensor is simulated. The raw, cheap sensor outputs are no longer visible to outside processes. The calibrated outputs will therefore simply be referred to as $\hat{\omega}$ in the remainder of this chapter.

Integration

Sensor outputs usually arrive at a regular sampling rate. For example, the Oculus Rift gyroscope provided a measurement every 1 ms (yielding a $1,000$ Hz sampling rate). Let $\hat{\omega}[k]$ refer to the kth sample, which arrives at time $k\Delta t$.

The orientation $\theta(t)$ at time $t = k\Delta t$ can be estimated by integration as

$$\hat{\theta}[k] = \theta(0) + \sum_{i=1}^{k} \hat{\omega}[i]\Delta t. \tag{9.8}$$

Each output $\hat{\omega}[i]$ causes a rotation of $\Delta\theta[i] = \hat{\omega}[i]\Delta t$. It is sometimes more convenient to write (9.8) in an incremental form, which indicates the update to $\hat{\theta}$ after each new sensor output arrives:

$$\hat{\theta}[k] = \hat{\omega}[k]\Delta t + \hat{\theta}[k-1]. \tag{9.9}$$

For the first case, $\hat{\theta}[0] = \theta(0)$.

If $\omega(t)$ varies substantially between $\theta(k\Delta t)$ and $\theta((k+1)\Delta t)$, then it is helpful to know what $\hat{\omega}[k]$ precisely corresponds to. It could be angular velocity at the start of the interval Δt, the end of the interval, or an average over the interval. If it is the start or end, then a trapezoidal approximation to the integral may yield less error over time [135].

Registration
In (9.8), the initial orientation $\theta(0)$ was assumed to be known. In practice, this corresponds to a *registration* problem, which is the initial alignment between the real and virtual worlds. To understand the issue, suppose that θ represents the yaw direction for a VR headset. One possibility is to assign $\theta(0) = 0$, which corresponds to whichever direction the headset is facing when the tracking system is turned on. This might be when the system is booted. If the headset has an "on head" sensor, then it could start when the user attaches the headset to his head. Often, the forward direction could be unintentionally set in a bad way. For example, if one person starts a VR demo and hands the headset to someone else, who is facing in another direction, then in VR the user would not be facing in the intended forward direction. This could be fixed by a simple option that causes "forward" (and hence $\theta(t)$) to be redefined as whichever direction the user is facing at provided.

An alternative to this entire problem is to declare $\theta(0) = 0$ to correspond to a direction that is fixed in the physical world. For example, if the user is sitting at a desk in front of a computer monitor, then the forward direction could be defined as the yaw angle for which the user and headset are facing the monitor. Implementing this solution requires a sensor that can measure the yaw orientation with respect to the surrounding physical world. For example, with the original Oculus Rift, the user faced a stationary camera, which corresponded to the forward direction.

Drift Correction
To make a useful tracking system, the drift error (9.3) cannot be allowed to accumulate. Even if the gyroscope were perfectly calibrated, drift error would nevertheless grow due to other factors such as quantized output values, sampling rate limitations, and unmodeled noise. The first problem is to estimate the drift error, which is usually accomplished with an additional sensor. Practical examples of this will be given in Section 9.2. For the simple merry-go-round example, imagine that an overhead camera takes a picture once in a while to measure the orientation. Let $\hat{\theta}_d[k]$ denote the estimated orientation from this single sensor measurement, arriving at stage k.

Because of drift error, there are now two conflicting sources of information: (1) the orientation $\hat{\theta}[k]$ estimated by integrating the gyroscope, and (2) the orientation $\hat{\theta}_d[k]$ instantaneously estimated by the camera (or some other, independent sensor). A classic approach to blending these two sources is a *complementary filter*, which mathematically interpolates between the two estimates:

$$\hat{\theta}_c[k] = \alpha\hat{\theta}_d[k] + (1 - \alpha)\hat{\theta}[k], \tag{9.10}$$

in which α is a *gain* parameter that must satisfy $0 < \alpha < 1$. Here, $\hat{\theta}_c[k]$ denotes the corrected estimate at stage k. Since the gyroscope is usually accurate over short times but gradually drifts, α is chosen to be close to zero (for example, $\alpha = 0.0001$). This causes the instantaneous estimate $\hat{\theta}_d[k]$ to have a gradual impact. At the other extreme, if α were close to 1, then the estimated orientation could wildly fluctuate due to errors in $\theta_d[k]$ in each stage. An additional consideration is that if the sensor output $\hat{\theta}_d[k]$ arrives at a much lower rate than the gyroscope sampling rate, then the most recently recorded output is used. For example, a camera image might produce an orientation estimate at 60 Hz, whereas the gyroscope produces outputs at 1000

Hz. In this case, $\hat{\theta}_d[k]$ would retain the same value for 16 or 17 stages, until a new camera image becomes available.

It is important to select the gain α to be high enough so that the drift is corrected, but low enough so that the user does not perceive the corrections. The gain could be selected "optimally" by employing a Kalman filter [45, 143, 161]; however, the optimality only holds if we have a linear stochastic system, which is not the case in human body tracking. The relationship between Kalman and complementary filters, for the exact models used in this chapter, appears in [121].

Using simple algebra, the complementary filter formulation in (9.10) can be reworked to yield the following equivalent expression:

$$\hat{\theta}_c[k] = \hat{\theta}[k] - \alpha \hat{d}[k] \tag{9.11}$$

in which

$$\hat{d}[k] = \hat{\theta}_d[k] - \hat{\theta}[k]. \tag{9.12}$$

Above, $\hat{d}[k]$ is just an estimate of the drift error at stage k. Thus, the complementary filter can alternatively be imagined as applying the negated, signed error, by a small, proportional amount α, to try to incrementally force it to zero.

9.2 Tracking 3D Orientation

IMUs

Recall from Section 2.1 (Figure 2.9) that IMUs have gone from large, heavy mechanical systems to cheap, microscopic MEMS circuits. This progression was a key enabler to high-quality orientation tracking. The gyroscope measures angular velocity along three orthogonal axes, to obtain $\hat{\omega}_x$, $\hat{\omega}_y$, and $\hat{\omega}_z$. For each axis, the sensing elements lie in the perpendicular plane, much like the semicircular canals in the vestibular organ (Section 8.2). The sensing elements in each case are micromachined mechanical elements that vibrate and operate like a tuning fork. If the sensor rotates in its direction of sensitivity, then the elements experience Coriolis forces, which are converted into electrical signals. These signals are calibrated to produce an output in degrees or radians per second; see Figure 9.1.

IMUs usually contain additional sensors that are useful for detecting drift errors. Most commonly, accelerometers measure linear acceleration along three axes to obtain $\hat{a}_x$, $\hat{a}_y$, and $\hat{a}_z$. The principle of their operation is shown in Figure 9.2. MEMS magnetometers also appear on many IMUs, which measure magnetic field strength along the three perpendicular axis. This is often accomplished by the mechanical motion of a MEMS structure that is subject to Lorentz force as it conducts inside of a magnetic field.

Calibration

Recall from Section 9.1 that the sensor outputs are distorted due to calibration issues. In the one-dimensional angular velocity case, there were only two parameters, for scale and offset, which appeared in (9.1). In the 3D setting, this would naturally extend to three scale and three offset parameters; however, the situation is worse because there may also be errors due to non-orthogonality of the MEMS elements. All of these can be accounted for by 12 parameters arranged in a homogeneous transform matrix:

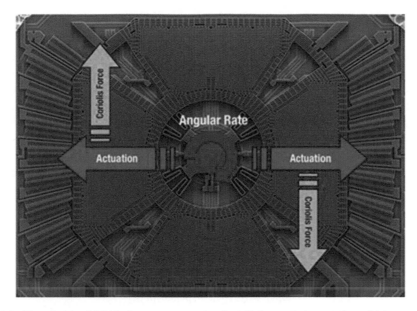

Figure 9.1 The vibrating MEMS elements respond to Coriolis forces during rotation, which are converted into an electrical signal.

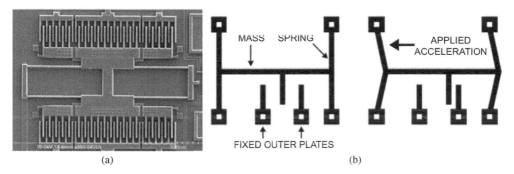

(a)   (b)

Figure 9.2 (a) A MEMS element for sensing linear acceleration (from [326]). (b) Due to linear acceleration in one direction, the plates shift and cause a change in capacitance as measured between the outer plates.

$$
\begin{bmatrix} \hat{\omega}_x \\ \hat{\omega}_y \\ \hat{\omega}_z \\ 1 \end{bmatrix} = \begin{bmatrix} a & b & c & j \\ d & e & f & k \\ g & h & i & \ell \\ 0 & 0 & 0 & 1 \end{bmatrix} \begin{bmatrix} \omega_x \\ \omega_y \\ \omega_z \\ 1 \end{bmatrix}.
\tag{9.13}
$$

There are 12 and not six DOFs because the upper left three-by-three matrix is not constrained to be a rotation matrix. The j, k, and ℓ parameters correspond to offset, whereas all others handle scale and non-orthogonality. Following the same methodology as in Section 9.1, the inverse of this transform can be estimated by minimizing the least squares error with respect to outputs of a better sensor, which provides ground truth. The outputs of the MEMS sensor are then adjusted by applying the estimated homogeneous transform to improve performance. (This is an extension of (9.7) to the 12-parameter case.) This general methodology applies to calibrating gyroscopes and accelerometers. Magnetometers may also be calibrated in this way but have further complications such as *soft iron bias*.

An additional challenge with MEMS sensors is dealing with other subtle dependencies. For example, the outputs are sensitive to the particular temperature of the MEMS elements. If a VR headset heats up during use, then calibration parameters are needed for every temperature that might arise in practice. Fortunately, IMUs usually contain a temperature sensor that can be used to associate the calibration parameters with the corresponding temperatures. Finally, MEMS elements may be sensitive to forces acting on the circuit board, which could be changed, for example, by a dangling connector. Care must be given to isolate external board forces from the MEMS circuit.

Integration

Now consider the problem of converting the sequence of gyroscope outputs into an estimate of the 3D orientation. At each stage k a vector,

$$\hat{\omega}[k] = (\hat{\omega}_x[k], \hat{\omega}_y[k], \hat{\omega}_z[k]), \tag{9.14}$$

arrives from the sensor. In Section 9.1, the sensor output $\hat{\omega}[k]$ was converted to a change $\Delta\theta[k]$ in orientation. For the 3D case, the change in orientation is expressed as a *quaternion*.

Let $q(v, \theta)$ be the quaternion obtained by the axis-angle conversion formula (3.30). Recall from Section 8.1.2 that the instantaneous axis of rotation is the magnitude of the angular velocity. Thus, if $\hat{\omega}[k]$ is the sensor output at stage k, then the estimated rotation axis (a unit vector) is

$$\hat{v}[k] = \hat{\omega}[k]/\|\hat{\omega}[k]\|. \tag{9.15}$$

Furthermore, the estimated amount of rotation that occurs during time Δt is

$$\Delta\hat{\theta}[k] = \|\hat{\omega}[k]\|\Delta t. \tag{9.16}$$

Using the estimated rotation axis (9.15) and amount (9.16), the orientation change over time Δt is estimated to be

$$\Delta\hat{q}[k] = q(\hat{v}[k], \Delta\hat{\theta}[k]). \tag{9.17}$$

Using (9.17) at each stage, the estimated orientation $\hat{q}[k]$ after obtaining the latest sensor output is calculated incrementally from $\hat{q}[k-1]$ as

$$\hat{q}[k] = \Delta\hat{q}[k] * \hat{q}[k-1], \tag{9.18}$$

in which $*$ denotes quaternion multiplication. This is the 3D generalization of (9.9), in which simple addition could be used to combine rotations in the 2D case. In (9.18), quaternion multiplication is needed to aggregate the change in orientation. (Simple addition is commutative, which is inappropriate for 3D rotations.)

Registration

The registration problem for the yaw component is the same as in Section 9.1. The forward direction may be chosen from the initial orientation of the rigid body or it could be determined with respect to a fixed direction in the world. The pitch and

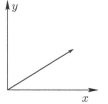 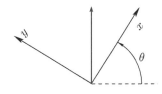 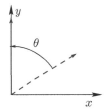

Up vector in sensor frame   Sensor frame with respect to world   Transformed sensor reading

Figure 9.3 If "up" is perfectly sensed by an accelerometer that is rotated by θ, then its output needs to be rotated by θ to view it from the world frame.

roll components should be determined so that they align with gravity. The virtual world should not appear to be tilted with respect to the real world (unless that is the desired effect, which is rarely the case).

Tilt Correction

The drift error $d(t)$ in (9.3) was a single angle, which could be positive or negative. If added to the estimate $\hat{\theta}(t)$, the true orientation $\theta(t)$ would be obtained. It is similar for the 3D case, but with quaternion algebra. The 3D drift error is expressed as

$$d(t) = q(t) * \hat{q}^{-1}(t), \tag{9.19}$$

which is equal to the identity rotation if $q(t) = \hat{q}(t)$. Furthermore, note that applying the drift error to the estimate yields $q(t) = d(t) * \hat{q}(t)$.

Since the drift error is a 3D rotation, it could be constructed as the product of a yaw, pitch, and a roll. Let *tilt error* refer to the part of the drift error that corresponds to pitch and roll. This will be detected using an "up" sensor. Let *yaw error* refer to the remaining part of the drift error, which will be detecting using a "compass." In reality, there do not exist perfect "up" and "compass" sensors, which will be addressed later.

Suppose that a sensor attached to the rigid body always reports an "up" vector that is parallel to the y-axis in the fixed, world-coordinate frame. In other words, it would be parallel to gravity. Since the sensor is mounted to the body, it reports its values in the coordinate frame of the body. For example, if the body were rolled 90 degrees so that its x-axis is pointing straight up, then the "up" vector would be reported as $(0, 0, 1)$ instead of $(0, 1, 0)$. To fix this, it would be convenient to transform the sensor output into the world frame. This involves rotating it by $q(t)$, the body orientation. For our example, this roll rotation would transform $(0, 0, 1)$ into $(0, 1, 0)$. Figure 9.3 shows a 2D example.

Now suppose that drift error has occurred and that $\hat{q}[k]$ is the estimated orientation. If this transform is applied to the "up" vector, then because of drift error, it might not be aligned with the y-axis, as shown in Figure 9.4. The up vector $\hat{u}$ is projected into the xz plane to obtain $(\hat{u}_x, 0, \hat{u}_z)$. The *tilt axis* lies in the xz plane and is constructed as the normal to the projected up vector: $\hat{t} = (\hat{u}_z, 0, -\hat{u}_x)$. Performing a rotation of ϕ about the axis $\hat{t}$ would move the up vector into alignment with the y-axis. Thus, the tilt error portion of the drift error is the quaternion $q(\hat{t}, \hat{\phi})$.

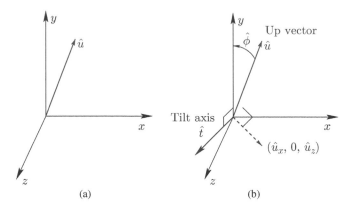

Figure 9.4 (a) Tilt error causes a discrepancy between the *y*-axis and the sensed up vector that is rotated using the estimate $\hat{q}[k]$ to obtain $\hat{u}$. (b) The *tilt axis* is normal to $\hat{u}$; a rotation of $-\hat{\phi}$ about the tilt axis would bring them into alignment, thereby eliminating the tilt error.

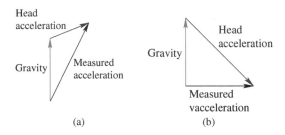

Figure 9.5 (a) There is no gravity sensor; the accelerometer measures the vector sum of apparent acceleration due to gravity and the true acceleration of the body. (b) A simple heuristic of accepting the reading as gravity only if the magnitude is approximately 9.8 m^2 will fail in some cases.

Unfortunately, there is no sensor that directly measures "up." In practice, the accelerometer is used to measure the "up" direction because gravity acts on the sensor, causing the sensation of upward acceleration at roughly 9.8m/s^2. The problem is that it also responds to true linear acceleration of the rigid body, and this cannot be separated from gravity due to the Einstein equivalence principle. It measures the vector sum of gravity and true linear acceleration, as shown in Figure 9.5. A simple heuristic is to trust accelerometer outputs as an estimate of the "up" direction only if its magnitude is close to 9.8 m^2 [76]. This could correspond to the common case in which the rigid body is stationary. However, this assumption is unreliable because downward and lateral linear accelerations can be combined to provide an output magnitude that is close to 9.8 m^2, but with a direction that is far from "up." Better heuristics may be built from simultaneously considering the outputs of other sensors or the rate at which "up" appears to change.

Assuming that the accelerometer is producing a reliable estimate of the gravity direction, the up vector $\hat{u}$ is calculated from the accelerometer output $\hat{a}$ by using (3.34), to obtain

$$\hat{u} = \hat{q}[k] * \hat{a} * \hat{q}[k]^{-1}. \tag{9.20}$$

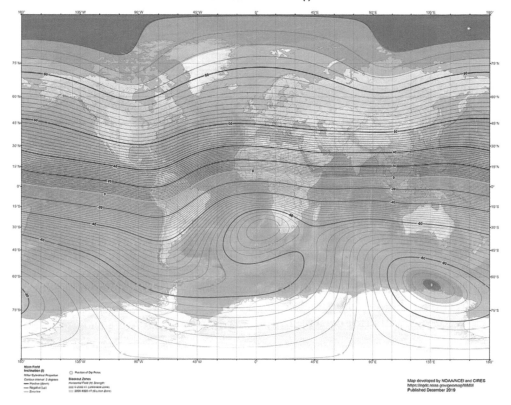

US/UK World Magnetic Model - Epoch 2020.0
Main Field Inclination (I)

Figure 9.6 The inclination angle of the Earth's magnetic field vector varies greatly over the Earth.

Yaw Correction

The remaining drift error component is detected by a "compass," which outputs a vector that lies in the world xz plane and always points "north." Suppose this is $\hat{n} = (0, 0, -1)$. Once again, the sensor output occurs in the coordinate frame of the body and needs to be transformed by $\hat{q}[k]$. The difference between $\hat{n}$ and the $-z$-axis is the resulting yaw drift error.

As in the case of the "up" sensor, there is no "compass" in the real world. Instead, there is a magnetometer, which measures a 3D magnetic field vector: $(\hat{m}_x, \hat{m}_y, \hat{m}_z)$. Suppose this is used to measure the Earth's magnetic field. It turns out that the field vectors do not "point" to the North pole. The Earth's magnetic field produces 3D vectors that generally do not lie in the horizontal plane, resulting in an *inclination angle*. Thus, the first problem is that the sensor output must be projected into the xz plane. Residents of Ecuador may enjoy magnetic field vectors that are nearly horizontal; however, in Finland they are closer to vertical; see Figure 9.6. If the magnetic field vector is close to vertical, then the horizontal component may become too small to be useful.

Another issue is that the projected vector in the horizontal plane does not point north, resulting in a *declination angle*; this is the deviation from north. Fortunately, reference to the true north is not important. It only matters that the sensor output is recorded in the registration stage to provide a fixed yaw reference.

The most significant problem is that the magnetometer measures the vector sum of *all* magnetic field sources. In addition to the Earth's field, a building generates its own field due to ferromagnetic metals. Furthermore, such materials usually exist on the circuit board that contains the sensor. For this case, the field moves with the sensor, generating a constant vector offset. Materials that serve as a source of magnetic fields are called *hard iron*. Other materials distort magnetic fields that pass through them; these are called *soft iron*. Magnetometer calibration methods mainly take into account offsets due to hard-iron bias and eccentricities due to soft-iron bias [93, 158].

After these magnetometer calibrations have been performed, the yaw drift error can be estimated from most locations with a few degrees of accuracy, which is sufficient to keep yaw errors from gradually accumulating. There are still problems. If a strong field is placed near the sensor, then the readings become dependent on small location changes. This could cause the measured direction to change as the rigid body translates back and forth. Another problem is that in some building locations, the vector sum of the Earth's magnetic field and the field generated by the building could be approximately zero (if they are of similar magnitude and pointing in opposite directions). In this unfortunate case, the magnetometer cannot produce useful outputs for yaw drift error detection.

Filtering
Using the detected drift error, filtering works in the same way as described in Section 9.1. The complementary filter (9.10) is upgraded to work with quaternions. It becomes slightly more complicated to represent the interpolation in terms of α. Let (v, θ) denote the axis-angle representation of the orientation $\hat{d}[k]$, which is the estimated drift error (a quaternion value). Let $q(v, \alpha\theta)$ represent the quaternion given by axis v and angle $\alpha\theta$. For a small value of α, this can be considered as a small step "toward" $\hat{d}[k]$.

The complementary filter in terms of quaternions becomes

$$\hat{q}_c[k] = q(v, -\alpha\theta) * \hat{q}[k], \qquad (9.21)$$

which is similar in form to (9.12). The simple subtraction from the 2D case has been replaced in (9.21) by multiplying an inverse quaternion from the left. The estimated drift error $\hat{d}[k]$ is obtained by multiplying the estimated tilt and yaw error quaternions. Alternatively, they could contribute separately to the complementary filter, with different gains for each, and even be combined with drift error estimates from more sources [200].

Setting the Viewpoint
The viewpoint is set using the estimated orientation $\hat{q}[k]$, although it might need to be adjusted to account for alternative timings, for the purpose of prediction or image warping, as discussed in Section 7.4. Let $\hat{q}(t)$ denote the estimated orientation for time t. In terms of the transformations from Section 3.4, we have just estimated R_{eye}. To calculate the correct viewpoint, the inverse is needed. Thus, $\hat{q}^{-1}(t)$ would correctly transform models to take the estimated viewpoint into account.

Yaw	Pitch	Roll	Error
+	+	+	None
−	+	+	L/R mix, flipped x
+	−	+	L/R mix, flipped y
+	+	−	L/R mix, flipped z
+	−	−	Inverse and L/R mix, flipped x
−	+	−	Inverse and L/R mix, flipped y
−	−	+	Inverse and L/R mix, flipped z
−	−	−	Inverse

Figure 9.7 A table to help debug common viewpoint transform errors. Each + means that the virtual world appears to move the correct way when performing the yaw, pitch, or roll. Each − means it moves in the opposite way. The first case is correct. All others are bugs. "L/R mix" means that left- and right-handed coordinate systems are getting mixed; the axis that was flipped is indicated.

A Debugging Tip

Programmers often make mistakes when connecting the tracked orientation to the viewpoint. Figure 9.7 shows a table of the common mistakes. To determine whether the transform has been correctly applied, one should put on the headset and try rotating about the three canonical axes: a pure yaw, a pure pitch, and a pure roll. Let + denote that the world is moving correctly with respect to a head rotation. Let − denote that it seems to move in the opposite direction. Figure 9.7 shows a table of the eight possible outcomes and the most likely cause of each problem.

A Head Model

The translation part of the head motion has not been addressed. Ideally, the head should be the same height in the virtual world as in the real world. This can be handled by the translation part of the T_{eye} matrix (3.36).

We must also account for the fact that as the head rotates, the eyes change their positions. For example, in a yaw head movement (nodding "no"), the pupils displace a few centimeters in the x direction. More accurately, they travel along a circular arc in a horizontal plane. To more closely mimic the real world, the movements of the eyes through space can be simulated by changing the center of rotation according to a fictitious *head model* [3]. This trick is needed until Section 9.3, where position is instead estimated from more sensors.

Recall from Section 3.5 that the cyclopean viewpoint was first considered and then modified to handle left and right eyes by applying horizontal offsets by inserting T_{left} (3.50) and T_{right} (3.52). In a similar way, offsets in the y and z directions can be added to account for displacement that would come from a rotating head. The result is to insert (9.22) before or after T_{right} and T_{left}:

$$T_{head} = \begin{bmatrix} 1 & 0 & 0 & 0 \\ 0 & 1 & 0 & h \\ 0 & 0 & 1 & p \\ 0 & 0 & 0 & 1 \end{bmatrix}, \tag{9.22}$$

in which h is a height parameter and p is a protrusion parameter. See Figure 9.8. The idea is to choose h and p that would correspond to the center of rotation of the head. The parameter h is the distance from the rotation center to the eye height,

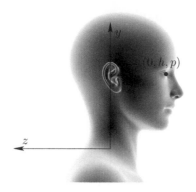

Figure 9.8 To obtain a *head model*, the rotation center is moved so that orientation changes induce a plausible translation of the eyes. The height *h* is along the *y*-axis, and the protrusion *p* is along the *z*-axis (which leads a negative number).

along the y-axis. A typical value is $h = 0.15$ m. The protrusion p is the distance from the rotation center to the cyclopean eye. A typical value is $p = -0.10$ m, which is negative because it extends opposite to the z-axis. Using a fake head model approximates the eye locations as the user rotates her head; however, it is far from perfect. If the torso moves, then this model completely breaks, resulting in a large mismatch between the real and virtual world head motions. Nevertheless, this head model was used in popular headsets, such as Samsung Gear VR.

An issue also exists with the y height of the head center. The user may be seated in the real world, but standing in the virtual world. This mismatch might be uncomfortable. The brain knows that the body is seated because of proprioception, regardless of the visual stimuli provided by VR. If the user is standing, then the head-center height could be set so that the eyes are at the same height as in the real world. This issue even exists for the case of full six-DOF tracking, which is covered next; the user might be sitting, and a vertical offset is added to make him appear to be standing in VR.

9.3 Tracking Position and Orientation

This section covers tracking of all six DOFs for a moving rigid body, with the most important case being head tracking. For convenience, we will refer to the position and orientation of a body as its *pose*. Six-DOF tracking enables T_{eye} from 3.4 to be fully derived from sensor data, rather than inventing positions from a plausible head model, as in (9.22). By estimating the position, the powerful depth cue of parallax becomes much stronger as the user moves her head from side to side. She could even approach a small object and look at it from any viewpoint, such as from above, below, or the sides. The methods in this section are also useful for tracking hands in space or objects that are manipulated during a VR experience.

Why Not Just Integrate the Accelerometer?
It seems natural to try to accomplish six-DOF tracking with an IMU alone. Recall from Figure 9.5 that the accelerometer measures the vector sum of true linear acceleration and acceleration due to gravity. If the gravity component is subtracted away

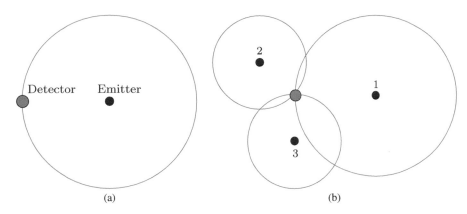

Figure 9.9 The principle of trilateration enables the detector location to be determined from estimates of distances to a known emitter. A 2D example is shown: (a) from a single emitter, the detector could be anywhere along a circle; (b) using three emitters, the position is uniquely determined.

from the output, as is heuristically accomplished for tilt correction, then it seems that the remaining part is pure body acceleration. Why not simply integrate this acceleration twice to obtain position estimates? The trouble is that the drift error rate is much larger than in the case of a gyroscope. A simple calibration error leads to linearly growing drift error in the gyroscope case because it is the result of a single integration. After a double integration, a calibration error leads to quadratically growing drift error. This becomes unbearable in practice after a fraction of a second. Furthermore, the true body acceleration cannot be accurately extracted, especially when the body quickly rotates. Finally, as drift accumulates, what sensors can be used to estimate the positional drift error? The IMU alone cannot help. Note that it cannot even distinguish motions at constant velocity, including zero motion; this is the same as our vestibular organs. Despite their shortcomings, modern IMUs remain an important part of six-DOF tracking systems because of their high sampling rates and ability to accurately handle the rotational component.

Make Your Own Waves
The IMU-based approach to tracking was *passive* in the sense that it relied on sources of information that already exist in the environment. Instead, an *active* approach can be taken by transmitting waves into the environment. Since humans operate in the same environment, waves that are perceptible, such as light and sound, are not preferred. Instead, common energy sources in active tracking systems include infrared, ultrasound, and electromagnetic fields.

Consider transmitting an ultrasound pulse (above 20,000 Hz) from a speaker and using a microphone to listen for its arrival. This is an example of an *emitter-detector pair*: The speaker is the emitter, and the microphone is the detector. If time measurement is synchronized between source and destination, then the *time of arrival* (*TOA* or *time of flight*) can be calculated. This is the time that it took for the pulse to travel the distance d between the emitter and detector. Based on the known propagation speed in the medium (330 m/s for ultrasound), the distance $\hat{d}$ is estimated. One frustrating limitation of ultrasound systems is reverberation between surfaces, causing the pulse to be received multiple times at each detector.

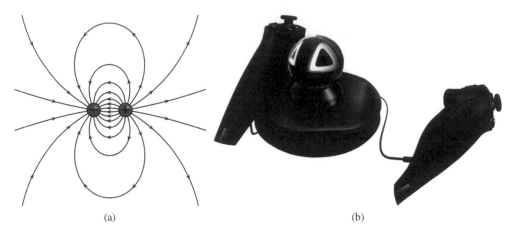

Figure 9.10 (a) A magnetic dipole offers a field that varies its magnitude and direction as the position changes.(b) The Razer Hydra, a game controller system that generates a weak magnetic field using a base station, enabling it to track the controller positions.

When functioning correctly, the position of the detector could then be narrowed down to a sphere of radius $\hat{d}$, centered at the transmitter; see Figure 9.9(a). By using two transmitters and one microphone, the position is narrowed down to the intersection of two spheres, resulting in a circle (assuming the transmitter locations are known). With three transmitters, the position is narrowed down to two points, and with four or more transmitters, the position is uniquely determined.[1] The emitter and detector roles could easily be reversed so that the object being tracked carries the emitter, and several receivers are placed around it. The method of combining these measurements to determine position is called *trilateration*. If electromagnetic waves, such as radio, light, or infrared, are used instead of ultrasound, then trilateration could still be applied even though it is impossible to measure the propagation time directly. If the transmitter amplitude is known then distance can be estimated based on power degradation, rather than TOA. Alternatively, a time-varying signal can be emitted and its reflected phase shift can be estimated when the received signal is superimposed onto the transmitted signal.

If the detectors do not know the precise time that the pulse started, then they could compare differences in arrival times between themselves; this is called *time difference of arrival* (*TDOA*). The set of possible locations is a hyperboloid instead of a sphere. Nevertheless, the hyperboloid sheets can be intersected for multiple emitter-detector pairs to obtain the method of *multilateration*. This was used in the Decca Navigation System in World War II to locate ships and aircraft. This principle is also used by our ears to localize the source of sounds, which will be covered in Section 11.3.

Finally, some methods could track position by emitting a complicated field that varies over the tracking area. For example, by creating a magnetic dipole, perhaps coded with a signal to distinguish it from background fields, the position and orientation of a body in the field could be estimated in the field; see Figure 9.10(a). This principle was used for video games in the Razer Hydra tracking system in a base

---

[1] Global positioning systems (*GPS*) work in this way, but using radio signals, the Earth surface constraint, and at least one more satellite eliminate time synchronization errors.

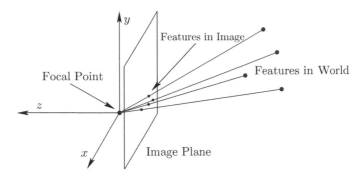

Figure 9.11 The real world contains special *features*, which are determined to lie along a line segment that connects to the focal point via perspective projection.

station that generated a magnetic field; see Figure 9.10(b). One drawback is that the field may become unpredictably warped in each environment, causing straight-line motions to be estimated as curved. Note that the requirements are the opposite of what was needed to use a magnetometer for yaw correction in Section 9.2; in that setting the field needed to be constant over the tracking area. For estimating position, the field should vary greatly across different locations.

The Power of Visibility

The most powerful paradigm for six-DOF tracking is *visibility*. The idea is to identify special parts of the physical world called *features* and calculate their positions along a line-of-sight ray to a known location. Figure 9.11 shows an example inspired by a camera, but other hardware could be used. One crucial aspect for tracking is *distinguishability*. If all features appear to be the same, then it may become difficult to determine and maintain "which is which" during the tracking process. Each feature should be assigned a unique label that is invariant over time, as rigid bodies in the world move. Confusing features with each other could cause catastrophically bad estimates to be made regarding the body pose.

The most common sensor used to detect features is a digital camera. Detecting, labeling, and tracking features are common tasks in computer vision or image processing. There are two options for features:

1. **Natural:** The features are automatically discovered, assigned labels, and maintained during the tracking process.
2. **Artificial:** The features are engineered and placed into the environment so that they can be easily detected, matched to preassigned labels, and tracked.

Natural features are advantageous because there are no setup costs. The environment does not need to be engineered. Unfortunately, they are also much more unreliable. Using a camera, this computer vision problem may be as challenging as it is for the human visual system. For some objects, textures, and lighting conditions, it could work well, but it is extremely hard to make it work reliably for *all* possible settings. Imagine trying to find and track features on an empty, white wall. Nevertheless, fairly robust tracking systems have been painstakingly developed and deployed in VR headsets, such as Oculus/Meta Quest 2, based on multiple cameras and natural features.

Figure 9.12 A sample QR code, which could be printed and used as an artificial feature.

Figure 9.13 The Oculus Rift headset contained IR LEDs hidden behind IR-transparent plastic.

For artificial features, one of the simplest solutions is to print a special tag onto the object to be tracked. For example, one could print bright red dots onto the object and then scan for their appearance as red blobs in the image. To solve the distinguishability problem, multiple colors, such as red, green, blue, and yellow dots, might be needed. Trouble may occur if these colors exist naturally in other parts of the image. A more reliable method is to design a specific *tag* that is clearly distinct from the rest of the image. Such tags can be coded to contain large amounts of information, including a unique identification number. One of the most common coded tags is the *QR code*, an example of which is shown in Figure 9.12.

The features described so far are called *passive* because they do not emit energy. The hope is that sufficient light is in the world so that enough reflects off of the feature and enters the camera sensor. A more reliable alternative is to engineer *active* features that emit their own light. For example, colored LEDs can be mounted on the surface of a headset or controller. This comes at the expense of requiring a power source and increasing overall object cost and weight. Furthermore, its industrial design may be compromised because it might light up like a Christmas tree.

Cloaking with Infrared
Fortunately, these tricks can be moved to the infrared (IR) part of the spectrum so that features are visible to cameras, but not to humans. Patterns can be painted

onto objects that highly reflect IR energy. Alternatively, IR LEDs can be mounted onto devices. This is the case for the Oculus Rift headset, and the IR LEDs were even hidden behind plastic that is transparent for IR energy, but appears black to humans; see Figure 9.13.

In some settings, it might be difficult to mount LEDs on the objects, as in the case of tracking the subtle motions of an entire human body. This is called *MOCAP* or *motion capture*, which is described in Section 9.4. In MOCAP systems, powerful IR LEDs are positioned around the camera so that they illuminate *retroreflective markers* that are placed in the scene. Each marker can be imagined as a spherical mirror in the IR part of the spectrum. One unfortunate drawback is that the range is limited because IR energy must travel from the camera location to the target and back again. Since energy dissipates quadratically as a function of distance, doubling the distance results on one-fourth of the energy level arriving at the camera.

At this point, it is natural to wonder why an entire image is being captured if the resulting image processing problem is trivial. The main reason is the proliferation of low-cost digital cameras and image processing software. Why not simply design an emitter-detector pair that produces a binary reading, indicating whether the visibility beam is occluded? This is precisely how the detection beam works in an automatic garage door system to ensure the door does not close on someone: an IR LED emits energy to a detection *photodiode*, which is essentially a switch that activates when it receives a sufficient level of energy for its target wavelength (in this case IR). To reduce the amount of energy dissipation, mirrors or lenses could be used to focus the energy.

Even better, an IR laser can be aimed directly at the detector. The next task is to use lenses and moving mirrors so that every detector that is visible from a fixed location will become illuminated at some point. The beam can be spread from a dot to a line using a lens, and then the line is moved through space using a spinning mirror. This was the basis of the *lighthouse tracking* system for the HTC Vive headset, which is covered later in this section.

The Perspective-n-Point (PnP) Problem

A moving rigid body needs to be "pinned down" using n observed features. This is called the *Perspective-n-Point* (or *PnP*) problem. We can borrow much of the math from Chapter 3; however, here we consider the placement of bodies in the *real* world, rather than the virtual world. Furthermore, we have an *inverse problem*, which is to determine the body placement based on points in the image. Up until now, the opposite problem was considered. For visual rendering in Chapter 7, an image was produced based on the known body placement in the (virtual) world.

The features could be placed on the body or in the surrounding world, depending on the sensing method. Suppose for now that they are on the body. Each feature corresponds to a point $p = (x, y, z)$ with coordinates defined in the frame of the body. Let T_{rb} be a homogeneous transformation matrix that contains the pose parameters, which are assumed to be unknown. Applying the transform T_{rb} to the point p as in (3.22) could place it anywhere in the real would. Recall the chain of transformations (3.41), which furthermore determines where each point on the body would appear in an image. The matrix T_{eye} held the camera pose, whereas T_{vp} and T_{can} contained the perspective projection and transformed the projected point into image coordinates.

Now suppose that a feature has been observed to be at location (i, j) in image coordinates. If T_{rb} is unknown, but all other transforms are given, then there would be six independent parameters to estimate, corresponding to the six DOFs. Observing (i, j) provides two independent constraints on the chain of transforms (3.41), one i and one for j. The rigid body therefore loses two DOFs, as shown in Figure 9.14. This was the P1P problem because n, the number of features, was one.

The P2P problem corresponds to observing two features in the image and results in four constraints. In this case, each constraint eliminates two DOFs, resulting in only two remaining DOFs; see Figure 9.14. Continuing further, if three features are observed, then for the P3P problem, zero DOFs remain (except for the case in which collinear features are chosen on the body). It may seem that the problem is completely solved; however, zero DOFs allows for multiple solutions. (They are isolated points in the space of solutions.) The P3P problem corresponds to trying to place a given triangle into a pyramid formed by rays so that each triangle vertex touches a different ray. This can be generally accomplished in four ways, which are hard to visualize. Imagine trying to slice a tall, thin pyramid (simplex) made of cheese so that four different slices have the exact same triangular size and shape. The cases of P4P and P5P also result in ambiguous solutions. Finally, in the case of P6P, unique solutions are always obtained if no four features are coplanar. All of the mathematical details are worked out in [363].

The PnP problem has been described in the ideal case of having perfect coordinate assignments to the feature points on the body and the perfect observation of those through the imaging process. In practice, small errors are made due to factors such as sensor noise, image quantization, and manufacturing tolerances. This results in ambiguities and errors in the estimated pose, which could deviate substantially from the correct answer [287]. Therefore, many more features may be used in practice to improve accuracy. Furthermore, a calibration procedure, such as *bundle adjustment* [113, 286, 333], may be applied before the device is used so that the feature point locations can be more accurately assigned before pose estimation is performed. Robustness may be improved by employing RANSAC [78].

Camera-Based Implementation

The visibility problem may be solved using a camera in two general ways, as indicated in Figure 9.15. Consider the *camera frame*, which is analogous to the eye frame from Figure 3.13 in Chapter 3. A *world-fixed camera* is usually stationary, meaning that the camera frame does not move relative to the world. A single transformation may be used to convert an object pose as estimated from the camera frame into a convenient world frame. For example, in the case of the Oculus Rift headset, the head pose could be converted to a world frame in which the $-z$ direction is pointing at the camera, y is "up," and the position is in the center of the camera's tracking region or a suitable default based on the user's initial head position. For an *object-fixed camera*, the estimated pose, derived from features that remain fixed in the world, is the transformation from the camera frame to the world frame. This case would be obtained, for example, if QR codes were placed on the walls.

As in the case of an IMU, calibration is important for improving sensing accuracy. The following homogeneous transformation matrix can be applied to the image produced by a camera:

Figure 9.14 Each feature that is visible eliminates two DOFs. On the left, a single feature is visible, and the resulting rigid body has only four DOFs remaining. On the right, two features are visible, resulting in only two DOFs. This can be visualized as follows. The edge that touches both segments can be moved back and forth while preserving its length if some rotation is also applied. Rotation about an axis common to the edge provides the second DOF.

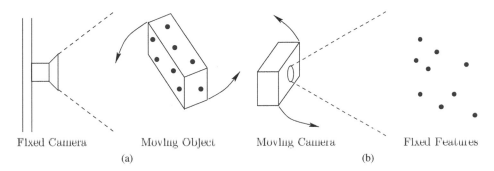

Figure 9.15 Two cases for camera placement. (a) A *world-fixed camera* is stationary, and the motions of objects relative to it are estimated using features on the objects. (b) An *object-fixed camera* is frequently under motion and features are ideally fixed to the world coordinate frame.

$$\begin{bmatrix} \alpha_x & \gamma & u_0 \\ 0 & \alpha_y & v_0 \\ 0 & 0 & 1 \end{bmatrix}. \tag{9.23}$$

The five variables appearing in the matrix are called *intrinsic parameters* of the camera. The α_x and α_y parameters handle scaling, γ handles shearing, and u_0 and v_0 handle offset of the optical axis. These parameters are typically estimated by taking images of an object for which all dimensions and distances have been carefully measured, and performing least-squares estimation to select the parameters that reduce the sum-of-squares error (as described in Section 9.1). For a wide-angle lens, further calibration may be needed to overcome optical distortions (recall Section 7.3).

Now suppose that a feature has been observed in the image, perhaps using some form of *blob detection* to extract the pixels that correspond to it from the rest of the image [286, 324]. This is easiest for a global shutter camera because all pixels will correspond to the same instant of time. In the case of a rolling shutter, the image may need to be transformed to undo the effects of motion (recall Figure 4.33). The location of the observed feature is calculated as a statistic of the blob pixel locations. Most commonly, the average over all blob pixels is used, resulting in non-integer image coordinates. Many issues affect performance: (1) quantization errors arise due to image coordinates for each blob pixel being integers; (2) if the feature does not cover enough pixels, then the quantization errors are worse; (3) changes in lighting conditions may make it difficult to extract the feature, especially in the case of natural features; (4) at some angles, two or more features may become close in the image, making it difficult to separate their corresponding blobs; (5) as various features enter

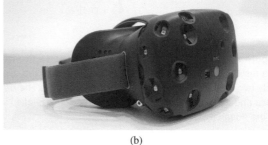

(a)   (b)

Figure 9.16 The laser-based tracking approach used in the HTC Vive headset. (a) A base station contains spinning drums that emit horizontal and vertical sheets of IR light. An array of IR LEDs appears in the upper left, which provide a synchronization flash. (b) Photodiodes in pockets on the front of the headset detect the incident IR light.

or leave the camera view, the resulting estimated pose may jump. Furthermore, errors tend to be larger along the direction of the optical axis, which is a key reason why some headsets have cameras facing in several directions.

Laser-Based Implementation

By designing a special emitter-detector pair, the visibility problem can be accurately solved over great distances. This was accomplished by the *lighthouse tracking* system of the 2016 HTC Vive headset, and the *Minnesota scanner* from 1989 [307]. Figure 9.16 shows the lighthouse tracking hardware for the HTC Vive. The operation of a camera is effectively simulated, as shown in Figure 9.17(a).

If the base station were a camera, then the sweeping vertical stripe would correspond to estimating the row of the pixel that corresponds to the feature; see Figure 9.17(a). Likewise, the sweeping horizontal stripe corresponds to the pixel column. The rotation rate of the spinning drum is known and is analogous to the camera frame rate. The precise timing is recorded as the beam hits each photodiode.

Think about polar coordinates (distance and angle) relative to the base station. Using the angular velocity of the sweep and the relative timing differences, the angle between the features as "observed" from the base station can be easily estimated. Although the angle between features is easily determined, their angles relative to some fixed direction from the base station must be determined. This is accomplished by an array of IR LEDs that are pulsed on simultaneously so that all photodiodes detect the flash (visible in Figure 9.16(a)). This could correspond, for example, to the instant of time at which each beam is at the 0 orientation. Based on the time from the flash until the beam hits a photodiode, and the known angular velocity, the angle of the observed feature is determined. To reduce temporal drift error, the flash may be periodically used during operation.

As in the case of the camera, the distances from the base station to the features are not known, but can be determined by solving the PnP problem. Multiple base stations can be used as well, in a way that is comparable to using multiple cameras or multiple eyes to infer depth. The result is accurate tracking over a large area, as shown in Figure 9.17(b).

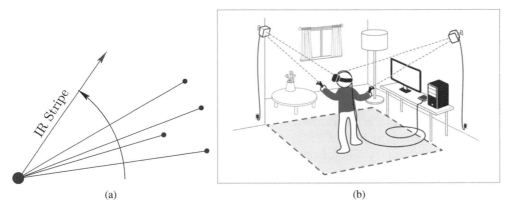

(a)   (b)

Figure 9.17 (a) This is a 2D view of the angular sweep of the IR stripe in the laser-based tracking approach (as in HTC Vive). This could correspond to a top-down view, in which a vertical stripe spins with a yaw rotation about the base. In this case, the angular locations in the horizontal direction are observed, similar to column coordinates of a camera image. This could also correspond to a side view, in which case the vertical stripe spins with a pitch rotation and the angular locations in the vertical direction are observed. As the beam hits the features, which are photodiodes, the direction is known because of the spinning rate and time since the synchronization flash. (b) By putting two base stations on top of poles at the corners of the tracking area, a large region can be accurately tracked for a headset and controllers.

Filtering

As in Section 9.2, outputs from sensors are combined over time by a filtering method to maintain the estimate. In the current setting, the pose can be maintained by combining both visibility information and outputs of an IMU. For the orientation component of the pose, the complementary filter from (9.10) could be used. The camera provides an additional source for detecting orientation drift error. The camera optical axis is a straightforward reference for yaw error estimation detection, which makes it a clear replacement for the magnetometer. If the camera tilt is known, then the camera can also provide accurate tilt error estimation.

The IMU was crucial for obtaining highly accurate orientation tracking because of accurate, high-frequency estimates of angular velocity provided by the gyroscope. If the frame rate for a camera or lighthouse system is very high, then sufficient sensor data may exist for accurate position tracking; however, it is preferable to directly measure derivatives. Unfortunately, IMUs do not measure linear velocity. However, the output of the linear accelerometer could be used as suggested in the beginning of this section. Suppose that the accelerometer estimates the body acceleration as

$$\hat{a}[k] = (\hat{a}_x[k], \hat{a}_y[k], \hat{a}_z[k]) \tag{9.24}$$

in the world frame. (This assumes the gravity component has been subtracted from the accelerometer output.)

By numerical integration, the velocity $\hat{v}[k]$ can be estimated from $\hat{a}[k]$. The position $\hat{p}[k]$ is estimated by integrating the velocity estimate. The updated equations using simple Euler integration are

$$\hat{v}[k] = \hat{a}[k]\Delta t + \hat{v}[k-1],$$
$$\hat{p}[k] = \hat{v}[k]\Delta t + \hat{p}[k-1]. \tag{9.25}$$

Note that each equation actually handles three components, x, y, and z, at the same time. The accuracy of the second equation can be further improved by adding $\frac{1}{2}\hat{a}[k]\Delta t^2$ to the right side.

As stated earlier, double integration of the acceleration leads to rapidly growing position drift error, denoted by $\hat{d}_p[k]$. The error detected from PnP solutions provide an estimate of $\hat{d}_p[k]$, but perhaps at a much lower rate than the IMU produces observations. For example, a camera might take pictures at 60 FPS and the IMU might report accelerations at 1,000 FPS.

The complementary filter from (9.10) can be extended to the case of double integration to obtain

$$p_c[k] = \hat{p}[k] - \alpha_p \hat{d}_p[k]$$
$$v_c[k] = \hat{v}[k] - \alpha_v \hat{d}_p[k]. \tag{9.26}$$

Here, $p_c[k]$ and $v_c[k]$ are the corrected position and velocity, respectively, which are each calculated by a complementary filter. The estimates $\hat{p}[k]$ and $\hat{v}[k]$ are calculated using (9.25). The parameters α_p and α_v control the amount of importance given to the drift error estimate in comparison to IMU updates.

Equation (9.26) is actually equivalent to a *Kalman filter*, which is the optimal filter (providing the most accurate estimates possible) for the case of a linear dynamical system with Gaussian noise, and sensors that also suffer from Gaussian noise. Let ω_d^2 represent the variance of the estimated Gaussian noise in the dynamical system, and let ω_s^2 represent the sensor noise variance. The complementary filter (9.26) is equivalent to the Kalman filter if the parameters are chosen as $\alpha_p = \sqrt{2\omega_d/\omega_s}$ and $\alpha_v = \omega_d/\omega_s$ [121]. A large variety of alternative filtering methods exist; however, the impact of using different filtering methods is usually small relative to calibration, sensor error models, and dynamical system models that are particular to the setup. Furthermore, the performance requirements are mainly *perceptually* based, which could be different than the classical criteria around which filtering methods were designed [170].

Once the filter is running, its pose estimates can be used to aid the PnP problem. The PnP problem can be solved incrementally by perturbing the pose estimated by the filter, using the most recent accelerometer outputs, so that the observed features are perfectly matched. Small adjustments can be made to the pose so that the sum-of-squares error is reduced to an acceptable level. In most cases, this improves reliability when there are so few features visible that the PnP problem has ambiguous solutions. Without determining the pose incrementally, a catastrophic jump to another PnP solution might occur.

9.4 Tracking Attached Bodies

Many tracking problems involve estimating the motion of one body relative to another attached, moving body. For example, an eye rotates inside its socket, which is part of the skull. Although the eye may have six DOFs when treated as a rigid body in space, its position and orientation are sufficiently characterized with two or three parameters once the head pose is given. Other examples include the head relative to the torso, a hand relative to the wrist, and the tip of a finger relative to its middle bone. The entire human body can even be arranged into a tree of attached bodies, based on a skeleton. Furthermore, bodies may be attached in a similar way for other

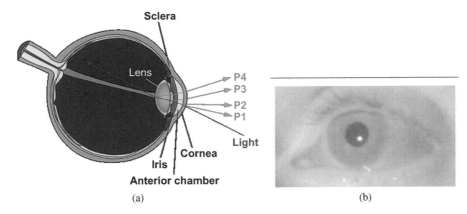

Figure 9.18 (a) The first and sometimes the fourth Purkinje images of an IR light source are used for eye tracking. (b) The first Purkinje image generates a bright reflection as shown.

organisms, such as dogs or monkeys, and machinery, such as robots or cars. In the case of a car, the wheels rotate relative to the body. In all of these cases, the result is a *multibody system*. The mathematical characterization of the poses of bodies relative to each other is called *multibody kinematics*, and the full determination of their velocities and accelerations is called *multibody dynamics*.

Eye Tracking
Eye tracking systems have been used by vision scientists for over a century to study eye movements. Three main uses for VR are: (1) To accomplish foveated rendering, as mentioned in Section 5.4, so that high-resolution rendering need only be performed for the part of the image that lands on the fovea. (2) To study human behavior by recording tracking data so that insights may be gained into VR sickness, attention, and effectiveness of experiences. (3) To render the eye orientations in VR so that social interaction may be improved by offering eye-contact and indicating someone's focus of attention; see Section 10.4.

Three general categories of eye-tracking approaches have been developed [65, 347]. The first is *electrooculography* (*EOG*), which obtains measurements from several electrodes placed on the facial skin around each eye. The recorded potentials correspond to eye muscle activity, from which the eye orientation relative to the head is determined through filtering. The second approach uses a contact lens, which contains a tiny magnetic coil that causes a potential change in a surrounding electromagnetic field. The third approach is called *video oculography* (*VOG*), which shines IR light onto the eye and senses its *corneal reflection* using a camera or photodiodes. The reflection is based on *Purkinje images*, as shown in Figure 9.18. Because of its low cost and minimal invasiveness, this has been the most commonly used method. The contact lens approach is the most accurate; however, it is also the most uncomfortable.

Forward Kinematics
Suppose that an eye tracking method has estimated the eye orientation relative to the human skull and it needs to be placed accordingly in the virtual world. This transformation must involve a combination of the head and eye transforms. For a

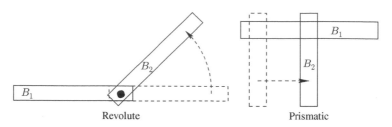

Figure 9.19 Two types of 2D joints: a revolute joint allows one link to rotate with respect to the other, and a prismatic joint allows one link to translate with respect to the other.

more complicated problem, consider placing the right index finger in the world by using the pose of the torso along with all of the angles formed between bones at each joint. To understand how these and other related problems are solved, it is helpful to first consider 2D examples.

Each body of a multibody system is called a *link*, and a pair of bodies are attached at a *joint*, which allows one or more DOFs of motion between them. Figure 9.19 shows two common ways that one planar body might move while attached to another. The *revolute joint* is most common and characterizes the motion allowed by a human elbow.

Consider defining a chain of m links, B_1 to B_m, and determining the location of a point on the last link. The points on each link are defined using coordinates of its own *body frame*. In this frame, the body appears as shown for B_{i-1} in Figure 9.20, with the origin at the joint that connects B_{i-1} to B_{i-2} and the x_{i-1} axis pointing through the joint that connects B_{i-1} to B_i. To move the points on B_i to the proper location in the body frame of B_{i-1}, the homogeneous transform

$$T_i = \begin{pmatrix} \cos\theta_i & -\sin\theta_i & a_{i-1} \\ \sin\theta_i & \cos\theta_i & 0 \\ 0 & 0 & 1 \end{pmatrix} \tag{9.27}$$

is applied. This rotates B_i by θ_i and then translates it along the x-axis by a_{i-1}. For a revolute joint, θ_i is a variable and a_{i-1} is a constant. For a prismatic joint, θ_i is constant and a_{i-1} is a variable.

Points on B_i are moved into the body frame for B_1 by applying the product $T_2 \cdots T_i$. A three-link example is shown in Figure 9.21. To move the first link B_1 into the world frame, a general 2D homogeneous transform can be applied:

$$T_1 = \begin{pmatrix} \cos\theta_1 & -\sin\theta_1 & x_t \\ \sin\theta_1 & \cos\theta_1 & y_t \\ 0 & 0 & 1 \end{pmatrix} . \tag{9.28}$$

This transform is simply added to the matrix product to move each B_i by applying $T_1 T_2 \cdots T_i$.

A chain of 3D links is handled in the same way conceptually, but the algebra becomes more complicated. See Section 3.3 of [166] for more details. Figure 9.22 shows six different kinds of joints that are obtained by allowing a pair of 3D links to slide against each other. Each link is assigned a convenient coordinate frame based

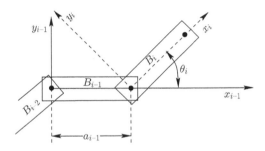

Figure 9.20 The body frame of each B_i, for $1 < i < m$, is based on the joints that connect B_i to B_{i-1} and B_{i+1}.

on the joints. Each homogeneous transform T_i contains a mixture of constants and variables in which the variables correspond to the freedom allowed by the joint. The most common assignment scheme is called *Denavit–Hartenberg parameters* [112]. In some settings, it might be preferable to replace each T_i by a parameterized quaternion that rotates the body, followed by a simple addition that translates the body.

A tree of links may also be considered; a common example is a human torso serving as the root, with a head, two arms, and two legs being chains that extend from it. The human hand is another example. Coordinate frames in this case are often assigned using *Kleinfinger–Khalil parameters* [151].

Constraints and Inverse Kinematics

Recall the PnP problem from Section 9.3, which involved calculating the pose of a body based on some observed constraints. A similar problem is to determine the joint parameters for a chain of bodies by considering the constraints on the bodies. A common example is to calculate the poses of the arm links by using only the pose of the hand. This is generally called the *inverse kinematics problem* (see [8] and Section 4.4 of [166]). As in the case of PnP, the number of solutions may be infinite, finite, one, or zero. Some 2D examples are shown in Figure 9.23. Generally, if the last link is constrained, then the freedom of motion for the intermediate links increases as the number of links increases. The *Chebychev–Grübler–Kutzbach criterion* gives the number of DOFs, assuming the links are not in some special, singular configurations [9]. A common problem in animating video game characters is to maintain a kinematic constraint, such as the hand grasping a doorknob, even though the torso or door is moving. In this case, *iterative optimization* is often applied to perturb each joint parameter until the error is sufficiently reduced. The error would measure the distance between the hand and the doorknob in our example.

Motion Capture Systems

Tracking systems for attached bodies use kinematic constraints to improve their accuracy. The most common application is tracking the human body, for which the skeleton is well understood in terms of links and joints [375]. Such motion capture systems have been an important technology for the movie industry as the motions

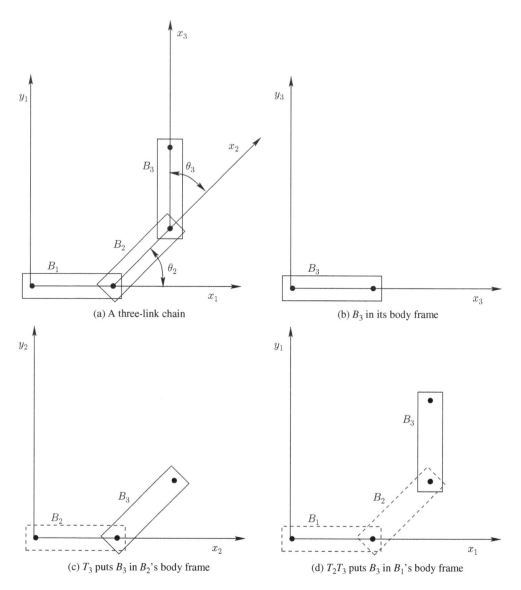

(a) A three-link chain

(b) B_3 in its body frame

(c) T_3 puts B_3 in B_2's body frame

(d) $T_2 T_3$ puts B_3 in B_1's body frame

Figure 9.21 Applying the transformation $T_2 T_3$ to the model of B_3. If T_1 is the identity matrix, then this yields the location in the virtual world of points in B_3.

of real actors are brought into a virtual world for animation. Figure 9.24 illustrates the operation. Features of the same kind as introduced in Section 9.3 are placed over the body and are visible to cameras mounted around the capture studio. The same options exist for visibility, with the most common approach over the past decades being to use cameras with surrounding IR LEDs and placing retroreflective markers on the actor.

To obtain a unique pose for each body part, it might seem that six features are needed (recall P6P from Section 9.3); however, many fewer are sufficient because of kinematic constraints. Additional features may nevertheless be used if the goal is to also capture skin motion as it moves along the skeleton. This is especially important

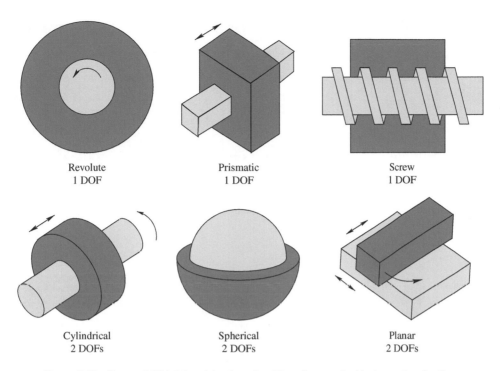

Figure 9.22 Types of 3D joints arising from the 2D surface contact between two bodies.

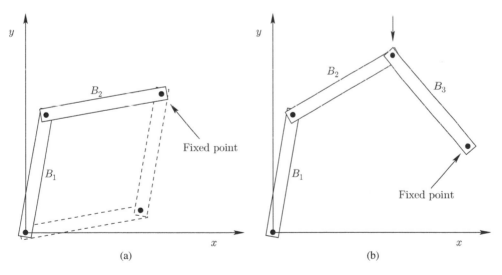

Figure 9.23 (a) The orientations of both links can be inferred from the position of the fixed point; however, there is a second solution if the angles are not restricted. (b) In the case of three links, a one-dimensional family of solutions exists when the end is fixed. This can be visualized by pushing down on the top joint, which would cause B_1 to rotate counterclockwise. This is equivalent to the classical *four-bar mechanism*, which was used to drive the wheels of a steam engine. (The fourth "link" is simply the fixed background).

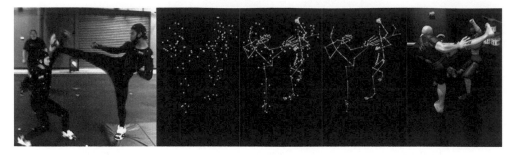

Figure 9.24 With a *motion capture* (*MOCAP*) system, artificial features are placed around the body of a human actor. The motions are extracted and matched to a kinematic model. Each rigid body in the model has an associated geometric model that is rendered to produce the final animated character.

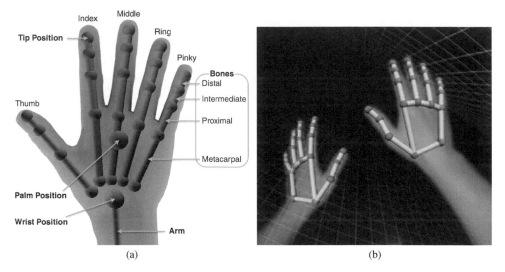

Figure 9.25 (a) The hand model used by Leap Motion tracking. (b) The tracked model superimposed in an image of the actual hands.

for facial movement. Many other MOCAP technologies have been developed. For example, a system developed by Noitom captures human body movement solely by placing IMUs on the body. Some systems capture motion by cameras alone, as in the case of Leap Motion (see Figure 9.25) for hand tracking, and systems by Microsoft and 8i for full-body tracking by extracting contours against a green screen. One challenge is to make highly accurate and reliable systems for low cost and installation effort.

9.5 3D Scanning of Environments

Up until now, this chapter has described how to use sensors to track the motions of one or more rigid bodies. By contrast, this section describes how sensors are used to build geometric models of rigid bodies. These could be movable or stationary

(a)   (b)

Figure 9.26 (a) The Afinia ES360 scanner, which produces a 3D model of an object while it spins on a turntable. (b) The Focus3D X 330 Laser Scanner, from FARO Technologies, is an outward-facing scanner for building accurate 3D models of large environments; it includes a GPS receiver to help fuse individual scans into a coherent map.

models, as introduced in Section 3.1. A movable model typically corresponds to an object that is being manipulated by the user, such as a sword, hammer, or coffee cup. These models are often built from a *3D scanner*, which images the object from many viewpoints in a controlled way. The object may be placed on a surface that is surrounded by cameras and other sensors, or it could be placed on a turntable that rotates the object so that it is observed from numerous viewpoints. Alternatively, the sensors may move around while the object remains stationary; see Figure 9.26(a).

SLAM

A 3D scanner is useful for smaller objects, with surrounding sensors facing inward. For larger objects and stationary models, the sensors are usually inside facing out; see Figure 9.26(b). A common example of a stationary model is the inside of a building. Scanning such models is becoming increasingly important for surveying, real estate, and forensics. This is also the classical robotics problem of *mapping*, in which a robot carrying sensors builds a 2D or 3D representation of its world for the purposes of navigation and collision avoidance. Robots usually need to estimate their locations based on sensors, which is called the *localization* problem. Robot localization and tracking bodies for VR are fundamentally the same problems, with the main distinction being that known motion commands are given to robots, but the corresponding human intent is not directly given. Robots often need to solve mapping and localization problems at the same time, which results in the *simultaneous localization and mapping* problem; the acronym *SLAM* is widely used. Due to the similarity of localization, mapping, and VR tracking problems, deep connections exist between robotics and VR. Therefore, many mathematical models, algorithms, and sensing technologies overlap.

Consider the possible uses of a large, stationary model for VR. It could be captured to provide a virtual world in which the user is placed at the current time or a later time. Image data could be combined with the 3D coordinates of the model, to produce a photorealistic model (recall Figure 2.14 from Section 2.2). This is achieved by texture mapping image patches onto the triangles of the model.

Live Capture of the Current Location

Rather than capturing a world in which to transport the user, sensors could alternatively be used to capture the physical world where the user is currently experiencing VR. This allows obstacles in the matched zone to be rendered in the virtual world, which might be useful for safety or to improve interactivity. For safety, the boundaries of the matched zone could be rendered to indicate that the user is about to reach the limit. Hazards such as a hot cup of coffee or a pet walking across the matched zone could be indicated. Interactivity can be improved by bringing fixed objects from the physical world into the virtual world. For example, if the user is sitting in front of a desk, then the desk can be drawn in the virtual world. If she touches the virtual desk, she will feel the real desk pushing back. This is a relatively easy way to provide touch feedback in VR.

Are Panoramas Sufficient?

Before embarking on the process of creating a large, detailed map of a surrounding 3D world, it is important to consider whether it is necessary. As mentioned in Section 7.5, panoramic images and videos are becoming increasingly simple to capture. In some applications, it might be sufficient to build an experience in which the user is transported between panoramas that were captured from many locations that are close to each other.

The Main Ingredients

Building a 3D model from sensor data involves three important steps:

1. Extracting a 3D *point cloud* from a fixed location.
2. Combining point clouds from multiple locations.
3. Converting a point cloud into a mesh of triangles.

For the first step, a sensor is placed at a fixed position and orientation while 3D points are extracted. This could be accomplished in a number of ways. In theory, any of the depth cues from Section 6.1 can be applied to camera images to extract 3D points. Variations in focus, texture, and shading are commonly used in computer vision as monocular cues. If two cameras are facing the same scene and their relative positions and orientations are known, then binocular cues are used to determine depth. By identifying the same natural feature in both images, the corresponding visibility rays from each image are intersected to identify a point in space; see Figure 9.27. As in Section 9.3, the choice between natural and artificial features exists. A single camera and an IR projector or laser scanner may be used in combination so

Figure 9.27 By using two cameras, *stereo vision* enables the location of a feature in the 3D world to be determined by intersecting the corresponding visibility ray from each camera. To accomplish this, the camera calibration parameters and relative poses must be known. Similarly, one camera could be replaced by a laser that illuminates the feature so that it is visible to the remaining camera. In either case, the principle is to intersect two visibility rays to obtain the result.

that depth is extracted by identifying where the lit point appears in the image. This is the basis of the Microsoft Kinect sensor (recall Figure 2.10 from Section 2.1). The resulting collection of 3D points is often called a *point cloud*.

In the second step, the problem is to merge scans from multiple locations. If the relative position and orientation of the scanner between scans is known, then the problem is solved. In the case of the object scanner shown in Figure 9.26(a), this was achieved by rotating the object on a turntable so that the position remains fixed and the orientation is precisely known for each scan. Suppose the sensor is instead carried by a robot, such as a drone. The robot usually maintains its own estimate of its pose for purposes of collision avoidance and determining whether its task is achieved. This is also useful for determining the pose that corresponds to the time at which the scan was performed. Typically, the pose estimates are not accurate enough, which leads to an optimization problem in which the estimated pose is varied until the data between overlapping scans nicely aligns. The *estimation-maximization (EM) algorithm* is typically used in this case, which incrementally adjusts the pose in a way that yields the maximum likelihood explanation of the data in a statistical sense. If the sensor is carried by a human, then extra sensors may be included with the scanning device, as in the case of GPS for the scanner in Figure 9.26(b); otherwise, the problem of fusing data from multiple scans could become too difficult.

In the third stage, a large point cloud has been obtained and the problem is to generate a clean geometric model. Many difficulties exist. The point density may vary greatly, especially where two or more overlapping scans were made. In this case, some points may be discarded. Another problem is that outliers may exist, which correspond to isolated points that are far from their correct location. Methods are needed to detect and reject outliers. Yet another problem is that large holes or gaps in the data may exist. Once the data has been sufficiently cleaned, surfaces are typically fit to the data, from which triangular meshes are formed. Each of these problems is a research area in itself. To gain some familiarity, consider experimenting with the open-source *Point Cloud Library*, which was developed to handle the operations that arise in the second and third stages. Once a triangular mesh is obtained, texture mapping may also be performed if image data is also available. One of the greatest challenges for VR is that the resulting models often contain numerous flaws, which are much more noticeable in VR than on a computer screen.

Further Reading

In addition to academic papers such as [83], some of the most useful coverage for IMU calibration appears in corporate white papers, such as [249]. For magnetometer calibration, see [93, 158, 168, 337]. Oculus Rift 3D orientation tracking is covered in [167, 169, 168, 171]. To fully understand vision-based tracking methods, see vision books [113, 194, 324]. Many approaches to PnP appear in research literature, such as [363, 376]. An excellent but older survey of tracking methods for VR/AR is [353]. One of the most highly cited works is [144]. See [240] for integration of IMU and visual data for tracking.

Eye tracking is surveyed in [65, 347]. Human body tracking is covered in [377]. To fully understand kinematic constraints and solutions to inverse kiematics problems, see [8, 10, 48]. SLAM from a robotics perspective is thoroughly presented in [329]. A survey of SLAM based on computer vision appears in [87]. Filtering or sensor fusion in the larger context can be more generally characterized in terms of *information spaces* (see chapter 11 of [166]).

CHAPTER TEN

Interaction

How should users interact with the virtual world? How should they move about? How can they grab and place objects? How should they interact with representations of each other? How should they interact with files or the Internet? The following insight suggests many possible interfaces.

Universal Simulation Principle:
Any interaction mechanism from the real world can be simulated in VR.

For example, the user might open a door by turning a knob and pulling. As another example, the user operates a virtual aircraft by sitting in a mock-up cockpit (as was shown in Figure 1.16). One could even simulate putting on a VR headset, leading to an experience that is comparable to a dream within a dream!

In spite of the universal simulation principle, recall from Section 1.1 that the goal is not necessarily realism. It is often preferable to make the interaction *better than reality*. Therefore, this chapter introduces *interaction mechanisms* that may not have a counterpart in the physical world.

Section 10.1 introduces general motor learning and control concepts. The most important concept is *remapping*, in which a motion in the real world may be mapped into a substantially different motion in the virtual world. This enables many powerful interaction mechanisms. The task is to develop ones that are easy to learn, easy to use, effective for the task, and provide a comfortable user experience. Section 10.2 discusses how the user may move himself in the virtual world, while remaining fixed in the real world. Section 10.3 presents ways in which the user may interact with other objects in the virtual world. Section 10.4 discusses social interaction mechanisms, which allow users to interact directly with each other. Section 10.5 briefly considers some additional interaction mechanisms, such as editing text, designing 3D structures, and Web browsing.

10.1 Motor Programs and Remapping

Motor Programs
Throughout our lives, we develop fine motor skills to accomplish many specific tasks, such as writing text, tying shoelaces, throwing a ball, and riding a bicycle. These are often called *motor programs* and are learned through repetitive trials, with

gradual improvements in precision and ease as the amount of practice increases [199]. Eventually, we produce the motions without even having to pay attention to them. For example, most people can drive a car without paying attention to particular operations of the steering wheel, brakes, and accelerator.

In the same way, most of us have learned how to use interfaces to computers, such as keyboards, mice, and game controllers. Some devices are easier to learn than others. For example, a mouse does not take long, but typing quickly on a keyboard takes years to master. What makes one skill harder to learn than another? This is not always easy to predict, as illustrated by the *backwards brain bicycle*, which was designed by Destin Sandlin by reversing the steering operation so that turning the handlebars left turns the front wheel to the right [21]. It took Sandlin six months learn how to ride it, and at the end he was unable to ride an ordinary bicycle. Thus, he unlearned how to ride a normal bicycle at the expense of learning the new one.

Design Considerations

In the development of interaction mechanisms for VR, the main considerations are:

1. Effectiveness for the task in terms of achieving the required speed, accuracy, and motion range, if applicable.
2. Difficulty of learning the new motor programs; ideally, the user should not be expected to spend many months mastering a new mechanism.
3. Ease of use in terms of cognitive load; in other words, the interaction mechanism should require little or no focused attention after some practice.
4. Overall comfort during use over extended periods; the user should not develop muscle fatigue, unless the task is to get some physical exercise.

To design and evaluate new interaction mechanisms, it is helpful to start by understanding the physiology and psychology of acquiring the motor skills and programs. Chapters 5 and 6 covered these for visual perception, which is the process of converting sensory *input* into a perceptual experience. We now consider the corresponding parts for generating *output* in the form of body motions in the physical world. In this case, the brain sends motor signals to the muscles, causing them to move, while at the same time incorporating sensory feedback by utilizing the perceptual processes.

The Neurophysiology of Movement

First consider the neural hardware involved in learning, control, and execution of voluntary movements. As shown in Figure 10.1(a), some parts of the cerebral cortex are devoted to motion. The *primary motor cortex* is the main source of neural signals that control movement, whereas the *premotor cortex* and *supplementary motor area* appear to be involved in the preparation and planning of movement. Many more parts are involved in motion and communicate through neural signals, as shown in Figure 10.1(b). The most interesting part is the *cerebellum*, meaning "little brain," which is located at the back of the skull. It seems to be a special processing unit that is mostly devoted to motion, but is also involved in functions such as attention and language. Damage to the cerebellum has been widely seen to affect fine motor control and learning of new motor programs. It has been estimated to contain around 101

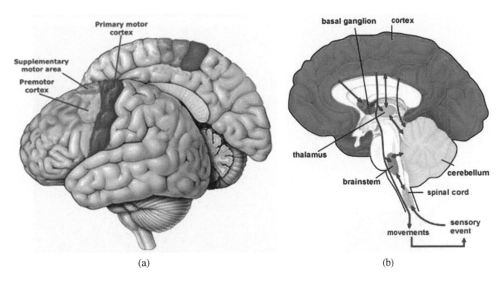

Figure 10.1 (a) Part of the cerebral cortex is devoted to motion. (b) Many other parts interact with the cortex to produce and execute motions, including the thalamus, spinal cord, basal ganglion, brain stem, and cerebellum.

billion neurons [7], far more than the entire cerebral cortex, which contains around 20 billion. Even though the cerebellum is much smaller, a large number is achieved through smaller, densely packed cells. In addition to coordinating fine movements, it appears to be the storage center for motor programs.

One of the most relevant uses of the cerebellum for VR is in learning *sensorimotor relationships*, which become encoded into a motor program. All body motions involve some kind of sensory *feedback*. The most common example is *hand-eye coordination*; however, even if you move your arms with your eyes closed, proprioception provides information in the form of efference copies of the motor signals. Developing a tight connection between motor control signals and sensory and perceptual signals is crucial to many tasks. This is also widely known in engineered systems, in which sensor-feedback and motor control are combined in applications such as robotics and aircraft stabilization; the subject that deals with this is called *control systems*. It is well-known that a *closed-loop* system is preferred in which sensor information provides feedback during execution, as opposed to *open-loop*, which specifies the motor signals as a function of time.

One of the most important factors is how long it takes to learn a motor program. As usual, there is great variation across humans. A key concept is *neuroplasticity*, which is the potential of the brain to reorganize its neural structures and form new pathways to adapt to new stimuli. Toddlers have a high level of neuroplasticity, which becomes greatly reduced over time through the process of *synaptic pruning*. This causes healthy adults to have about half as many synapses per neuron than a child of age two or three [100]. Unfortunately, the result is that adults have a harder time acquiring new skills such as learning a new language or learning how to use a complicated interface. In addition to the reduction of neuroplasticity with age, it also greatly varies among people of the same age.

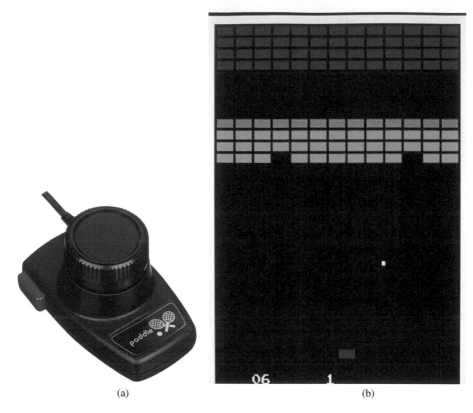

(a)   (b)

Figure 10.2 (a) Atari 2600 Paddle controller. (b) The Atari Breakout game, in which the bottom line segment is a virtual paddle that allows the ball to bounce to the top and eliminate bricks upon contacts.

Learning Motor Programs

Now consider learning a motor program for a computer interface. A simple, classic example is the video game *Breakout*, which was developed by Atari in 1976. The player turns a knob, shown in Figure 10.2. This causes a line segment on the bottom of the screen to move horizontally. The Paddle contains a potentiometer that with calibration allows the knob orientation to be reliably estimated. The player sees the line segment positioned on the bottom of the screen and quickly associates the knob orientations. The learning process therefore involves taking information from visual perception and the proprioception signals from turning the knob and determining the sensorimotor relationships. Skilled players could quickly turn the knob so that they could move the line segment much more quickly than one could move a small tray back and forth in the real world. Thus, we already have an example where the virtual world version allows better performance than in reality.

In the Breakout example, a one-dimensional *mapping* was learned between the knob orientation and the line segment position. Many alternative control schemes could be developed; however, they are likely to be more frustrating. If you find an emulator to try Breakout, it will most likely involve using keys on a keyboard to move the segment. In this case, the amount of time that a key is held down corresponds to the segment displacement. The segment velocity is set by the program, rather than the user. A reasonable alternative using modern hardware might be to

—— 248 ——

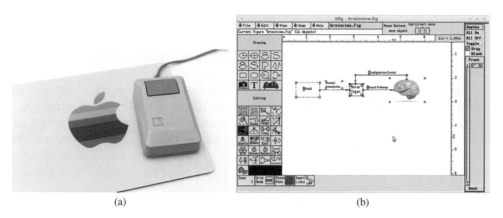

Figure 10.3 (a) The Apple Macintosh mouse. (b) As a mouse moves across the table, the virtual finger on the screen moves correspondingly but is rotated by 90° and travels over longer distances.

move a finger back and forth over a touch screen while the segment appears directly above it. The finger would not be constrained enough due to extra DOFs and the rapid back-and-forth motions of the finger may lead to unnecessary fatigue, especially if the screen is large. Furthermore, there are conflicting goals in positioning the screen: Making it as visible as possible versus making it comfortable for rapid hand movement over a long period of time. In the case of the Paddle, the motion is accomplished by the fingers, which have high dexterity, while the forearm moves much less. The mapping provides an association between body movement and virtual object placement that achieves high accuracy, fast placement, and long-term comfort.

Figure 10.3 shows a more familiar example, which is the computer mouse. As the mouse is pushed around on a table, encoders determine the position, which is converted into a pointer position on the screen. The sensorimotor mapping seems a bit more complex than in the Breakout example. Young children seem to immediately learn how to use the mouse, whereas older adults require some practice. The 2D position of the mouse is mapped to a 2D position on the screen, with two fundamental distortions: (1) The screen is rotated 90 degrees in comparison to the table (horizontal to vertical motion. (2) The motion is scaled so that small physical motions produce larger screen motions. The advantages of the original Xerox Alto mouse were scientifically argued in [39] in terms of human skill learning and *Fitts' law* [79, 195], which mathematically relates pointing task difficulty to the time required to reach targets.

For a final example, suppose that by pressing a key, the letter "h" is instantly placed on the screen in a familiar font. Our visual perception system recognizes the "h" as being equivalent to the version on paper. Thus, typing the key results in the perception of "h." This is quite a comfortable, fast, and powerful operation. The amount of learning required seems justified by the value of the output.

Motor Programs for VR

The examples given so far already seem closely related to VR. A perceptual experience is controlled by body movement that is sensed through a hardware device.

Using the universal simulation principle, any of these and more could be brought into a VR system. The physical interaction part might be identical (you could really be holding an Atari Paddle), or it could be simulated through another controller. Think about possible designs.

Using the tracking methods of Chapter 9, the position and orientation of body parts could be reliably estimated and brought into VR. For the case of head tracking, it is essential to accurately maintain the viewpoint with high accuracy and zero effective latency; otherwise, the VR experience is significantly degraded. This is essential because the perception of stationarity must be maintained for believability and comfort. The motion of the sense organ must be matched by a tracking system.

Remapping

For the motions of other body parts, this perfect matching is not critical. Our neural systems can instead learn associations that are preferable in terms of comfort, in the same way as the Atari Paddle, mouse, and keyboard work in the real world. Thus, we want to do *remapping*, which involves learning a sensorimotor mapping that produces different results in a virtual world than one would expect from the real world. The keyboard example above is one of the most common examples of remapping. The process of pushing a pencil across paper to produce a letter has been replaced by pressing a key. The term remapping is even used with keyboards to mean the assignment of one or more keys to another key.

Remapping is natural for VR. For example, rather than reaching out to grab a virtual door knob, one could press a button to open the door. For a simpler case, consider holding a controller for which the pose is tracked through. A scaling parameter could be set so that one centimeter of hand displacement in the real world corresponds to two centimeters of displacement in the virtual world. This is similar to the scaling parameter for the mouse. Section 10.2 covers the remapping from natural walking in the real world to achieving the equivalent in a virtual world by using a controller. Section 10.3 covers object interaction methods, which are again achieved by remappings. You can expect to see many new remapping methods for VR in the coming years.

10.2 Locomotion

Suppose that the virtual world covers a much larger area than the part of the real world that is tracked. In other words, the matched zone is small relative to the virtual world. In this case, some form of interaction mechanism is needed to move the user in the virtual world while she remains fixed within the tracked area in the real world. An interaction mechanism that moves the user in this way is called *locomotion*. It is as if the user is riding in a virtual vehicle that is steered through the virtual world.

Figure 10.4 shows a spectrum of common locomotion scenarios. At the left, the user walks around in an open space while wearing a headset. No locomotion is needed unless the virtual world is larger than the open space. This case involves no mismatch between real and virtual motions.

The two center cases correspond to a seated user wearing a headset. In these cases, an interaction mechanism is used to change the position of the matched zone in the

All matched motions	LOCOMOTION SPECTRUM		All remapped motion
Real walking with headset	Seated in swivel chair with headset	Seated in fixed chair with headset Yaw and translation handled by controller	Seated in fixed chair and viewing a screen Entire lookat handle by controller
HTC Vive CAVE system	Gear VR Google Daydream Oculus Rift		FPS game on screen Nintendo Virtual Boy

Figure 10.4 Moving from left to right, the amount of viewpoint mismatch between real and virtual motions increases.

virtual world. If the user is seated in a swivel chair, then he could change the direction he is facing (yaw orientation) by rotating the chair. This can be considered as orienting the user's torso in the virtual world. If the user is seated in a fixed chair, then the virtual torso orientation is typically changed using a controller, which results in more mismatch. The limiting case is on the right of Figure 10.4, in which there is not even head tracking. If the user is facing a screen, as in the case of a first-person shooter game on a screen, then a game controller is used to change the position and orientation of the user in the virtual world. This is the largest amount of mismatch because all changes in viewpoint are generated by the controller.

Redirected Walking

If the user is tracked through a very large space, such as a square region of at least 30 meters on each side, then it is possible to make her think she is walking in straight lines for kilometers while she is in fact walking in circles. This technique is called *redirected walking* [266]. Walking along a straight line over long distances without visual cues is virtually impossible for humans (and robots!) because in the real world it is impossible to achieve perfect symmetry. One direction will tend to dominate through an imbalance in motor strength and sensory signals, causing people to travel in circles.

Imagine a VR experience in which a virtual city contains long, straight streets. As the user walks down the street, the yaw direction of the viewpoint can be gradually varied. This represents a small amount of mismatch between the real and virtual worlds, and it causes the user to walk along circular arcs. The main trouble with this technique is that the user has free will and might decide to walk to the edge of the matched zone in the real world, even if he cannot directly perceive it. In this case, an unfortunate, disruptive warning might appear, suggesting that he must rotate to reset the yaw orientation.

Locomotion Implementation

Now consider the middle cases from Figure 10.4 of sitting down and wearing a headset. Locomotion can then be simply achieved by moving the viewpoint with a controller. It is helpful to think of the matched zone as a controllable cart that moves across the ground of the virtual environment; see Figure 10.5. First consider the simple case in which the ground is a horizontal plane. Let T_{track} denote the homogeneous transform that represents the tracked position and orientation of the

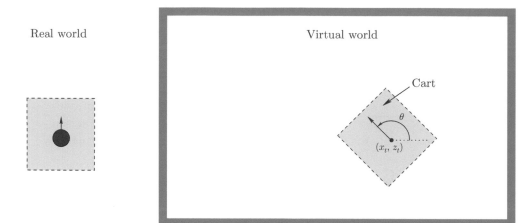

Figure 10.5 Locomotion along a horizontal terrain can be modeled as steering a cart through the virtual world. A top-down view is shown. The yellow region is the matched zone (recall Figure 2.15), in which the user's viewpoint is tracked. The values of x_t, z_t, and θ are changed by using a controller.

cyclopean (center) eye in the physical world. The methods described in Section 9.3 could be used to provide T_{track} for the current time.

The position and orientation of the cart is determined by a controller. The homogeneous matrix

$$T_{cart} = \begin{bmatrix} \cos\theta & 0 & \sin\theta & x_t \\ 0 & 1 & 0 & 0 \\ -\sin\theta & 0 & \cos\theta & z_t \\ 0 & 0 & 0 & 1 \end{bmatrix} \tag{10.1}$$

encodes the position (x_t, z_t) and orientation θ of the cart (as a yaw rotation, borrowed from (3.18)). The height is set at $y_t = 0$ in (10.1) so that it does not change the height determined by tracking or other systems. (Recall from Section 9.2 that the height might be set artificially if the user is sitting in the real world, but standing in the virtual world.)

The eye transform is obtained by chaining T_{track} and T_{cart} to obtain

$$T_{eye} = (T_{track} T_{cart})^{-1} = T_{cart}^{-1} T_{track}^{-1}. \tag{10.2}$$

Recall from Section 3.4 that the eye transform is the *inverse* of the transform that places the geometric models. Therefore, (10.2) corresponds to changing the perspective due to the cart, followed by the perspective of the tracked head on the cart.

To move the viewpoint for a fixed direction θ, the x_t and z_t components are obtained by integrating a differential equation:

$$\begin{aligned} \dot{x}_t &= s\cos\theta, \\ \dot{z}_t &= s\sin\theta. \end{aligned} \tag{10.3}$$

Integrating (10.3) over a time step Δt, the position update appears as

$$x_t[k + 1] = x_t[k] + \dot{x}_t \Delta t$$
$$z_t[k + 1] = z_t[k] + \dot{z}_t \Delta t. \tag{10.4}$$

The variable s in (10.3) is the forward speed. The average human walking speed is about 1.4 meters per second. The virtual cart can be moved forward by pressing a button or key that sets $s = 1.4$. Another button can be used to assign $s = -1.4$, which would result in backward motion. If no key or button is held down, then $s = 0$, which causes the cart to remain stopped. An alternative control scheme is to use the two buttons to increase or decrease the speed, until some maximum limit is reached. In this case, motion is sustained without holding down a key.

Keys could also be used to provide lateral motion, in addition to forward/backward motion. This is called *strafing* in video games. It should be avoided, if possible, because it causes unnecessary lateral vection.

Issues with Changing Direction

Now consider the orientation θ. To move in a different direction, θ needs to be reassigned. The assignment could be made based on the user's head yaw direction. This becomes convenient and comfortable when the user is sitting in a swivel chair and looking forward. By rotating the swivel chair, the direction can be set. (However, this could become a problem for a wired headset because the cable could wrap around the user.)

In a fixed chair, it may become frustrating to control θ because the comfortable head yaw range is limited to only 60° in each direction (recall Figure 5.21). In this case, buttons can be used to change θ by small increments in clockwise or counterclockwise directions. Unfortunately, changing θ according to constant angular velocity causes yaw vection, which is nauseating to many people. Some users prefer to tap a button to instantly yaw about 10 degrees each time. If the increments are too small, then vection appears again, and if the increments are too large, then users become confused about their orientation.

Another issue is where to locate the center of rotation, as shown in Figure 10.6. What happens when the user moves his head away from the center of the chair in the real world? Should the center of rotation be about the original head center or the new head center? If it is chosen as the original center, then the user will perceive a large translation as θ is changed. However, this would also happen in the real world if the user were leaning over while riding in a cart. If it is chosen as the new head center, then the amount of translation is less, but might not correspond as closely to reality.

For another variation, the car-like motion model (8.30) from Section 8.3.2 could be used so that the viewpoint cannot be rotated without translating. In other words, the avatar would have a minimum turning radius. In general, the viewpoint could be changed by controlling any virtual vehicle model. Figure 1.1 from Chapter 1 showed an example in which the "vehicle" is a bird.

Vection Reduction Strategies

The main problem with locomotion is vection, which leads to VR sickness. Recall from Section 8.4 that six different kinds of vection occur, one for each DOF.

Sitting upright   Learning in the chair

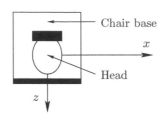
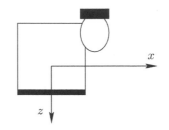

Rotation axis is head center.   Should rotation axis be new head
                                  center or original xz origin?

Figure 10.6 On the right the yaw rotation axis is centered on the head, for a user who is upright in the chair. On the left, the user is leaning over in the chair. Should the rotation axis remain fixed or move with the user?

Furthermore, numerous factors were given that affect the sensitivity to vection. Reducing the intensity of these factors should reduce vection and, hopefully, VR sickness.

Several strategies for reducing vection-based VR sickness are:

1. If the field of view for the optical flow is reduced, then the vection is weakened. A common example is to make a cockpit or car interior that blocks most of the optical flow.
2. If the viewpoint is too close to the ground, then the magnitudes of velocity and acceleration vectors of moving features are higher. This is why you might feel as if you are traveling faster in a small car that is low to the ground in comparison to riding at the same speed in a truck or minivan.
3. Surprisingly, a larger mismatch for a short period of time may be preferable to a smaller mismatch over a long period of time; see Figure 10.7.
4. Having high spatial frequency will yield more features for the human vision system to track. Therefore, if the passing environment is smoother, with less detail, then vection should be reduced. Consider the case of traveling up a staircase. If the steps are clearly visible so that they appear as moving horizontal stripes, then the user may quickly come nauseated by the strong vertical vection signal.
5. Reducing contrast, such as making the world seem hazy or foggy while accelerating, may help.
6. Providing other sensory cues such as blowing wind or moving audio sources might provide stronger evidence of motion. Including vestibular stimulation in the form of a rumble or vibration may also help lower the confidence of the vestibular signal. Even using head tilts to induce changes in virtual-world motion may help because it would cause distracting vestibular signals.
7. If the *world* is supposed to be moving, rather than the user, then making it clear through cues or special instructions can help.
8. Providing specific tasks, such as firing a laser at flying insects, may provide enough distraction from the vestibular conflict. If the user is instead focused entirely on the motion, then she might become sick more quickly.

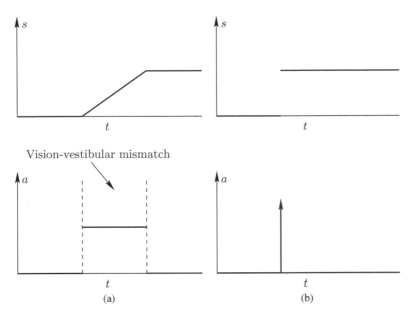

Figure 10.7 (a) Applying constant acceleration over a time interval to bring the stopped avatar up to a speed limit. The upper plot shows the speed over time. The lower plot shows the acceleration. The interval of time over which there is nonzero acceleration corresponds to a mismatch with the vestibular sense. (b) In this case, an acceleration impulse is applied, resulting in the desired speed limit being immediately achieved. In this case, the mismatch occurs over a time interval that is effectively zero length. In practice, the perceived speed changes in a single pair of consecutive frames. Surprisingly, most people consider case (b) to be more comfortable than (a). Perhaps the brain prefers an outlier mismatch for a very short time interval, as supposed to a smaller, sustained mismatch over a longer time interval (such as 5 seconds).

9. The adverse effects of vection may decrease through repeated practice. People who regularly play FPS games in front of a large screen already seem to have reduced sensitivity to vection in VR. Requiring users to practice before sickness is reduced might not be a wise strategy for companies hoping to introduce new products. Imagine trying some new food that makes you nauseated after the first 20 times of eating it, but then gradually becomes more acceptable. Who would keep trying it?

A final suggestion is to avoid locomotion wherever possible! Try to design experiences that do not critically depend on it.

Nonplanar Locomotion

Now consider more complicated locomotion cases. If the user is walking over a terrain, then the y component can be simply increased or decreased to reflect the change in altitude. This may seem realistic, but keep in mind that it increases the amount of mismatch between the real and virtual worlds because vertical vection is combined with forward vection.

In the case of moving through a 3D medium, all six forms of vection from Section 8.4 become enabled. Common settings include a virtual spacecraft, aircraft, or scuba

(a)   (b)

Figure 10.8   (a) An omnidirectional treadmill used in a CAVE system by the US Army for training. (b) A home-brew bicycle riding system connected to a VR headset, developed by Paul Dyan.

diver. Yaw, pitch, and roll vection can be easily generated. For example, imagine flying a virtual spacecraft. By rolling the craft, roll vection can be caused as the stars spin around in a circular pattern. If a developer must make a craft move in these ways, then the prior suggestions for reducing vection intensity should be followed. Furthermore, careful experimentation with human subjects should be performed to determine which forms of vection are worse in the particular application; see Chapter 12. To avoid singularities, for systems in which all 3 DOFs of rotational motion are possible, the virtual vehicle transformations are best maintained in terms of quaternions (recall the issues from Section 3.3).

Adding special effects that move the viewpoint will cause further difficulty with vection. For example, making an avatar jump up and down will cause vertical vection. It is also a bad idea to account for swaying head motions while walking because of the increased mismatch. Imagine a far worse case of looking out through the eyes of an avatar that performs gymnastics. The view of the world may become unbearable during multiple flips.

Specialized Hardware

Many kinds of hardware have been developed to support locomotion. One of the oldest examples is to create an entire cockpit for aircraft flight simulation (recall Figure 1.16). Figure 10.8(a) shows an *omnidirectional treadmill* that enables walking in any direction and over any distance. Exercise machines, such as a stationary bicycle have been connected to VR systems so that the user can pedal and steer to guide herself through a large virtual world, as shown in Figure 10.8(b). Figure 1.1 showed a mechanical platform for virtual flying like a bird.

Teleportation

The locomotion methods covered so far have mainly focused on reproducing experiences that are familiar in the real world, which provide instances of the universal simulation principle. In VR, however, we could also move in ways that are physically implausible. The most common is *teleportation*, which it works like a transporter in the TV series Star Trek. The user is immediately transported to another location.

Figure 10.9 A virtual "laser pointer" that follows a parabolic arc so that a destination for teleportation can be easily specified as a point on the floor.

How is the desired location determined? One simple mechanism is a *virtual laser pointer* (or *3D mouse*), which is accomplished by the user holding a controller that is similar in shape to a laser pointer in the real world. A smart phone could even be used. The user rotates the controller to move a laser dot in the virtual world. This requires performing a ray casting operation (recall from Section 7.1) to find the nearest visible triangle along the ray that corresponds to the laser light.

To select a location where the user would prefer to stand, she could simply point the virtual laser and press a key to be instantly teleported. To make pointing at the floor easier, the beam could actually be a parabolic arc that follows gravity, similar to a stream of water; see Figure 10.9. Places that are not visible can be selected by using a pop-up map, or even performing a text-based search. (Voice commands could be used instead of typing.) One method, called *world in miniature*, involves showing the user a virtual small-scale version of the environment [318]. This is effectively a 3D map.

Wayfinding

The cognitive problem of learning a spatial representation and using it to navigate is called *wayfinding*. This is a higher-level process than the low-level locomotion mechanism, but the two are closely related. One issue with locomotion systems that are not familiar in the real world is that users might not learn the spatial arrangement of the world around them. Would your brain still form place cells for an environment in the real world if you were able to teleport from place to place? We often observe this phenomenon with people who learn to navigate a city using only GPS or taxi services rather than doing their own wayfinding.

The teleportation mechanism reduces vection, and therefore VR sickness; however, it may come at the cost of reduced learning of the spatial arrangement of the environment. When performing teleportation, it is important not to change the yaw orientation of the viewpoint; otherwise, the user may become even more disoriented. He might not understand where he is now positioned and oriented in the virtual world relative to the previous location.

Note that the universal simulation principle can once again be employed to borrow any effective navigation tools from the real world. If virtual buildings and cities are laid out in ways that are common in the real world, then they should be easier to navigate. Signs and landmarks can even be placed into the virtual world to help with navigation. In the real world, signs often tell us the locations of exits, the names of streets, or the boundary of a district. Landmarks such as tall buildings, windmills, or towers provide visual cues that are effective for navigation over long distances. Many of these ideas are discussed in chapter 7 of [31].

10.3 Manipulation

We interact with objects in the real world for many reasons. You might eat a bowl of soup by moving a spoon between the bowl and your mouth. You might pick up a rock and throw it as far as possible. You might put on a pair of pants. These examples and many more fall under the topic of *manipulation*. In the real world, manipulation involves complex sensorimotor relationships, which, through evolution and experience, enable us to manipulate objects under a wide variety of settings. The variation of objects includes differences in size, weight, friction, flexibility, temperature, fragility, and so on. Somehow our bodies can handle that. Getting robots to perform the manipulation in the ways that humans do has been a long and frustrating road, with only limited success [206].

Because of manipulation complexity in the real world, it is an ideal candidate for applying the remapping concepts from Section 10.1 to make manipulation as simple as possible in VR. The virtual world does not have to follow the complicated physics of manipulation. It is instead preferable to make operations such as selecting, grasping, manipulating, carrying, and placing an object as fast and easy as possible. Furthermore, extensive reaching or other forms of muscle strain should be avoided, unless the VR experience is designed to provide exercise.

Avoid Gorilla Arms
One of the most common misconceptions among the public is that the interface used by Tom Cruise in the movie *Minority Report* is desirable; see Figure 10.10. In fact, it quickly leads to the well-known problem of *gorilla arms*, in which the user quickly feels fatigue from extended arms. How long can you hold your arms directly in front of yourself without becoming fatigued?

Selection
One of the simplest ways to select an object in the virtual world is with the virtual laser pointer, which was described in Section 10.2. Several variations may help to improve the selection process. For example, the user might instead hold a virtual flashlight that illuminates potential selections. The field of view of the flashlight

Figure 10.10 Tom Cruise moving windows around on a holographic display in the 2002 movie *Minority Report*. It is a great-looking interaction mechanism for Hollywood, but it is terribly tiring in reality. The user would quickly experience *gorilla arms*.

could be adjustable [84]. A virtual mirror could be placed so that a selection could be made around a corner. Chapter 5 of [31] offers many other suggestions.

With a pointer, the user simply illuminates the object of interest and presses a button. If the goal is to retrieve the object, then it can be immediately placed in the user's virtual hand or inventory. If the goal is to manipulate the object in a standard, repetitive way, then pressing the button could cause a virtual motor program to be executed. This could be used, for example, to turn a doorknob, thereby opening a door. In uses such as this, developers might want to set a limit on the depth of the laser pointer, so that the user must be standing close enough to enable the interaction. It might seem inappropriate, for example, to turn doorknobs from across the room!

If the object is hard to see, then the selection process may be complicated. It might be behind the user's head, which might require uncomfortable turning. The object could be so small or far away that it occupies only a few pixels on the screen, making it difficult to precisely select it. The problem gets significantly worse if there is substantial clutter around the object of interest, particularly if other selectable objects are nearby. Finally, the object may be partially or totally occluded from view.

Manipulation

If the user carries an object over a long distance, then it is not necessary for him to squeeze or clutch the controller; this would yield unnecessary fatigue. In some cases,

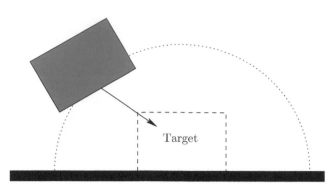

Figure 10.11 To make life easier on the user, a *basin of attraction* can be defined around an object so that when the basin is entered, the dropped object is attracted directly to the target pose.

the user might be expected to carefully inspect the object while having it in possession. For example, he might want to move it around in his hand to determine its 3D structure. The object orientation could be set to follow exactly the 3D orientation of a controller that the user holds. The user could even hold a real object in hand that is tracked by external cameras but has a different appearance in the virtual world. This enables familiar force feedback to the user, a concept that is revisited in Section 13.1. Note that an object could even be manipulated directly in its original place in the virtual world without bringing it close to the user's virtual body [30]. In this case, the virtual hand is brought to the object, while the physical hand remains in place. Having a longer arm than normal can also be simulated [259], to retrieve and place objects over greater distances.

Placement

Now consider ungrasping the object and placing it into the world. An easy case for the user is to press a button and have the object simply fall into the right place. This is accomplished by a *basin of attraction*, which is an attractive potential function defined in a neighborhood of the target pose (position and orientation); see Figure 10.11. The minimum of the potential function is at the target. After the object is released, the object falls into the target pose by moving so that the potential is reduced to its minimum. This behavior is seen in many 2D drawing programs so that the endpoints of line segments conveniently meet. An example of convenient object placement is in the 2011 Minecraft sandbox game by Markus Persson (Notch), in which building blocks simply fall into place. Children have built millions of virtual worlds in this way.

Alternatively, the user may be required to delicately place the object. Perhaps the application involves stacking and balancing objects as high as possible. In this case, the precision requirements would be very high, placing a burden on both the controller tracking system and the user.

Remapping

Now consider the power of remapping, as described in Section 10.1. The simplest case is the use of the button to select, grasp, and place objects. Instead of a button, continuous motions could be generated by the user and tracked by systems. Examples include turning a knob, moving a slider bar, moving a finger over a touch screen, and moving a free-floating body through space. Recall that one of the most important aspects of remapping is easy learnability. Reducing the number of degrees of freedom that are remapped will generally ease the learning process. To avoid gorilla arms and related problems, a scaling factor could be imposed on the tracked device so that a small amount of position change in the controller corresponds to a large motion in the virtual world. This problem could again be studied using Fitts's law as in the case of the computer mouse. Note that this might have an adverse effect on precision in the virtual world. In some settings orientation scaling might also be desirable. In this case, the 3D angular velocity ($\omega_x, \omega_y, \omega_z$) could be scaled by a factor to induce more rotation in the virtual world than in the real world.

Common systems
The development of interaction mechanisms for manipulation remains one of the greatest challenges for VR. Consumer VR headsets may either leverage existing game controllers, as in the bundling of the XBox 360 controller with the Oculus Rift in 2016, or introduce systems that assume large hand motions are the norm, as in the HTC Vive headset controller, as shown in Figure 10.12. Controllers that have users moving their hands through space seem not too far from the *Minority Report* interaction mechanism shown in Figure 10.10. Others have developed gesturing systems that involve no hardware in the hands, as in the Leap Motion system that was shown in Figure 9.25 from Section 9.4. These are perhaps updated versions of the vision of "goggles and gloves" that was popular in the 1990s (recall Figure 1.30(c) from Section 1.3). Rapid evolution of methods and technologies for manipulation can be expected in the coming years, with increasing emphasis on user comfort and ease of use.

10.4 Social Interaction

Communication and social interaction are vast subjects that extend well outside the scope of this book. Furthermore, social interaction in VR, or *social VR*, remains in a stage of infancy, with substantial experimentation and rethinking of paradigms occurring. Nevertheless, connecting humans together is one of the greatest potentials for VR technology. Although it might seem isolating to put displays between ourselves and the world around us, we can also be brought closer together through successful interaction mechanisms. This section highlights several key issues with regard to social interaction, rather than providing a complete review.

Beyond Shannon–Weaver Communication
An important factor is how many people will be interacting through the medium. Start with a pair of people. One of the most powerful mathematical models ever developed is the *Shannon–Weaver model of communication*, which for decades has been the basis of design for communication systems in engineering; see Figure 10.13. The model involves a *sender* and a *recipient*. The communication system *encodes* a message from the sender, which is then sent over a noisy *channel*. At the other end, the system *decodes* the message and it arrives to the recipient. The recipient

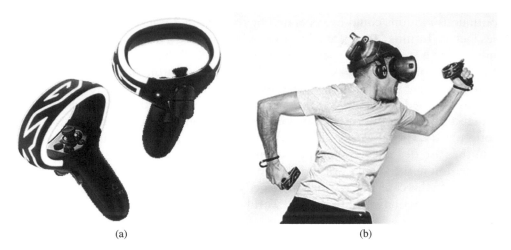

(a)   (b)

Figure 10.12   (a) A pair of hand-held controllers that came with the HTC Vive Cosmos headset; the device included side buttons, a trigger, and a touch pad for the thumb. (b) A user trying the controllers.

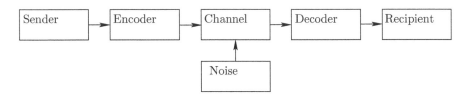

Figure 10.13   The classical Shannon–Weaver model of communication (from 1948). The sender provides a message to the encoder, which transmits the message through a channel corrupted by noise. At the other end, a decoder converts the message into a suitable format for the receiver. This model serves as the basis of communication theory in engineering.

could give *feedback* to indicate whether the message has been received intact. This communication model gave rise to the field of *information theory*, which enabled a well-defined notion of *bandwidth* for a communication channel and revealed the limits of data compression.

This model is powerful in that it mathematically quantifies human interaction, but it is also inadequate for covering the kinds of interactions that are possible in VR. By once again following the universal simulation principle, any kind of human interaction that exists in the real world could be brought into VR. The Shannon–Weaver model is inspired by interaction mechanisms such as the nineteenth-century telegraph or twentieth-century *handheld receiver* (or *walkie-talkie*). In these cases, the humans are completely isolated from each other, and the technology provides a burst of information that is similar to writing a letter. We have gone from text to audio to video communication, and could extend even further by incorporating displays for other senses, such as touch and smell. There are also many opportunities to use synthetic models, possibly in combination with actual captured information from cameras and microphones. Simple gestures and mannerisms can provide subtle but important components of interaction that are not captured by the classical communication model.

In spite of its shortcomings for VR, keep in mind that the Shannon–Weaver model provides powerful analysis of bandwidth and latency for computer networks and systems, which ultimately support any form of social interaction. Therefore, it has far reaching implications on what can or cannot be accomplished in a VR system. This occurs because all "communication" is converted into streams of bits that are sent through cables or network connections. One key problem is to ensure that the targeted social interaction VR experience is comfortable, convincing, and reliably supported over the computer network.

From Avatars to Visual Capture

How should others see you in VR? This is one of the most intriguing questions because it depends on both the social context and on the technological limitations. A clear spectrum of possibilities exists. At one extreme, a user may represent himself through an *avatar*, which is a 3D representation that might not correspond at all to his visible, audible, and behavioral characteristics; see Figure 10.14. At the other extreme, a user might be captured using imaging technology and reproduced in the virtual world with a highly accurate 3D representation; see Figure 10.15. In this case, it may seem as if the person were teleported directly from the real world to the virtual world. Many other possibilities exist along this spectrum, and it is worth considering the trade-offs.

One major appeal of an avatar is anonymity, which offers the chance to play a different role or exhibit different personality traits in a social setting. In a phenomenon called the *Proteus effect*, it has been observed that a person's behavior changes based on the virtual characteristics of the avatar, which is similar to the way in which people have been known to behave differently when wearing a uniform or costume [369]. The user might want to live a fantasy, or try to see the world from a different perspective. For example, people might develop a sense of empathy if they are able to experience the world from an avatar that appears to be different in terms of race, gender, height, weight, age, and so on.

Users may also want to experiment with other forms of embodiment. For example, a group of children might want to inhabit the bodies of animals while talking and moving about. Imagine if you could have people perceive you as if you were an alien, an insect, an automobile, or even a talking block of cheese. People were delightfully surprised in 1986 when Pixar brought a desk lamp to life in the animated short Luxo Jr. Hollywood movies over the past decades have been filled with animated characters, and we have the opportunity to embody some of them while inhabiting a virtual world!

Now consider moving toward physical realism. Based on the current technology, three major kinds of similarity can be independently considered:

1. **Visual appearance:** How close does the avatar seem to the actual person in terms of visible characteristics?
2. **Auditory appearance:** How much does the sound coming from the avatar match the voice, language, and speech patterns of the person?
3. **Behavioral appearance:** How closely do the avatar's motions match the body language, gait, facial expressions, and other motions of the person?

Figure 10.14 A sampling of avatars, shown in a Nonprofit Commons meeting in Second Life.

The first kind of similarity could start to match the person by making a kinematic model in the virtual world (recall Section 9.4) that corresponds in size and mobility to the actual person. Other simple matching such as hair color, skin tone, and eye color could be performed. To further improve realism, texture mapping could be used to map skin and clothes onto the avatar. For example, a picture of the user's face could be texture mapped onto the avatar face. Highly accurate matching might also be done by constructing synthetic models, or combining information from both imaging and synthetic sources. Accurate synthetic matching has been performed by researchers at the USC Institute for Creative Technologies; see Figure 10.16. A frustrating problem, as mentioned in Section 1.1, is the uncanny valley. People often describe computer-generated animation that tends toward human realism as seeing zombies or talking cadavers. Thus, being far from perfectly matched is usually much better than "almost" matched in terms of visual appearance.

For the auditory part, users of Second Life and similar systems have preferred text messaging. This interaction is treated as if they were talking aloud, in the sense that text messages can only be seen by avatars that would have been close enough to hear it at the same distance in the real world. Texting helps to ensure anonymity. Recording and reproducing voice is simple in VR, making it much simpler to match auditory appearance than visual appearance. One must take care to render the audio

Figure 10.15 Holographic communication research from Microsoft in 2016. A 3D representation of a person is extracted in real time and superimposed in the world, as seen through augmented reality glasses (Hololens).

with proper localization, so that it appears to others to be coming from the mouth of the avatar; see Chapter 11. If desired, anonymity can be easily preserved in spite of audio recording by using real-time voice-changing software (such as MorphVOX or Voxal Voice Changer); this might be preferred to texting in some settings.

Finally, note that the behavioral experience could be matched perfectly, while the avatar has a completely different visual appearance. This is the main motivation for motion capture systems, in which the movements of a real actor are recorded and then used to animate an avatar in a motion picture. Note that movie production is usually a long, off-line process. Accurate, real-time performance that perfectly matches the visual and behavioral appearance of a person is currently unattainable in low-cost VR systems. Furthermore, capturing the user's face is difficult if part of it is covered by a headset, although some progress has been made in this area [183].

On the other hand, tracking systems can be leveraged to provide accurately matched behavioral appearance in some instances. For example, head tracking can be directly linked to the avatar head so that others can know where the head is turned. Users can also understand head nods or gestures, such as "yes" or "no." Figure 10.17 shows a simple VR experience in which friends can watch a movie together while being represented by avatar heads that are tracked. (They can also talk to each other.) In some systems, eye tracking could also be used so that users can see where the avatar is looking; however, in some cases, this might enter back into the uncanny valley. If the hands are tracked, which could be done using controllers such as those shown in Figure 10.12, then they can also be brought into the virtual world.

(a)　　　　　　　　　　　　　　　(b)

Figure 10.16 The Digital Emily project from 2009. (a) A real person is imaged. (b) Geometric models are animated along with sophisticated rendering techniques to produce realistic facial movement.

Figure 10.17 Multiple users could meet in a virtual world and socialize. In this case, they are watching a movie together in a theater. Their head movements are provided using head tracking data. They are also able to talk to each other with localized audio.

From One-on-One to Societies

Now consider social interaction on different scales. The vast majority of one-on-one interaction that we have in the real world is with people we know. Likewise, it is the same when interacting through technology, whether through text messaging, phone calls, or video chat. Most of our interaction through technology is targeted in that there is a specific purpose to the engagement. This suggests that VR can be used to take a video chat to the next level, where two people feel like they are face-to-face in a virtual world, or even in a panoramic capture of the real world. Note, however, that in the real world, we may casually interact simply by being in close proximity while engaged in other activities, rather than having a targeted engagement.

One important aspect of one-on-one communication is whether the relationship between the two people is *symmetrical* or *complementary* (from Paul Watzlawick's

Axioms of Communication). In a symmetrical relationship the two people are of equal status, whereas in a complementary relationship one person is in a superior position, as in the case of a boss and employee or a parent and a child. This greatly affects the style of interaction, particularly in a targeted activity.

Now consider interactions within a small group of people in the real world. Perhaps a family or coworkers are sharing a meal together. Perhaps children are together on a playground. Perhaps friends and family have gathered for a holiday or birthday celebration. VR versions of such interactions could focus on a targeted activity, such as gathering for a party. Perhaps you are the one who could not attend in person, but will instead "hang out" with the group through some VR interface. Perhaps there is a meeting, and a few people need to attend remotely, which is currently handled by *teleconferencing*, in which voice and video are transmitted over the network. The common scenario that is closest to VR is schoolchildren meeting in a networked video game, with some social interaction occurring while they play. They might form teams and interact through text messaging or voice while playing.

As the number of people increases to over a dozen, the case of a complementary relationship leads to a presentation or interview. Some examples are a teacher lecturing to a class of students, and a politician speaking in front of a group of reporters. In these interactions, a leader has been clearly assigned to communicate with the group. These settings could be reproduced in VR by allowing people to attend through panoramic video capture. Alternatively, the entire event could take place in a virtual world. In the case of a symmetrical relationship, people might mingle at a large reception and carry on conversations in small groups. This could also be reproduced in VR.

In the limiting case, an online community may emerge, which could connect millions of users. Several examples were given in Section 1.3, including MMORPGs and Second Life. People may have casual interactions by bumping into each other while spending a significant amount of time living or working in a networked virtual world. One issue, which exists in any online community, is membership. Is it open to everyone, or only to a closed group?

Transformed Social Interaction

Two common themes in this book have been that VR can produce experiences that are better than reality, and that our perceptual systems adapt to new stimuli. It is therefore natural to wonder how social interaction can be altered or improved through VR. The notion of *transformed social interaction* has been introduced Jeremy Bailenson [16]. A thought-provoking example is shown in Figure 10.18. In a virtual world, a teacher could look at every student simultaneously, directly in the eyes, while lecturing to the class. This is physically impossible in the real world, but it is easy to make in VR because each student could see a different version of the virtual world. Of course, the students might reason that the teacher could not possibly be paying attention to *all* of them, but the chance that she *might* be watching could have a significant effect on learning outcomes. The classroom could also appear to have a small number of students, while in reality thousands of students are in attendance. How many more mechanisms for social interaction can be introduced that are impossible to achieve in the real world? How quickly will our brains adapt to them?

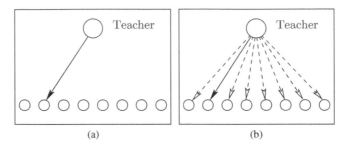

Figure 10.18 (a) A top-down depiction of an ordinary classroom is shown, in which a teacher can look directly at one student. (b) In a VR classroom, the teacher could be looking at each student simultaneously, at least from the perspective of each student.

In what settings would we prefer such interaction to meeting in the real world? The future should bring about many exciting new mechanisms for social interaction.

10.5 Additional Interaction Mechanisms

This chapter has covered three families of interaction mechanisms: locomotion, manipulation, and social. These families emerged from decades of research and development, but do not completely cover every kind of interaction. Many systems demand a custom interaction mechanism be constructed that does not fall into the three families. Furthermore, with the widespread current use of low-cost VR systems, we expect that new families will emerge. A few examples of other interaction mechanisms and associated challenges are presented here.

Interaction with Information and Media

The content of the Internet can be brought into VR in numerous ways by following the universal simulation principle. Figure 1.8 from Section 1.2 showed a movie screen in a virtual movie theater. In this case, simple interaction may be needed to pause or change the movie. As a more complex example, a web browser could appear on a public display in the virtual world or on any other device that is familiar to users in the real world. Alternatively, a virtual screen may float directly in front of the user, while a stable, familiar background is provided.

For decades, people have interacted with their computers and web browsers using two input devices, one for typing and the other for pointing. In the case of a PC, this has taken the form of a keyboard and mouse. With modern smartphones, people are expected to type on small touch screens or use alternatives such as voice or swipe-to-type. They use their fingers to point by touching, and additionally zoom with a pair of fingers.

Text Entry and Editing

The typing options on a smartphone are sufficient for entering search terms or typing a brief message, but they are woefully inadequate for writing a novel. For professionals who currently sit in front of keyboards to write reports, computer programs, newspaper articles, and so on, what kind of interfaces are needed to entice them to work in VR?

One option is to track a real keyboard and mouse, making them visible VR. Tracking of fingertips may also be needed to provide visual feedback. This enables a system to be developed that magically transforms the desk and surrounding environment into anything. Much like the use of a background image on a desktop system, a relaxing panoramic image or video could envelop the user while she works. For the actual work part, rather than having one screen in front of the user, a number of screens or windows could appear all around and at different depths.

It is easy to borrow interface concepts from existing desktop windowing systems, but much research remains to design and evaluate completely novel interfaces for improved productivity and comfort while writing. What could word processing look like in VR? What could an integrated development environment (IDE) for writing and debugging software look like? If the keyboard and mouse are replaced by other interfaces, then the user might not even need to sit at a desk to work. One challenge would be to get users to learn a method that offers text entry speeds that are comparable to using a keyboard, but enables them to work more comfortably.

3D Design and Visualization

What are the professional benefits to being able to inhabit a 3D virtual world? In addition to video games, several other fields have motivated the development of computer graphics. Prior to *computer-aided design* (*CAD*), architects and engineers spent many hours with pencil and paper to painstakingly draw accurate lines on paper. The computer has proved to be an indispensable tool for design. Data visualization has been a key use of computers over the past years. Examples are medical, scientific, and market data. With all of these uses, we are still forced to view designs and data sets by manipulating 2D projections on screens.

VR offers the ability to interact with and view 3D versions of a design or data set. This could be from the outside looking in, perhaps at the design of a new kitchen utensil. It could also be from the inside looking out, perhaps at the design of a new kitchen. If the perceptual concepts from Chapter 6 are carefully addressed, then the difference between the designed object or environment and the real one may be less than ever before. Viewing a design in VR can be considered as a kind of *virtual prototyping*, before a physical prototype is constructed. This enables rapid, low-cost advances in product development cycles.

A fundamental challenge to achieving VR-based design and visualization is the interaction mechanism. What will allow an architect, artist, game developer, movie set builder, or engineer to comfortably build 3D worlds over long periods of time? What tools will allow people to manipulate high-dimensional data sets as they project onto a 3D world?

The Future

Many more forms of interaction can be imagined, even by just applying the universal simulation principle. Video games have already provided many ideas for interaction via a standard game controller. Beyond that, the Nintendo Wii remote has been especially effective in making virtual versions of sports activities such as bowling a ball or swinging a tennis racket. What new interaction mechanisms will be comfortable and effective for VR? If displays are presented to senses other than vision, then even more possibilities emerge. For example, could you give someone a meaningful hug on the other side of the world if they are wearing a suit that applies the appropriate forces to the body?

Further Reading

For overviews of human motor control and learning, see [199, 276]. Proprioception issues in the context of VR are covered in [62]. For more on locomotion and wayfinding see [53] and chapters 6 and 7 of [31]. For grasping issues in robotics, see [206].

For more on locomotion and wayfinding, see [53] and chapters 6 and 7 of [31]. The limits of hand-eye coordination were studied in the following seminal papers: [57, 71, 355]. The *power law of practice* was introduced in [234], which indicates that the logarithm of reaction time reduces linearly with the amount of practice. Research that relates Fitts's law to pointing device operation includes [73, 196, 197, 308]. For broad coverage of human-computer interaction, see [37, 40]. For additional references on social interaction through avatars, see [20, 214, 336].

CHAPTER ELEVEN

Audio

Hearing is an important sense for VR and has been unfortunately neglected up until this chapter. Developers of VR systems tend to focus mainly on the vision part because it is our strongest sense; however, the audio component of VR is powerful and the technology exists to bring high-fidelity audio experiences into VR. In the real world, audio is crucial to art, entertainment, and oral communication. As mentioned in Section 2.1, audio recording and reproduction can be considered as a VR experience by itself, with both a CAVE-like version (surround sound) and a headset version (wearing headphones). When combined consistently with the visual component, audio helps provide a compelling and comfortable VR experience.

Each section of this chapter is the auditory (or audio) complement to one of Chapters 4 through 7. The progression again goes from physics to physiology, and then from perception to rendering. Section 11.1 explains the physics of sound in terms of waves, propagation, and frequency analysis. Section 11.2 describes the parts of the human ear and their function. This naturally leads to auditory perception, which is the subject of Section 11.3. Section 11.4 concludes by presenting auditory rendering, which can produce sounds synthetically from models or reproduce captured sounds. When reading these sections, it is important to keep in mind the visual counterpart of each subject. The similarities make it easier to quickly understand and the differences lead to unusual engineering solutions.

11.1 The Physics of Sound

This section parallels many concepts from Chapter 4, which covered the basic physics of light. Sound wave propagation is similar in many ways to light, but with some key differences that have major perceptual and engineering consequences. Whereas light is a *transverse wave*, which oscillates in a direction perpendicular to its propagation, sound is a *longitudinal wave*, which oscillates in a direction parallel to its propagation. Figure 11.1 shows an example of this for a parallel wavefront.

Sound corresponds to vibration in a medium, which is usually air, but could also be water or any other gases, liquids, or solids. There is no sound in a vacuum, which is unlike light propagation. For sound, the molecules in the medium displace, causing variations in pressure that range from a *compression* extreme to a decompressed, *rarefaction* extreme. At a fixed point in space, the pressure varies as a function of time. Most importantly, this could be the pressure variation on a human eardrum, which

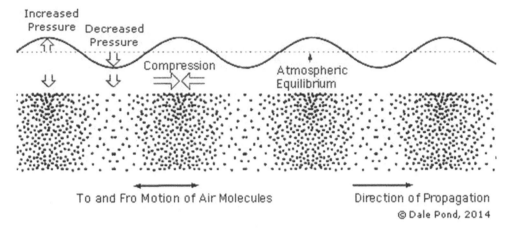

Figure 11.1 Sound is a longitudinal wave of compression and rarefaction of air molecules. The case of a pure tone is shown here, which leads to a sinusoidal pressure function. (Figure by Dale Pond.)

is converted into a perceptual experience. The sound pressure level is frequently reported in *decibels* (abbreviated as *dB*), which is defined as

$$N_{db} = 20 * \log_{10}(p_e/p_r),\qquad(11.1)$$

in which p_e is the pressure level of the peak compression and p_r is a reference pressure level, which is usually taken as 2×10^{-7} newtons/square meter.

Sound waves are typically produced by vibrating solid materials, especially as they collide or interact with each other. A simple example is striking a large bell, which causes it to vibrate for many seconds. Materials may also be forced into sound vibration by sufficient air flow, as in the case of a flute. Human bodies are designed to produce sound by using the lungs to force air through the vocal cords, which causes them to vibrate. This enables talking, singing, screaming, and so on.

Sound Sources and Attenuation
As in the case of light, we can consider rays, for which each *sound ray* is perpendicular to the sound propagation wavefront. A point sound source can be defined, which produces emanating rays with equal power in all directions. This also results in power reduction at a quadratic rate as a function of distance from the source. Such a point source is useful for modeling, but cannot be easily achieved in the real world. Planar wavefronts can be achieved by vibrating a large, flat plate, which results in the acoustic equivalent of collimated light. An important distinction, however, is the *attenuation* of sound as it propagates through a medium. Due to energy lost in the vibration of molecules, the sound intensity decreases by a constant factor (or fixed percentage) for every unit of distance from the planar source; this is an example of *exponential decay*.

Propagation Speed
Sound waves propagate at 343.2 meters per second through air at 20° C (68° F). For comparison, light propagation is about 874,000 times faster. We have planes and

cars that can surpass the speed of sound, but are nowhere near traveling at the speed of light. This is perhaps the most important difference between sound and light for making VR systems. The result is that human senses and engineered sensors easily measure differences in arrival times of sound waves, leading to stronger emphasis on temporal information.

Frequency and Wavelength

As in Section 4.1, the decomposition of waves into frequency components becomes important. For sound, the frequency is the number of compressions per second and is called *pitch*. The range is generally considered to be from 20 Hz to 20,000 Hz, which is based on human hearing, much in the same way that the frequency range for light is based on human vision. Vibrations above 20,000 Hz are called *ultrasound* and are audible to some animals. Vibrations below 20 Hz are called *infrasound*.

Using (4.1) from Section 4.1 and the propagation speed $s = 343.2$, the wavelength of a sound wave can also be determined. At 20 Hz the wavelength is $\lambda = 343.2/20 = 17.1$ m. At 20,000 Hz, it becomes $\lambda = 17.1$ mm. The waves are the sizes of objects in our world. This causes the sound to interfere with objects in a complicated way that is difficult to model when trying to reproduce the behavior in VR. By comparison, light waves are tiny, ranging from 400 nm to 700 nm.

Doppler Effect

The sound pressure variations previously described were for a fixed receiving point. If the point is moving away from the source, then the wavefronts will arrive at a reduced frequency. For example, if the receiver moves at 43.2 m/s away from the source, then the waves would seem to be traveling at only $343.2 - 43.2 = 300$ meters per second. The received frequency shifts due to the relative motion between the source and receiver. This is known as the *Doppler effect*, and the frequency as measured at the receiver can be calculated as

$$f_r = \left(\frac{s + v_r}{s + v_s}\right) f_s, \tag{11.2}$$

in which s is the propagation speed in the medium, v_r is the velocity of the receiver, v_s is the velocity of the source, and f_s is the frequency of the source. In our example, $s = 343.2$, $v_r = -43.2$, and $v_s = 0$. The result is that a sound source with frequency $f_s = 1,000$ Hz would be perceived by the receiver as having frequency $f_r \approx 876.7$. This is the reason why a siren seems to change pitch as a police car passes by. The Doppler effect also applies to light, but the effect is negligible in normal VR contexts (unless developers want to experiment with virtual time dilation, space travel, and so on).

Reflection and Transmission

As with light, wave propagation is strongly affected by propagation through media. Imagine a sound wave hitting an interior wall as someone yells from inside a room. It may be helpful to think about a ray of sound approaching the wall. Due to reflection, much of the sound will bounce as if the wall were an acoustic mirror. However, some of the sound energy will penetrate the wall. Sound propagates more quickly

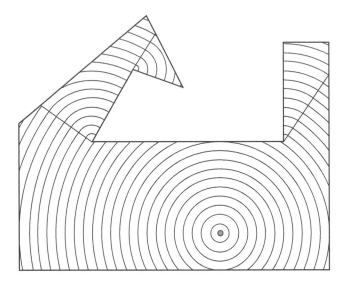

Figure 11.2 Waves can even bend around corners, due to *diffraction*. A top-down view of a room is shown. At each of the three interior corners, the propagating wavefront expands around it.

through more solid materials, resulting in a bending of the ray as it penetrates. This is refraction. Some of the sound escapes the far side of the wall and propagates through the air in an adjacent room, resulting in transmission. Thus, someone in the adjacent room can hear yelling. The total amount of energy contained in the sound waves before they hit the wall is split by reflection and transmission, with additional loss due to attenuation.

Diffraction

Wavefronts can also bend around corners, which is called *diffraction*; see Figure 11.2. This would enable someone to hear a sound that is around the corner of a building, without relying on any reflection or transmission. More diffraction occurs for longer wavelengths; thus, a lower-pitched sound bends around corners more easily. This also explains why we are more concerned about acoustic diffraction in a room than light diffraction, although the latter is often important for lenses. (Recall the Fresnel lens drawback of Section 7.3.)

Fourier Analysis

Spectral decompositions were important for characterizing light sources and reflections in Section 4.1. In the case of sound, they are even more important. A sinusoidal wave, as shown in Figure 11.3(a), corresponds to a *pure tone*, which has a single associated frequency; this is analogous to a color from the light spectrum. A more complex waveform, such the sound of a piano note, can be constructed from a combination of various pure tones. Figures 11.3(b) to 11.3(d) provide a simple example. This principle is derived from *Fourier analysis*, which enables any periodic function to be decomposed into sinusoids (pure tones in our case) by simply adding them up. Each pure tone has a particular *frequency*, *amplitude* or scaling factor, and a possible timing for its peak, which is called its *phase*. By adding up a finite number of

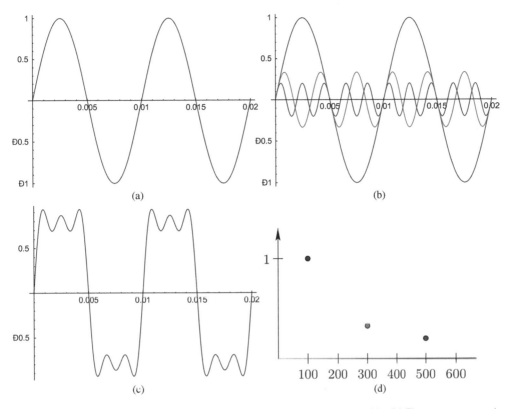

Figure 11.3 (a) A pure tone (sinusoid) of unit amplitude and frequency 100 Hz. (b) Three pure tones; in addition to the original blue, the green sinusoid has amplitude 1/3 and frequency 300 Hz, and the red one has amplitude 1/5 and frequency 500 Hz. (c) Directly adding the three pure tones approximates a square-like waveform. (d) In the frequency spectrum, there are three nonzero points, one for each pure tone.

pure tones, virtually any useful waveform can be closely approximated. The higher-frequency, lower-amplitude sinusoids are often called *higher-order harmonics*; the largest-amplitude wave is called the *fundamental frequency*. The plot of amplitude and phase as a function of frequency is obtained by applying the *Fourier transform*, which will be briefly covered in Section 11.4.

Where Are the Lenses?

At this point, the most obvious omission in comparison to Chapter 4 is the acoustic equivalent of lenses. As stated earlier, refraction occurs for sound. Why is it that human ears do not focus sounds onto a spatial image in the same way as the eyes? One problem is the long wavelengths in comparison to light. Recall from Section 5.1 that the photoreceptor density in the fovea is close to the wavelength of visible light. It is likely that an "ear fovea" would have to be several meters across or more, which would make our heads too large. Another problem is that low-frequency sound waves interact with objects in the world in a more complicated way. Thus, rather than forming an image, our ears instead work by performing Fourier analysis to sift out the structure of sound waves in terms of sinusoids of various frequencies, amplitudes, and phases. Each ear is more like a single-pixel camera operating

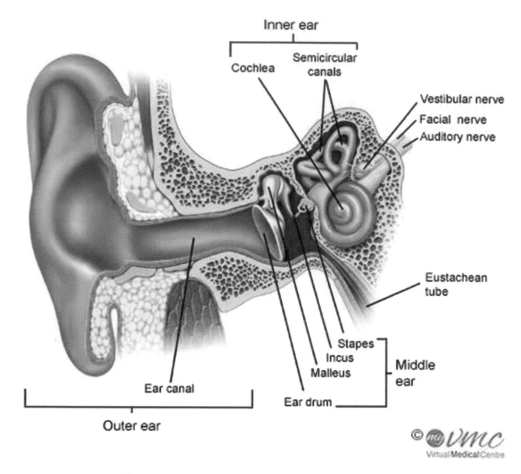

Figure 11.4 The physiology of the human auditory system.

at tens of thousands of "frames per second," rather than capturing a large image at a slower frame rate. The emphasis for hearing is the distribution over *time*, whereas the emphasis is mainly on *space* for vision. Nevertheless, both time and space are important for both hearing and vision.

11.2 The Physiology of Human Hearing

Human ears convert sound pressure waves into neural impulses, which ultimately lead to a perceptual experience. The anatomy of the human ear is shown in Figure 11.4. The ear is divided into outer, middle, and inner parts, based on the flow of sound waves. Recall from Section 5.3 the complications of eye movements. Although cats and some other animals can rotate their ears, humans cannot, which simplifies this part of the VR engineering problem.

Outer Ear
The floppy part of the ear that protrudes from the human head is called the *pinna*. It mainly serves as a funnel for collecting sound waves and guiding them into the

ear canal. It has the effect of amplifying sounds in the 1,500 to 7,500 Hz frequency range [371]. It also performs subtle filtering of the sound, causing some variation in the high-frequency range that depends on the incoming direction of the sound source. This provides a powerful cue regarding the direction of a sound source.

After traveling down the ear canal, the sound waves cause the *eardrum* to vibrate. The eardrum is a cone-shaped membrane that separates the outer ear from the middle ear. Its covers only 55 mm^2 of area. If this were a camera, it would have a resolution of one pixel at this point because no additional spatial information exists other than what can be inferred from the membrane vibrations.

Middle Ear

The main function of the middle ear is to convert vibrating air molecules in the outer ear into vibrating liquid in the inner ear. This is accomplished by bones that connect the eardrum to the inner ear. The air and the liquid of the inner ear have differing *impedance*, which is the resistance to vibration. The bones are called the malleus (hammer), incus (anvil), and stapes (stirrup), and they are connected in series via muscles and ligaments that allow relative movement. The purpose of the bones is to match the impedance so that the pressure waves are transmitted to the inner ear with as little power loss as possible. This avoids the tendency of a higher-impedance material to reflect the sound away. An example of this is voices reflecting over the surface of a lake, rather than being transmitted into the water.

Inner Ear

The inner ear contains both the vestibular organs, which were covered in Section 8.2, and the *cochlea*, which is the sense organ for hearing. The cochlea converts sound energy into neural impulses via mechanoreceptors. This is accomplished in a beautiful way that performs a spectral decomposition in the process so that the neural impulses encode amplitudes and phases of frequency components.

Figure 11.5 illustrates its operation. As seen in Figure 11.5(a), eardrum vibration is converted into oscillations of the *oval window* at the base of the cochlea. A tube that contains a liquid called *perilymph* runs from the oval window to the *round window* at the other end. The *basilar membrane* is a structure that runs through the center of the cochlea, which roughly doubles the length of the tube containing perilymph. The first part of the tube is called the *scala vestibuli*, and the second part is called the *scala tympani*. As the oval window vibrates, waves travel down the tube, which causes the basilar membrane to displace. The membrane is thin and stiff near the base (near the oval and round windows) and gradually becomes soft and floppy at the furthest away point, called the *apex*; see Figure 11.5(b). This causes each point on the membrane to vibrate only over a particular narrow range of frequencies.

Mechanoreceptors

The basilar membrane is surrounded by a larger and complicated structure called the *organ of Corti*, which additionally contains mechanoreceptors that are similar to those shown in Section 8.2. See Figure 11.6. The mechanoreceptors convert

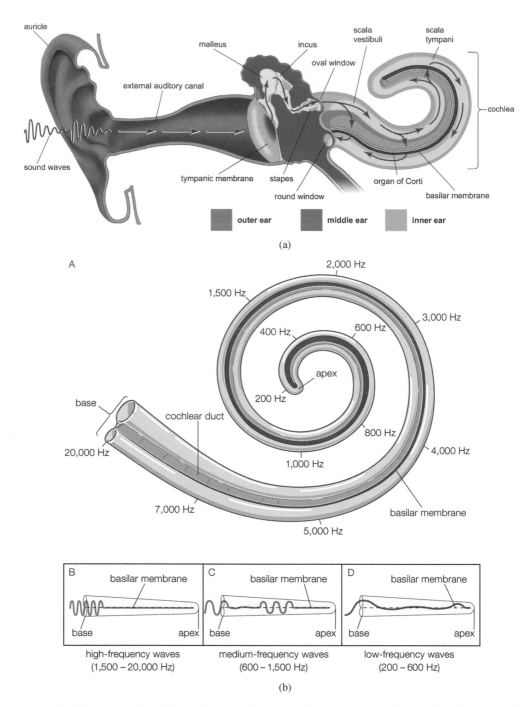

Figure 11.5 The operation of the cochlea. (a) The perilymph transmits waves that are forced by the oval window through a tube that extends the length of the cochlea and back again, to the round window. (b) Because of varying thickness and stiffness, the central spine (basilar membrane) is sensitive to particular frequencies of vibration; this causes the mechanoreceptors, and ultimately auditory perception, to be frequency sensitive.

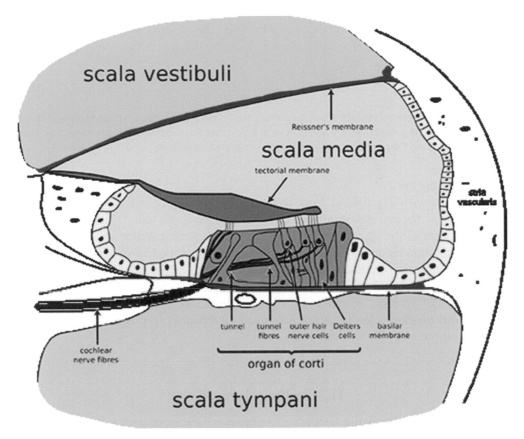

Figure 11.6 A cross section of the *organ of Corti*. The basilar and tectorial membranes move relative to each other, causing the hairs in the mechanoreceptors to bend.

displacements of hairs into neural impulses. The hairs are displaced as the basilar membrane vibrates because the ends of some are attached to the *tectorial membrane*. The relative motions of the basilar and tectorial membranes causes a shearing action that moves the hairs. Each ear contains around 20,000 mechanoreceptors, which is considerably less than the 100 million photoreceptors in the eye.

Spectral Decomposition
By exploiting the frequency-based sensitivity of the basilar membrane, the brain effectively has access to a spectral decomposition of the incoming sound waves. It is similar to, but not exactly the same as, the Fourier decomposition discussed in Section 11.1. Several differences are mentioned in chapter 4 of [207]. If pure tones at two different frequencies are simultaneously presented to the ear, then the basilar membrane produces a third tone, which is sometimes audible [152]. Also, the neural impulses that result from mechanoreceptor output are not linearly proportional to the frequency amplitude. Furthermore, the detection of one tone may cause detections of nearby tones (in terms of frequency) to be inhibited [282], much like lateral inhibition in horizontal cells (recall from Section 5.2). Section 11.4.1 will clarify how these differences make the ear more complex in terms of filtering.

Left   Right

Figure 11.7 Due to the *precedence effect*, an auditory illusion occurs if the head is placed between stereo speakers so that one is much closer than the other. If they output the same sound at the same time, then the person perceives the sound arriving from the closer speaker rather than perceiving an echo.

Auditory Pathways

The neural pulses are routed from the left and right cochleae up to the highest level, which is the *primary auditory cortex* in the brain. As usual, hierarchical processing occurs as the signals are combined through neural structures. This enables multiple frequencies and phase shifts to be analyzed. An early structure called the *superior olive* receives signals from both ears so that differences in amplitude and phase can be processed. This will become important in Section 11.3 for determining the location of an audio source. At the highest level, the primary auditory cortex is mapped out *tonotopically* (locations are based on frequency), much in the same way as topographic mapping of the visual cortex.

11.3 Auditory Perception

Now that we have seen the hardware for hearing, the next part is to understand how we perceive sound. In the visual case, we saw that perceptual experiences are often surprising because they are based on adaptation, missing data, assumptions filled in by neural structures, and many other factors. The same is true for auditory experiences. Furthermore, *auditory illusions* exist in the same way as optical illusions. The McGurk effect from Section 6.4 was an example that used vision to induce incorrect auditory perception.

Precedence Effect

A more common auditory illusion is the *precedence effect*, in which only one sound is perceived if two nearly identical sounds arrive at slightly different times; see Figure 11.7. Sounds often reflect from surfaces, causing *reverberation*, which is the delayed arrival at the ears of many "copies" of the sound due to the different propagation paths that were taken from reflections, transmissions, and diffraction. Rather than hearing a jumble, people perceive a single sound. This is based on the first arrival, which usually has the largest amplitude. An echo is perceived if the timing difference is larger than the *echo threshold* (in one study it ranged from 3 to 61 ms [367]). Other auditory illusions involve incorrect localization (*Franssen effect* and *Glissando illusion* [61]), illusory continuity of tones [348], and forever increasing tones (*Shepard tone illusion* [291]).

Psychoacoustics and Loudness Perception

The area of psychophysics, which was introduced in Section 2.3, becomes specialized to *psychoacoustics* for the case of auditory perception. Stevens' law of perceived

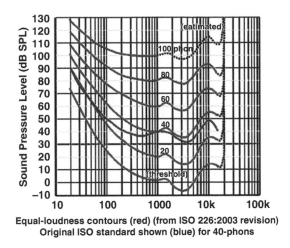

Equal-loudness contours (red) (from ISO 226:2003 revision)
Original ISO standard shown (blue) for 40-phons

Figure 11.8 Contours of equal loudness perception as a function of frequency.

stimulus magnitude and Weber's law of just noticeable differences (JNDs) appear throughout the subject. For example, the exponent for Stevens' law (recall (2.1)), for perceived loudness of a 3,000 Hz pure tone, is $x = 0.67$ [317]. This roughly means that if a sound increases to a much higher pressure level, we perceive it as only a bit louder. A more complicated example from psychoacoustics is shown in Figure 11.8, a chart of contours that correspond to equal loudness perception as a function of frequency. In other words, as the frequency varies, at what levels are the sounds perceived to be the same loudness? This requires careful design of experiments with human subjects, a problem that is common throughout VR development as well; see Section 12.4.

Pitch Perception
When considering perception, the frequency of a sound wave is referred to as *pitch*. Perceptual psychologists have studied the ability of people to detect a targeted pitch in spite of confusion from sounds consisting of other wavelengths and phases. One fundamental observation is that the auditory perception system performs *critical band masking* to effectively block out waves that have frequencies outside a particular range of interest. Another well-studied problem is the perception of differences in pitch (or frequency). For example, for a pure tone at 1,000 Hz, could someone distinguish it from a tone at 1,010 Hz? This is an example of JND. It turns out that for frequencies below 1,000 Hz, humans can detect a change of frequency that is less than 1 Hz. The discrimination ability decreases as the frequency increases. At 10,000 Hz, the JND is about 100 Hz. In terms of percentages, this means that pitch perception is better than a 0.1 percent difference at low frequencies, but increases to 1.0 percent for higher frequencies.

Also regarding pitch perception, a surprising auditory illusion occurs when the fundamental frequency is removed from a complex waveform. Recall from Figure 11.3 that a square wave can be approximately represented by adding sinusoids of smaller and smaller amplitudes, but higher frequencies. It turns out that people perceive the tone of the fundamental frequency, even when it is removed, and only the

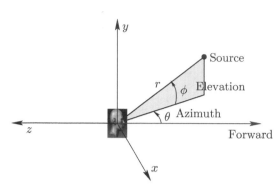

Figure 11.9 Spherical coordinates are used for the source point in auditory localization. Suppose the head is centered on the origin and facing in the $-z$ direction. The *azimuth* θ is the angle with respect to the forward direction after projecting the source into the *xz* plane. The *elevation* ϕ is the interior angle formed by a vertical triangle that connects the origin to the source and to the projection of the source into the plane. The radius *r* is the distance from the origin to the source.

higher-order harmonics remain; several theories for this are summarized in chapter 5 of [207].

Localization

One of the main areas of psychoacoustics is *localization*, which means estimating the location of a sound source by hearing it. This is crucial for many VR experiences. For example, if people are socializing, then their voices should seem to come from the mouths of corresponding avatars. In other words, the auditory and visual cues should match. Any kind of sound effect, such as a car or zombie approaching, should also have matched cues.

The JND concept is applied for localization to obtain the *minimum audible angle* (MAA), which is the minimum amount of angular variation that can be detected by a human listener. A spherical coordinate system is usually used for localization, in which the listener's head is at the origin; see Figure 11.9. The angle in the horizontal plane between the forward direction and the source is called the *azimuth*, which extends from -180 to 180 degrees. The angle corresponding to deviation of the source from the horizontal plane is called the *elevation*, which extends from -90 to 90 degrees. The third coordinate is the *radius* or *distance* from the origin (head center) to the source. The MAA depends on both frequency and the direction of the source. Figure 11.10 shows a plot of the MAA as a function of frequency, at several values for azimuth. The amount of variation is surprising. At some frequencies and locations, the MAA is down to 1 degree; however, at other combinations, localization is extremely bad.

Monaural Cues

Auditory localization is analogous to depth and scale perception for vision, which was covered in Section 6.1. Since humans have a pair of ears, localization cues can be divided into ones that use a single ear and others that require both ears. This is analogous to monocular and binocular cues for vision. A *monaural cue* relies on sounds reaching a single ear to constrain the set of possible sound sources. Several monaural cues are [372]:

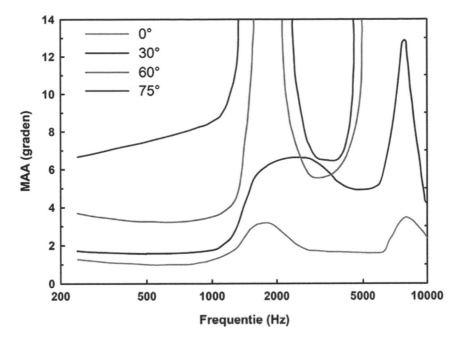

Figure 11.10 Plots of the *minimum audible angle* (*MAA*) as a function of frequency. Each plot corresponds to a different azimuth angle.

1. The pinna is shaped asymmetrically so that incoming sound is distorted in a way that depends on the direction from which it arrives, especially the elevation. Although people are not consciously aware of this distortion, the auditory system uses it for localization.
2. The amplitude of a sound decreases quadratically with distance. If it is a familiar sound, then its distance can be estimated from the perceived amplitude. Familiarity affects the power of this cue in the same way that familiarity with an object allows depth and scale perception to be separated.
3. For distant sounds, a distortion of the frequency spectrum occurs because higher-frequency components attenuate more quickly than low-frequency components. For example, distant thunder is perceived as a deep rumble, but nearby thunder includes a higher-pitched popping sound.
4. Finally, a powerful monaural cue is provided by the reverberations entering the ear as the sounds bounce around; this is especially strong in a room. Even though the precedence effect prevents us from perceiving these reverberations, the brain nevertheless uses the information for localization. This cue alone is called *echolocation*, which is used naturally by some animals, including bats. Some people can perform this by making clicking sounds or other sharp noises; this allows *acoustic wayfinding* for blind people.

Binaural Cues
If both ears become involved, then a *binaural cue* for localization results. The simplest case is the *interaural level difference* (*ILD*), which is the difference in sound

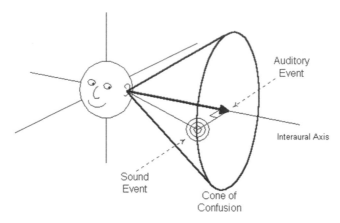

Figure 11.11 The *cone of confusion* is the set of locations where a point source might lie after using the ITD binaural cue. It is technically a hyberboloid, but approximately looks like a cone.

magnitude as heard by each ear. For example, one ear may be facing a sound source, while the other is in the *acoustic shadow*. (The shadow caused by an object in front of a sound source is similar to the shadow from a light source.) The closer ear would receive a much stronger vibration than the other.

Another binaural cue is *interaural time difference* (*ITD*), which is closely related to the TDOA sensing approach described in Section 9.3. The distance between the two ears is approximately 21.5 cm, which results in different arrival times of the sound from a source. Note that sound travels 21.5 cm in about 0.6 ms, which means that surprisingly small differences are used for localization.

Suppose that the brain measures the difference in arrival times as 0.3 ms. What is the set of possible places where the source could have originated? This can be solved by setting up algebraic equations, which results in a conical surface known as a hyperboloid. If it is not known which sound came first, then the set of possible places is a hyperboloid of two disjoint sheets. Since the brain knows which one came first, the two sheets are narrowed down to one hyperboloid sheet, which is called the *cone of confusion*; see Figure 11.11. (In most cases, it approximately looks like a cone, even though it is hyperboloid.) Uncertainty within this cone can be partly resolved, however, by using the distortions of the pinna.

The Power of Motion

More importantly, humans resolve much ambiguity by simply moving their heads. Just as head movement allows the powerful vision depth cue of parallax, it also provides better auditory localization. In fact, *auditory parallax* even provides another localization cue because nearby audio sources change their azimuth and elevation faster than distant ones. With regard to ITD, imagine having a different cone of confusion for every head pose, all within a short time. By integrating other senses, the relative head poses can be estimated, which roughly allows for an intersection of multiple cones of confusion to be made, until the sound source is precisely pinpointed. Finally, recall that the motion of a source relative to the receiver causes the Doppler effect. As in the case of vision, the issue of perceived self motion versus the

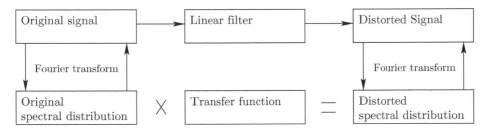

Figure 11.12 An overview of a linear filter and its relationship to Fourier analysis. The top row of blocks corresponds to the time domain, whereas the bottom row is the frequency (or spectral) domain.

motion of objects emerges based on the auditory input arises. This could contribute to vection (recall Section 8.2).

11.4 Auditory Rendering

We now arrive at the problem of producing sounds for the virtual world, and sending them to aural displays (speakers) so that the user perceives them as they were designed for the VR experience. They should be consistent with visual cues and with past auditory experiences in the real world. Whether recorded sounds, synthetic sounds, or a combination, the virtual pressure waves and their rendering to speakers should sufficiently fool the user's brain.

11.4.1 Basic Signal Processing

The importance of frequency components in sound waves should be clear by now. This remains true for the engineering problem of synthesizing sounds for VR, which falls under the area of *signal processing*. A brief overview is given here; see [11, 192] for further reading. As the core of this subject is the characterization or design of *filters* that transform or distort signals. In our case the signals are sound waves that could be fully synthesized, captured using microphones, or some combination. (Recall that both synthetic and captured models exist for the visual case as well.)

Figure 11.12 shows the overall scheme, which will be presented over this section. The original signal appears in the upper left. First, follow the path from left to right. The signal enters a black box labeled *linear filter* and becomes distorted, as shown in the right. What is a linear filter? Some background concepts are needed before returning to that question.

Sampling Rates
Signal processing formulations exist for both *continuous-time*, which makes nice formulations and mathematical proofs, and *discrete-time*, which has an uglier appearance, but corresponds directly to the way computers process signals. Because of its practical value, we will focus on the discrete-time case.

Start with a signal as a function of time, with values represented as $x(t)$. Using digital processing, it will be sampled at regular time intervals. Let Δt be the sampling interval. The *sampling rate* or (*sampling frequency*) is roughly $1/\Delta t$ Hz. For example, with 1,000 Hz sampling frequency, Δt is one millisecond. According to the *Nyquist–Shannon sampling theorem*, the sampling rate should be at least two times the highest frequency component in the signal. Since the highest frequency component for audio is 20,000 Hz, this suggests that the sampling rate should be at least 40,000 Hz. By no coincidence, the sampling rates of CDs and DVDs are 44,100 Hz and 48,000 Hz, respectively.

By sampling the signal, an array of values is produced.[1] At 1,000 Hz, the array would contain a thousand values for every second. Using an index variable k, we can refer to the kth sample as $x[k]$, which corresponds to $x(k\Delta t)$. Arbitrarily, the first sample is $x[0] = x(0)$.

Linear Filters

In the context of signal processing, a *filter* is a transformation that maps one signal to another. Each signal is a function of time, and the filter is like a black box that receives the one signal as input, and produces another as output. If x represents an entire signal (over all times), then let $F(x)$ represent the resulting signal after running it through the filter.

A *linear filter* is a special kind of filter that satisfies two algebraic properties. The first algebraic property is *additivity*, which means that if two signals are added and sent through the filter, the result should be the same as if they were each sent through the filter independently, and then the resulting transformed signals were added. Using notation, this is $F(x + x') = F(x) + F(x')$ for any two signals x and x'. For example, if two different sounds are sent into the filter, the result should be the same whether they are combined before or after the filtering. This concept will become useful as multiple sinusoids are sent through the filter.

The second algebraic property is *homogeneity*, which means that if the signal is scaled by a constant factor before being sent though the filter, the result would be the same as if it were scaled by the same factor afterwards. Using notation, this means that $cF(x) = F(cx)$ for every constant c and signal x. For example, this means that if we double the sound amplitude, then the output sound from the filter doubles its amplitude as well.

A linear filter generally takes the form

$$y[k] = c_0 x[k] + c_1 x[k-1] + c_2 x[k-2] + c_3 x[k-3] + \cdots + c_n x[k-n], \quad (11.3)$$

in which each c_i is a constant, and $n+1$ is the number of samples involved in the filter. One may consider the case in which n tends to infinity, but it will not be pursued here. Not surprisingly, (11.3) is a linear equation. This particular form is a *causal filter* because the samples on the left occur no later than the sample $y[k]$. A non-causal filter would require dependency on future samples, which is reasonable for a recorded signal, but not for live sampling. (The future is usually unpredictable!)

Here are some examples of linear filters (special cases of (11.3)). This one takes a moving average of the last three samples:

$$y[k] = \frac{1}{3}x[k] + \frac{1}{3}x[k-1] + \frac{1}{3}x[k-2]. \quad (11.4)$$

---

[1] The values are also discretized, and are represented using floating-point numbers. This level of discretization will be ignored.

Alternatively, this is an example of *exponential smoothing* (also called *exponentially weighted moving average*):

$$y[k] = \frac{1}{2}x[k] + \frac{1}{4}x[k-1] + \frac{1}{8}x[k-2] + \frac{1}{16}x[k-3]. \qquad (11.5)$$

Finite Impulse Response
An important and useful result is that the behavior of a linear filter can be fully characterized in terms of its *finite impulse response* (*FIR*). The filter in (11.3) is often called an *FIR filter*. A *finite impulse* is a signal for which $x[0] = 1$ and $x[k] = 0$ for all $k > 0$. Any other signal can be expressed as a linear combination of time-shifted finite impulses. If a finite impulse is shifted, for example $x[2] = 1$, with $x[k] = 0$ for all other $k \neq 2$, then a linear filter produces the same result, but it is just delayed two steps later. A finite impulse can be rescaled due to filter linearity, with the output simply being rescaled. The results of sending scaled and shifted impulses through the filter are also obtained directly due to linearity.

Nonlinear Filters
Any (causal) filter that does not follow the form (11.3) is called a *nonlinear filter*. Recall from Section 11.2 that the operation of the human auditory system is almost a linear filter, but exhibits characteristics that make it into a nonlinear filter. Linear filters are preferred because of their close connection to spectral analysis, or frequency components, of the signal. Even if the human auditory system contains some nonlinear behavior, analysis based on linear filters is nevertheless valuable.

Returning to Fourier Analysis
Now consider the bottom part of Figure 11.12. The operation of a linear filter is easy to understand and compute in the *frequency domain*. This is the function obtained by performing the Fourier transform on the signal, which provides an amplitude for every combination of frequency and phase. This transform was briefly introduced in Section 11.1 and is illustrated in Figure 11.3. Formally, it is defined for discrete-time systems as

$$X(f) = \sum_{k=-\infty}^{\infty} x[k]e^{-i2\pi f k}, \qquad (11.6)$$

in which $X(f)$ is the resulting spectral distribution, which is a function of the frequency f. The exponent involves $i = \sqrt{-1}$ and is related to sinusoids through Euler's formula:

$$e^{-i2\pi f k} = \cos(-2\pi f k) + i\sin(-2\pi f k). \qquad (11.7)$$

Unit complex numbers are used as an algebraic trick to represent the phase. The *inverse Fourier transform* is similar in form and converts the spectral distribution back into the time domain. These calculations are quickly performed in practice by using the *Fast Fourier Transform* (*FFT*) [11, 192].

(a)   (b)

Figure 11.13 An audio model (b) is usually simpler than a visual model (a) [253].

Transfer Function

In some cases, a linear filter is designed by expressing how it modifies the spectral distribution. It could amplify some frequencies, while suppressing others. In this case, the filter is defined in terms of a *transfer function*, which is applied as follows: (1) transforming the original signal using the Fourier transform, (2) multiplying the result by the transfer function to obtain the distorted spectral distribution, and then (3) applying the inverse Fourier transform to obtain the result as a function of time. The transfer function can be calculated from the linear filter by applying the discrete Laplace transform (called *z-transform*) to the finite impulse response [11, 192].

11.4.2 Acoustic Modeling

The geometric modeling concepts from Section 3.1 apply to the auditory side of VR, in addition to the visual side. In fact, the same models could be used for both. Walls that reflect light in the virtual world also reflect sound waves. Therefore, both could be represented by the same triangular mesh. This is fine in theory, but fine levels of detail or spatial resolution do not matter as much for audio. Due to high visual acuity, geometric models designed for visual rendering may have a high level of detail. Recall from Section 5.4 that humans can distinguish 30 stripes or more per degree of viewing angle. In the case of sound waves, small structures are essentially invisible to sound. One recommendation is that the acoustic model needs to have a spatial resolution of only 0.5 m [343]. Figure 11.13 shows an example. Thus, any small corrugations, door knobs, or other fine structures can be simplified away. It remains an open challenge to automatically convert a 3D model designed for visual rendering into one optimized for auditory rendering.

Now consider a sound source in the virtual environment. This could, for example, be a "magical" point that emits sound waves or a vibrating planar surface. The equivalent of white light is called *white noise*, which in theory contains equal weight of all frequencies in the audible spectrum. Pure static from an analog TV or radio is an approximate example of this. In practical settings, the sound of interest has a high concentration among specific frequencies, rather than being uniformly distributed.

How does the sound interact with the surface? This is analogous to the shading problem from Section 7.1. In the case of light, diffuse and specular reflections occur with a dependency on color. In the case of sound, the same two possibilities exist, again with a dependency on the wavelength (or equivalently, the frequency). For a large, smooth, flat surface, a specular reflection of sound waves occurs, with the outgoing angle being equal to the incoming angle. The reflected sound usually has a different amplitude and phase. The amplitude may be decreased by a constant factor due to absorption of sound into the material. The factor usually depends on the wavelength (or frequency). The back of [343] contains coefficients of absorption, given with different frequencies, for many common materials.

In the case of smaller objects, or surfaces with repeated structures such as bricks or corrugations, the sound waves may scatter in a way that is difficult to characterize. This is similar to diffuse reflection of light, but the scattering pattern for sound may be hard to model and calculate. One unfortunate problem is that the scattering behavior depends on the wavelength. If the wavelength is much smaller or much larger than the size of the structure (entire object or corrugation), then the sound waves will mainly reflect. If the wavelength is close to the structure size, then significant, complicated scattering may occur.

At the extreme end of modeling burdens, a *bidirectional scattering distribution function* (*BSDF*) could be constructed. The BSDF could be estimated from equivalent materials in the real world by a combination of a speaker placed in different locations and a microphone array to measure the scattering in a particular direction. This might work well for flat materials that are large with respect to the wavelength, but it will still not handle the vast variety of complicated structures and patterns that can appear on a surface.

Capturing Sound

Sounds could also be captured in the real world using microphones and then brought into the physical world. For example, the matched zone might contain microphones that become speakers at the equivalent poses in the real world. As in the case of video capture, making a system that fully captures the sound field is challenging. Simple but effective techniques based on interpolation of sounds captured by multiple microphones are proposed in [261].

11.4.3 Auralization

Propagation of Sound in the Virtual World

As in visual rendering, there are two main ways to handle the propagation of waves. The most expensive way is based on simulating the physics as accurately as possible, which involves computing numerical solutions to partial differential equations that precisely model wave propagation. The cheaper way is to shoot visibility rays and characterize the dominant interactions between sound sources, surfaces, and ears. The choice between the two methods also depends on the particular setting; some systems involve both kinds of computations [212, 343]. If the waves are large relative to the objects in the environment, then numerical methods are preferred. In other words, the frequencies are low and the geometric models have a high level of detail. At higher frequencies or with larger, simpler models, visibility-based methods are preferable.

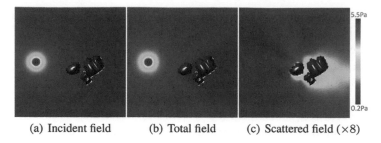

(a) Incident field   (b) Total field   (c) Scattered field ($\times 8$)

Figure 11.14 Computed results for sound propagation by numerically solving the Helmholtz wave equation (taken from [212]). (a) The pressure magnitude before obstacle interaction is considered. (b) The pressure after taking into account scattering. (c) The scattering component, which is the pressure from (b) minus the pressure from (a).

Numerical Wave Propagation

The *Helmholtz wave equation* expresses constraints at every point in $\mathbb{R}^3$ in terms of partial derivatives of the pressure function. Its frequency-dependent form is

$$\nabla^2 p + \frac{\omega^2}{s^2} p = 0, \qquad (11.8)$$

in which p is the sound pressure, ∇^2 is the Laplacian operator from calculus, and ω is related to the frequency f as $\omega = 2\pi f$.

Closed-form solutions to (11.8) do not exist, except in trivial cases. Therefore, numerical computations are performed by iteratively updating values over the space; a brief survey of methods in the context of auditory rendering appears in [212]. The wave equation is defined over the obstacle-free portion of the virtual world. The edge of this space becomes complicated, leading to *boundary conditions*. One or more parts of the boundary correspond to sound sources, which can be considered as vibrating objects or obstacles that force energy into the world. At these locations, the 0 in (11.8) is replaced by a *forcing function*. At the other boundaries, the wave may undergo some combination of absorption, reflection, scattering, and diffraction. These are extremely difficult to model; see [269] for details. In some rendering applications, these boundary interactions may simplified and handled with simple *Dirichlet boundary conditions* and *Neumann boundary conditions* [370]. If the virtual world is unbounded, then an additional *Sommerfield radiation condition* is needed. For detailed models and equations for sound propagation in a variety of settings, see [269]. An example of a numerically computed sound field is shown in Figure 11.14.

Visibility-Based Wave Propagation

The alternative to numerical computations, which gradually propagate the pressure numbers through the space, is visibility-based methods, which consider the paths of sound rays that emanate from the source and bounce between obstacles. The methods involve determining ray intersections with the geometric model primitives, which is analogous to ray tracing operations from Section 7.1.

It is insightful to look at the impulse response of a sound source in a virtual world. If the environment is considered as a linear filter, then the impulse response

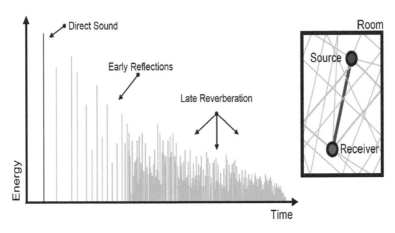

Figure 11.15 A simulation of reverberations [253].

provides a complete characterization for any other sound signal [213, 253, 263]. Figure 11.15 shows the simple case of the impulse response for reflections in a rectangular room. Visibility-based methods are particularly good at simulating the reverberations, which are important to reproduce for perceptual reasons. More generally, visibility-based methods may consider rays that correspond to all of the cases of reflection, absorption, scattering, and diffraction. Due to the high computational cost of characterizing all rays, *stochastic ray tracing* offers a practical alternative by randomly sampling rays and their interactions with materials [343]; this falls under the general family of Monte Carlo methods, which are used, for example, to approximate solutions to high-dimensional integration and optimization problems.

Entering the Ear
Sound that is generated in the virtual world must be transmitted to each ear in the physical world. It is as if a virtual microphone positioned in the virtual world captures the simulated sound waves. These are then converted into audio output through a speaker that is positioned in front of the ear. Recall from Section 11.3 that humans are able to localize sound sources from auditory cues. How would this occur for VR if all of the sound emanates from a fixed speaker? The ILD and ITD cues could be simulated by ensuring that each ear receives the appropriate sound magnitude and phase so that differences in amplitude and timing are correct. This implies that the physical head must be reproduced at some level of detail in the virtual world so that these differences are correctly calculated. For example, the distance between the ears and the size of the head may become important.

HRTFs
This solution would still be insufficient to resolve ambiguity within the cone of confusion. Recall from Section 11.3 that the pinna shape distorts sounds in a direction-dependent way. To fully take into account the pinna and other parts of the head that may distort the incoming sound, the solution is to develop a *head-related transfer function* (*HRTF*). The idea is to treat this distortion as a linear filter, which

can be characterized in terms of its transfer function (recall Figure 11.12). This is accomplished by placing a human subject into an anechoic chamber and placing sound sources at different locations in the space surrounding the head. At each location, an impulse is generated on a speaker, and the impulse response is recorded with a small microphone placed inside the ear canal of a human or dummy. The locations are selected by incrementally varying the distance, azimuth, and elevation; recall the coordinates for localization from Figure 11.10. In many cases, a *far-field approximation* may be appropriate, in which case a large value is fixed for the distance. This results in an HRTF that depends on only the azimuth and elevation.

It is, of course, impractical to build an HRTF for every user. There is significant motivation to use a single HRTF that represents the "average listener"; however, the difficulty is that it might not be sufficient in some applications because it is not designed for individual users (see Section 6.3.2 of [343]). One compromise might be to offer a small selection of HRTFs to users to account for variation among the population, but they may be incapable of picking the one most suitable for their particular pinnae and head. Another issue is that the transfer function may depend on factors that frequently change, such as wearing a hat, putting on a jacket with a hood or large collar, or getting a haircut. Recall that adaptation occurs throughout human perception and nearly all aspects of VR. If people adapt to frequent changes in the vicinity of their heads in the real world, then perhaps they would also adapt to an HRTF that is not perfect. Significant research questions remain in this area.

Tracking Issues
The final challenge is to ensure that the physical and virtual ears align in the matched zone. If the user turns her head, then the sound should be adjusted accordingly. If the sound emanates from a fixed source, then it should be perceived as fixed while turning the head. This is another example of the perception of stationarity. Accordingly, tracking of the ear pose (position and orientation) is needed to determine the appropriate "viewpoint." This is equivalent to head tracking with simple position and orientation offsets for the right and left ears. As for vision, there are two choices. The head orientation alone may be tracked, with the full pose of each ear determined by a head model (recall Figure 9.8). Alternatively, the full head pose may be tracked, directly providing the pose of each ear through offset transforms. To optimize performance, user-specific parameters can provide a perfect match: the distance along the z-axis from the eyes to the ears and the distance between ears. The latter is analogous to the IPD, the distance between pupils for the case of vision.

Further Reading

For mathematical and computational foundations of acoustics, see [269, 328]. Physiology and psychoacoustics are covered in [223, 371] and chapters 4 and 5 of [207]. Localization is covered thoroughly in [23]. The cone of confusion is discussed in [296]. Echo thresholds are covered in [273, 367].

Some basic signal processing texts are [11, 192]. For an overview of auditory displays, see [344]. Convenient placement of audio sound sources from a psychophysical perspective is covered in [261]. Auditory rendering is covered in detail in the book [343]. Some key articles on auditory rendering are [88, 213, 253, 262, 263].

CHAPTER TWELVE

Evaluating VR Systems and Experiences

Which headset is better? Which VR experience is more comfortable over a long period of time? How much field of view is enough? What is the most appropriate interaction mechanism? Engineers and developers want to know the answers to these kinds of questions; however, it should be clear at this point that these are difficult to answer because of the way that human physiology and perception operate and interact with engineered systems. By contrast, pure engineering questions such as "What is the estimated battery life?" or "What is the vehicle's top speed on level ground?" are much more approachable.

Recall the definition of VR from Section 1.1, which involves an *organism*. When VR is applied by scientists to study the neural structures and perception of a rat, there is a clear separation between the rat and the scientist. However, in the case of VR for humans, the developer frequently tries out his own creations. In this case, the developer alternates between the role of scientist and rat. This introduces numerous problems, especially if the developer is naive about perceptual issues.

Further complicating matters is adaptation, which occurs on all scales. For example, a person evaluating a VR experience many times over several weeks may initially find it uncomfortable, but later become accustomed to it. Of course this does not imply that its likelihood of making a fresh user sick is lower. There is also great variation across people. Any one person, including the developer, provides just one data point. People who are immune to sickness from vection will have no trouble developing such systems and inflicting them upon others.

Another factor is that most people who create systems are biased toward liking what they create. Furthermore, as discussed in Section 8.4, just having the knowledge of what the experience represents can affect vection. These issues fall under the general heading of *human factors*, which has been studied for decades. One closely related area is *human–computer interaction* (*HCI*), which uses the methods discussed in this section. However, since VR works by disrupting the low-level operation of sensory systems that we have trusted for our entire lives, the level of complications from the lowest-level side effects to the highest-level cognitive effects seems unprecedented.

Opportunities for failure exist at all levels, from hardware, to low-level software, to content creation engines. As hardware and low-level software rapidly improve, the burden is shifting more to developers of software engines and VR experiences. This chapter presents several topics that may aid engineers and developers in their quest to build better VR systems and experiences. Section 12.1 introduces methods for guiding them to improve their discriminatory power. Rather than adapting to become oblivious to a problem, a developer could train herself to become more sensitive to problems. Section 12.2 applies the fundamentals from this book to provide simple advice for VR developers. Section 12.3 covers VR sickness, including the main symptoms and causes, so that VR systems and experiences may be improved. Section 12.4 introduces general methods for designing experiments that involve human subjects, and includes some specific methods from psychophysics. All of the concepts from this chapter should be used to gain critical feedback and avoid pitfalls in an iterative VR development process.

12.1 Perceptual Training

Most people who try VR for the first time are unaware of technical flaws that would be obvious to some experienced engineers and developers. If the VR experience is functioning as it should, then the user should be overwhelmed by dominant visual stimuli and feel as if he is inhabiting the virtual world. Minor flaws may be subtle or unnoticeable as attention is focused mainly on the targeted experience (as considered in the definition of VR from Section 1.1). Some parts might not be functioning as designed or some perceptual issues might have been neglected. This might result in an experience that is not as good as it could have been after performing some simple adjustments. Even worse, the flaws might cause the user to become fatigued or sick. At the end, such users are usually not consciously aware of what went wrong. They might blame anything, such as particular visual stimuli, a particular experience, the headset hardware, or even the whole concept of VR.

This problem can be mitigated by training specific users and developers to notice common types of flaws. By developing a program of *perceptual training*, a user could be requested to look for a particular artifact or shortcoming, or to repeatedly practice performing some task. Throughout this book, we have seen the importance of adaptation in human perceptual processes. For example, if a constant stimulus is presented over a long period of time, then its perceived intensity diminishes.

Through repeated and guided exposure to a particular VR system and experience, users can adapt their perceptual systems. This is a form of *perceptual learning*, which is a branch of perceptual psychology that studies long-lasting changes to the perceptual systems of an organism in response to its environment. As VR becomes a new environment for the organism, the opportunities and limits of perceptual learning remain largely unexplored. Through active training, the way in which users adapt can be controlled so that their perceptual abilities and discrimination power increases. This in turn can be used to train *evaluators* who provide frequent feedback in the development process. An alternative is to develop an automated system that can detect flaws without human intervention. It is likely that a combination of both human and automatic evaluation will be remain important.

Examples of Perceptual Learning

In everyday life we encounter many examples of perceptual learning, for each of the senses. Regarding vision, doctors and medical technicians are trained to extract relevant information from images that appear to be a confusing jumble to the untrained eye. A cancer specialist can spot tumors in CT and MRI scans. An obstetrician can effortlessly determine, from a hand-held ultrasound scanner, whether structures in a fetus are developing normally. Regarding hearing, musicians learn to distinguish and classify various musical notes after extensive practice. Audiophiles learn to notice particular flaws in music reproduction due to recording, compression, speaker, and room-acoustic issues. Regarding taste and smell, a sommelier learns to distinguish subtle differences between wines. Regarding touch, the blind learn to read Braille, which is expressed as tiny patterns of raised dots that are felt with fingertips. All of these examples seem impossible to a newcomer, to the point that it would seem we do not even have the neural hardware for accomplishing it. Nevertheless, through established perceptual training programs and/or repeated practice, people can acquire surprisingly powerful perceptual abilities. Why not do the same for evaluating VR?

Perceptual Learning Factors and Mechanisms
What happens to human perceptual systems when these forms of learning occur? One important factor is *neuroplasticity*, which enables human brains to develop specialized neural structures as an adaptation to environmental stimuli. Although this is much stronger with small children, as exhibited in the case of native language learning, neuroplasticity remains through adults' lives; the amount may highly vary across individuals.

Another factor is the way in which the learning occurs. Adaptations might occur from casual observation or targeted strategies that focus on the stimulus. The time and repetition involved for the learning to take place might vary greatly, depending on the task, performance requirements, stimuli, and person. Furthermore, the person might be given *supervised training*, in which feedback is directly provided as she attempts to improve her performance. Alternatively, *unsupervised training* may occur, in which the trainer has placed sufficient stimuli in the learner's environment, but does not interfere with the learning process.

Four basic mechanisms have been developed to explain perceptual learning [99]:

1. **Attentional weighting:** The amount of attention paid to features that are relevant to the task is increased, while decreasing attention to others.
2. **Stimulus imprinting:** Specialized receptors are developed that identify part or all of the relevant stimuli. These could be neurological structures or abstract processes that function as such.
3. **Differentiation:** Differing stimuli that were once fused together perceptually become separated. Subtle differences appear to be amplified.
4. **Unitization:** This process combines or compresses many different stimuli into a single response. This is in contrast to differentiation and becomes useful for classifications in which the differences within a unit become irrelevant.

The remainder of this section offers examples and useful suggestions in the context of VR. The field is far from having standard perceptual training programs that resemble medical image or musical training. Instead, we offer suggestions on how to move and where to focus attention while trying to spot errors in a VR experience. This requires the human to remain aware of the interference caused by artificial stimuli, which goes against the stated definition of VR from Section 1.1.

Figure 12.1 A butterfly appears in the image that is presented to the left eye, but there is not one in the corresponding right image.

Stereo Problems

Figure 12.1 shows a simple error in which an object appears in the scene for one eye but not the other. The rest of the virtual world is rendered correctly. This may go completely unnoticed by untrained eyes. Solution: close the left eye, while keeping the right one open; after that, switch to having the left eye open and the right eye closed. By switching back and forth between having a single eye open, the mismatch should become clear. This will be called the *eye-closing trick*.

Another common error is to have the right and left eye images reversed. It is easy to have this problem after making a sign error in (3.50), or misunderstanding which way the viewpoint needs to shift for each eye. The phenomenon is known as *pseudoscopic vision*, in which the perceived concavity of objects may seem reversed. In many cases, however, it is difficult to visually detect the error. Solution: approach the edge of an object so that one side of it is visible to one eye only. This can be verified by using the eye-closing trick. Based on the geometry of the object, make sure that the side is visible to the correct eye. For example, the left eye should not be the only one to see the right side of a box.

Finally, stereoscopic vision could have an incorrect distance between the virtual pupils (the t parameter in (3.50)). If $t = 0$, then the eye closing trick could be used to detect that the two images look identical. If t is too large or too small, then depth and scale perception (Section 6.1) are affected. A larger separation t would cause the world to appear smaller; a smaller t would cause the opposite.

Canonical Head Motions

Now consider errors that involve movement, which could be caused by head tracking errors, the rendering perspective, or some combination. It is helpful to make careful, repeatable motions, which will be called *canonical head motions*. If rotation alone is tracked, then there are three rotational DOFs. To spot various kinds of motion or viewpoint errors, the evaluator should be trained to carefully perform individual, basic rotations. A pure yaw can be performed by nodding a "no" gesture. A pure pitch appears as a pure "yes" gesture. A pure roll is more difficult to accomplish, which involves turning the head back and forth so that one eye is higher than the other at the extremes. In any of these movements, it may be beneficial to translate the cyclopean viewpoint (point between the center of the eyes) as little as possible, or follow as closely to the translation induced by the head model of Section 9.1.

For each of these basic rotations, the evaluator should practice performing them at various, constant angular velocities and amplitudes. For example, she should try to yaw her head very slowly, at a constant rate, up to 45 each way. Alternatively, she should try to rotate at a fast rate, up to 10 degrees each way, perhaps with a frequency of 2 Hz. Using canonical head motions, common errors that were given in Figure 9.7 could be determined. Other problems, such as a discontinuity in the tracking, tilt errors, latency, and the incorrect depth of the viewpoint can be more easily detected in this way.

If position is tracked as well, then three more kinds of canonical head motions become important, one for each position DOF. Thus, horizontal, vertical, and depth changing motions can be performed to identify problems. For example, with horizontal, side-to-side motions, it can be determined whether motion parallax is functioning correctly.

VOR versus Smooth Pursuit

Recall from Sections 5.3, 5.4, and 6.2 that eye movements play an important role in visual perception. An evaluator should keep in mind the particular eye movement mode when evaluating whether an object in the virtual world is actually stationary when it is supposed to be. If a canonical yaw motion is made while eyes are fixated on the object, then the vestibulo-ocular reflex (VOR) is invoked. In this case, then the evaluator can determine whether the object appears to move or distort its shape while the image of the object is fixed on the retina. Similarly, if an object is slowly moving by and the head is fixed, the evaluator performs smooth pursuit to keep the object on the retina. As indicated in Section 5.4, the way in which an object appears to distort for a line-by-line scanout display depends on whether the motion is due to VOR or smooth pursuit. If the object moves by very quickly and the eyes do not keep it fixed on the retina, then it may be possible to perceive the zipper effect.

Peripheral Problems

The current generation of VR headsets have significant optical aberration issues; recall from Section 4.3 that these become worse as the distance from the optical axis increases. It is important to distinguish between two cases: (1) looking through the center of the lens while detecting distortion at the periphery, and (2) rotating the eyes to look directly through the edge of the lens. Distortion might be less noticeable in the first case because of lower photoreceptor density at the periphery; however, mismatches could nevertheless have an impact on comfort and sickness. Optical flow signals are strong at the periphery, and mismatched values may be perceived as incorrect motions.

In the second case, looking directly through the lens might reveal lack of focus at the periphery, caused by spherical aberration. Also, chromatic aberration may

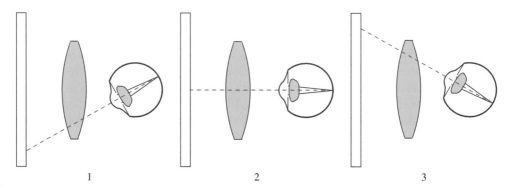

1   2   3

Figure 12.2 A top-down view that shows how the eye rotates when fixated on a stationary object in the virtual world, and the head is yawed counterclockwise (facing right to facing left). Lens distortions at the periphery interfere with the perception of stationarity.

become visible, especially for sharp white lines against a black background. Furthermore, errors in pincushion distortion correction may become evident as a straight line appears to become curved. These problems cannot be fixed by a single distortion correction function (as covered in Section 7.3) because the pupil translates away from the optical axis when the eye rotates. A different, asymmetric correction function would be needed for each eye orientation, which would require eye tracking to determine which correction function to use at each time instant.

To observe pincushion or barrel distortion, the evaluator should apply a canonical yaw motion over as large an amplitude as possible, while fixating on an object. In this case, the VOR will cause the eye to rotate over a large range while sweeping its view across the lens from side to side, as shown in Figure 12.2. If the virtual world contains a large, flat wall with significant texture or spatial frequency, then distortions could become clearly visible as the wall appears to be "breathing" during the motion. The effect may be more noticeable if the wall has a regular grid pattern painted on it.

Finally, many users do not even notice the limited field of view of the lens. Recall from Section 5.4 that any flat screen placed in front of the eye will only cover some of the eye's field of view. Therefore, photoreceptors at the periphery will not receive any direct light rays from the display. In most cases, it is dark inside the headset, which results in the perception of a black band around the visible portion of the display. Once this is pointed out to users, it becomes difficult for them to ignore it.

Latency Perception

The direct perception of latency varies wildly among people. Even when it is not perceptible, it has been one of the main contributors to VR sickness [174]. Adaptation causes great difficulty because people can adjust to a constant amount of latency through long exposure; returning to the real world might be difficult in this case. For a period of time, most of the real world may not appear to be stationary!

In my own efforts at Oculus VR, I could detect latency down to about 40 ms when I started working with the prototype Oculus Rift in 2012. By 2014, I was able to detect latency down to as little as 2 ms by the following procedure. The first step is to face a vertical edge, such as a door frame, in the virtual world. The evaluator should keep a comfortable distance, such as two meters. While fixated on the edge, a canonical yaw motion should be performed with very low amplitude, such as a few degrees, and a frequency of about 2 Hz. The amplitude and frequency of motions are important. If the amplitude is too large, then optical distortions may interfere. If the speed is too high, then the headset might start to flop around with respect to the head. If the speed is too low, then the latency might not be easily noticeable. When performing this motion, the edge should appear to be moving out of phase with the head if there is significant latency.

Recall that many VR systems today achieve zero effective latency, as mentioned in Section 7.4; nevertheless, perceptible latency may occur on many systems due to the particular combination of hardware, software, and VR content. By using prediction, it is even possible to obtain negative effective latency. Using arrow keys that increment or decrement the prediction interval, I was able to tune the effective latency down to 2 ms by applying the method above. The method is closely related to the psychophysical method of adjustment, which is covered later in Section 12.4. I was later able to immediately spot latencies down to 10 ms without any other adjustments or comparisons. Although this is not a scientific conclusion (see Section 12.4), it seems that I experienced a form of perceptual learning after spending nearly two years debugging tracking and rendering systems at Oculus VR to bring the effective latency down to zero.

Conclusions

This section provided some suggestions for training people to spot problems in VR systems. Many more can be expected to emerge in the future. For example, to evaluate auditory localization in a virtual world, evaluators should close their eyes and move their heads in canonical motions. To detect lens glare in systems that use Fresnel lenses, they should look for patterns formed by bright lights against dark backgrounds. To detect display flicker (recall from Section 6.2), especially if it is as low as 60 Hz, then the evaluator should enter a bright virtual world, preferably white, and relax the eyes until vibrations are noticeable at the periphery. To notice vergence-accommodation mismatch (recall from Section 5.4), virtual objects can be placed very close to the eyes. As the eyes converge, it may seem unusual that they are already in focus, or the eyes attempt to focus as they would in the real world, which would cause the object to be blurred.

There is also a need to have formal training mechanisms or courses that engineers and developers could use to improve their perceptive powers. In this case, evaluators could improve their skills through repeated practice. Imagine a VR experience that is a competitive game designed to enhance your perceptive abilities in spotting VR flaws.

12.2 Recommendations for Developers

With the widespread availability and affordability of VR headsets, the number of people developing VR experiences has grown dramatically over the years. Most developers have come from the video game industry, where their skills and experience in developing games and game engines are "ported over" to VR. In some cases, simple adaptations are sufficient, but game developers have been repeatedly surprised at how a highly successful and popular game experience does not translate directly to a comfortable, or even fun, VR experience. Most of the surprises are due to a lack of understanding human physiology and perception. As the field progresses, developers are coming from an increasing variety of backgrounds, including cinema, broadcasting, communications, social networking, visualization, and engineering. Artists and hobbyists have also joined in to make some of the most innovative experiences.

This section provides some useful recommendations, which are based on a combination of the principles covered in this book, and recommendations from other developer guides (especially [368]). This is undoubtedly an incomplete list that should evolve as new kinds of hardware and experiences are developed. Most VR experiences to date are based on successful 3D video games, which is evident in the kinds of recommendations being made by developers in recent years. Most of the following recommendations link to prior parts of this book, which provide scientific motivation or further explanation.

Virtual Worlds

- Set units in the virtual world that match the real world so that scales can be easily matched. For example, one unit equals one meter in the virtual world. This helps with depth and scale perception (Section 6.1).
- Make sure that objects are completely modeled so that missing parts are not noticeable as the user looks at them from viewpoints that would have been unexpected for graphics on a screen.
- Very thin objects, such as leaves on a tree, might look incorrect in VR due to varying viewpoints.
- Design the environment so that less locomotion is required; for example, a virtual elevator would be more comfortable than virtual stairs (Sections 8.4 and 10.2).
- Consider visual and auditory rendering performance issues and simplify the geometric models as needed to maintain the proper frame rates on targeted hardware (Sections 7.4 and 11.4).

Visual Rendering

- The only difference between the left and right views should be the viewpoint, not models, textures, colors, and so on (Sections 3.5 and 12.1).
- Never allow words, objects, or images to be fixed to part of the screen; all content should appear to be embedded in the virtual world. Recall from Section 2.1 that being stationary on the screen is not the same as being perceived as stationary in the virtual world.
- Be careful when adjusting the field of view for rendering or any parameters that affect lens distortion so that the result does not cause further mismatch (Sections 7.3 and 12.1).
- Re-evaluate common graphics tricks such as texture mapping and normal mapping, to ensure that they are effective in VR as the user has stereoscopic viewing and is able to quickly change viewpoints (Section 7.2).
- Anti-aliasing techniques are much more critical for VR because of the varying viewpoint and stereoscopic viewing (Section 7.2).

- The rendering system should be optimized so that the desired virtual world can be updated at a frame rate that is at least as high as the hardware requirements (for example, 90 FPS); otherwise, the frame rate may decrease and vary, which causes discomfort (Section 7.4.)
- Avoid movements of objects that cause most of the visual field to change in the same way; otherwise, the user might feel as if she is moving (Section 8.4).
- Determine how to cull away geometry that is too close to the face of the user; otherwise, substantial vergence-accommodation mismatch will occur (Section 5.4).
- Unlike in games and cinematography, the viewpoint should not change in a way that is not matched to head tracking, unless the intention is for the user to feel as if she is moving in the virtual world, which itself can be uncomfortable (Section 10.2).
- For proper depth and scale perception, the interpupillary distance of the user in the real world should match the corresponding viewpoint distance between eyes in the virtual world (Section 6.1).
- In comparison to graphics on a screen, reduce the brightness and contrast of the models to increase VR comfort.

Tracking and the Matched Zone
- Never allow head tracking to be frozen or delayed; otherwise, the user might immediately perceive self-motion (Section 8.4).
- Make sure that the eye viewpoints are correctly located, considering stereo offsets (Section 3.5), head models (Section 9.1), and locomotion (Section 10.2).
- Beware of obstacles in the real world that do not exist in the virtual world; a warning system may be necessary as the user approaches an obstacle (Section 8.3.1).
- Likewise, beware of obstacles in the virtual world that do not exist in the real world. For example, it may have unwanted consequences if a user decides to poke his head through a wall (Section 8.3.1).
- As the edge of the tracking region is reached, it is more comfortable to gradually reduce contrast and brightness than to simply hold the position fixed (Section 8.4).

Interaction
- Consider interaction mechanisms that are better than reality by giving people superhuman powers, rather than applying the universal simulation principle (Chapter 10).
- For locomotion, follow the suggestions in Section 10.2 to reduce vection side effects.
- For manipulation in the virtual world, try to require the user to move as little as possible in the physical world; avoid giving the user a case of gorilla arms (Section 10.3).
- With regard to social interaction, higher degrees of realism are not necessarily better, due to the uncanny valley (Section 10.4).

User Interfaces

- If a floating menu, web browser, or other kind of virtual display appears, then it should be rendered at least two meters away from the user's viewpoint to minimize vergence-accommodation mismatch (Section 5.4).
- Such a virtual display should be centered and have a relatively narrow field of view, approximately one-third of the total viewing area, to minimize eye and head movement (Section 5.3).
- Embedding menus, options, game status, and other information may be most comfortable if it appears to be written into the virtual world in ways that are familiar; this follows the universal simulation principle (Chapter 10).

Audio

- Be aware of the difference between a user listening over fixed, external speakers versus attached headphones; sound source localization will not function correctly over headphones without tracking (Section 2.1).
- Both position and orientation from tracking and avatar locomotion should be taken into account for auralization (Section 11.4).
- The Doppler effect provides a strong motion cue (Section 11.1).
- Geometric models can be greatly simplified for audio in comparison to visual rendering; a spatial resolution of 0.5 meters is usually sufficient (Section 11.4).

Self Appearance

- The feeling of being present in the virtual world and the ability to judge scale in it are enhanced if the user is able to see her corresponding body in VR.
- A simple virtual body is much better than having none at all.
- Unexpected differences between the virtual body and real body may be alarming. They could have a different gender, body type, or species. This could lead to a powerful experience, or could be an accidental distraction.
- If only head tracking is performed, then the virtual body should satisfy some basic kinematic constraints, rather than decapitating the user in the virtual world (Section 9.4).
- Users' self-appearance will affect their social behavior, as well as the way people around them react to them (Section 10.4).

12.3 Comfort and VR Sickness

Experiencing discomfort as a side effect of using VR systems has been the largest threat to widespread adoption of the technology over the past decades. It is considered the main reason for its failure to live up to overblown expectations in the early 1990s. Few people want a technology that causes them to suffer while using it, and in many cases long after using it. It has also been frustrating for researchers to characterize VR sickness because of many factors such as variation among people, adaptation over repeated use, difficulty of measuring symptoms, rapidly changing technology, and content-dependent sensitivity. Advances in display, sensing, and computing technologies have caused the adverse side effects due to hardware to reduce; however, they nevertheless remain today in consumer VR headsets.

As hardware-based side effects reduce, the burden has been shifting more toward software engineers and content developers. This is occurring because the VR experience itself has the opportunity to make people sick, even though the hardware may be deemed to be perfectly comfortable. In fact, the best VR headset available may enable developers to make people more sick than ever before! For these reasons, it is critical for engineers and developers of VR systems to understand these unfortunate side effects so that they determine how to reduce or eliminate them for the vast majority of users.

Sickness or Syndrome

In this book, we refer to any unintended, uncomfortable side effects of using a VR system as a form of *VR sickness*. This might include many symptoms that are not ordinarily associated with sickness, such as fatigue. A more accurate phrase might therefore be VR *maladaptation syndrome*, in which *maladaptation* refers to being more harmful than helpful, and *syndrome* refers to a group of symptoms that consistently occur together in association with the activity.

Motion Sickness Variants

It is helpful to know terms that are closely related to VR sickness because they are associated with similar activities, sets of symptoms, and potential causes. This helps in searching for related research. The broadest area of relevance is *motion sickness*, which refers to symptoms that are associated with exposure to real and/or apparent motion. It generally involves the vestibular organs (Section 8.2), which implies that they involve sensory input or conflict regarding accelerations; in fact, people without functioning vestibular organs do not experience motion sickness [148]. Motion sickness due to real motion occurs because of unusual forces that are experienced. This could happen from spinning oneself around in circles, resulting in dizziness and nausea. Similarly, the symptoms occur from being transported by a vehicle that can produce forces that are extreme or uncommon. The self-spinning episode could be replaced by a hand-powered merry-go-round. More extreme experiences and side effects can be generated by a variety of motorized amusement park rides.

Unfortunately, motion sickness extends well beyond entertainment, as many people suffer from motion sickness while riding in vehicles designed for transportation. People experience *car sickness*, *sea sickness*, and *air sickness*, from cars, boats, and airplanes, respectively. It is estimated that only about 10 percent of people have never experienced significant nausea during transportation [174]. Militaries have performed the largest motion sickness studies because of soldiers spending long tours of duty on sea vessels and flying high-speed combat aircraft. About 70 percent of naval personnel experience seasickness, and about 80 percent of those have decreased work efficiency or motivation [254]. Finally, another example of unusual forces is space travel, in which astronauts who experience microgravity complain of nausea and other symptoms; this is called *space sickness*.

Visually Induced Motion Sickness

The motion sickness examples so far have involved real motion. By contrast, motion sickness may occur by exposure to stimuli that convince the brain that accelerations are occurring, even though they are not. This is called *apparent motion*. The most commonly studied case is *visually induced apparent motion*, which is also called vection and was covered in Sections 8.4 and 10.2. Symptoms associated with this are part of *visually induced motion sickness*.

Vection (more generally, optical flow) can be generated in many ways. Recall from Figure 2.20 of Section 2.3 that extreme vection was caused by a room that swung while people remained fixed inside. Scientists use an *optokinetic drum* to conduct controlled experiments in vection and motion sickness by surrounding the subject with movable visual stimuli. Across a variety of studies that involve particular moving visual fields, only a few subjects are immune to side effects. About 50 percent to 100 percent experience dizziness and about 20 percent to 60 percent experience stomach symptoms; the exact level depends on the particular experiment [174].

Alternatively, displays may be used to generate vection. Recall from Section 6.2 that the optical flow perceived in this case is stroboscopic apparent motion due to a rapid succession of frames. The case of using displays is obviously of more interest to us; however, sickness studies that use optokinetic drums remain relevant because they serve as an important point of reference. They reveal how bad visually induced motion sickness can become, even in the limit of having no hardware artifacts such as display resolution and low frame rates.

Simulator Sickness and Cybersickness

Once displays are used, the choices discussed in Section 2.1 reappear: They may be fixed screens that surround the user (as in a CAVE VR system) or a head-mounted display that requires tracking. Vehicle *simulators* are perhaps the first important application of VR, with the most common examples being driving a car and flying an airplane or helicopter. The user may sit on a fixed base, or a motorized base that responds to controls. The latter case provides vestibular stimulation, for which time synchronization of motion and visual information is crucial to minimize sickness. Usually, the entire cockpit is rebuilt in the real world, and the visual stimuli appear at or outside the windows. The head could be tracked to provide stereopsis and varying viewpoints, but most often this is not done so that comfort is maximized and technological side effects are minimized. The branch of visually induced motion sickness that results from this activity is aptly called *simulator sickness*, which has been well studied by the US military.

The term *cybersickness* [210] was proposed to cover any sickness associated with VR (or virtual environments), which properly includes simulator sickness. Unfortunately, the meaning of the term has expanded in recent times to include sickness associated with spending too much time interacting with smartphones or computers in general. Furthermore, the term *cyber* has accumulated many odd connotations over the decades. Therefore, we refer to visually induced motion sickness, and any other forms of discomfort that arise from VR, as *VR sickness*.

Common Symptoms of VR Sickness

A variety of terms are used to refer to symptoms throughout various motion and VR sickness studies. The most common are (based on [146, 148, 172, 174, 311]):

- **Nausea:** In mild form, users may start having unpleasant sensations associated with the stomach, upper abdomen, esophagus, or throat. As the intensity increases, it gradually leads to the feeling of needing to vomit. This is the most negative and intimidating symptom of VR sickness.

- **Dizziness:** Users may feel a sensation of movement, such as spinning, tumbling, or swaying, even after the stimulus is removed. This may also include *vertigo*, which is similar and often associated with malfunctioning vestibular organs.
- **Drowsiness:** Users may become less alert, yawn, and eventually start to fall asleep.
- **Increased salivation:** The amount of saliva in the mouth increases, causing more swallowing that usual.
- **Cold sweating:** Users begin to sweat or increase their sweat, but not in response to increased ambient temperature.
- **Pallor:** Users experience a whitening or loss of normal skin color in the face, and possibly ears, neck, and chest.
- **Warmth/flushing:** This corresponds to a sudden increase in perceived warmth, similar to a wave of fever.
- **Headache:** Users develop headaches that may gradually increase in intensity and remain long after use.
- **Fatigue:** Users may become tired or exhausted after a long experience.
- **Eyestrain:** Users may feel that their eyes are tired, fatigued, sore, or aching.
- **Accommodation issues:** Users may have blurred vision or have difficulty focusing.

After reading this daunting list, it is important to associate it with *worst-case* analysis. These are the symptoms reported by at least *some* people for *some* VR experiences. The goal is to make VR systems and experiences that eliminate these symptoms for as many people as possible. Furthermore, most symptoms may be greatly reduced through repeated exposure and adaptation.

Other Side Effects

In addition to the direct symptoms just listed, several other phenomena are closely associated with motion and VR sickness, and potentially persist long after usage. One of them is *Sopite syndrome* [103], which is closely related to drowsiness but may include other symptoms, such as laziness, lack of social participation, mood changes, apathy, and sleep disturbances. These symptoms may persist even after adaptation to the systems previously listed have been greatly reduced or eliminated. Another phenomenon is *postural disequilibrium*, which adversely affects balance and coordination [174]. Finally, another phenomenon is loss of visual acuity during head or body motion [174], which seems to be a natural consequence of the VOR (Section 5.3) becoming adapted to the flaws in a VR system. This arises from forcing the perception of stationarity in spite of issues in resolution, latency, frame rates, optical distortion, and so on.

After Effects

One of the most troubling aspects of VR sickness is that symptoms might last for hours or even days after usage [310]. Most users who experience symptoms immediately after withdrawal from a VR experience still show some sickness, though at diminished levels, 30 minutes later. Only a very small number of outlier users may continue to experience symptoms for hours or days. Similarly, some people who experience sea sickness complain of *land sickness* for extended periods after

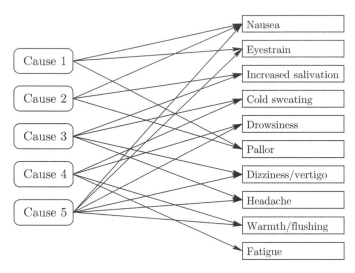

Figure 12.3 The symptoms are observed, but the causes are not directly measured. Researchers face an *inverse problem*, which is to speculate on the causes based on observed symptoms. The trouble is that each symptom may have many possible causes, some of which might not be related to the VR experience.

returning to stable ground. This corresponds to postural instability and perceived instability of the visual world; the world might appear to be rocking [174].

From Symptoms to Causes

The symptoms are the *effect*, but what are their *causes*? See Figure 12.3. The unfortunate problem for the scientist or evaluator of a VR system is that only the symptoms are observable. Any symptom could have any number of direct possible causes. Some of them may be known and others may be impossible to determine. Suppose, for example, that a user has developed mild nausea after 5 minutes of a VR experience. What are the chances that he would have gotten nauseated anyway because he rode his bicycle to the test session and forgot to eat breakfast? What if he has a hangover from alcoholic drinks the night before? Perhaps a few users such as this could be discarded as outliers, but what if there was a large festival the night before, which increased the number of people who are fatigued before the experiment? Some of these problems can be handled by breaking them into groups that are expected to have low variability; see Section 12.4. At the very least, one should probably ask them beforehand if they feel nauseated; however, this could even cause them to pay more attention to nausea, which generates a bias.

Even if it is narrowed down that the cause was the VR experience, this determination may not be narrow enough to be useful. Which part of the experience caused it? The user might have had no problems were it not for 10 seconds of stimulus during a 15-minute session. How much of the blame was due to the hardware versus the particular content? The hardware might be as comfortable as an optokinetic drum, which essentially shifts the blame to the particular images on the drum.

Questions relating to cause are answered by finding statistical correlations in the data obtained before, during, and after the exposure to VR. Thus, causation is not determined through directly witnessing the cause and its effect in the way that it is with witnessing the effect of a shattered glass that is clearly caused by dropping it on the floor. Eliminating irrelevant causes is an important part of the experimental design, which involves selecting users carefully and gathering appropriate data from them in advance. Determining more specific causes requires more experimental trials. This is complicated by the fact that different trials cannot be easily applied to the same user. Once people are sick, they will not be able to participate, or would at least give biased results that are difficult to compensate for. They could return on different days for different trials, but there could again be issues because of adaptation to VR, including the particular experiment, and simply being in a different health or emotional state on another occasion.

Variation among Users
A further complication is the wide variability among people to VR sickness susceptibility. Individual differences among groups must be accounted for in the design of the experiment; see Section 12.4. Most researchers believe that women are more susceptible to motion sickness than men [146, 246]; however, this conclusion is disputed in [174]. Regarding age, it seems that susceptibility is highest in children under 12, which then rapidly decreases as they mature to adulthood, and then gradually decreases further over their lifetime [267]. One study even concludes that Chinese people are more susceptible than some other ethnic groups [315]. The best predictor of an individual's susceptibility to motion sickness is to determine whether she or he has had it before. Finally, note that there may also be variability across groups, such as in the severity of the symptoms, the speed of their onset, the time they last after the experiment, and the rate at which the users adapt to VR.

Sensory Conflict Theory
In addition to determining the link between cause and effect in terms of offending stimuli, we should also try to understand *why* the body is reacting adversely to VR. What physiological and psychological mechanisms are involved in the process? Why might one person be unable to quickly adapt to certain stimuli, while other people are fine? What is particularly bad about the stimulus that might be easily fixed without significantly degrading the experience? The determination of these mechanisms and their reasons for existing falls under *etiology*. Although there is no widely encompassing and accepted theory that explains motion sickness or VR sickness, some useful and accepted theories exist.

One of must relevant and powerful theories for understanding VR sickness is *sensory conflict theory* [134, 148]. Recall the high-level depiction of VR systems from Figure 2.1 of Section 2.1. For VR, two kinds of mismatch exist:

1. The engineered stimuli do not closely enough match that which is expected by the central nervous system and brain in comparison to natural stimuli. Examples include artifacts due to display resolution, aliasing, frame rates, optical distortion, limited colors, synthetic lighting models, and latency.
2. Some sensory systems receive no engineered stimuli. They continue to sense the surrounding physical world in a natural way and send their neural signals accordingly. Examples include signals from the vestibular and proprioceptive systems.

Real-world accelerations continue to be sensed by the vestibular organs, and the poses of body parts can be roughly estimated from motor signals.

Unsurprisingly, the most important conflict for VR involves accelerations. In the case of vection, the human vision system provides optical flow readings consistent with motion, but the signals from the vestibular organ do not match. Note that this is the reverse of a common form of motion sickness, which is traveling in a moving vehicle without looking outside of it. For example, imagine reading a book while a passenger in a car. In this case, the vestibular system reports the accelerations of the car, but there is no corresponding optical flow.

Forced Fusion and Fatigue
Recall from Section 6.4 that our perceptual systems integrate cues from different sources, across different sensing modalities, to obtain a coherent perceptual interpretation. In the case of minor discrepancies between the cues, the resulting interpretation can be considered as *forced fusion* [122], in which the perceptual systems appear to work harder to form a match in spite of errors. The situation is similar in engineering systems that perform sensor fusion or visual scene interpretation; the optimization or search for possible interpretations may be much larger in the presence of more noise or incomplete information. Forced fusion appears to lead directly to fatigue and eyestrain. By analogy to computation, it may be not unlike a CPU or GPU heating up as computations intensify for a more difficult problem. Thus, human bodies are forced to work harder as they learn to interpret virtual worlds in spite of engineering flaws. Fortunately, repeated exposure leads to learning or adaptation, which might ultimately reduce fatigue.

Poison Hypotheses
Sensory conflict might seem to be enough to explain why extra burden arises, but it does not seem to imply that nausea would result. Scientists wonder what evolutionary origins might be responsible for this and related symptoms. Note that humans have the ability to naturally nauseate themselves from spinning motions that do not involve technology. The indirect *poison hypothesis* asserts that nausea associated with motion sickness is a by-product of a mechanism that evolved in humans so that they would vomit an accidentally ingested toxin [331]. The symptoms of such toxins frequently involve conflict between visual and vestibular cues. Scientists have considered alternative evolutionary explanations, such as *tree sickness* in primates so that they avoid swaying, unstable branches. Another explanation is the *direct* poison hypothesis, which asserts that nausea became associated with toxins because they were correlated throughout evolution with activities that involved increased or prolonged accelerations. A detailed assessment of these alternative hypotheses and their incompleteness is given in Section 23.9 of [174].

Levels of VR Sickness
To improve VR systems and experiences, we must first be able to properly compare them in terms of their adverse side effects. Thus, the resulting symptoms need to be quantified. Rather than a simple yes/no response for each symptom, it is more

precise to obtain numbers that correspond to relative severity. Several important quantities, for a particular symptom, include

- The intensity of the symptom.
- The rate of symptom onset or intensity increase while the stimulus is presented.
- The rate of symptom decay or intensity decrease after the stimulus is removed.
- The percentage of users who experience the symptom at a fixed level or higher.

The first three can be visualized as a plot of intensity over time. The last one is a statistical property; many other statistics could be calculated from the raw data.

Questionnaires

The most popular way to gather quantitative data is to have users fill out a questionnaire. Researchers have designed many questionnaires over the years [173]; the most widely known and utilized is the *simulator sickness questionnaire (SSQ)* [147]. It was designed for simulator sickness studies for the US military but has been used much more broadly. The users are asked to score each of 16 standard symptoms on a four-point scale: 0 none, 1 slight, 2 moderate, and 3 severe. The results are often aggregated by summing the scores for a selection of the questions. To determine onset or decay rates, the SSQ must be administered multiple times, such as before, after 10 minutes, after 30 minutes, immediately after the experiment, and then 60 minutes afterwards.

Questionnaires suffer from four main drawbacks. The first is that the answers are subjective. For example, there is no clear way to calibrate what it means across the users to feel nausea at level "1" versus level "2." A single user might give different ratings based on emotion or even the onset of other symptoms. The second drawback is that users are asked to pay attention to their symptoms, which could bias their perceived onset. (They may accidentally become like perceptually trained evaluators, as discussed in Section 12.1.) The third drawback is that users must be interrupted so that they can provide scores *during* a session. The final drawback is that the intensity over time must be sampled coarsely because a new questionnaire must be filled out at each time instant of interest.

Physiological Measurements

The alternative is to attach sensors to the user so that physiological measurements are automatically obtained before, during, and after the VR session. The data can be obtained continuously without interrupting the user or asking him to pay attention to symptoms. There may, however, be some discomfort or fear associated with the placement of sensors on the body. Researchers typically purchase a standard sensing system, such as the Biopac MP150, which contains a pack of sensors, records the data, and transmits them to a computer for analysis.

Some physiological measures have been used for studying VR sickness:

- **Electrocardiogram (ECG):** This sensor records the electrical activity of the heart through electrodes placed on the skin. Heart rate typically increases during a VR session.
- **Electrogastrogram (EGG):** This is similar to the ECG, but the electrodes are placed near the stomach so that gastrointestinal discomfort can be estimated.

- **Electrooculogram (EOG):** Electrodes are placed around the eyes so that eye movement can be estimated. Alternatively, a camera-based eye tracking system may be used (Section 9.4). Eye rotations and blinking rates can be determined.
- **Photoplethysmogram (PPG):** This provides additional data on heart movement and is obtained by using a *pulse oximeter*. Typically this device is clamped onto a fingertip and monitors the oxygen saturation of the blood.
- **Galvanic skin response (GSR):** This sensor measures electrical resistance across the surface of the skin. As a person sweats, the moisture of the skin surface increases conductivity. This offers a way to measure cold sweating.
- **Respiratory effort:** The breathing rate and amplitude are measured from a patch on the chest that responds to differential pressure or expansion. The rate of breathing may increase during the VR session.
- **Skin pallor:** This can be measured using a camera and image processing. In the simplest case, an IR LED and photodiode serves as an emitter-detector pair that measures skin reflectance.
- **Head motion:** A head tracking system is a rich source of movement data, which can help to estimate fatigue or postural instability with no additional cost, or distraction to the user.

A comparison of physiological measures and questionnaires appears in [60], and it is even concluded that one can determine whether a person is experiencing VR from the physiological data alone.

Sickness Reduction Strategies
Through experimental studies that determine VR sickness frequencies and intensities across users, engineers and developers can iterate and produce more comfortable VR experiences. Improvements are needed at all levels. Recall the challenge of the perception of stationarity. Most of the real world is perceived as stationary, and it should be the same way for virtual worlds. Improvements in visual displays, rendering, and tracking should help reduce sickness by ever improving the perception of stationarity. Optical distortions, aliasing, latencies, and other artifacts should be reduced or eliminated. When they cannot be eliminated, then comfortable trade-offs should be found. New display technologies should also be pursued that reduce vergence-accommodation mismatch, which causes substantial discomfort when close objects appear on a headset that uses a traditional screen and lens combination (recall from Section 5.4).

Even for an ideally functioning headset, locomotion can cause sickness because of vection. Following the strategies suggested in Section 10.2 should reduce the sickness symptoms. A better idea is to design VR experiences that require little or no locomotion.

As last resorts, two other strategies may help to alleviate VR sickness [148]. The first is to regularly practice, which causes adaptation. The amount of fatigue from forced fusion should be expected to decrease as the body becomes adjusted to the unusual combination of stimuli. Of course, if the VR experience makes most people sick, then asking them to "power through" it a dozen times or more may be a bad idea. Finally, users could take drugs that reduce susceptibility, much in the way that some people take air sickness pills before boarding a plane. These pills are usually antihistamines or anticholinergics, which have unfortunate side effects such as fatigue, drowsiness, impaired cognitive performance, and potential for addiction in some cases.

12.4 Experiments on Human Subjects

Imagine that you have developed a new locomotion method with hopes that it reduces VR sickness. You and a few friends may try it and believe it is better than the default method. How do you convince the skeptical world that it is better, which includes people who are less likely to be biased toward preferring your presumably clever new method? You could argue that it is better because it respects known issues from human physiology and perception, which would be a decent start. This would have provided good motivation for trying the method in the first place; however, it is not sufficient by itself because there is so much uncertainty in how the body interacts with technology. The solution is to design an experiment that scientifically establishes whether your method is better. This leads to many challenges, such as determining how many people should try it, what exactly they should do, how long they should do it for, who should be assigned to which method, and how their sickness will be measured afterward. Some of these difficulties emerged in Section 12.3. If the experiment is designed well, then scientists will be on your side to support the results. If some people are still not convinced, then at least you will have the support of those who believe in the scientific method! Fortunately, this includes the psychologists and neuroscientists, and even the researchers in the closely related field of human–computer interaction [37, 40].

The Scientific Method

The *scientific method* has been around since ancient times, and continues to be refined and improved in particular sciences. Figure 12.4 depicts how it could appear for VR development. Imagine trying to climb a ladder. The first step is accomplished by studying the appropriate literature or gaining the background necessary to design a new method that is likely to be an improvement. This will reduce the chances of falling from the ladder. The second step is to design and implement the new method. This step could include some simple evaluation on a few users just to make sure it is worth proceeding further.

The third step is to precisely formulate the hypothesis, regarding how it is an improvement. Examples are (1) a reduction in adverse symptoms, (2) improved comfort, (3) greater efficiency at solving tasks, (4) stronger belief that the virtual world is real, and (5) a greater enjoyment of the activity. It often makes sense to evaluate multiple criteria, but the result may be that the new method is better in some ways and worse in others. This is a common outcome, but it is preferable to failing to improve in any way! The hypothesis could even involve improving future experimental procedures; an example is [60], in which researchers determined cases in which physiological measures are better indicators of VR sickness than questionnaires. Finally, the hypothesis should be selected in a way that simplifies the fourth step, the experiment, as much as possible while remaining useful.

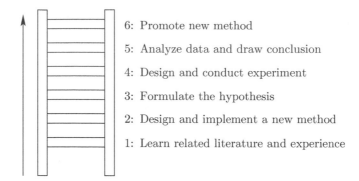

6: Promote new method

5: Analyze data and draw conclusion

4: Design and conduct experiment

3: Formulate the hypothesis

2: Design and implement a new method

1: Learn related literature and experience

Figure 12.4 The scientific process is much like climbing a ladder. Be careful not to fall too far down with each failure!

For the fourth step, the experiment should be designed and conducted to test the hypothesis. The fifth step is to analyze the data and draw a conclusion. If the result is a "better" method in terms of the criteria of interest, then the six step is reached, at which point the new method should be presented to the world.

At any step, failure could occur. For example, right after the experiment is conducted, it might be realized that the pool of subjects is too biased. This requires falling down one step and redesigning or reimplementing the experiment. It is unfortunate if the conclusion at the fifth step is that the method is not a clear improvement, or is even worse. This might require returning to level two or even one. The key is to keep from falling too many steps down the ladder per failure by being careful at each step!

Human Subjects
Dealing with people is difficult, especially if they are participants in a scientific experiment. They may differ wildly in terms of their prior VR experience, susceptibility to motion sickness, suspicion of technology, moodiness, and eagerness to make the scientist happy. They may agree to be participants in the experiment out of curiosity, financial compensation, boredom, or academic degree requirements (psychology students are often forced to participate in experiments). A scientist might be able to guess how some people will fare in the experiment based on factors such as gender, age, or profession. The subject of applying the scientific method to formulate and evaluate hypotheses regarding groups of people (or animals) is called *behavioral science* [155].

One of the greatest challenges is whether they are being observed "in the wild" (without even knowing they are part of an experiment) or if the experiment presents stimuli or situations they would never encounter in the real world. The contrived setting sometimes causes scientists to object to the *ecological validity* of the experiment. Fortunately, VR is a particular contrived setting that we want to evaluate. Thus, conclusions made about VR usage are more likely to be ecologically valid, especially if experimental data can be obtained without users even being aware of the experiment. Head tracking data could be collected on a server while millions of people try a VR experience.

Ethical Standards

This leads to the next challenge, which is the rights of humans, who presumably have more of them than animals. Experiments that affect their privacy or health must be avoided. Scientific experiments that involve human subjects must uphold high standards of ethics, which is a lesson that was painfully learned from Nazi medical experiments and the Tuskegee syphilis experiment in the mid-twentieth century. The Nazi War Crimes Tribunal outcomes resulted in the *Nuremberg code*, which states a set of ethical principles for experimentation on human subjects. Today, ethical standards for human subject research are taken seriously around the world, with ongoing debate or differences in particulars [241]. In the United States, experiments involving human subjects are required by law to be approved by an *institutional review board* (*IRB*). Typically, the term IRB is also used to refer to the proposal for an experiment or set of experiments that has been approved by the review board, as in the statement, "That requires an IRB." Experiments involving VR are usually not controversial and are similar to experiments on simulator sickness that have been widely approved for decades.

Variables

Behavioral scientists are always concerned with *variables*. Each variable takes on values in a set, which might be numerical, as in real numbers, or symbolic, as in colors, labels, or names. From their perspective, the following are the three most important classes of variables:

- **Dependent:** These are the main objects of interest for the hypothesis.
- **Independent:** These have values that are directly changed or manipulated by the scientist.
- **Nuisance:** As these vary, their values might affect the values of the dependent variable, but the scientist has less control over them and they are not the objects of interest.

The high-level task is to formulate a hypothesis that can be evaluated in terms of the relationship between independent and dependent variables, and then design an experiment that can keep the nuisance variables under control and can be conducted within the budget of time, resources, and access to subjects.

The underlying mathematics for formulating models of how the variables behave and predicting their behavior is probability theory, which was introduced in Section 6.4. Unfortunately, we are faced with an inverse problem, as was noted in Figure 12.3. Most of the behavior is not directly observable, which means that we must gather data and make inferences about the underlying models and try to obtain as much confidence as possible. Thus, resolving the hypothesis is a problem in *applied statistics*, which is the natural complement or inverse of probability theory.

Formulating a Hypothesis

In the simplest case, scientists want to determine a binary outcome for a hypothesis of interest: *true* or *false*. In more complicated cases, there may be many mutually exclusive hypotheses, and scientists want to determine which one is true. For example, which among 17 different locomotion methods is the most comfortable?

Proceeding with the simpler case, suppose that a potentially better locomotion method has been determined in terms of VR sickness. Let x_1 denote the use of the original method and let x_2 denote the use of the new method.

The set $x = \{x_1, x_2\}$ is the independent variable. Each x_i is sometimes called the *treatment* (or *level* if x_i takes on real values). The subjects who receive the original method are considered to be the *control group*. If a drug were being evaluated against applying no drug, then they would receive the *placebo*.

Recall from Section 12.3 that levels of VR sickness could be assessed in a variety of ways. Suppose, for the sake of example, that EGG voltage measurements averaged over a time interval is chosen as the dependent variable y. This indicates the amount of gastrointestinal discomfort in response to the treatment, x_1 or x_2.

The hypothesis is a logical true/false statement that relates x to y. For example, it might be

$$H_0 : \mu_1 - \mu_2 = 0, \tag{12.1}$$

in which each μ_i denotes the "true" average value of y at the same point in the experiment, by applying treatment x_i to all people in the world.[1] The hypothesis H_0 implies that the new method has no effect on y and is generally called a *null hypothesis*. The negative of H_0 is called an *alternative hypothesis*. In our case this is

$$H_1 : \mu_1 - \mu_2 \neq 0, \tag{12.2}$$

which implies that the new method has an impact on gastrointestinal discomfort; however, it could be better or worse.

Testing the Hypothesis

Unfortunately, the scientist is not able to perform the same experiment at the same time on *all* people. She must instead draw a small set of people from the population and make a determination about whether the hypothesis is true. Let the index j refer to a particular chosen participant, and let $y[j]$ be his or her response for the experiment; each participant's response is a dependent variable. Two statistics are important for combining information from the dependent variables: the *mean*,

$$\hat{\mu} = \frac{1}{n} \sum_{j=1}^{n} y[j], \tag{12.3}$$

which is simply the average of $y[j]$ over the subjects, and the *variance*, which is

$$\hat{\sigma}^2 = \frac{1}{n} \sum_{j=1}^{n} (y[j] - \hat{\mu})^2. \tag{12.4}$$

The variance estimate (12.4) is considered to be a *biased estimator* for the "true" variance; therefore, *Bessel's correction* is sometimes applied, which places $n - 1$ into the denominator instead of n, resulting in an *unbiased estimator*.

To test the hypothesis, *Student's t-distribution* ("Student" was William Sealy Gosset) is widely used, which is a probability distribution that captures how the mean μ is distributed if n subjects are chosen at random and their responses $y[j]$ are averaged; see Figure 12.5. This assumes that the response $y[j]$ for each individual j is a *normal distribution* (called *Gaussian distribution* in engineering), which is the most

---

[1] To be more mathematically precise, μ_i is the limiting case of applying x_i to an infinite number of people with the assumption that they all respond according to a normal distribution with the same mean.

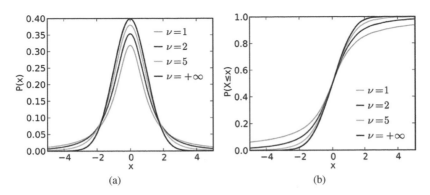

Figure 12.5 Student's t distribution: (a) probability density function (pdf); (b) cumulative distribution function (cdf). In the figures, ν is called the *degrees of freedom*, and $\nu = n - 1$ for the number of subjects n. When ν is small, the pdf has larger tails than the normal distribution; however, in the limit as ν approaches ∞, the Student t distribution converges to the normal distribution.

basic and common probability distribution. It is fully characterized in terms of its mean μ and standard deviation σ. The exact expressions for these distributions are not given here, but are widely available; see [126] and other books on mathematical statistics for these and many more.

The *Student's t-test* [320] involves calculating the following:

$$t = \frac{\hat{\mu}_1 - \hat{\mu}_2}{\hat{\sigma}_p \sqrt{\frac{1}{n_1} + \frac{1}{n_2}}}, \tag{12.5}$$

in which

$$\hat{\sigma}_p = \sqrt{\frac{(n_1 - 1)\hat{\sigma}_1^2 + (n_2 - 1)\hat{\sigma}_2^2}{n_1 + n_2 - 2}} \tag{12.6}$$

and n_i is the number of subjects who received treatment x_i. The subtractions of 1 and 2 in the expressions are due to Bessel's correction. Based on the value of t, the confidence α in the null hypothesis H_0 is determined by looking in a table of the Student's t cdf (Figure 12.5(b)). Typically, $\alpha = 0.05$ or lower is sufficient to declare that H_1 is true (corresponding to 95 percent confidence). Such tables are usually arranged so that for a given ν and α, the minimum t value needed to confirm H_1 with confidence $1 - \alpha$ is presented. Note that if t is negative, then the effect that x has on y runs in the opposite direction, and $-t$ is applied to the table.

The binary outcome might not be satisfying enough. This is not a problem because difference in means, $\hat{\mu}_1 - \hat{\mu}_2$, is an estimate of the amount of change that applying x_2 had in comparison to x_1. This is called the *average treatment effect*. Thus, in addition to determining *whether* the H_1 is true via the t-test, we also obtain an estimate of *how much* it affects the outcome.

Student's t-test assumed that the variance within each group is identical. If it is not, then *Welch's t-test* is used [352]. Note that the variances were not given in advance in either case. They are estimated "on the fly" from the experimental data. Welch's t-test gives the same result as Student's t-test if the variances happen to be the same; therefore, when in doubt, it may be best to apply Welch's *t*-test. Many other tests can be used and are debated in particular contexts by scientists; see [126].

Correlation Coefficient
In many cases, the independent variable x and the dependent variable y are both continuous (taking on real values). This enables another important measure called the *Pearson correlation coefficient* (or *Pearson's r*). This estimates the amount of linear dependency between the two variables. For each subject i, the treatment (or level) $x[i]$ is applied and the response is $y[i]$. Note that in this case, there are no groups (or every subject is a unique group). Also, any treatment could potentially be applied to any subject; the index i only denotes the particular subject.

The *r-value* is calculated as the estimated covariance between x and y when treated as random variables:

$$r = \frac{\sum_{i=1}^{n}(x[i] - \hat{\mu}_x)(y[i] - \hat{\mu}_y)}{\sqrt{\sum_{i=1}^{n}(x[i] - \hat{\mu}_x)^2}\sqrt{\sum_{i=1}^{n}(y[i] - \hat{\mu}_y)^2}}, \tag{12.7}$$

in which $\hat{\mu}_x$ and $\hat{\mu}_y$ are the averages of $x[i]$ and $y[i]$, respectively, for the set of all subjects. The denominator is just the product of the estimated standard deviations: $\hat{\sigma}_x\hat{\sigma}_y$.

The possible r-values range between -1 and 1. Three qualitatively different outcomes can occur:

- $r > 0$: This means that x and y are *positively correlated*. As x increases, y tends to increase. A larger value of r implies a stronger effect.
- $r = 0$: This means that x and y are *uncorrelated*, which is theoretically equivalent to a null hypothesis.
- $r < 0$: This means that x and y are *negatively correlated*. As x increases, y tends to decrease. A smaller value of r implies a stronger effect.

In practice, it is highly unlikely to obtain $r = 0$ from experimental data; therefore, the absolute value $|r|$ gives an important indication of the likelihood that y depends on x. The theoretical equivalence to the null hypothesis ($r = 0$) would happen only as the number of subjects tends to infinity.

Dealing with Nuisance Variables
We have considered dependent and independent variables, but have neglected the nuisance variables. This is the most challenging part of experimental design. Only the general idea is given here; see [155, 198] for exhaustive presentations. Suppose that when looking through the data it is noted that the dependent variable y depends heavily on an identifiable property of the subjects, such as gender. This property would become a nuisance variable, z. We could imagine designing an experiment just to determine whether and how much z affects y, but the interest is in some independent variable x, not z.

The dependency on z drives the variance high across the subjects; however, if they are divided into groups that have the same z value inside each group, then the variance could be considerably lower. For example, if gender is the nuisance variable, then we would divide the subjects into groups of men and women and discover that the variance is smaller in each group. This technique is called *blocking*, and each group is called a *block*. Inside a block, the variance of y should be low if the independent variable x is held fixed.

The next problem is to determine which treatment should be applied to which subjects. Continuing with the example, it would be a horrible idea to give treatment x_1 to women and treatment x_2 to men. This completely confounds the nuisance variable z and independent variable x dependencies on the dependent variable y. The clear alternative would be to apply x_1 to half of the women and men, and x_2 to the other half, which is significantly better. Another alternative is to use a *randomized design*, in which the subjects are assigned x_1 or x_2 at random. This safely eliminates accidental bias and is easy for an experimenter to implement.

If there is more than one nuisance variable, then the assignment process becomes more complicated, which tends to cause a greater preference for randomization. If the subjects participate in a multiple-stage experiment where the different treatments are applied at various times, then the treatments must be carefully assigned. One way to handle it is by assigning the treatments according to a *Latin square*, which is an m-by-m matrix in which every row and column is a permutation of m labels (in this case, treatments).

Analysis of Variance
The main remaining challenge is to identify nuisance variables that would have a significant impact on the variance. This is called *analysis of variance* (or *ANOVA*, pronounced "ay nova"), and methods that take this into account are called *ANOVA design*. Gender was an easy factor to imagine, but others may be more subtle, such as the amount of FPS games played among the subjects, or the time of day that the subjects participate. The topic is far too complex to cover here (see [155]), but the important intuition is that low-variance clusters must be discovered among the subjects, which serves as a basis for dividing them into blocks. This is closely related to the problem of *unsupervised clustering* (or *unsupervised learning*) because classes are being discovered without the use of a "teacher" who identifies them in advance. ANOVA is also considered as a generalization of the t-test to three or more variables.

More Variables
Variables other than independent, dependent, and nuisance sometimes become important in the experiment. A *control variable* is essentially a nuisance variable that is held fixed through the selection of subjects or experimental trials. For example, the variance may be held low by controlling the subject selection so that only males between the ages of 18 and 21 are used in the experiment. The approach helps to improve the confidence in the conclusions from the experiment, possibly with a smaller number of subjects or trials, but might prevent its findings from being generalized to settings outside of the control.

A *confounding variable* is an extraneous variable that causes the independent and dependent variables to be correlated, but they become uncorrelated once the value of the confounding variable is given. For example, having a larger shoe size may correlate to better speaking ability. In this case the confounding variable is the person's age. Once the age is known, we realize that older people have larger feet than small children, and are also better at speaking. This illustrates the danger of inferring causal relationships from statistical correlations.

Psychophysical Methods

Recall from Section 2.3 that psychophysics relates perceptual phenomena to the original stimuli, which makes it crucial for understanding VR. Stevens' power law (2.1) related the perceived stimulus magnitude to the actual magnitude. The JND involved determining a *differential threshold*, which is the smallest amount of stimulus change that is detectable. A special case of this is an *absolute threshold*, which is the smallest magnitude stimulus (in comparison to zero) that is detectable.

Psychophysical laws or relationships are gained through specific experiments on human participants. The term *psychophysics* and research area were introduced by Gustav Fechner [77], who formulated three basic experimental approaches, which will described next. Suppose that x represents the stimulus magnitude. The task is to determine how small Δx can become so that subjects perceive a difference. The classical approaches are the following:

- **Method of constant stimuli:** In this case, stimuli at various magnitudes are presented in succession, along with the reference stimulus. The subject is asked for each stimulus pair where he can perceive a difference between them. The magnitudes are usually presented in random order to suppress adaptation. Based on the responses over many trials, a best-fitting psychometric function is calculated, as was shown in Figure 2.21.
- **Method of limits:** The experimenter varies the stimulus magnitude in small increments, starting with an upper or lower limit. The subject is asked in each case whether the new stimulus has less, equal, or more magnitude than the reference stimulus.
- **Method of adjustment:** The subject is allowed to adjust the stimulus magnitude up and down within a short amount of time, while also being able to compare to the reference stimulus. The subject stops when she reports that the adjusted and reference stimuli appear to have equal magnitude.

Although these methods are effective and widely used, several problems exist. All of them may be prone to some kinds of bias. For the last two, adaptation may interfere with the outcome. For the last one, there is no way to control how the subject makes decisions. Another problem is efficiency, in that many iterations may be wasted in the methods by considering stimuli that are far away from the reference stimulus.

Adaptive Methods

Due to these shortcomings, researchers have found numerous ways to improve the experimental methods over the past few decades. A large number of these are surveyed and compared in [332], and fall under the heading of *adaptive psychophysical methods*. Most improved methods perform *staircase procedures*, in which the stimulus magnitude starts off with an easy case for the subject and is gradually decreased (or increased if the reference magnitude is larger) until the subject makes a mistake [91]. At this point, the direction is reversed and the steps are increased until another mistake is made. The process of making a mistake and changing directions continues until the subject makes many mistakes in a small number of iterations. The step size must be carefully chosen, and could even be reduced gradually during the experiment. The direction (increase or decrease) could alternatively be decided using Bayesian or maximum-likelihood procedures that provide an estimate for the threshold as the data are collected in each iteration [115, 157, 351]. These methods generally fall under the heading of the *stochastic approximation method* [271].

Stimulus Magnitude Estimation

Recall that Stevens' power law is not about detection thresholds, but is instead about the perceived magnitude of a stimulus. For example, one plate might feel twice as hot as another. In this case, subjects are asked to estimate the relative difference in magnitude between stimuli. Over a sufficient number of trials, the exponent of Stevens' power law (2.1) can be estimated by choosing a value for x (the exponent) that minimizes the least-squares error (recall from Section 9.1).

Further Reading

For surveys on perceptual learning, see [95, 99, 110, 258]. Hyperacuity through perceptual learning is investigated in [102, 258]. In [289] it is established that perceptual learning can occur even without focused attention.

Human sensitivity to latency in VR and computer interfaces is analyzed in [64, 68, 203, 366]. Comfort issues in stereo displays are studied in [295]. For connections between postural sway and sickness, see [300, 319].

For some important studies related to VR sickness, see [13, 149, 150, 156, 228, 268]. General overviews of VR sickness are given in [146, 172, 311]. Motion sickness is surveyed in [267]. See [56, 122, 141, 260] for additional coverage of forced fusion.

For coverage of the mathematical methods and statistics for human subjects experimentation, see [155]. The book [198] is highly popular for its coverage of hypothesis testing in the context of psychology. For treatment of psychophysical methods, see [179, 332, 358] and chapter 3 of [94].

CHAPTER THIRTEEN

Frontiers

We arrive at the final chapter, which surveys some topics that could influence widespread VR usage in the future, but are mostly in a research and development stage. Sections 13.1 and 13.2 cover the forgotten senses. Earlier in this book, we covered vision, hearing, and balance (vestibular) senses, which leaves touch, smell, and taste. Section 13.1 covers touch, or more generally, the *somatosensory system*. This includes physiology, perception, and engineering technology that stimulates the somatosensory system. Section 13.2 covers the two *chemical senses*, smell and taste, along with attempts to engineer "displays" for them. Section 13.3 discusses how robots are used for telepresence and how they may ultimately become our *surrogate selves* through which the real world can be explored with a VR interface. Just like there are avatars in a virtual world (Section 10.4), the robot becomes a kind of physical avatar in the real world. Finally, Section 13.4 discusses steps toward the ultimate level of human augmentation and interaction: brain–machine interfaces.

13.1 Touch and Proprioception

Visual and auditory senses are the main focus of VR systems because of their relative ease to stimulate using current technology. Their organs are concentrated in a small place on the head, and head tracking technology is cheap and accurate. Unfortunately, this neglects the powerful senses of *touch* and *proprioception*, and related systems, which provide an intimate connection to the world around us. Our eyes and ears enable us to perceive the world from a distance, but touch seems to allow us to directly *feel* it. Furthermore, proprioception gives the body a sense of where it is anywhere in the world with respect to gravity and the relative placement or configuration of limbs and other structures that can be moved by our muscles. We will therefore consider these neglected senses, from their receptors to perception, and then to engineering systems that try to overtake them.

The Somatosensory System

The *body senses* provide signals to the brain about the human body itself, including direct contact with the skin, the body's configuration and movement in the world, and the ambient temperature. Within this category, the vestibular system (Section 8.2) handles balance, and the *somatosensory system* handles touch, proprioception,

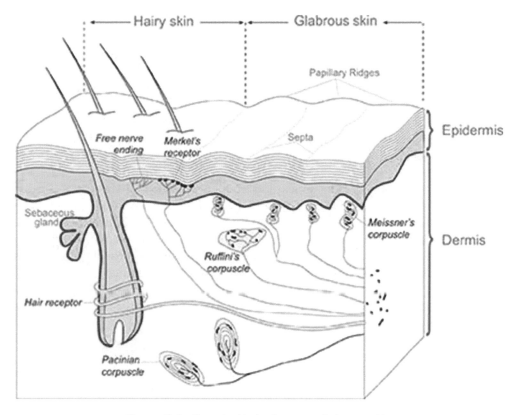

Figure 13.1 Six major kinds of receptors in human skin.

and kinesthesis. Consider the human body and all of its movable parts, such as the legs, arms, fingers, tongue, mouth, and lips. Proprioception corresponds to the awareness of the *pose* of each part relative to others, whereas *kinesthesis* is the counterpart for the movement itself. In other words, kinesthesis provides information on velocities, accelerations, and forces.

The somatosensory system has at least nine major kinds of receptors, six of which are devoted to touch, and the remaining three are devoted to proprioception and kinesthesis. Figure 13.1 depicts the six main touch receptors, which are embedded in the skin (*dermis*). Their names, structures, and functions are as follows:

- **Free nerve endings:** These are neurons with no specialized structure. They have axons that extend up into the outer skin (*epidermis*), with the primary function of sensing temperature extremes (hot and cold), and pain from tissue damage. These neurons are special (called *pseudounipolar*) in that axons perform the role of both dendrites and axons in a typical neural cell.
- **Ruffini's endings or corpuscles:** These are embedded deeply in the skin and signal the amount of stretching that is occurring at any moment. They have a sluggish temporal response.
- **Pacinian corpuscles:** These are small bodies filled with fluid and respond to pressure. Their response is fast, allowing them to sense vibrations (pressure variations) of up to 250 to 350 Hz.

- **Merkel's disks:** These structures appear just below the epidermis and respond to static pressure (little or no variation over time), with a slow temporal response.
- **Meissner's corpuscles:** These are also just below the epidermis and respond to lighter touch. Their response is faster than Merkel's discs and Ruffini's corpuscles, allowing vibrations up to 30 to 50 Hz to be sensed; this is not as high as is possible with the Pacinian corpuscles.
- **Hair follicle receptors:** These correspond to nerve endings that wrap closely around the hair root; they contribute to light touch sensation and also pain if the hair is removed.

The first four of these receptors appear in skin all over the body. Meissner's corpuscles are only in parts where there are no hair follicles (*glabrous skin*), and the hair follicle receptors obviously appear only where there is hair. In some critical places, such as eyelids, lips, and tongue, thermoreceptors called the *end-bulbs of Krause* also appear in the skin. Yet another class is *nocireceptors*, which appear in joint tissues and cause a pain sensation from overstretching, injury, or inflammation.

Touch has both spatial and temporal resolutions. The spatial resolution or acuity corresponds to the density, or number of receptors per square area, which varies over the body. The density is high at the fingertips and very low on the back. This has implications for touch perception, which will be covered shortly. The temporal resolution is not the same as for hearing, which extends up to 20,000 Hz; the Pacinian corpuscles allow vibrations up to a few hundred hertz to be distinguished from a static pressure.

Regarding proprioception (and kinesthesis), there are three kinds of receptors:

- **Muscle spindles:** As the name suggests, these are embedded inside of each muscle so that changes in their length can be reported to the central nervous system (which includes the brain).
- **Golgi tendon organs:** These are embedded in tendons, which are each a tough band of fibrous tissue that usually connects a muscle to bone. The organs report changes in muscle tension.
- **Joint receptors:** These lie at the joints between bones and help coordinate muscle movement while also providing information to the central nervous system regarding relative bone positions.

Through these receptors, the body is aware of the relative positions, orientations, and velocities of its various moving parts.

The neural pathways for the somatosensory system work in a way that is similar to the visual pathways of Section 5.2. The signals are routed through the thalamus, with relevant information eventually arriving at the *primary somatosensory cortex* in the brain, where the higher-level processing occurs. Long before the thalamus, some of the signals are also routed through the spinal cord to motor neurons that control muscles. This enables rapid motor response for the purpose of withdrawing from painful stimuli quickly, and for the *knee-jerk reflex*. Inside the primary somatosensory cortex, neurons fire in a spatial arrangement that corresponds to their location on the body (topographic mapping). Some neurons also have receptive fields that correspond to local patches on the skin, much in the same way as receptive fields work for vision (recall Figure 5.8 from Section 5.2). Once again, lateral inhibition and spatial opponency exist and form detectors that allow people to estimate sharp pressure features along the surface of the skin.

Somatosensory Perception

We now transition from physiology to *somatosensory perception*. The familiar concepts from psychophysics (Sections 2.3 and 12.4) appear again, resulting in determinations of detection thresholds, perceived stimulus magnitude, and acuity or resolution along temporal and spatial axes. For example, the ability to detect the presence of a vibration, presented at different frequencies and temperatures, was studied in [26].

Two-Point Acuity

Spatial resolution has been studied by the *two-point acuity test*, in which the skin is poked in two nearby places by a pair of sharp calipers. The subjects are asked whether they perceive a single poke, or two pokes in different places at the same time. The detection thresholds are then arranged by the location on the body to understand how the spatial resolution varies. The sharpest acuity is on the tongue and fingers, where points can be distinguished if they are as close as 2 or 3mm. For the forehead, the threshold is around 20 mm. The back has the lowest acuity, resulting in a threshold of around 60 mm. These results have also been shown to correspond directly to the sizes of receptive fields in the somatosensory cortex. For example, neurons that correspond to the back have much larger fields (in terms of skin area) than those of the fingertip.

Texture Perception

By running fingers over a surface, *texture perception* results. The size, shape, arrangement, and density of small elements that protrude from, or indent into, the surface affect the resulting perceived texture. The *duplex theory* states that coarser textures (larger elements) are mainly perceived by spatial cues, whereas finer textures are mainly perceived through temporal cues [127, 145]. By *spatial cue*, it means that the structure can be inferred by pressing the finger against the surface. By *temporal cue*, the finger is slid across the surface, resulting in a pressure vibration that can be sensed by the Pacinian and Meissner's corpuscles. For a finer texture, a slower motion may be necessary so that the vibration frequency remains below 250 to 350 Hz. Recall from Section 12.1 that people can learn to improve their texture perception and acuity when reading Braille. Thus, perceptual learning may be applied to improve tactile (touch) perception.

Haptic Perception

For a larger object, its overall geometric shape can be inferred through *haptic exploration*, which involves handling the object. Imagine that someone hands you an unknown object, and you must determine its shape while blindfolded. Figure 13.2 shows six different qualitative types of haptic exploration, each of which involves different kinds of receptors and combinations of spatial and temporal information. By integrating the somatosensory signals from this in-hand manipulation, a geometric model of the object is learned.

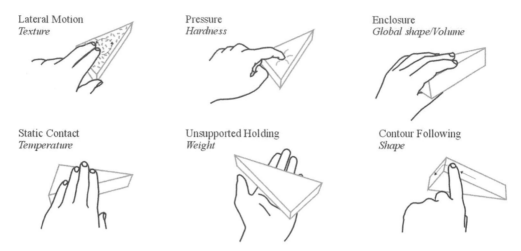

Figure 13.2 Haptic exploration involves several different kinds interaction between the hand and an object to learn the object properties, such as size, shape, weight, firmness, and surface texture.

Somatosensory Illusions

Recall from Section 6.4 that the brain combines signals across multiple sensing modalities to provide a perceptual experience. Just as the McGurk effect uses mismatches between visual and auditory cues, illusions have also been discovered by mismatching cues between vision and somatosensory systems. The *rubber hand illusion* is one of the most widely known [67]. In this case, scientists conducted an experiment in which the subjects were seated at a table with both arms resting on it. The subjects' left arm was covered, but a substitute rubber forearm was placed nearby on the table and remained visible so that it appeared as if it were their own left arm. The experimenter stroked both the real and fake forearms with a paint brush to help build up visual and touch association with the fake forearm. Using a functional MRI scanner, scientists determined that the same parts of the brain are activated whether it is the real or fake forearm. Furthermore, they even learned that making a stabbing gesture with a needle causes anticipation of pain and the tendency to withdraw the real left arm, which was actually not threatened [67, 299], and that hot or cold sensations can even be perceived by association [297].

More generally, this is called a *body transfer illusion* [256, 299]. An example of this was shown in Figure 1.15 of Section 1.2 for a VR system in which men and women were convinced that they were swapping bodies, while the visual information from a camera was coupled with coordinated hand motions to provide tactile sensory stimulation. Applications of this phenomenon include empathy and helping amputees to overcome phantom limb sensations. This illusion also gives insights into the kinds of motor programs that might be learnable, as discussed in Sections 10.1 and 10.3, by controlling muscles while getting visual feedback from VR. It furthermore affects the perception of oneself in VR, which was discussed in Sections 10.4 and 12.2.

Haptic Interfaces

Touch sensations through engineered devices are provided through many disparate systems. Figure 1.1 from Section 1.1 showed a system in which force feedback is

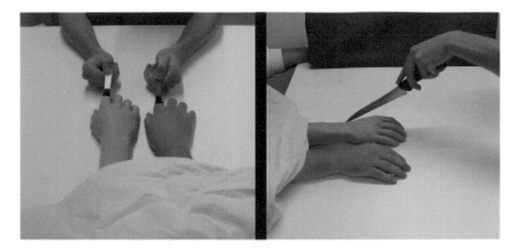

Figure 13.3 The *rubber hand illusion*, in which a person reacts to a fake hand as if it were her own [108].

provided by allowing the user to push mechanical wings to fly. Furthermore, a fan simulates wind with intensity that is proportional to the speed of the person virtually flying. The entire body also tilts so that appropriate vestibular stimulation is provided.

Figure 13.4 shows several more examples. Figure 13.4(a) shows a PC mouse with a scroll wheel. As the wheel is rotated with the middle finger, discrete bumps are felt so that a more carefully calibrated movement can be generated. Figure 13.4(b) shows a game controller attachment that provides vibration at key points during an experience, such as an explosion or body contact.

Many haptic systems involve using a robot arm to apply force or pressure at precise locations and directions within a small region. Figure 13.4(c) shows such a system in which the user holds a pen that is attached to the robot arm. Forces are communicated from the robot to the pen to the fingers. As the pen strikes a virtual surface, the robot provides force feedback to the user by blocking its motion. The pen could be dragged across the virtual surface to feel any kind of texture [242]; a variety of simulated textures are presented in [51]. Providing such force feedback is important in the development of medical devices that enable doctors to perform surgical procedures through an interface that is connected to a real device. Without accurate and timely haptic feedback, it is difficult for doctors to perform many procedures. Imagine cutting into layers of tissue without being able to feel the resistant forces on the scalpel. It would be easy to push a bit too far!

Figure 13.4(d) shows a haptic display that is arranged much like a visual display. A rectangular region is indexed by rows and columns, and at each location a small pin can be forced outward. This enables shapes to appear above the surface, while also allowing various levels of pressure and frequencies of vibration.

All of the examples involve haptic feedback applied to the hands; however, touch receptors appear all over the human body. To provide stimulation over a larger fraction of receptors, a *haptic suit* may be needed, which provides forces, vibrations, or even electrical stimulation at various points on the suit. A drawback of these systems is the cumbersome effort of putting on and removing the suit with each session.

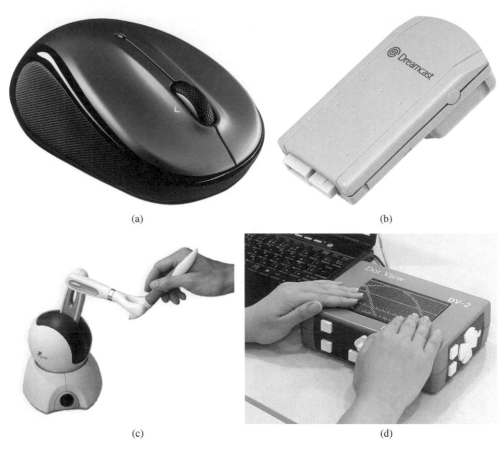

Figure 13.4 (a) The Logitech M325 wireless mouse with a scroll wheel that provides tactile feedback in the form of 72 bumps as the wheel performs a full revolution. (b) The Sega Dreamcast Jump Pack (1999), which attaches to a game controller and provides vibrations during game play. (c) Haptic Omni, from 3D Systems, a pen-guiding haptic device, which communicates pressure and vibrations through the pen to the fingers. (d) The KGS Dot View Model DV-2, which is a haptic pin array. The pins are forced upward to simulate various textures as the finger tip scans across its surface.

Touch Feedback via Augmented Reality
Given the difficulties of engineering haptic displays, an alternative is to rely on real objects in the match zone to provide feedback to the somatosensory system. This is sometimes called a *tangible user interface* [335]. As mentioned in Section 8.3.3, a powerful experience is made by aligning the real and virtual worlds. At one extreme, a see-through display, such as Microsoft Hololens, which was shown in Section 1.2, enables users to see and interact with the physical world around them. The display simply adds virtual objects to the real world or visually enhances real objects.

13.2 Smell and Taste

The only human senses not considered so far are smell and taste. They are formally known as *olfaction* and *gustation*, respectively [63]. Furthermore, they are usually grouped together as the *chemical senses* because their receptors work by chemical interactions with molecules that arrive upon them. The resulting *chemoreceptors* respond to particular substances and sufficiently high levels of concentration. Compared to the other senses, much less research has been done about them and there are much fewer electronic devices that "display" stimuli to the nose and tongue. Nevertheless, these senses are extremely important. The design of artificial smells is a huge business, which includes perfumes, deodorants, air fresheners, cleaners, and incense. Likewise, designing tastes is the basis of the modern food industry (for better or worse).

Smell Physiology and Perception

Odors are important for several biological purposes, which includes detecting prey and predators, selecting potential mates, and judging whether food is safe to eat. The *olfactory receptor* neurons lie in the roof of the nasal cavity, covering an area of 2 to 4 cm^2. There are around 6 million receptors, which are believed to span 500 to 1,000 different types depending on their responsiveness to specific chemical compositions [207]. Airborne molecules dissolve into the olfactory mucus, which triggers detection by cilia (small hairs) that are part of the receptor. The olfactory receptors are constantly regenerating, with an average lifespan of about 60 days. In addition to receptors, some free nerve endings lie in the olfactory mucus as well. The sensory pathways are unusual in that they do not connect through the thalamus before reaching their highest-level destination, which for smell is the *primary olfactory cortex*. There is also a direct route from the receptors to the *amygdala*, which is associated with emotional response. This may help explain the close connection between smell and emotional reactions.

In terms of perception, humans can recognize thousands of different smells [292], and women generally perform better than men [36]. The discrimination ability depends on the concentration of the smell (in terms of molecules per cubic area). If the concentration is weaker, then discrimination ability decreases. Furthermore, what is considered to be a high concentration for one odor may be barely detectable for another. Consequently, the detection thresholds vary by a factor of a thousand or more, depending on the substance. Adaptation is also important for smell. People are continuously adapting to surrounding smells, especially those of their own body or home, so that they become unnoticeable. Smokers also adapt so that they do not perceive the polluted air in the way that nonsmokers can.

It seems that humans can recognize many more smells than the number of olfactory receptor types. This is possible because of combinatorial encoding. Any single odor (or chemical compound) may trigger multiple types of receptors. Likewise, each receptor may be triggered by multiple odors. Thus, a many-to-many mapping exists between odors and receptor types. This enables far more odors to be distinguished based on the distinct subsets of receptor types that become activated.

Olfactory Interfaces

Adding scent to films can be traced back to the early twentieth century. One system, from 1960, was called *Smell-O-Vision* and injected 30 different odors into the movie theater seats at different points during the film. The Sensorama system mentioned in

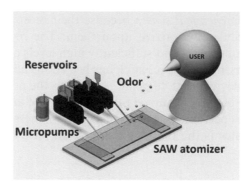

Figure 13.5 A depiction of a wearable olfactory display from [116]. Micropumps force bits of liquid from small reservoirs. The SAW atomizer is a surface acoustic wave device that converts droplets into an atomized odor.

Figure 1.29(c) of Section 1.3 also included smells. In addition, the military has used smells as part of simulators for many decades.

A survey of previous olfactory displays and interfaces appears in [138], along with current challenges and issues. Olfactory displays have been shown to induce strong cognitive and emotional responses from people, which makes them attractive for increasing immersion in VR [140].

It also offers advantages in some forms of medical treatments that involve cravings and emotional responses. Surprisingly, there is even evidence that pleasant odors help reduce visually induced motion sickness [150].

Olfactory displays usually involve air pumps that can spray chemical compounds into air. The presentation of such engineered odors could be delivered close to the nose for a personal experience. In this case, the canisters and distribution system could be worn on the body [365]. A system is depicted in Figure 13.5. Alternatively, the smells could be delivered on the scale of a room. This would be preferable for a CAVE setting, but it is generally hard to control the intensity and uniformity of the odor, especially in light of air flow that occurs from open windows and air vents. It might also be desirable to vary the concentration of odors over a large area so that localization can be performed, but this is again difficult to achieve with accuracy.

Taste Physiology and Perception
We now jump from smell to taste. On the human tongue lie about 10,000 *taste buds*, each of which contains a group of about 50 to 150 *taste receptors* [301]. The receptors live for an average of 10 days, with regeneration constantly occurring. Five basic types of taste receptors have been identified:

- **Umami:** This one is sensitive to amino acids, such as *monosodium glutamate* (*MSG*), and is responsible for an overall sense of tastiness. This enables food manufacturers to cheaply add chemicals that make food seem to taste better. The biological motivation is likely to be that amino acids are important building blocks for proteins.
- **Sweet:** This is useful for identifying a food source in terms of its valuable sugar content.

Figure 13.6 A *digital lollipop* was developed at the National University of Singapore [265].

- **Salty:** This is useful for determining whether a food source has sufficient salt content, which is required for normal neural functions.
- **Sour:** This is useful for determining the amount of acidity in a food, which could imply useful vitamins, unripeness, or even bacteria in spoiled food.
- **Bitter:** This is often associated with toxic plants, which may trigger a natural aversion to them.

All of these work by dissolving food and generating a response based on chemical decomposition. The sensory pathways connect through the thalamus to the *gustatory cortex* and to the amygdala, which affects emotional responses.

Taste perception is closely related to the taste receptor types. One of the most widely known models is *Henning's tetrahedron* from 1927, which is a 3D space of tastes that is generated using barycentric coordinates (Section 7.2) over four extreme vertices that each represent pure sweet, salty, sour, or bitter. Thus, each taste is a linear interpolation the four components. This, of course, neglects umami, which was more recently added to the list of receptor types [43, 233]. Adaptation occurs for taste, including an aversion to foods that might have been coincident with sickness. The concept of *flavor* is a perceptual experience that combines cues from taste, smell, temperature, touch, vision, and sound. Therefore, it is challenging to understand the mechanisms that create a flavor experience [58].

Gustatory Interfaces
Relatively little has been done to date on simulating taste electronically. Figure 13.6 shows one example, in which electrodes are placed over and under the tongue to provide stimulation that simulates the main taste types. In another work, taste illusions are formed by accompanying eating with incorrect visual and olfactory cues [231]. It is generally difficult to develop *gustatory interfaces* for VR without actually causing people to eat food during the experience. There are clearly health and hygienic issues as well.

13.3 Robotic Interfaces

Robots are programmable devices that involve a mixture of sensors, actuators (motors), and computational devices. They are usually expected to interpret high-level commands, use sensors to learn about the world around them, and plan and execute actions that move them safely to accomplish the goals set out by their commanders. Their components mimic those of humans in many ways. Robots have sensors and humans have senses. For some specific correspondences, robots have cameras, IMUs, and joint encoders, whereas humans measure the same quantities via vision, vestibular, and proprioceptive senses. Most robots have motors and humans have muscles, both of which serve the same purpose. Robots perform computations to relate high-level goals to low-level motor commands while interpreting data from sensors. Humans reason about high-level goals as well, while sending motor signals to muscles and turning stimuli from senses into perceptual phenomena. After making so many parallels between robots and humans, a natural question is: Why not use VR technology to allow a human to inhabit the body of a robot? We could use robots as our *surrogate selves*.

Teleoperation

The first step toward this vision is to interact with robots over large distances. Vehicles have been operated by remote control for well over a century. One of the earliest examples is a radio-controlled boat that was publicly demonstrated in New York by Nicola Tesla in 1898. Across the twentieth century, numerous teleoperated robots were developed for navigation in remote or hazardous situations, such as handling radioactive materials, space travel, and undersea exploration. Space agencies (such as NASA) and militaries have conducted extensive research and development of remote controlled vehicles. Another intriguing example of teleoperation is the *TeleGarden* from 1995, which was a robot arm hovering over a real garden, at the University of Southern California, that was connected to the Internet. Remote visitors could plant seeds and generally take care of the garden. In 2001, teleoperated robots were deployed to the World Trade Center bombing site to search for victims. In current times, remote controlled vehicles of all kinds are widely available to hobbyists, including cars, fixed-wing aircraft, quadrotors (drones), boats, and submarines. Operation is often difficult because the user must control the vehicle from a third-person view while handling the controller. Therefore, many vehicles have been equipped with wireless cameras so that the user obtains a *first-person view* (*FPV*) on a screen. This is an important step toward telepresence. Teleoperation need not be limited to vehicles. Health care is one of the largest and growing fields for teleoperation, which usually involves a fixed-based robot arm that manipulates medical instruments. For a general survey of networked robotics, see [306].

Modern Robots

Thousands of different robots have been designed and built, some with very special purposes, such as cleaning windows of a building, and others for more general purposes, such as assisted living. Figure 13.7 shows *humanoid robots* that strive for *anthropomorphic* or a human-like appearance. Figure 13.8 shows a sampling of other kinds of robots. Figure 1.12 in Section 1.2 showed two more examples, which were a stereoscopic pan-tilt module and a video-streaming drone.

In addition to hardware, substantial software infrastructure exists to help developers, such as ROS (Robot Operating System) and Gazebo. Almost any robot is a candidate platform from which a telerobotic VR interface could be attached. Cameras and microphones serve as the surrogate eyes and ears of the user. A gripper (also called *end-effector*) could serve as remote hands, if feasible and important

Figure 13.7 The HRP-4 *humanoid robots*, which are produced in Japan by National Institute of Advanced Industrial Science and Technology (AIST) and Kawada Industries.

for the application. The user can command the robot's motions and actions via keyboards, controllers, voice, or body motions. For a humanoid robot, the human body could even be tracked using motion capture (Section 9.4) and mapped directly onto motions of the humanoid. More generally, any anthropomorphic aspects of a robot could become part of the matched zone. At the other extreme, the robot allows many nonhuman experiences, such as becoming the size of a small insect and flying around the room, or swimming like a fish in the sea.

Telepresence

The term and concept of *telepresence* is attributed to Marvin Minsky, pioneer of artificial intelligence [218]; see also [270, 293, 316]. In the most idealized case, which we are far from achieving with current technology, it could completely eliminate the

(a)   (b)

(c)   (d)

Figure 13.8 A sampling of commercial and university robots. (a) Neato XV vacuum cleaning robot. (b) Kuka YouBot, which is an omnidirectional mobile base with a manipulator arm on top. (c) Aqua, an underwater robot from McGill University [66]. (d) A flying microrobot from the Harvard Microrobotics Lab [193].

need to physically travel. It could also revolutionize the lives of people who have limited mobility due to disabilities or advanced age. In terms of technical challenges, telepresence involves the integration of two components: *teleoperation* and VR.

Figure 13.9 shows a telepresence system that is commercially available and serves as a useful point of reference. Similar robots have appeared in telepresence research [139, 175, 248, 325]. The robot is controlled by the user through a tablet or smartphone, while at the remote site the robot carries a tablet that provides a wide-angle camera and a screen to show the user's face. The base is designed to roll through typical office spaces, and the tablet height is adjustable to allow face-to-face interaction. The vehicle is top-heavy, which requires a control mechanism called the *inverted pendulum* to stabilize the tablet.

Several aspects come to mind regarding a telepresence robot:

- **Sensory input:** What will it sense from the remote physical world? For visual input, it could contain cameras that directly map the eye viewpoints and are even matched to user head motions (as was shown in Figure 1.12(a)). Alternatively, it

Figure 13.9 The Double telepresence robot is a screen and camera on a stick. The robot costs around $2,500, and the screen is a tablet, such as an iPad. The height can even be adjusted remotely so that the person may appear to be sitting or standing.

could capture and transmit an entire panorama. Going even further, this could be extended to depth and light fields. Auditory input is captured using one or more microphones, depending on the importance of localization. Some other possible inputs for telepresence are temperature, contact forces, humidity, odors, and the robot's remaining battery life.

- **Mobility:** Where can the robot go? With no mobility, telepresence is reduced to a stationary camera and microphone. If the task is to interact with people, then it should be able to move into the same places that people are capable of entering. In other settings, many modes of mobility may be desirable, such as flying, swimming, or even crawling through pipes.

- **Audiovisual output:** At one extreme, the telepresence system could seem like a "fly on the wall" and not disrupt life at the remote site. More commonly, it is designed to interact with people, which could be accomplished by a screen and a speaker. If the robot has some anthropomorphic characteristics, then it may also be able to make gestures that communicate emotion or intent with other people.

- **Manipulation:** The telepresence system shown in Figure 13.9 targets face-to-face interaction and therefore neglects being able to manipulate objects at the remote site. A telepresence robot is much more powerful if it can grasp, manipulate, carry, and ungrasp objects. It could then open doors, operate elevators, go grocery shopping, and so on.

The remainder of this section covers ongoing challenges in the development of better telepresence systems.

Tele-embodiment Issues
Imagine how people would react to the robotic surrogate version of yourself. It is highly unlikely that they would treat you exactly in the same way as if you were

physically present. Recall from Section 10.4 that social interaction in VR depends on the avatars that people chose to represent themselves. With telepresence, you would be perceived as a *robotic avatar*, which leads to the same kinds of social issues [247]. The remote person may seem handicapped or awkward in a way that causes avoidance by others. Unfortunately, there is much less freedom to choose how you want to look in comparison to interaction in a purely virtual world. You may have to be perceived by everyone as an awkward screen on a stick if that is the platform. Research in *social robotics* and *human–robot interaction* may be useful in helping improve social interactions through such a robotic avatar [82, 131, 279].

Remote-Control versus Autonomy
Assuming that the robot may roam over a larger area than the matched zone, a locomotion method is needed. This implies that the user controls the robot motion through an interface. In Section 10.2, locomotion was presented for navigating in a large virtual world and was explained as controlling a cart (Figure 10.5). The robot in the real world behaves geometrically like the cart in the pure virtual world; however, there are some differences: (1) The robot cannot simply teleport to another location. It is, however, possible to connect to a different robot, if many are available, which would feel like teleportation to the user. (2) The robot is subject to constraints based on its physical design and its environment. It may have rolling wheels or walking legs, and may or may not be able to easily traverse parts of the environment. It will also have limited driving speed, turning speed, and battery life. (3) A high cost is usually associated with crashing the robot into people or obstacles.

A spectrum of choices exists for the user who teleoperates the robot. At one extreme, the user may continuously control the movements, in the way that a radio-controlled car is driven using the remote. Latency becomes critical for some applications, especially telesurgery [191, 364]. At the other extreme, the user may simply point out the location on a map or use a virtual laser pointer (Section 10.2) to point to a visible location. In this case, the robot could execute all of the motions by itself and take the user along for the ride. This requires a higher degree of autonomy for the robot because it must plan its own route that accomplishes the goals without running into obstacles; this is known in robotics as *motion planning* [166]. This frees the user from having to focus attention on the minor robot movements, but it may be difficult to obtain reliable performance for some combinations of robot platforms and environments. It could also lower the sense of presence and wayfinding ability.

VR Sickness Issues
Because of the connection to locomotion, vection once again arises (Section 8.4). Many of the suggestions from Section 10.2 to reduce vection can be applied here, such as reducing the contrast or the field of view while the robot is moving. Now consider some robot-specific suggestions. Users may be more comfortable controlling the robot themselves rather than having a higher level of autonomy, even though it involves tedious concentration. Furthermore, the path itself determined by a motion planning algorithm could be optimized to reduce sickness by shortening times over which accelerations occur or by avoiding close proximity to walls or objects that have high spatial frequency and contrast. Another idea is to show the motion on a 2D or

3D map while the robot is moving, from a third-person perspective. The user could conceivably be shown anything, such as news feeds, while the robot is moving. As in the case of locomotion for virtual worlds, one must be careful not to disorient the user by failing to provide enough information to easily infer the new position and orientation relative to the old one by the time the user has arrived.

Latency Issues

As expected, time delays threaten the performance and comfort of telepresence systems. Such latencies have already been discussed in terms of visual rendering (Section 7.4) and virtual world simulation (Section 8.3.2). A networked system causes new latency to be added to that of the VR system because information must travel from the client to the server and back again. Furthermore, bandwidth (bits per second) is limited, which might cause further delays or degradation in quality. For reference, the average worldwide travel time to Google and back was around 100 ms in 2012 (it was 50 to 60 ms in the US) [224]. Note that by transmitting an entire panoramic view to the user, the network latency should not contribute to head tracking and rendering latencies.

However, latency has a dramatic impact on *interactivity*, which is a well-known problem to networked gamers. On the other hand, it has been found that people generally tolerate latencies in phone calls of up to 200 ms before complaining of difficulty conversing; however, they may become frustrated if they expect the robot to immediately respond to their movement commands. Completing a manipulation task is even more difficult because of delays in hand-eye coordination. In some cases people can be trained to overcome high latencies through adaptation, assuming the latencies do not substantially vary during and across the trials [69]. The latency poses a considerable challenge for medical applications of telepresence. Imagine if you were a doctor pushing on a scalpel via a telepresence system, but could not see or feel that it is time to stop cutting until 500 ms later. This might be too late!

13.4 Brain–Machine Interfaces

The ultimate interface between humans and machines could be through direct sensing and stimulation of neurons. One step in this direction is to extract physiological measures, which were introduced in Section 12.3. Rather than using them to study VR sickness, we could apply measures such as heart rate, galvanic skin response, and respiration to adjust the VR experience dynamically. Various goals would be optimized, such as excitement, fear, comfort, or relaxation. Continuing further, we could apply technology that is designed to read the firings of neurons so that the VR system responds to it by altering the visual and auditory displays. The users can learn that certain thoughts have an associated effect in VR, resulting in mind control. The powers of neuroplasticity and perceptual learning (Section 12.1) could enable them to comfortably and efficiently move their avatar bodies in the virtual world. This might sound like pure science fiction, but substantial progress has been made. For example, monkeys have been trained by neuroscientists at Duke University to drive wheelchairs using only their thoughts [264]. In the field of *brain–machine interfaces* (alternatively, *BMI*, *brain–computer interfaces*, or *BCI*), numerous other experiments

visual faces   left   right

visual pictures

auditory

olfactory

gustatory

somatosensory

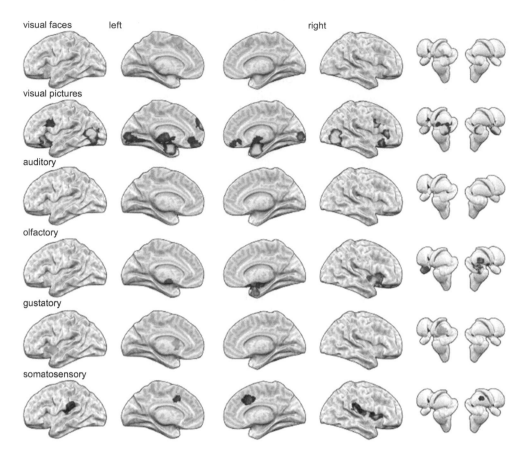

Figure 13.10   fMRI-based images that show brain areas that respond to various sensory activity [284].

have been performed, which connect humans and animals to mechanical systems and VR experiences via their thoughts [176, 178, 188]. Surveys of this area include [90, 237, 360].

Measurement Methods

The goal of devices that measure neural activity is to decipher the voluntary intentions and decisions of the user. They are usually divided into two categories: *noninvasive* (attaching sensors to the skin is allowed) and *invasive* (drilling into the skull is allowed).

First consider the noninvasive case, which is by far the most appropriate for humans. The most accurate way to measure full brain activity to date is by *functional magnetic resonance imaging* (*fMRI*), which is shown in Figure 13.10. This is related to MRI, which most people are familiar with as a common medical scanning method. Ordinary MRI differs in that it provides an image of the static structures to identify abnormalities, whereas an fMRI provides images that show activities of parts of the brain over time. Unfortunately, fMRI is too slow, expensive, and cumbersome for everyday use as a VR interface [176]. Furthermore, users must

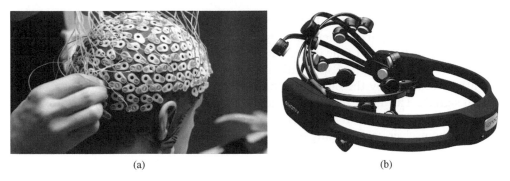

Figure 13.11 EEG systems place electrodes around the skull. (a) A skull cap that allows up to a few dozen signals to be measured. (b) Emotive wireless EEG device.

remain rigidly fixed, and sometimes they ingest a dye that increases contrast due to variations in blood flow.

Thus, the most common way to measure brain activity for BMI is via *electroencephalogram* (*EEG*), which involves placing electrodes along the scalp to measure electrical field fluctuations that emanate from neural activity; see Figure 13.11. The signal-to-noise ratio is unfortunately poor because the brain tissue, bone, and skin effectively perform low-pass filtering that destroys most of the signal. There is also significant attenuation and interference with other neural structures. The transfer rate of information via EEG is between 5 and 25 bits per second [176, 360]. This is roughly equivalent to one to a few characters per second, which is two orders of magnitude slower than the average typing rate. Extracting the information from EEG signals involves difficult signal processing [283]; open-source libraries exist, such as OpenVibe from INRIA Rennes.

For the invasive case, electrodes are implanted intracranially (inside the skull). This provides much more information for scientists but is limited to studies on animals (and some humans suffering from neural disorders such as Parkinson's disease). Thus, invasive methods are not suitable for the vast majority of people as a VR interface. The simplest case is to perform a single-unit recording for a particular neuron; however, this often increases the number of required trials because the neural response typically switches between different neurons across trials. As the number of neurons increases, the problem of deciphering the thoughts becomes more reliable. Numerous recordings could be from a single site that performs a known function, or could come from multiple sites to help understand the distributed processing performed by the brain [176].

Medical Motivation

It is important to understand the difference between VR users and the main targeted community for BMI. The field of BMI has rapidly developed because it may give mobility to people who suffer from neuromuscular disabilities [360]. Examples include driving a wheelchair and moving a prosthetic limb by using thoughts alone. The first mental control system was built by Jacques Vidal in the 1970s [339, 340], and since that time many systems have been built using several kinds of neural signals. In all cases, it takes a significant amount of training and skill to operate these interfaces. People with motor disabilities may be highly motivated to include hours of daily practice as part of their therapy routine, but this would not be the case for the majority of VR users. One interesting problem in training is that trainees require *feedback*, which is a perfect application of VR. The controller in the VR system is essentially replaced by the output of the signal processing system that analyzes the neural signals. The user can thus practice moving a virtual wheelchair or prosthetic limb while receiving visual feedback from a VR system. This prevents them from injuring themselves or damaging equipment or furnishings while practicing.

Learning New Body Schema

What happens to the human's perception of her own body when controlling a prosthetic limb? The internal brain representation of the body is referred to as a *body schema*. It was proposed over a century ago [117] that when people skillfully use tools, the body schema adapts accordingly so that the brain operates as if there is a new, extended body. This results in perceptual assimilation of the tool and hand, which was confirmed from neural signals in [133]. This raises a fascinating question for VR research: What sort of body schema could our brains learn through different visual body representations (avatars) and interaction mechanisms for locomotion and manipulation?

BMI in VR

In the context of VR, most systems have used one of three different kinds of EEG signals [85, 177, 188, 189, 275]: (1) motor imagery, (2) SSVEP, and (3) P300. The most common is *motor imagery*, which is a mental process that a person performs before executing an action. During this time, the person rehearses or simulates the motion in the brain, which leads to measurable activations in the primary motor cortex. Users imagine rotating in place or making footsteps to achieve locomotion in the virtual world. Unfortunately, most successful systems are limited to a couple of simple commands, such as starting and stopping walking. Nevertheless, users have been able to explore maze-like environments by simply imagining the motions.

One advantage of motor imagery is that it does not require any interference or special stimulus from the system, thereby allowing the user to proceed without disruption or particular timing. The other two kinds of signals unfortunately require a stimulus to be generated, and then the response is measured by EEG. One of them is *SSVEP* (*steady state visually evoked potential*), which occurs when a flashing visual stimulus is presented in the range of 3.5 to 75 Hz. The signal-to-noise ratio is very strong for SSVEP, and the user can affect its outcome based on attention paid to the flashing. The decision of whether to pay attention is used as the basis of the command. The other signal is *P300*, which appears about 300 ms after a rare and relevant stimulus is presented. Once again, the response is measured based on how much attention the user pays to the stimulus.

Research Challenges

Although BMIs are rapidly maturing, several challenges remain before they could come into widespread use:

- Better technologies for measuring neural signals while remaining non-invasive. Ideally, one would like to measure outputs of thousands of neurons with a high signal-to-noise ratio. One alternative to fMRI is *functional near-infrared spectroscopy (fNIRS)*. Such signals can be used in combination with EEG to enhance measurement [136, 232].

- Improved bandwidth in terms of bits per second that can be commanded by the user so that there are clear advantages over using body movements or controllers. VR systems with noninvasive BMI typically offer up to one bit per second, which is woefully inadequate [178].

- Better classification techniques that can recognize the intentions and decisions of the user with higher accuracy and detail. Modern machine learning methods may help advance this.

- Dramatic reduction in the amount of training that is required before using an interface. If it requires more work than learning how to type, then widespread adoption would be unlikely.

- A better understanding of what kinds of body schemas can be learned through the feedback provided by VR systems so that the brain accepts the virtual body as being natural.

Thus, with the exception of helping people with motor disabilities, BMI has a long way to go before reaching levels of mind control that are expected from science fiction.

Toward a Brain in a Vat

To build a widespread, networked VR society, it is tempting to consider invasive BMI possibilities in a distant future. Before proceeding, recall the discussion of ethical standards from Section 12.4 and consider whether such a future is preferable. Suppose that in addition to measuring neural outputs, direct neural stimulation were also used. This would forgo the need to place displays in front of senses. For the eye, signals could be sent directly to the photoreceptors. This technology is called *retinal implants* and already exists for the purpose of helping the blind to see. Similarly, *cochlear* implants help the deaf to hear. Neuroscientists, such as David Eagleman from Stanford, have even proposed that we could learn to develop completely new senses. An example is perceiving infrared or radio signals by remapping their frequencies, amplitudes, and spatial arrangements to other collections of receptors on the body, such as the back. The limits of neuroplasticity have yet to be fully understood in this way.

Rather than stimulating receptors, the engineered stimulus could even be placed at higher neural levels. For example, why bother with stimulating photoreceptors if the optic nerve could be directly stimulated? This would involve mimicking the processing performed by the ganglion cells, which is challenging, but would also reduce the bandwidth requirements in comparison to stimulating the rods and cones. Ultimately, direct neural measurement and stimulation could lead to the brain in a vat, which was mentioned in Section 1.1.

How do you know you are not already a brain in a vat, and an evil scientist has been taunting you while you read this VR book?

References

[1] M. Abrash. Raster scan displays: More than meets the eye. Blog post. Accessed January 10, 2016 at http://blogs.valvesoftware.com/abrash/raster-scan-displays-more-than-meets-the-eye/, January 2013.

[2] Z. M. Aghajan, L. Acharya, J. J. Moore et al. Impaired spatial selectivity and intact phase precession in two-dimensional virtual reality. *Nature Neuroscience*, 18(1):121–128, 2015.

[3] Y. Akatsuka and G. A. Bekey. Compensation for end to end delays in a VR system. In *Proceedings IEEE Virtual Reality Annual International Symposium*, pages 156–159, 1998.

[4] K. Akeley, S. J. Watt, A. Reza Girschick, and M. S. Banks. A stereo display prototype with multiple focal distances. *ACM Transactions on Graphics*, 23(3): 804–813, 2004.

[5] T. Akenine-Möller, E. Haines, and N. Hoffman. *Real-Time Rendering*. CRC Press, Boca Raton, FL, 2008.

[6] D. Alais, C. Morrone, and D. Burr. Separate attentional resources for vision and audition. *Proceedings of the Royal Society B: Biological Sciences*, 273(1592):1339–1345, 2006.

[7] B. B. Andersen, L. Korbo, and B. Pakkenberg. A quantitative study of the human cerebellum with unbiased stereological techniques. *Journal of Comparative Neurology*, 326(4):549–560, 1992.

[8] J. Angeles. Spatial Kinematic Chains. Analysis, Synthesis, and Optimisation. Springer-Verlag, Berlin, 1982.

[9] J. Angeles. *Rotational Kinematics*. Springer-Verlag, Berlin, 1989.

[10] J. Angeles. *Fundamentals of Robotic Mechanical Systems: Theory, Methods, and Algorithms*. Springer-Verlag, Berlin, 2003.

[11] A. Antoniou. *Digital Signal Processing: Signals, Systems, and Filters*. McGraw-Hill Education, Columbus, OH, 2005.

[12] D. K. Arrowsmith and C. M. Place. *Dynamical Systems: Differential Equations, Maps, and Chaotic Behaviour*. Chapman & Hall/CRC, New York, 1992.

[13] K. W. Arthur. Effects of Field of View on Performance with Head-Mounted Displays. PhD thesis, University of North Carolina at Chapel Hill, 2000.

[14] K. J. Astrom and R. Murray. *Feedback Systems: An Introduction for Scientists and Engineers*. Princeton University Press, Princeton, NJ, 2008.

[15] F. A. Azevedo, L. R. Carvalho, L. T. Grinberg et al. Equal numbers of neuronal and nonneuronal cells make the human brain an isometrically scaled-up primate brain. *Journal of Computational Neurology*, 513(5):532–541, 2009.

[16] J. N. Bailenson, A. C. Beall, J. Loomis, J. Blascovich, and M. Turk. Transformed social interaction: Decoupling representation from behavior and form in collaborative virtual environments. *PRESENCE: Teleoperators and Virtual Environments*, 13(4):428–441, 2004.

REFERENCES

[17] M. S. Banks, J. Kim, and T. Shibata. Insight into vergence-accommodation mismatch. In *Proceedings of SPIE*, vol. 8735, 873509P1- 873509P-12, 2013.

[18] H. B. Barlow and R. M. Hill. Evidence for a physiological explanation of the waterfall illusion. *Nature*, 200:1345–1347, 1963.

[19] H. H. Barrett and K. J. Myers. *Foundations of Image Science*. Wiley, Hoboken, NJ, 2004.

[20] E. P. Becerra and M. A. Stutts. Ugly duckling by day, super model by night: The influence of body image on the use of virtual worlds. *Journal of Virtual Worlds Research*, 1(2):1–19, 2008.

[21] C. Bergland. The wacky neuroscience of forgetting how to ride a bicycle. *Psychology Today*, May 2015. www.psychologytoday.com/intl/blog/the-athletes-way/201505/the-wacky-neuroscience-forgetting-how-ride-bicycle

[22] J. Birn. *Digital Lighting and Rendering, 3rd Ed.* New Riders, San Francisco, CA, 2013.

[23] J. Blauert. *Spatial Hearing: Psychophysics of Human Sound Localization*. Massachusetts Institute of Technology Press, Cambridge, MA, 1996.

[24] J. F. Blinn. Models of light reflection for computer synthesized pictures. In *Proceedings Annual Conference on Computer Graphics and Interactive Techniques*, pages 192–198, 1977.

[25] I. Bogost and N. Monfort. *Racing the Beam: The Atari Video Computer System*. Massachusetts Institute of Technology Press, Cambridge, MA, 2009.

[26] S. J. Bolanowski, G. A. Gescheider, R. T. Verillo, and C. M. Checkosky. Four channels mediate the aspects of touch. *Journal of the Acoustical Society of America*, 84(5):1680–1694, 1988.

[27] W. M. Boothby. *An Introduction to Differentiable Manifolds and Riemannian Geometry. Revised 2nd Ed.* Academic, New York, 2003.

[28] D. Bordwell and K. Thompson. *Film History: An Introduction, 3rd Ed.* McGraw-Hill, New York, 2010.

[29] J. K. Bowmaker and H. J. A. Dartnall. Visual pigment of rods and cones in a human retina. *Journal of Physiology*, 298:501–511, 1980.

[30] D. Bowman and L. Hodges. An evaluation of techniques for grabbing and manipulating remote objects in immersive virtual environments. In *Proceedings ACM Symposium on Interactive 3D Graphics*, pages 35–38, 1997.

[31] D. A. Bowman, E. Kruijff, J. J. LaViola, and I. Poupyrev. *3D User Interfaces*. Addison-Wesley, Boston, MA, 2005.

[32] K. Brown. Silent films: What was the right speed? *Sight and Sound*, 49(3):164–167, 1980.

[33] M. Brown and D. G. Lowe. Automatic panoramic image stitching using invariant features. *International Journal of Computer Vision*, 74(1):59–73, 2007.

[34] N. C. Burbules. Rethinking the virtual. In J. Weiss, J. Nolan, and P. Trifonas, editors, *The International Handbook of Virtual Learning Environments*, pages 3–24. Kluwer Publishers, Dordrecht, 2005.

[35] D. C. Burr, M. C. Morrone, and L. M. Vaina. Large receptive fields for optic flow detection in humans. *Vision Research*, 38(12):1731–1743, 1998.

[36] W. S. Cain. Odor identification by males and females: Predictions vs performance. *Chemical Senses*, 7(2):129–142, 1994.

[37] P. Cairns and A. L. Cox. *Research Methods for Human-Computer Interaction*. Cambridge University Press, Cambridge, 2008.

[38] F. W. Campbell and D. G. Green. Optical and retinal factors affecting visual resolution. *Journal of Physiology*, 181(3):576–593, 1965.

[39] S. K. Card, W. K. English, and B. J. Burr. Evaluation of mouse, rate-controlled isometric joystick, step keys, and text keys for text selection on a CRT. *Ergonomics*, 20(8):601–613, 1978.

[40] J. M. Caroll. *HCI Models, Theories, and Frameworks: Toward a Multidisciplinary Science*. Morgan Kaufmann, San Francisco, CA, 2003.

[41] E. Catmull. A Subdivision Algorithm for Computer Display of Curved Surfaces. PhD thesis, University of Utah, 1974.

[42] A. Y. Chang. A survey of geometric data structures for ray tracing. Technical Report TR-CIS-2001-06, Brooklyn Polytechnic University, 2001.

[43] N. Chaudhari, A. M. Landin, and S. D. Roper. A metabotropic glutamate receptor variant functions as a taste receptor. *Nature Neuroscience*, 3(3):113–119, 2000.

[44] G. Chen, J. A. King, N. Burgess, and J. O'Keefe. How vision and movement combine in the hippocampal place code. *Proceedings of the National Academy of Science USA*, 110(1):378–383, 2013.

[45] C. K. Chui and G. Chen. *Kalman Filtering*. Springer-Verlag, Berlin, 1991.

[46] D. Claus and A. W. Fitzgibbon. A rational function lens distortion model for general cameras. In *Proceedings of the IEEE Conference on Computer Vision and Pattern Recognition*, pages 213–219, 2005.

[47] E. Cline. *Ready Player One*. Random House, New York, 2011.

[48] D. Cox, J. Little, and D. O'Shea. *Ideals, Varieties, and Algorithms*. Springer-Verlag, Berlin, 1992.

[49] C. Cruz-Neira, D. J. Sandin, T. A. DeFanti, R. V. Kenyon, and J. C. Hart. The CAVE: Audio visual experience automatic virtual environment. *Communications of the ACM*, 35(6):64–72, 1992.

[50] W. Cui and L. Gao. Optical mapping near-eye three-dimensional display with correct focus cues. *Optics Letters*, 42(13):2475–2478, 2017.

[51] H. Culbertson, J. J. Lopez Delgado, and K. J. Kuchenbecker. One hundred data-driven haptic texture models and open-source methods for rendering on 3D objects. In *Proceedings IEEE Haptics Symposium*, pages 319–325, 2014.

[52] C. A. Curcio, K. R. Sloan, R. E. Kalina, and A. E. Hendrickson. Human photoreceptor topography. *Journal of Comparative Neurobiology*, 292(4):497–523, 1990.

[53] R. P. Darken and B. Peterson. Spatial orientation, wayfinding, and representation. In K. S. Hale and K. M. Stanney, editors, *Handbook of Virtual Environments, 2nd Edition*, pages 131–161. CRC Press, Boca Raton, FL, 2015.

[54] R. Darwin. New experiments on the ocular spectra of light and colours. *Philosophical Transactions of the Royal Society of London*, 76:313–348, 1786. https://archive.org/details/philtrans07762880.

[55] M. de Berg, M. van Kreveld, M. Overmars, and O. Schwarzkopf. *Computational Geometry: Algorithms and Applications, 2nd Ed*. Springer-Verlag, Berlin, 2000.

[56] K. N. de Winkel, M. Katliar, and H. H. Bülthoff. Forced fusion in multisensory heading estimation. *PloS ONE*, 10(5), 2015. DOI: https://doi.org/10.1371/journal.pone.0127104.

[57] J. R. Dejong. The effects of increasing skill on cycle time and its consequences for time standards. *Ergonomics*, 1(1):51–60, 1957.

[58] J. Delwiche. The impact of perceptual interactions on perceived flavor. *Food Quality and Preferences*, 15, 137–146. https://citeseerx.ist.psu.edu/document?repid=rep1&type=pdf&doi=718913163f7fe43a00fa0fe3b2d37d33a816b215.

[59] J. L. Demer, J. Goldberg, H. A. Jenkins, and F. I. Porter. Vestibulo-ocular reflex during magnified vision: Adaptation to reduce visual-vestibular conflict. *Aviation, Space, and Environmental Medicine*, 58(9 Pt 2):A175–A179, 1987.

[60] M. Dennison, Z. Wisti, and M. D'Zmura. Use of physiological signals to predict cybersickness. *Displays*, 44:52–52, 2016. www.sciencedirect.com/science/article/abs/pii/S0141938216301081.

[61] D. Deutsch, T. Hamaoui, and T. Henthorn. The glissando illusion and handedness. *Neuropsychologia*, 45(13):2981–2988, 2007.

[62] P. DiZio, J. R. Lackner, and R. K. Champney. Proprioceptive adaptation and aftereffects. In K. S. Hale and K. M. Stanney, editors, *Handbook of Virtual Environments, 2nd Edition*. CRC Press, Boca Raton, FL, 2015.

[63] R. L. Doty (Ed.). *Handbook of Olfaction and Gustation, 3rd Ed.* Wiley-Blackwell, Hoboken, NJ, 2015.

[64] M. H. Draper, E. S. Viire, T. A. Furness, and V. J. Gawron. Effects of image scale and system time delay on simulator sickness with head-coupled virtual environments. *Human Factors*, 43(1):129–146, 2001.

[65] A. T. Duchowski. *Eye Tracking Methodology: Theory and Practice, 2nd Ed.* Springer-Verlag, Berlin, 2007.

[66] G. Dudek, P. Giguere, C. Prahacs et al. Aqua: An amphibious autonomous robot. *IEEE Computer Magazine*, 40(1):46–53, 2007.

[67] H. H. Ehrsson, C. Spence, and R. E. Passingham. That's my hand! Activity in premotor cortex reflects feeling of ownership of a limb. *Science*, 305(5685):875–877, 2004.

[68] S. R. Ellis, K. Mania, B. D. Adelstein, and M. I. Hill. Generalizeability of latency detection in a variety of virtual environments. In *Proceedings of the Human Factors and Ergonomics Society Annual Meeting*, pages 2632–2636, 2004.

[69] S. R. Ellis, M. J. Young, B. D. Adelstein, and S. M. Ehrlich. Discrimination of changes in latency during head movement. In *Proceedings Computer Human Interfaces*, pages 1129–1133, 1999.

[70] M. Emoto, K. Masaoka, M. Sugawara, and F. Okano. Viewing angle effects from wide field video projection images on the human equilibrium. *Displays*, 26(1):9–14, 2005.

[71] D. J. Encross. Control of skilled movement. *Psychological Bulletin*, 84(1):14–29, 1977.

[72] R. Engbert and K. Mergenthaler. Microsaccades are triggered by low retinal image slip. *Proceedings of the National Academy of Sciences of the United States of America*, 103(18):7192–7197, 2008.

[73] B. W. Epps. Comparison of six cursor control devices based on Fitts' law models. In *Proceedings of the 30th Annual Meeting of the Human Factors Society*, pages 327–331, 1986.

[74] C. J. Erkelens. Coordination of smooth pursuit and saccades. *Vision Research*, 46(1–2):163–170, 2006.

[75] D. Fattal, Z. Peng, T. Tran et al. A multi-directional backlight for a wide-angle, glasses-free three-dimensional display. *Nature*, 495:348–351, 2013.

[76] J. Favre, B. M. Jolles, O. Siegrist, and K. Aminian. Quaternion-based fusion of gyroscopes and accelerometers to improve 3D angle measurement. *Electronics Letters*, 32(11):612–614, 2006.

[77] G. T. Fechner. *Elements of Psychophysics (in German)*. Breitkopf and Härtel, Leipzig, 1860.

[78] M. A. Fischler and R. C. Bolles. Random sample consensus: A paradigm for model fitting with applications to image analysis and automated cartography. *Communications of the ACM*, 24(6):381–395, 1981.

[79] P. M. Fitts. The information capacity of the human motor system in controlling the amplitude of movement. *Journal of Experimental Psychology*, 47(6):381–391, 1956.

[80] R. C. Fitzpatrick and B. L. Day. Probing the human vestibular system with galvanic stimulation. *Journal of Applied Physiology*, 96(6):2301–2316, 2004.

[81] R. C. Fitzpatrick, J. Marsden, S. R. Lord, and B. L. Day. Galvanic vestibular stimulation evokes sensations of body rotation. *NeuroReport*, 13(18):2379–2383, 2002.

[82] T. Fong, I. Nourbakhsh, and K. Dautenhahn. A survey of socially interactive robots: Concepts, design, and applications. *Robotics and Autonomous Systems*, 42(3–4):143–166, 2003.

[83] W. T. Fong, S. K. Ong, and A. Y. C. Nee. Methods for in-field user calibration of an inertial measurement unit without external equipment. *Measurement Science and Technology*, 19(8), 2008. DOI: https://doi.org/10.1088/0957-0233/19/8/085202.

[84] A. K. Forsberg, K. Herndon, and R. Zelznik. Aperture based selection for immersive virtual environments. In *Proceedings ACM Symposium on User Interface Software and Technology*, pages 95–96, 1996.

[85] D. Friedman, R. Leeb, C. Guger et al. Navigating virtual reality by thought: What is it like? *Presence: Teleoperators and Virtual Environments*, 16(1):100–110, 2007.

[86] H. Fuchs, Z. M. Kedem, and B. F. Naylor. On visible surface generation by a priori tree structures. In *Proceedings ACM SIGGRAPH*, pages 124–133, 1980.

[87] J. Fuentes-Pacheco, J. Ruiz-Ascencio, and J. M. Rendon-Mancha. Visual simultaneous localization and mapping: a survey. *Journal Artificial Intelligence Review*, 43(1):55–81, 2015.

[88] T. Funkhouser, I. Carlbom, G. Elko, G. Pingali, M. Sondhi, and J. West. A beam tracing approach to acoustic modeling for interactive virtual environments. In *Proceedings ACM Annual Conference on Computer Graphics and Interactive Techniques*, pages 21–32, 1998.

[89] J. Gallier. *Curves and Surfaces in Geometric Modeling*. Morgan Kaufmann, San Francisco, CA, 2000.

[90] S. Gao, Y. Wang, X. Gao, and B. Hong. Visual and auditory brain-computer interfaces. *IEEE Transactions on Biomedical Engineering*, 61(5):1436–1447, 2014.

[91] M. A. Garcia-Perez. Forced-choice staircases with fixed step sizes: asymptotic and small-sample properties. *Vision Research*, 38(12):1861–81, 1998.

[92] G. M. Gauthier and D. A. Robinson. Adaptation of the human vestibuloocular reflex to magnifying lenses. *Brain Research*, 92(2):331–335, 1975.

[93] D. Gebre-Egziabher, G. Elkaim, J. David Powell, and B. Parkinson. Calibration of strapdown magnetometers in magnetic field domain. *Journal of Aerospace Engineering*, 19(2):87–102, 2006.

[94] G. Gescheider. *Psychophysics: The Fundamentals, 3rd Ed.* Lawrence Erlbaum Associates, Mahwah, NJ, 2015.

[95] E. Gibson. *Principles of Perceptual Learning and Development*. Appleton-Century-Crofts, New York, 1969.

[96] W. Gibson. *Neuromancer*. Ace Books, 1984.

[97] W. C. Gogel. An analysis of perceptions from changes in optical size. *Perception and Psychophysics*, 60(5):805–820, 1998.

[98] E. B. Goldstein. *Sensation and Perception, 9th Ed.* Wadsworth, Belmont, CA, 2014.

[99] R. L. Goldstone. Perceptual learning. *Annual Review of Psychology*, 49:585–612, 1998.

[100] A. Gopnik, A. N. Meltzoff, and P. K. Kuhl. *The Scientist in the Crib: What Early Learning Tells Us About the Mind*. HarperCollins, New York, 2000.

[101] S. Gottschalk, M. C. Lin, and D. Manocha. Obbtree: A hierarchical structure for rapid interference detection. In *Proceedings ACM SIGGRAPH*, pages 171–180, 1996.

[102] A. C. Grant, M. C. Thiagarajah, and K. Sathian. Tactile perception in blind Braille readers: A psychophysical study of acuity and hyperacuity using gratings and dot patterns. *Perception and Psychophysics*, 62(2):301–312, 2000.

[103] A. Graybiel and J. Knepton. Sopite syndrome – sometimes sole manifestation of motion sickness. *Aviation, Space, and Environmental Medicine*, 47(8):873–882, 1976.

[104] J. Gregory. *Game Engine Architecture, 2nd Ed.* CRC Press, Boca Raton, FL, 2014.

[105] J. E. Greivenkamp. *Field Guide to Geometrical Optics*. SPIE Press, Bellingham, WA, 2004.

[106] B. Guentner, M. Finch, S. Drucker, D. Tan, and J. Snyder. Foveated 3D graphics. Technical report, Microsoft Research, 2012. Available at http://research.microsoft.com/.

[107] P. Guigue and O. Devillers. Fast and robust triangle-triangle overlap test using orientation predicates. *Journal of Graphics Tools*, 8(1):25–32, 2003.

[108] A. Guterstam, V. I. Petkova, and H. H. Ehrsson. The illusion of owning a third arm. *PloS ONE*, 6(2), 2011.

[109] K. S. Hale and K. M. Stanney. *Handbook of Virtual Environments, 2nd Edition*. CRC Press, Boca Raton, FL, 2015.

[110] G. Hall. *Perceptual and Associative Learning*. Oxford University Press, Oxford, 1991.

[111] B. J. Harris. *The History of the Future: Oculus, Facebook, and the Revolution that Swept Virtual Reality*. HarperCollins, New York, NY, 2019.

[112] R. S. Hartenberg and J. Denavit. A kinematic notation for lower pair mechanisms based on matrices. *Journal of Applied Mechanics*, 77:215–221, 1955.

[113] R. I. Hartley and A. Zisserman. *Multiple View Geometry in Computer Vision, 2nd Ed.* Cambridge University Press, Cambridge, UK, 2004.

[114] C. D. Harvey, F. Collman, D. A. Dombeck, and D. W. Tank. Intracellular dynamics of hippocampal place cells during virtual navigation. *Nature*, 461(7266):941–946, 2009.

[115] J. O. Harvey. Efficient estimation of sensory thresholds with ml-pest. *Spatial Vision*, 11(1):121–128, 1997.

[116] K. Hashimoto, Y. Maruno, and T. Nakamoto. Brief demonstration of olfactory and visual presentation using wearable olfactory display and head mounted display. In *Proceedings IEEE Virtual Reality Conference*, page Abstract, 2016.

[117] H. Head and G. Holmes. Sensory disturbances from cerebral lesion. *Brain*, 34(2-3):102–254, 1911.

[118] E. G. Heckenmueller. Stabilization of the retinal image: A review of method, effects, and theory. *Psychological Bulletin*, 63(3):157–169, 1965.

[119] J. Heikkilä. Geometric camera calibration using circular control points. *IEEE Transactions on Pattern Analysis and Machine Intelligence*, 22(10):1066–1077, 2000.

[120] J. Heikkilä and O. Silvén. A four-step camera calibration procedure with implicit image correction. In *Proc. Computer Vision and Pattern Recognition*, pages 1106–1112, 1997.

[121] W. T. Higgins. A comparison of complementary and Kalman filtering. *IEEE Transactions on Aerospace and Electronic Systems*, 11(3):321–325, 1975.

[122] J. M. Hillis, M. O. Ernst, M. S. Banks, and M. S. Landy. Combining sensory information: mandatory fusion within, but not between, senses. *Science*, 298(5098):1627–30, 2002.

[123] P. Hoberman, D. M. Krum, E. A. Suma, and M. Bolas. Immersive training games for smartphone-based head mounted displays. In *IEEE Virtual Reality Short Papers and Posters*, 2012.

[124] J. G. Hocking and G. S. Young. *Topology*. Dover, New York, 1988.

[125] C. M. Hoffmann. *Geometric and Solid Modeling*. Morgan Kaufmann, San Francisco, CA, 1989.

[126] R. V. Hogg, J. McKean, and A. T. Craig. *Introduction to Mathematical Statistics, 7th Ed.* Pearson, New York, NY, 2012.

[127] M. Hollins, M. H. Buonocore, and G. R. Mangun. The neural mechanisms of top-down attentional control. *Nature Neuroscience*, 3(3):284–291, 2002.

[128] G. C. Holst and T. S. Lomheim. *CMOS/CCD Sensors and Camera Systems*. SPIE Press, Bellingham, WA, 2011.

[129] X. Hu and H. Hua. Design and assessment of a depth-fused multi-focal-plane display prototype. *Journal of Display Technology*, 10(4):308–316, 2014.

[130] A. S. Huang, A. Bachrach, P. Henry et al. Visual odometry and mapping for autonomous flight using an RGB-D camera. In *Proceedings International Symposium on Robotics Research*, 2011.

[131] C.-M. Huang and B. Mutlu. The repertoire of robot behavior: Enabling robots to achieve interaction goals through social behavior. *Journal of Human-Robot Interaction*, 2(2), 2013.

[132] W. Hugemann. Correcting lens distortions in digital photographs. In *European Association for Accident Research and Analysis (EVU) Conference*, 2010.

[133] A. Iriki, M. Tanaka, and Y. Iwamura. Coding of modified body schema during tool use by macaque postcentral neurones. *Neuroreport*, 7(14):2325–2330, 1996.

[134] J. A. Irwin. The pathology of sea-sickness. *The Lancet*, 118(3039):907–909, 1878.

[135] A. Iserles. *A First Course in the Numerical Analysis of Differential Equations, 2nd Ed.* Cambridge University Press, Cambridge, UK, 2008.

[136] M. Izzetoglu, K. Izzetoglu, S. Bunce et al. Functional near-infrared neuroimaging. *IEEE Transactions on Neural Systems and Rehabilitation Engineering*, 13(2):153–159, 2005.

[137] J. Jerald. *The VR Book*. Association of Computer Machinery and Morgan & Claypool Publishers, 2015.

[138] D. L. Jones, S. Dechmerowski, R. Oden et al. In K. S. Hale and K. M. Stanney, editors, *Handbook of Virtual Environments, 2nd Edition*, pages 131–161. CRC Press, Boca Raton, FL, 2015.

[139] N. P. Jouppi and S. Thomas. Telepresence systems with automatic preservation of user head height, local rotation, and remote translation. In *Proc. IEEE International Conference on Robotics and Automation*, pages 62–68, 2005.

[140] P. Isokoski M. Lehtonen P. Muller et al. Olfactory display prototype for presenting and sensing authentic and synthetic odors. In *Proceedings ACM International Conference on Multimodal Interaction*, pages 73–77, 2018.

[141] M. Kaliuzhna, M. Prsa, S. Gale, S. J. Lee, and O. Blanke. Learning to integrate contradictory multisensory self-motion cue pairings. *Journal of Vision*, 15(10), 2015.

[142] M. Kalloniatis and C. Luu. Visual acuity. In H. Kolb, R. Nelson, E. Fernandez, and B. Jones, editors, *Webvision: The Organization of the Retina and Visual System*. 2007. Last retrieved on October 18, 2016.

[143] R. Kalman. A new approach to linear filtering and prediction problems. *Transactions of the ASME, Journal of Basic Engineering*, 82:35–45, 1960.

[144] H. Kato and M. Billinghurst. Marker tracking and hmd calibration for a video-based augmented reality conferencing system. In *Proceedings of IEEE and ACM International Workshop on Augmented Reality*, pages 85–94, 1999. doi: https://doi.org/10.1109/IWAR.1999.803809.

[145] D. Katz. Der aufbau der tastwelt. *Zeitschrift für Psychologie*, Ergänzungsband 11, 1925.

[146] R. S. Kennedy and L. H. Frank. A review of motion sickness with special reference to simulator sickness. Technical Report NAVTRAEQUIPCEN 81-C-0105-16, United States Navy, 1985.

[147] R. S. Kennedy, N. E. Lane, K. S. Berbaum, and M. G. Lilienthal. Simulator sickness questionnaire: An enhanced method for quantifying simulator sickness. *International Journal of Aviation Psychology*, 3(3):203–220, 1993.

[148] B. Keshavarz, H. Hecht, and B. D. Lawson. Visually induced motion sickness: Causes, characteristics, and countermeasures. In K. S. Hale and K. M. Stanney, editors, *Handbook of Virtual Environments, 2nd Edition*, pages 647–698. CRC Press, Boca Raton, FL, 2015.

[149] B. Keshavarz, B. E. Riecke, L. J. Hettinger, and J. L. Campos. Vection and visually induced motion sickness: How are they related? *Frontiers in Psychology*, 6(472), 2015.

[150] B. Keshavarz, D. Stelzmann, A. Paillard, and H. Hecht. Visually induced motion sickness can be alleviated by pleasant odors. *Experimental Brain Research*, 233(5):1353–1364, 2015.

[151] W. Khalil and J. F. Kleinfinger. A new geometric notation for open and closed-loop robots. In *Proceedings IEEE International Conference on Robotics & Automation*, volume 3, pages 1174–1179, 1986.

[152] D. O. Kim, C. E. Molnar, and J. W. Matthews. Cochlear mechanics: Nonlinear behaviour in two-tone responses as reflected in cochlear-new-fibre responses and in ear-canal sound pressure. *Journal of the Acoustical Society of America*, 67(5):1704–1721, 1980.

[153] H. Kingma and M. Janssen. Biophysics of the vestibular system. In A. M. Bronstein, editor, *Oxford Textbook of Vertigo and Imbalance*. Oxford University Press, Oxford, UK, 2013.

[154] C. L. Kinsey. *Topology of Surfaces*. Springer-Verlag, Berlin, 1993.

[155] R. E. Kirk. *Experimental Design, 4th Ed.* Sage, Thousand Oaks, CA, 2013.

[156] E. M. Kolasinski. Simulator sickness in virtual environments. Technical Report 2017, U.S. Army Research Institute, 1995.

[157] L. L. Kontsevich and C. W. Tyler. Bayesian adaptive estimation of psychometric slope and threshold. *Vision Research*, 39(16):2729–2737, 1999.

[158] C. Konvalin. Compensating for tilt, hard-iron, and soft-iron effects. Accessed May 30, 2016, at www.sensorsmag.com/sensors/motion-velocity-displacement/compensating-tilt-hard-iron-and-soft-iron-effects-6475, December 2009.

[159] B. C. Kress and P. Meyrueis. *Applied Digital Optics: From Micro-optics to Nanophotonics*. Wiley, Hoboken, NJ, 2009.

[160] J. B. Kuipers. *Quaternions and Rotation Sequences*. Princeton University Press, Princeton, NJ, 1999.

[161] P. R. Kumar and P. Varaiya. *Stochastic Systems*. Prentice-Hall, Englewood Cliffs, NJ, 1986.

[162] R. Lafer-Sousa, K. L. Hermann, and B. R. Conway. Striking individual differences in color perception uncovered by 'the dress' photograph. *Current Biology*, 25(13):R545–R546, 2015.

[163] M. F. Land and S.-E. Nilsson. *Animal Eyes*. Oxford University Press, Oxford, UK, 2002.

[164] D. Lanman and D. Luebke. Near-eye light field displays. *ACM Transactions on Graphics*, 32(6), 2013.

[165] J. Lanman, E. Bizzi, and J. Allum. The coordination of eye and head movement during smooth pursuit. *Brain Research*, 153(1):39–53, 1978.

[166] S. M. LaValle. *Planning Algorithms*. Cambridge University Press, Cambridge, UK, 2006. Available at http://planning.cs.uiuc.edu/.

[167] S. M. LaValle. Help! My cockpit is drifting away. Oculus blog post, December 2013. Accessed January 10, 2016, at https://developer.oculus.com/blog/magnetometer/

[168] S. M. LaValle. The latent power of prediction. Oculus blog post, July 2013. Accessed January 10, 2016, at https://developer.oculus.com/blog/the-latent-power-of-prediction/

[169] S. M. LaValle. Sensor fusion: Keeping it simple. Oculus blog post. Accessed January 10, 2016, at https://developer.oculus.com/blog/sensor-fusion-keeping-it-simple/, May 2013.

[170] S. M. LaValle and P. Giokaris. Perception based predictive tracking for head mounted displays. US Patent 20140354515A1, December 2014.

[171] S. M. LaValle, A. Yershova, M. Katsev, and M. Antonov. Head tracking for the Oculus Rift. In *Proc. IEEE International Conference on Robotics and Automation*, pages 187–194, 2014.

[172] J. J. LaViola. A discussion of cybersickness in virtual environments. *ACM SIGCHI Bulletin*, 32:47–56, 2000.

[173] B. D. Lawson. Motion sickness scaling. In K. S. Hale and K. M. Stanney, editors, *Handbook of Virtual Environments, 2nd Edition*, pages 601–626. CRC Press, Boca Raton, FL, 2015.

[174] B. D. Lawson. Motion sickness symptomatology and origins. In K. S. Hale and K. M. Stanney, editors, *Handbook of Virtual Environments, 2nd Edition*, pages 531–600. CRC Press, Boca Raton, FL, 2015.

[175] D. Lazewatsky and W. Smart. An inexpensive robot platform for teleoperation and experimentation. In *Proc. IEEE International Conference on Robotics and Automation*, pages 1211–1216, 2011.

[176] M. A. Lebedev and M. A. L. Nicolelis. Brain-machine interfaces: Past, present, and future. *TRENDS in Neurosciences*, 29(9):536–546, 2006.

[177] A. Lecuyer, L. George, and M. Marchal. Toward adaptive VR simulators combining visual, haptic, and brain-computer interfaces. In *IEEE Computer Graphics and Applications*, pages 3318–3323, 2013.

[178] A. Lécuyer, F. Lotte, R. B. Reilly et al. Brain-computer interfaces, virtual reality, and videogames. *IEEE Computer*, 41(10):66–72, 2008.

[179] M. R. Leek. Adaptive procedures in psychophysical research. *Perception and Psychophysics*, 63(8):1279–1292, 2001.

[180] R. J. Leigh and D. S. Zee. *The Neurology of Eye Movements, 5th Ed.* Oxford University Press, 2015.

[181] J.-C. Lepecq, I. Giannopulu, and P.-M. Baudonniere. Cognitive effects on visually induced body motion in children. *Perception*, 24(4):435–449, 1995.

[182] J.-C. Lepecq, I. Giannopulu, S. Mertz, and P.-M. Baudonniere. Vestibular sensitivity and vection chronometry along the spinal axis in erect man. *Perception*, 28(1):63–72, 1999.

[183] H. Li, L. Trutoiu, K. Olszewski, L. Wei, T. Trutna, P.-L. Hsieh, A. Nicholls, and C. Ma. Facial performance sensing head mounted display. In *Proceedings ACM SIGGRAPH*, 2015.

[184] M. C. Lin and J. F. Canny. Efficient algorithms for incremental distance computation. In *Proceedings IEEE International Conference on Robotics & Automation*, vol. 2, pages 1008–1014, 1991.

[185] M. C. Lin and D. Manocha. Collision and proximity queries. In J. E. Goodman and J. O'Rourke, editors, *Handbook of Discrete and Computational Geometry, 2nd Ed.*, pages 787–807. Chapman and Hall/CRC Press, New York, 2004.

[186] J. Linowes. *Unity Virtual Reality Projects*. Packt, Birmingham, UK, 2015.

[187] S. Liversedge, I. Gilchrist, and S. Everling (eds.). *Oxford Handbook of Eye Movements*. Oxford University Press, 2011.

[188] F. Lotte, J. Faller, C. Guger et al. Combining BCI with virtual reality: Towards new applications and improved BCI. In B. Z. Allison, S. Dunne, R. Leeb, J. Del R. Millán, and A. Nijholt, editors, *Towards Practical Brain-Computer Interfaces*, pages 197–220. Springer-Verlag, Berlin, 2012.

[189] F. Lotte, A. van Langhenhove et al. Exploring large virtual environments by thoughts using a brain–computer interface based on motor imagery and high-level commands. *Presence: Teleoperators and Virtual Environments*, 19(1):154–170, 2010.

[190] G. D. Love, D. M. Hoffman, P. J. H. Hands et al. High-speed switchable lens enables the development of a volumetric stereoscopic display. *Optics Express*, 17(18):15716–15725, 2009.

[191] M. J. Lum, J. Rosen, H. King et al. Telepresence systems with automatic preservation of user head height, local rotation, and remote translation. In *Proc. IEEE Conference on Engineering in Medicine and Biology Society*, pages 6860–6863, 2009.

[192] R. G. Lyons. *Understanding Digital Signal Processing, 3rd Ed.* Prentice-Hall, Englewood Cliffs, NJ, 2010.

[193] K. Y. Ma, P. Chirarattananon, and R. J. Wood. Design and fabrication of an insect-scale flying robot for control autonomy. In *Proc. IEEE/RSJ International Conference on Intelligent Robots and Systems*, pages 1133–1140, 2012.

[194] Y. Ma, S. Soatto, J. Kosecka, and S. S. Sastry. *An Invitation to 3-D Vision*. Springer-Verlag, Berlin, 2003.

[195] I. S. MacKenzie. Fitts' law as a research and design tool in human-computer interaction. *Human-Computer Interaction*, 7(1):91–139, 1992.

[196] I. S. Mackenzie. Movement time prediction in human-computer interfaces. In R. M. Baecker, J. Grudin, W. A. S. Buxton, and S. Greenberg, editors, *Readings in Human-Computer Interaction*, pages 483–492. Morgan Kaufmann, San Francisco, 1995.

[197] I. S. MacKenzie and W. Buxton. Extending Fitts' Law to 2D tasks. In *Proceedings of the SIGCHI Conference on Human Factors in Computing Systems*, pages 219–226, 1992.

[198] N. A. Macmillan and C. D. Creelman. *Dection Theory: A User's Guide, 2nd Ed.* Lawrence Erlbaum Associates, Mahwah, NJ, 2005.

[199] R. Magill and D. Anderson. *Motor Learning and Control: Concepts and Applications*. McGraw-Hill, New York, NY, 2013.

[200] R. Mahoney, T. Hamel, and J.-M. Pflimlin. Nonlinear complementary filters on the special orthogonal group. *IEEE Transactions on Automatic Control*, 53(5):1203–1218, 2008.

[201] A. Maimone, D. Lanman, K. Rathinavel et al. Pinlight displays: Wide field of view augmented-reality eyeglasses using defocused point light sources. *ACM Transactions on Graphics*, 33(4), 2014.

[202] K. Mallon and P. F. Whelan. Precise radial un-distortion of images. In *Proc. Computer Vision and Pattern Recognition*, pages 18–21, 2004.

[203] K. Mania, B. D. Adelstein, S. R. Ellis, and M. I. Hill. Perceptual sensitivity to head tracking latency in virtual environments with varying degrees of scene complexity. In *Proceedings of Symposium on Applied Perception in Graphics and Visualization*, pages 39–47, 2004.

[204] W. R. Mark, L. McMillan, and G. Bishop. Post-rendering 3D warping. In *Proceedings of the Symposium on Interactive 3D Graphics*, pages 7–16, 1997.

[205] S. Marschner and P. Shirley. *Fundamentals of Computer Graphics, 4th Ed.* CRC Press, Boca Raton, FL, 2015.

[206] M. T. Mason. *Mechanics of Robotic Manipulation*. Massachusetts Institute of Technology Press, Cambridge, MA, 2001.

[207] G. Mather. *Foundations of Sensation and Perception*. Psychology Press, Hove, UK, 2008.

[208] G. Mather, F. Verstraten, and S. Anstis. *The motion aftereffect: A modern perspective*. Massachusetts Institute of Technology Press, Boston, MA, 1998.

[209] N. Matsuda, A. Fix, and D. Lanman. Focal surface displays. *ACM Transactions on Graphics*, 36(4), 2017.

[210] M. E. McCauley and T. J. Sharkey. Cybersickness: Perception of self-motion in virtual environments. *Presence*, 1(3):311–318, 1992.

[211] H. McGurk and J. MacDonald. Hearing lips and seeing voices. *Nature*, 264:746–748, 1976.

[212] R. Mehra, N. Raghuvanshi, L. Antani et al. Wave-based sound propagation in large open scenes using an equivalent source formulation. *ACM Transactions on Graphics*, 32(2), 2013.

[213] J. Merimaa and V. Pulkki. Spatial impulse response rendering I: Analysis and synthesis. *Journal of the Audio Engineering Society*, 53(12):1115–1127, 2005.

[214] P. R. Messinger, E. Stroulia, K. Lyons et al. Virtual worlds – past, present, and future: New directions in social computing. *Decision Support Systems*, 47(3):204–228, 2009.

[215] A. Mikami, W. T. Newsome, and R. H. Wurtz. Motion selectivity in macaque visual cortex. II. Spatiotemporal range of directional interactions in MT and V1. *Journal of Neurophysiology*, 55(6):1328–1339, 1986.

[216] P. Milgram, H. Takemura, A. Utsumi, and F. Kishino. Augmented reality: A class of displays on the reality-virtuality continuum. H. Das, ed., *Telemanipulator and Telepresence Technologies*, SPIE Vol. 2351, pages 282–292, 1994.

[217] M. Mine and G. Bishop. Just-in-time pixels. Technical Report TR93-005, University of North Carolina, Chapel Hill, NC, 1993.

[218] M. Minsky. Telepresence. *Omni magazine*, pages 44–52, June 1980.

[219] B. Mirtich. V-Clip: Fast and robust polyhedral collision detection. Technical Report TR97-05, Mitsubishi Electronics Research Laboratory, 1997.

[220] B. Mirtich. Efficient algorithms for two-phase collision detection. In K. Gupta and A.P. del Pobil, editors, *Practical Motion Planning in Robotics: Current Approaches and Future Directions*, pages 203–223. Wiley, Hoboken, NJ, 1998.

[221] T. Möller. A fast triangle-triangle intersection test. *Journal of Graphics Tools*, 2(2):25–30, 1997.

[222] T. Möller and N. Trumbore. Fast, minimum storage ray/triangle intersection. *Journal of Graphics Tools*, 2(1):21–28, 1997.

[223] B. Moore. *An Introduction to the Psychology of Hearing, 6th Ed.* Brill, Somerville, MA, 2012.

[224] G. Morrison. Input lag: How important is it? *CNET*, June 2013. Posted online at www.cnet.com/news/input-lag-how-important-is-it/.

[225] H. S. Mortensen, B. Pakkenberg, M. Dam et al. Quantitative relationships in delphinid neocortex. *Frontiers in Neuroanatomy*, 8, 2014. https://doi.org/10.3389/fnana.2014.00132.

[226] M. E. Mortenson. *Geometric Modeling, 2nd Ed.* Wiley, Hoboken, NJ, 1997.

[227] E. I. Moser, E. Kropff, and M.-B. Moser. Place cells, grid cells, and the brain's spatial representation system. *Annual Reviews of Neuroscience*, 31:69–89, 2008.

[228] J. D. Moss and E. R. Muth. Characteristics of head-mounted displays and their effects on simulator sickness. *Human Factors*, 53(3):308–319, 2011.

[229] D. E. Muller and F. P. Preparata. Finding the intersection of two convex polyhedra. *Theoretical Computer Science*, 7(2):217–236, 1978.

[230] D. Mustafi, A. H. Engel, and Palczewski. Structure of cone photoreceptors. *Progress in Retinal and Eye Research*, 28(4):289–302, 2009.

[231] T. Narumi, S. Nishizaka, T. Kajinami, T. Tanikawa, and M. Hirose. Augmented reality flavors: gustatory display based on edible marker and cross-modal interaction. In *Proceedings of the SIGCHI Conference on Human Factors in Computing Systems*, pages 93–102, 2011.

[232] N. Naseer and K.-S. Hong. fNIRS-based brain-computer interfaces: A review. *Frontiers in Human Neuroscience*, 9(3), 2015.

[233] G. Nelson, J. Chandrashekar, M. A. Hoon et al. An amino-acid taste receptor. *Nature*, 416(6877):199–202, 2002.

[234] A. Newell and P. S. Rosenbloom. Mechanisms of skill acquisition and the law of practice. In J. R. Anderson, editor, *Cognitive Skills and Their Acquisition,*, pages 1–55. Erlbaum, Hillsdale, NJ, 1981.

[235] Y. M. H. Ng and C. P. Kwong. Correcting the chromatic aberration in barrel distortion of endoscopic images. *Journal of Systemics, Cybernetics, and Informatics*, 2003.

[236] F. Nicodemus. Directional reflectance and emissivity of an opaque surface. *Applied Optics*, 4(7):767–775, 1965.

[237] L. F. Nicolas-Alonso and J. Gomez-Gil. Brain computer interfaces, a review. *Sensors*, 12(2):1211–1279, 2012.

[238] J. Ninio. *The Science of Illusions*. Cornell University Press, Ithaca, NY, 2001.

[239] D. Nitz. A place for motion in mapping. *Nature Neuroscience*, 18(1):6–7, 2010.

[240] G. Nützi, S. Weiss, D. Scaramuzza, and R. Siegwart. Fusion of IMU and vision for absolute scale estimation in monocular SLAM. *Journal of Intelligent and Robotic Systems*, 61(1):287–299, 2011.

[241] Office for Human Research Protections. International compilation of human research standards. Technical report, U.S. Department of Health and Human Services, 2016. http://www.hhs.gov/ohrp/international/compilation-human-research-standards.

[242] A. M. Okamura, J. T. Dennerlein, and R. D. Howe. Vibration feedback models for virtual environments. In *Proc. IEEE International Conference on Robotics and Automation*, volume 1, pages 674–679, 1998.

[243] J. O'Keefe and J. Dosytovsky. The hippocampus as a spatial map. preliminary evidence from unit activity in the freely-moving rat. *Brain Research*, 34(1):171–175, 1971.

[244] J. L. Olson, D. M. Krum, E. A. Suma, and M. Bolas. A design for a smartphone-based head mounted display. In *Proceedings IEEE Virtual Reality Conference*, pages 233–234, 2011.

[245] G. Osterberg. Topography of the layer of rods and cones in the human retina. *Acta Ophthalmologica, Supplement*, 6:1–103, 1935.

[246] G. D. Park, R. W. Allen, D. Fiorentino, T. J. Rosenthal, and M. L. Cook. Simulator sickness scores according to symptom susceptibility, age, and gender for an older driver assessment study. In *Proceedings of the Human Factors and Ergonomics Society Annual Meeting*, pages 2702–2706, 2006.

[247] E. Paulos and J. Canny. Prop: Personal roving presence. In *Proceedings of the SIGCHI Conference on Human Factors in Computing Systems*, pages 296–303, 1995.

[248] E. Paulos and J. Canny. Social tele-embodiment: Understanding presence. *Autnomous Robots*, 11(1):87–95, 2000.

[249] M. Pedley. High-precision calibration of a three-axis accelerometer. Technical report, Freescale Semiconductor, 2015. Available at http://cache.freescale.com/files/sensors/doc/app_note/AN4399.pdf.

[250] E. Peli. The visual effects of head-mounted display (HMD) are not distinguishable from those of desk-top computer display. *Vision Research*, 38(13):2053–2066, 1998.

[251] E. Peli. Optometric and perceptual issues with head-mounted displays. In P. Mouroulis, editor, *Visual instrumentation : Optical design and engineering principles*. McGraw-Hill, New York, NY, 1999.

[252] J. Pelz, M. Hayhoe, and R. Loeber. The coordination of eye, head, and hand movements in a natural task. *Experimental Brain Research*, 139(3):266–277, 2001.

[253] S. Pelzer, L. Aspöck, D. Schröder, and M. Vorländer. Integrating real-time room acoustics simulation into a cad modeling software to enhance the architectural design process. *Buildings*, 4(2):113–138, 2014. https://doi.org/10.3390/buildings4020113.

[254] R. J. Pethybridge. Sea sickness incidence in royal navy ships. Technical Report 37/82, Institute of Naval Medicine, Gosport, Hants, UK, 1982.

[255] S. Petitjean, D. Kriegman, and J. Ponce. Computing exact aspect graphs of curved objects: Algebraic surfaces. *International Journal of Computer Vision*, 9:231–255, December 1992.

[256] V. I. Petkova and H. H. Ehrsson. If I Were You: Perceptual Illusion of Body Swapping. *PloS ONE*, 3(12), 2008.

[257] M. Pocchiola and G. Vegter. The visibility complex. *International Journal Computational Geometry & Applications*, 6(3):279–308, 1996.

[258] T. Poggio, M. Fahle, and S. Edelman. Fast perceptual learning in visual hyperacuity. *Science*, 256(5059):1018–1021, 1992.

[259] I. Poupyrev, M. Billinghust, S. Weghorst, and T. Ichikawa. The go-go interaction technique: non-linear mapping for direct manipulation in VR. In *Proceedings ACM Symposium on User Interface Software and Technology*, pages 79–80, 1996.

[260] M. Prsa, S. Gale, and O. Blanke. Self-motion leads to mandatory cue fusion across sensory modalities. *Journal of Neurophysiology*, 108(8):2282–2291, 2012.

[261] V. Pulkki. Virtual sound source positioning using vector base amplitude panning. *Journal of the Audio Engineering Society*, 45(6):456–466, 1997.

[262] V. Pulkki. Virtual sound source positioning using vector base amplitude panning. *Journal of the Audio Engineering Society*, 55(6):503–516, 2007.

[263] V. Pulkki and J. Merimaa. Spatial impulse response rendering II: Reproduction of diffuse sound and listening tests. *Journal of the Audio Engineering Society*, 54(1/2):3–20, 2006.

[264] S. Rajangam, P. H. Tseng, A. Yin et al. Wireless cortical brain-machine interface for whole-body navigation in primates. *Scientific Reports*, 2016.

[265] N. Ranasinghe, R. Nakatsu, N. Hieaki, and P. Gopalakrishnakone. Tongue mounted interface for digitally actuating the sense of taste. In *Proceedings IEEE International Symposium on Wearable Computers*, pages 80–87, 2012.

[266] S. Razzaque, Z. Kohn, and M C. Whitton. Redirected walking. In *Proceedings of Eurographics*, pages 289–294, 2001.

[267] J. T. Reason and J. J. Brand. *Motion Sickness*. Academic, New York, 1975.

[268] M. F. Reschke, J. T. Somers, and G. Ford. Stroboscopic vision as a treatment for motion sickness: Strobe lighting vs. shutter glasses. *Aviation, Space, and Environmental Medicine*, 77(1):2–7, 2006.

[269] S. W. Rienstra and A. Hirschberg. *An Introduction to Acoustics*. Endhoven University of Technology, 2016. www.win.tue.nl/~sjoerdr/papers/boek.pdf.

[270] K. J. Ritchey. Panoramic image based virtual reality/telepresence audio-visual system and method. US Patent 5495576A, February 1996.

[271] H. Robbins and S. Monro. Stochastic iteration: A stochastic approximation method. *Annals of Mathematical Statistics*, 22(3):400–407, 1951.

[272] C. P. Robert. *The Bayesian Choice, 2nd. Ed.* Springer-Verlag, Berlin, 2001.

[273] P. Robinson, A. Walther, C. Faller, and J. Braasch. Echo thresholds for reflections from acoustically diffusive architectural surfaces. *Journal of the Acoustical Society of America*, 134(4):2755–2764, 2013.

[274] M. Rolfs. Microsaccades: Small steps on a long way. *Psychological Bulletin*, 49(20):2415–2441, 2009.

[275] R. Ron-Angevin and A. Diaz-Estrella. Brain–computer interface: Changes in performance using virtual reality techniques. *Neuroscience Letters*, 449(2):123–127, 2009.

[276] D. Rosenbaum. *Human Motor Control, 2nd Ed.* Elsevier, Amsterdam, 2009.

[277] S. Ross. *A First Course in Probability, 9th Ed.* Pearson, New York, NY, 2012.

[278] G. Roth and U. Dicke. Evolution of the brain and intelligence. *Trends in Cognitive Sciences*, 9(5):250–257, 2005.

[279] K. Ruhland, C. E. Peters, S. Andrist et al. A review of eye gaze in virtual agents, social robotics and hci: Behaviour generation, user interaction and perception. *Computer Graphics Forum*, 34(6):299–326, 2015.

[280] A. Ruina and R. Pratap. *Introduction to Statics and Dynamics*. Oxford University Press, Oxford, UK, 2015. http://ruina.tam.cornell.edu/Book/.

[281] W. Rushton. Effect of humming on vision. *Nature*, 216:1173–1175, 2009.

[282] M. B. Sachs and N. Y. S. Kiang. Two-tone inhibition in auditory nerve fibres. *Journal of the Acoustical Society of America*, 43(5):1120–1128, 1968.

[283] S. Sanei and J. A. Chambers. *EEG Signal Processing*. Wiley, Hoboken, NJ, 2007.

[284] A. B. Satpute, J. Kang, K. C. Bickhart et al. Involvement of sensory regions in affective experience: A meta-analysis. *Front. Psychol.*, 6, 2015. https://doi.org/10.3389/fpsyg.2015.01860.

[285] X. M. Sauvan and C. Bonnet. Spatiotemporal boundaries of linear vection. *Perception and Psychophysics*, 57(6):898–904, 1995.

[286] D. Schmalsteig and T. Höllerer. *Augmented Reality: Principles and Practice*. Mendeley Ltd., London, 2015.

[287] G. Schweighofer and A. Pinz. Robust pose estimation from a planar target. *IEEE Transactions on Pattern Analysis and Machine Intelligence*, 28(12):2024–2030, 2006.

[288] A. R. Seitz, J. E. Nanez, S. R. Halloway, and T. Watanabe. Perceptual learning of motion leads to faster-flicker perception. *Journal of Vision*, 6(6):158, 2015.

[289] A. R. Seitz and T. Watanabe. The phenomenon of task-irrelevant perceptual learning. *Vision Research*, 49(21):2604–2610, 2009.

[290] M. Shelhamer, D. A. Robinson, and H. S. Tan. Context-specific adaptation of the gain of the vestibulo-ocular reflex in humans. *Journal of Vestibular Research: Equilibrium and Orientation*, 2(1):89–96, 1992.

[291] R. N. Shepard. Circularity in judgements of relative pitch. *Journal of the Acoustical Society of America*, 36(12):2346–2453, 1964.

[292] G. M. Shepherd. Discrimination of molecular signals by the olfactory receptor neuron. *Neuron*, 13(4):771–790, 1994.

[293] T. B. Sheridan. Musings on telepresence and virtual presence. *Presence: Teleoperators and Virtual Environments*, 1(1):120–126, 1992.

[294] W. R. Sherman and A. B. Craig. *Understanding Virtual Reality: Interface, Application, and Design*. Morgan Kaufmann, San Francisco, CA, 2002.

[295] T. Shibata, J. Kim, D. M. Hoffman, and M. S. Banks. The zone of comfort: predicting visual discomfort with stereo displays. *Journal of Vision*, 11(8):1–29, 2011.

[296] B. G. Shinn-Cunningham, S. Santarelli, and N. Kopco. Tori of confusion: Binaural localization cues for sources within reach of a listener. *Journal of the Acoustical Society of America*, 107(3):1627–1636, 2002.

[297] M. Siedlecka, A. Klumza, M. Lukowska, and M. Wierzchon. Rubber hand illusion reduces discomfort caused by cold stimulus. *PloS ONE*, 9(10), 2014.

[298] P. Signell. Predicting and specifying the perceived colors of reflective objects. Technical Report MISN-0-270, Michigan State University, East Lansing, MI, 2000. //www.physnet.org/.

[299] M. Slater, B. Spanlang, M. V. Sanchez-Vives, and O. Blanke. Experience of body transfer in virtual reality. *PloS ONE*, 5(5), 2010.

[300] L. J. Smart, T. A. Stoffregen, and B. G. Bardy. Visually induced motion sickness predicted by postural instability. *Human Factors*, 44(3):451–465, 2002.

[301] C. U. M. Smith. *Biology of Sensory Systems, 2nd Ed*. Wiley, Hoboken, NJ, 2008.

[302] G. Smith and D. A. Atchison. *The Eye and Visual Optical Instruments*. Cambridge University Press, Cambridge, UK, 1997.

[303] R. Sawdon Smith and A. Fox. *Langford's Basic Photography, 10th Ed*. Focal Press, Oxford, UK, 2016.

[304] W. J. Smith. *Modern Optical Engineering, 4th Ed*. SPIE Press, Bellingham, WA, 2008.

[305] N. Snavely, S. M. Seitz, and R. Szeliski. Photo tourism: exploring photo collections in 3D. *ACM Transactions on Graphics*, 25(3):835–846, 2006.

[306] D. Song, K. Goldberg, and N. Y. Chong. Networked telerobots. In O. Khatib and B. Siciliano, editors, *Springer Handbook of Robotics*, pages 759–771. Springer-Verlag, Berlin, 2008.

[307] B. R. Sorensen, M. Donath, G.-B. Yanf, and R. C. Starr. The Minnesota scanner: A prototype sensor for three-dimensional tracking of moving body segments. *IEEE Transactions on Robotics*, 5(4):499–509, 1989.

[308] R. W. Soukoreff and I. S. MacKenzie. Towards a standard for pointing device evaluation, perspectives on 27 years of Fitts' law research in HCI. *International Journal of Human-Computer Studies*, 61:751–759, 2004.

[309] M. W. Spong, S. Hutchinson, and M. Vidyasagar. *Robot Modeling and Control*. Wiley, Hoboken, NJ, 2005.

[310] K. M. Stanney and R. S. Kennedy. Aftereffects from virtual environment expore: How long do they last? In *Proceedings of the Human Factors and Ergonomics Society Annual Meeting*, pages 48(2): 1476–1480, 1998.

[311] K. M. Stanney and R. S. Kennedy. Simulation sickness. In D. A. Vincenzi, J. A. Wise, M. Mouloua, and P. A. Hancock, editors, *Human Factors in Simulation and Training*, pages 117–127. CRC Press, Boca Raton, FL, 2009.

[312] A. Steed and S. Julier. Design and implementation of an immersive virtual reality system based on a smartphone platform. In *Proceedings IEEE Symposium on 3D User Interfaces*, pages 43–46, 2013.

[313] R. M. Steinman, Z. Pizlo, and F. J. Pizlo. Phi is not beta, and why Wertheimer's discovery launched the Gestalt revolution. *Vision Research*, 40(17):2257–2264, 2000.

[314] N. Stephenson. *Snow Crash*. Bantam Books, 1996.

[315] R. M. Stern, S. Hu, R. LeBlanc, and K. L. Koch. Chinese hyper-susceptibility to vection-induced motion sickness. *Aviation, Space, and Environmental Medicine*, 64(9 Pt 1):827–830, 1993.

[316] J. Steuer. Defining virtual reality: Dimensions determining telepresence. *Journal of Communication*, 42(4):73–93, 1992.

[317] S. S. Stevenson. On the psychophysical law. *Psychological Review*, 64(3):153–181, 1957.

[318] R. Stoakley, M. J. Conway, and R. Pausch. Virtual reality on a WIM: interative worlds in minature. In *Proceedings of the SIGCHI Conference on Human Factors in Computing Systems*, pages 265–272, 1995.

[319] T. A. Stoffregen, E. Faugloire, K. Yoshida, M. B. Flanagan, and O. Merhi. Motion sickness and postural sway in console video games. human factors. *Human Factors*, 50(2):322–331, 2008.

[320] Student. The probable error of a mean. *Biometrika*, 6(1):1–25, 1908.

[321] I. E. Sutherland. The ultimate display. In *Proceedings of the IFIP Congress*, pages 506–508, 1965.

[322] I. E. Sutherland. A head-mounted three dimensional display. In *Proceedings of AFIPS*, pages 757–764, 1968.

[323] R. Szeliski. Image alignment and stitching: A tutorial. Technical Report MSR-TR-2004-92, Microsoft Research, 2004. Available at http://research.microsoft.com/.

[324] R. Szeliski. *Computer Vision: Algorithms and Applications*. Springer-Verlag, Berlin, 2010.

[325] L. Takayama, E. Marder-Eppstein, H. Harris, and J. Beer. Assisted driving of a mobile remote presence system: System design and controlled user evaluation. In *Proc. IEEE International Conference on Robotics and Automation*, pages 1883–1889, 2011.

[326] F. Tejada. Silicon on Insulator CMOS and Microelectromechanical Systems: Mechanical Devices, Sensing Techniques and System Electronics. PhD thesis, The Johns Hopkins University, 2006.

[327] Thomas and Finney. *Calculus and Analytic Geomtry, 9th Ed.* Addison-Wesley, Boston, MA, 1995.

[328] L. L. Thompson and P. M. Pinsky. Acoustics. *Encyclopedia of Computational Mechanics*, 2(22), 2004.

[329] S. Thrun, W. Burgard, and D. Fox. *Probabilistic Robotics*. Massachusetts Institute of Technology Press, Cambridge, MA, 2005.

[330] K. Thurley and A. Ayaz. Virtual reality systems for rodents. *Current Zoology*, 63(1), 2017.

[331] A. Treisman. Focused attention in the perception and retrieval of multidimensional stimuli. *Attention, Perception, and Psychophysics*, 22(1):1–11, 1977.

[332] B. Treutwein. Minireview: Adaptive psycholphysical procedures. *Vision Research*, 35(17):2503–2522, 1995.

[333] B. Triggs, P. McLauchlan, R. Hartley, and A. Fitzbiggon. Bundle adjustment – a modern synthesis. In *Proceedings IEEE International Workshop on Vision Algorithms*, pages 298–372, 1999.

[334] R. Y. Tsai. A versatile camera calibration technique for high-accuracy 3D machine vision metrology using off-the-shelf TV cameras and lenses. *IEEE Journal of Robotics and Automation*, 3(4):323–344, 1987.

[335] B. Ullmer and H. Ishii. Emerging frameworks for tangible user interfaces. In J. M. Caroll, editor, *Human-Computer Interaction for Tanglible User Interfaces*, pages 579–601. Addison-Wesley, Boston, MA, 2001.

[336] A. Vasalou and A. Joinson. Me, myself and I: The role of interactional context on self-presentation through avatars. *Computers in Human Behavior*, 25(2):510–520, 2009.

[337] J. F. Vasconcelos, G. Elkaim, C. Silvestre, P. Oliveira, and B. Cardeira. Geometric approach to strapdown magnetometer calibration in sensor frame. *Transactions on Aerospace and Electronic Systems*, 47(2):1293–1306, 2011.

[338] G. Vass and T. Perlaki. Applying and removing lens distortion in post production. Technical report, Colorfont, Ltd., Budapest, 2003.

[339] J. Vidal. Toward direct brain – computer communication. *Annual Review of Biophysics and Bioengineering*, 2:157–180, 1973.

[340] J. J. Vidal. Real-time detection of brain events in EEG. *Proceedings of the IEEE*, 65(5):633–664, 1977.

[341] E. S. Viirre, H. Pryor, S. Nagata, and T. Furness. The virtual retinal display: A new technology for virtual reality and augmented vision in medicine. *Studies in Health Technology and Informatics*, 50:252 257, 1998.

[342] S. T. von Soemmerring. *Über das Organ der Seele*. Königsberg, 1796. With afterword by Immanuel Kant.

[343] M. Vorländer. *Auralization*. Springer-Verlag, Berlin, 2010.

[344] M. Vorländer and B. Shinn-Cunningham. Virtual auditory displays. In K. S. Hale and K. M. Stanney, editors, *Handbook of Virtual Environments, 2nd Edition*. CRC Press, Boca Raton, FL, 2015.

[345] C. Wächter and A. Keller. Instant ray tracing: The bounding interval hierarchy. In T. Akenine-Möller and W. Heidrich, editors, *Eurographics Symposium on Rendering*, pages 139–149. 2006.

[346] B. A. Wandell. *Foundations of Vision*. Sinauer Associates, 1995. Available at https://foundationsofvision.stanford.edu/.

[347] X. Wang and B. Winslow. Eye tracking in virtual environments. In K. S. Hale and K. M. Stanney, editors, *Handbook of Virtual Environments, 2nd Edition*. CRC Press, Boca Raton, FL, 2015.

[348] R. M. Warren, J. M. Wrightson, and J. Puretz. Illusory continuity of tonal and infratonal periodic sounds. *Journal of the Acoustical Society of America*, 84(4):1338–1142, 1964.

[349] W. H. Warren and K. J. Kurtz. The role of central and peripheral vision in perceiving the direction of self-motion. *Perception and Psychophysics*, 51(5):443–454, 1992.

[350] D. S. Watkins. *Fundamentals of Matrix Computations*. Wiley, Hoboken, NJ, 2002.

[351] A. B. Watson and D. G. Pelli. QUEST: A Bayesian adaptive psychometric method. *Perception and Psychophysics*, 33(2):113–120, 1983.

[352] B. L. Welch. The generalization of "Student's" problem when several different population variances are involved. *Biometrika*, 34(1–2):28–35, 1947.

[353] G. Welch and E. Foxlin. Motion tracking: No silver bullet, but a respectable arsenal. *IEEE Computer Graphics and Applications*, 22(6):24–28, 2002.

[354] R. B. Welch and B. J. Mohler. Adapting to virtual environments. In K. S. Hale and K. M. Stanney, editors, *Handbook of Virtual Environments, 2nd Edition*. CRC Press, Boca Raton, FL, 2015.

[355] A. T. Welford. *Fundamentals of Skill*. Methuen Publishing, London, 1968.

[356] M. Wertheimer. Experimentelle Studien über das Sehen von Bewegung (Experimental Studies on the Perception of Motion). *Zeitschrift für Psychologie*, 61:161–265, 1912.

[357] J. Westerhoff. *Reality: A Very Short Introduction*. Oxford University Press, Oxford, UK, 2011.

[358] F. A. Wichman and N. J. Hill. The psychometric function: I. fitting, sampling, and goodness of fit. *Perception and Psychophysics*, 63(8):1293–1313, 2001.

[359] J. M. Wolfe, K. R. Kluender, and D. M. Levi. *Sensation and Perception, 4th Ed.* Sinauer, Sunderland, MA, 2015.

[360] J. R. Wolpaw, N. Birbaumer, D. J. McFarland, G. Pfurtscheller, and T. M. Vaughan. Brain–computer interfaces for communication and control. *Clinical Neurophysiology*, 113(6):767–791, 2002.

[361] A. F. Wright, C. F. Chakarova, M. M. Abd El-Aziz, and S. S. Bhattacharya. Photoreceptor degeneration: Genetic and mechanistic dissection of a complex trait. *Nature Reviews Genetics*, 11:273–284, 2010.

[362] F. E. Wright. *The Methods of Petrographic-Microscopic Research*. Carnegie Institution of Washington, 1911.

[363] Y. Wu and Z. Hu. PnP problem revisited. *Journal of Mathematical Imaging and Vision*, 24(1):131–141, 2006.

[364] S. Xu, M. Perez, K. Yang et al. Determination of the latency effects on surgical performance and the acceptable latency levels in telesurgery using the dV-Trainer simulator. *Surgical Endoscopy*, 28(9):2569–2576, 2014.

[365] T. Yamada, S. Yokoyama, T. Tanikawa, K. Hirota, and M. Hirose. Wearable olfactory display: Using odor in outdoor environment. In *Proceedings IEEE Virtual Reality Conference*, pages 199–206, 2006.

[366] E. Yang and M. Dorneich. The effect of time delay on emotion, arousal, and satisfaction in human-robot interaction. In *Proceedings of the Human Factors and Ergonomics Society Annual Meeting*, pages 443–447, 2015.

[367] X. Yang and W. Grantham. Effects of center frequency and bandwidth on echo threshold and buildup of echo suppression. *Journal of the Acoustical Society of America*, 95(5):2917, 1994.

[368] R. Yao, T. Heath, A. Davies et al. Oculus VR Best Practices Guide, March 2014. Accessed July 10, 2016, at http://brianschrank.com/vrgames/resources/Oculus BestPractices.pdf.

[369] N. Yee and J. Bailenson. The Proteus effect: The effect of transformed self-representation on behavior. *Human Communication Research*, 33:271–290, 2007.

[370] H. Yeh, R. Mehra, Z. Ren et al. Wave-ray coupling for interactive sound propagation in large complex scenes. *ACM Transactions on Graphics*, 32(6), 2013.

[371] W. A. Yost. *Fundamentals of Hearing: An Introduction, 5th Ed.* Emerald Group, Somerville, MA, 2006.

[372] P. Zahorik. Assessing auditory distance perception using virtual acoustics. *Journal of the Acoustical Society of America*, 111(4):1832–1846, 2002.

[373] V. M. Zatsiorsky. *Kinematics of Human Motion*. Human Kinetics, Champaign, IL, 1997.

[374] V. M. Zatsiorsky. *Kinetics of Human Motion*. Human Kinetics, Champaign, IL, 2002.

[375] V. M. Zatsiorsky and B. I. Prilutsky. *Biomechanics of Skeletal Muscles*. Human Kinetics, Champaign, IL, 2012.

[376] Y. Zheng, Y. Kuang, S. Sugimoto, and K. Aström. Revisiting the PnP problem: A fast, general and optimal solution. In *Proceedings IEEE International Conference on Computer Vision*, pages 2344–2351, 2013.

[377] H. Zhou and H. Hu. Human motion tracking for rehabilitation – A survey. *Biomedical Signal Processing and Control*, 3(1):1–18, 2007.

Image Credits

Figure 1.01 Courtesy Max Reihner, Somniacs.co

Figure 1.02a Kay Thurley, Aslô Ayaz, figure adapted from 'Virtual reality systems for rodents', Current Zoology, Volume 63, Issue 1, February 2017, pp 109–119. https://doi.org/10.1093/cz/zow070

Figure 1.02b Photo courtesy Dr. Kay Thurley.

Figure 1.03a Created by Stuart Layton, released under CC BY-SA 3.0, https://upload.wikimedia.org/wikipedia/commons/5/5e/Place_Cell_Spiking_Activity_Example.png

Figure 1.03b Torkel Hafting, https://commons.wikimedia.org/wiki/File:Autocorrelationplot_grid_cell.JPG CC-BY-SA-3.0

Figure 1.04 Alexander Wikel, https://commons.wikimedia.org/wiki/File:Braininvat.jpg CC-BY-3.0

Figure 1.06a Courtesy Alex Wivel

Figure 1.06b © Virtuix, used with permission

Figure 1.06c © Playful Corp, used with permission

Figure 1.06d courtesy of Brian Schrank

Figures 1.07, 1.8 Facebook Technologies, LLC © 2020. All rights reserved. Content used with permission by Facebook Technologies, LLC.

Figure 1.09a Padaguan, 'Google Street View camera car' (https://commons.wikimedia.org/wiki/File:Google_Street_View_camera_car.jpg), (CC BY-SA 3.0). https://creativecommons.org/licenses/by-sa/3.0/legalcode

Figure 1.09b Picture courtesy of Insta360.

Figure 1.10a © silkfactory / iStockphoto.

Figure 1.10b © Luke Woods, used with permission

Figure 1.11 (background) © Taya Ovod / Shutterstock.

Figure 1.11 (inset) © Jordi Vidal / Redferns / Getty Images.

Figure 1.12a Courtesy of John Nappo, DORA platform

Figure 1.12b © DreamQii, used with permission

Figure 1.13 HyacintheLuynes, 'Second Life 11th Birthday Live Drax Files Radio Hour' (https://commons.wikimedia.org/wiki/File:Second_Life_11th_Birthday_Live_Drax_Files_Radio_Hour.jpg), (CC BY-SA 3.0). https://creativecommons.org/licenses/by-sa/3.0/legalcode

Figure 1.14 Figure by Within, Clouds over Sidra, used with permission

Figure 1.15 courtesy of BeAnotherLab

Figure 1.16 photo by Javier Garcia, US Air Force

Figure 1.17 Dunhuang Mogao Caves VR Experience, Lijun Ma, Xiaobo Lu, Academy of Arts and Design, Tsinghua University, Beijing, 2016–2019. https://dunhuang.design

Figure 1.18 Courtesy IVR-NATION

Figure 1.19 Courtesy Dr. Kesh Kesavadas, University of Illinois.

Figure 1.21a © PG / Bauer-Griffin / Getty Images.

Figure 1.22a Courtesy of shane4games

Figure 1.22b Copyright Erkki Trummel, used with permission

Figure 1.23a Courtesy of the Archeological Society of India

Figure 1.23b Copyright © The British Library. Used with permission.

Figure 1.23c © DeAgostini / Getty Images.

Figure 1.23d © Fine Art Images / Heritage Images / Getty Images.

Figure 1.25a © Association Freres Lumiere / Roger Viollet via Getty Images.

Figure 1.25b Still from 'Le voyage dans la lune' Georges Méliès, 1902.

Figure 1.25c © Sunset Boulevard / Corbis via Getty Images.

Figure 1.25d © Allstar Picture Library / Alamy Stock Photo.

Figure 1.26b © LMPC via Getty Images.

Figure 1.26c © Lucasfilm Animation / Photo 12 / Alamy Stock Photo.

Figure 1.26d © Getty Images / Handout.

Figure 1.27 National Archives and Records Administration, United States Information Service. Evert F. Bumgarder, photographer.

Figure 1.28b © ilbusca/Getty Images

Figure 1.28c Bethesda Softworks LLC.

Figure 1.28d Courtesy of Joel Hruschka

Figure 1.28e © Rovio Entertainment Corporation. All Rights Reserved.

Figure 1.28f Minecraft screenshot © Microsoft Corporation. Used with permission from Microsoft. https://www.minecraft.net/en-us/about-minecraft

Figure 1.29a © ilbusca / iStockphoto.

Figure 1.29b © trekandshoot / Shutterstock.

Figure 1.29d © Science & Society Picture Library / Getty Images.

Figure 1.30a 2014 CAVE virtual environment, Illinois Simulator Laboratory, Beckman Institute, University of Illinois at Urbana-Champaign (photo by Hank Kaczmarski)

Figure 1.30b Courtesy Ivan Sutherland, Bob Sproull, and Quintin Foster. Used with permission.

Figure 1.30c Courtesy Jeff Reinking

Figure 1.30d © Andrew Taylor / Fairfax Media via Getty Images.

Figure 1.30e Evan-Amos, 'Virtual-Boy-wController' (https://commons.wikimedia.org/wiki/File:Virtual-Boy-wController.jpg), marked as Public Domain.

Figure 1.30f Evan-Amos, 'Oculus-Rift-CV1-Headset Back' (https://commons.wikimedia.org/wiki/File:Oculus-Rift-CV1-Headset-Back.jpg), Public Domain.

Figure 2.06 © Manfred Majewski / EyeEm / Getty Images.

Figure 2.7a courtesy Teesside University

Figure 2.7b courtesy Jean Rivot

Figure 2.8a courtesy 3DSystems.com

Figure 2.8b courtesy Drilnoth

Figure 2.9a Klu andre, en.wikipedia; https://commons.wikimedia.org/wiki/File:LN3-2A_Platform_MVC-876X.JPG CC BY-SA-3.0

Figure 2.09b Courtesy Bosch Sensortec GmbH.

Figure 2.10a Evan-Amos, 'Xbox-360-Kinect-Standalone' (https://commons.wiki media.org/wiki/File:Xbox-360-Kinect-Standalone.png), marked as Public Domain.

Figure 2.10b courtesy Microsoft

Figure 2.11a Evan-Amos, 'Google-Cardboard' (https://commons.wikimedia.org/ wiki/File:Google-Cardboard.jpg), marked as Public Domain.

Figure 2.11b Maurizio Pesce, 'Samsung Gear VR (15247457825)' (https://commons .wikimedia.org/wiki/File:Samsung_Gear_VR_(15247457825).jpg), (CC BY 2.0). https://creativecommons.org/licenses/by/2.0/legalcode

Figure 2.12 courtesy iFixit, https://www.ifixit.com/Teardown/Oculus+Rift+Develop ment+Kit+2+Teardown/27613

Figure 2.14 Courtesy Dieter Fox and Nicholas Roy

Figure 2.16a Tony Phillips, NASA

Figure 2.16b Edward H Adelson https://commons.wikimedia.org/wiki/File:Checker_ shadow_illusion.svg CC-BY-SA 4.0

Figure 2.18 www.wpclipart.com

Figure 2.20 From Magic: Stage Illusions and Scientific Diversions, Including Trick Photography,compiled and edited by Albert A. Hopkins, Munn & Co., Publishers (1898)

Figure 3.2 created by Yutsi and released as public domain

Figure 4.5 By Gringer (Own work) [Public domain], via Wikimedia Commons

Figure 4.6 Figure 1 from Signell, 'Predicting and specifying the perceived colors of reflective objects' Technical Report MISN-0-270, Michigan State University, East Lansing, MI. © 2001, Peter Signell for Project PHYSNET. http://www.physnet.org/

Figure 4.7 Title figure from Signell, 'Predicting and specifying the perceived colors of reflective objects' Technical Report MISN-0-270, Michigan State University, East Lansing, MI. © 2001, Peter Signell for Project PHYSNET. http://www.physnet.org

Figure 4.08a Geni, 'Nimrud lens British Museum' (https://commons.wikimedia.org/ wiki/File:Nimrud_lens_British_Museum.jpg), (CC BY-SA 4.0). https://creativecom mons.org/licenses/by-sa/4.0/legalcode.

Figure 4.08b Dierk Schaefer, 'Stadtkirche Bad Wildungen, Pfingsten, Detail: Brillenapostel' (https://www.flickr.com/photos/dierkschaefer/6273179191/in/photo stream/), (CC BY 2.0). https://creativecommons.org/licenses/by/2.0/legalcode

Figure 4.18 Stan Zurek, https://commons.wikimedia.org/wiki/File:Chromatic_aber ration_(comparison).jpg CC-BY-SA-2.5

Figure 4.21 Ilveon (Own work) https://commons.wikimedia.org/wiki/File:Vlg_shop .jpg CC BY-SA 3.0

Figure 4.22 Figure 22 from F. E. Wright, The Methods of Petrographic-microscopic Research. Carnegie Institution of Washington, 1911.

Figure 4.23 used per license terms at https://en.wikipedia.org/wiki/File:Astigmatism_ text_blur.png

Figure 4.31 from timeanddate.com, used with permission

Figure 4.32a Filya1, 'Matrixw' (https://commons.wikimedia.org/wiki/File:Matrixw .jpg#globalusage), (CC BY-SA 3.0). https://creativecommons.org/licenses/by-sa/3.0/ legalcode

Figure 4.32b courtesy of Sparkfun

Figure 6.1 placed in public domain by the Art Institute of Chicago

Figure 6.2a Tony Philips, NASA

Figure 6.05b Courtesy Nadia S. Inturias P.

Figure 6.7c Courtesy of Todd Terry

Figure 6.07d © primeimages / Getty Images.

Figure 6.08 Rainer Zenz, 'Horopter' (https://commons.wikimedia.org/wiki/File: Horopter.png), (CC BY-SA 3.0). https://creativecommons.org/licenses/by-sa/3.0/ legalcode

Figure 6.09 Facebook Technologies, LLC © 2020. All rights reserved. Content used with permission by Facebook Technologies, LLC.

Figure 6.10a Courtesy of camera-obscura.co.uk

Figure 6.11 Photo © Julien Viry / Dreamstime.com. Illustration by Deborah Nicholls.

Figure 6.20 SharkD, 'HSV color solid cylinder' (https://commons.wikimedia.org/ wiki/File:HSV_color_solid_cylinder.png), (CC BY-SA 3.0). https://creativecom mons.org/licenses/by-sa/3.0/legalcode

Figure 6.21 Courtesy Jeff Yurek and Nanosys, Inc.

Figure 6.22a © Heather Stirratt / EyeEm / Getty Images.

Figure 6.22b © Peter Hermes Furian / Dreamstime.com.

Figure 6.23 original by Jurohi

Figure 6.25b J. Jastrow, from 'The mind's eye' Popular Science Monthly, 54, 299–312 (1899).

Figure 7.8 by Anynobody https://commons.wikimedia.org/wiki/File:Textured m1a2.png CC-BY-SA-4.0

Figure 7.09 Courtesy Matti Pouke.

Figure 7.11 NASA.

Figure 7.12a Courtesy Matti Pouke.

Figure 7.12b Courtesy Matti Pouke.

Figure 7.14 Pko, 'Fresnel lens' (https://commons.wikimedia.org/wiki/File:Fresnel_ lens.svg), released as Public Domain.

Figure 7.15 Courtesy NVIDIA Corporation.

Figure 7.17 Courtesy of Forceman

Figure 7.18 Cmglee, 'Comparison double triple buffering' (https://commons.wiki media.org/wiki/File:Comparison_double_triple_buffering.svg), https://creativecom mons.org/licenses/by-sa/3.0/legalcode

Figure 7.22 Image courtesy Bigscreen, Inc.

Figure 7.23a 360 Rize

Figure 7.23b © Neil Godwin / Shutterstock.

Figure 8.2a Courtesy Seattle Parks and Recreation

Figure 8.03 © Encyclopaedia Britannica / UIG / Getty Images.

Figure 8.4 Courtesy Elias Munir

Figure 8.05 © Pattarawit Chompipat / Dreamstime.com.

Figure 8.08a Aston Martin 'Vulcan' model from Forza Horizon 4 Series 19 Update, AMR Pro track package. © Microsoft Corporation. Used with permission from Microsoft. https://www.forzamotorsport.net/en-us/news/fh4_Series_19.

Figure 8.8b Courtesy of softkinetic.com

Figure 8.13 courtesy Andreas Geiger

Figure 9.1 Courtesy STMicroelectronics

Figure 9.2a Courtesy Francisco Tejada

Figure 9.2b Drawing courtesy of Mouser Electronics

Figure 9.06 Map developed by NOAA/NCEI and CIRES. https://ngdc.noaa.gov/geomag/WMM

Figure 9.08 © Alfred Pasieka / Science Photo Library / Getty Images.

Figure 9.10a 2010 Geek3 / GNU-FDL, commons.wikimedia.org/wiki/File:VFPt_cylindrical_magnet_thumb.svg

Figure 9.10b Image created by http://GamingShogun.com

Figure 9.13 Courtesy ifixit https://www.ifixit.com/Teardown/Oculus+Rift+CV1+Teardown/60612

Figure 9.16a Photograph by Ben Lang for RoadtoVR.com, used with permission

Figure 9.16b Courtesy Maurizio Pesce

Figure 9.18a Z22, 'Diagram of four Purkinje images' (https://commons.wikimedia.org/wiki/File:Diagram_of_four_Purkinje_images.svg), (CC BY-SA 4.0). https://creativecommons.org/licenses/by-sa/4.0/legalcode

Figure 9.18b © 2012 Massimo Gneo et al, Figure 1 from 'A Free Geometry Model-Independent Neural Eye-Gaze Tracking System' Journal of Neuroengineering and Rehabilitation, (https://www.ncbi.nlm.nih.gov/pmc/articles/PMC3543256/figure/F1/), (CC BY 2.0). https://creativecommons.org/licenses/by/2.0/legalcode

Figure 9.24 Courtesy Motus Digital LLC. www.mocaponline.com

Figure 9.25 Courtesy of Leap Motion

Figure 9.26a Courtesy of Afinia

Figure 9.26b provided by FARO Technologies, Inc.

Figure 10.1 Courtesy of www.thebrain.mcgill.ca

Figure 10.02a Evan-Amos, 'Atari-2600-Paddle-Controller-FR' (https://commons.wikimedia.org/wiki/File:Atari-2600-Paddle-Controller-FR.jpg), marked as Public Domain.

Figure 10.02b © ArcadeImages / Alamy Stock Photo.

Figure 10.03a © Mariakray / Dreamstime.com.

Figure 10.08a Douglas G. LaFon, U.S. Army Photo.

Figure 10.8b Courtesy of Paul Dyan

Figure 10.09 Courtesy NeCo Software AB.

Figure 10.10 © CBS Photo Archive / Getty Images.

Figure 10.12 Courtesy HTC Corporation.

Figure 10.14 Second Life image courtesy of Linden Research, Inc. 'Virtual Reality' is not affiliated with nor sponsored by Linden Research.

Figure 10.15 © Chesnot / Getty Images.

Figure 10.16a USC ICT

Figure 10.17 Image courtesy Bigscreen, Inc.

Figure 11.1 Courtesy of Dale Pond

Figure 11.4 www.myvmc.com, used with permission

Figure 11.05a, b © Encyclopaedia Britannica / UIG / Getty Images.

Figure 11.06 Original: Oarih Ropshkow, Vector: Fred the Oyster, 'Cochlea-crosssection' (https://commons.wikimedia.org/wiki/File:Cochlea-crosssection.svg), (CC BY-SA 3.0). https://creativecommons.org/licenses/by-sa/3.0/legalcode

Figure 11.08 Lindosland, 'Lindos1,' (https://commons.wikimedia.org/wiki/File:Lindos1.svg), Public Domain.

Figure 11.10 Courtesy Dutch Society of Audiology (NVA). https://audiologieboek.nl

Figure 11.13 Courtesy Sönke Pelzer, Lukas Aspöck, Dirk Schröder, and Michael Vorländer

Figure 11.14 Ravish Mehra, Nikunj Raghuvanshi, Lakulish Antani, Anish Chandak, Sean Curtis, and Dinesh Manocha, 2013. 'Wave-based sound propagation in large open scenes using an equivalent source formulation' ACM Trans. Graph. 32, 2, Article 19 (April 2013) DOI: https://doi.org/10.1145/2451236.2451245. Used with permission.

Figure 11.15 Courtesy Sönke Pelzer, Lukas Aspöck, Dirk Schröder, and Michael Vorländer

Figure 12.1 © Image by Ann Latham Cudworth, used with permission

Figure 12.05 Skbkekas, 'Student t pdf' (https://commons.wikimedia.org/wiki/File: Student_t_pdf.svg) and 'Student t cdf' (https://commons.wikimedia.org/wiki/File: Student_t_cdf.svg), (CC BY-SA 3.0). https://creativecommons.org/licenses/by/3.0/ legalcode

Figure 13.01 Thomas.haslwanter, 'Skin proprioception' (https://commons.wikimedia .org/wiki/File:Skin_proprioception.jpg), (CC BY-SA 4.0). https://creativecommons org/licenses/by-sa/4.0/legalcode

Figure 13.2 Alison Okamura, adapted from S. Lederman, R. Klatzky: Hand movements: A window into haptic object recognition, Cogn. Psychol. 19(3), 342–368 (1987)

Figure 13.3 courtesy of Arvid Guterstam

Figure 13.4a Courtesy of Logitech

Figure 13.04b Evan-Amos, 'Dreamcast-Jump-Pack' (https://commons.wikimedia .org/wiki/File:Dreamcast-Jump-Pack.jpg), (CC BY-SA 3.0). https://creativecom mons.org/licenses/by-sa/3.0/legalcode

Figure 13.4c Courtesy of 3D Systems

Figure 13.4d Courtesy KGS Corporation.

Figure 13.5 © 2016 IEEE. Reprinted, with permission, from K. Hashimoto and T. Nakamoto, 'Tiny Olfactory Display Using Surface Acoustic Wave Device and Micropumps for Wearable Applications' IEEE Sensors Journal, 16:12, 4974-4980.

Figure 13.6 courtesy of Nimesha Ramasinghe

Figure 13.07 © Toshifumi Kitamura / AFP via Getty Images.

Figure 13.8a Courtesy of bestrobothooverreviews.com

Figure 13.8b Courtesy Kuka Robotics.

Figure 13.8d Ben Finio: The Harvard Microrobotics Lab

Figure 13.9 Courtesy of Double Robotics

Figure 13.10 © 2015 Ajay B. Satpute, et al., 'Involvement of Sensory Regions in Affective Experience: A Meta-Analysis' Frontiers in Psychology, vol. 6, 1860, 15 Dec. 2015, doi: https://dx.doi.org/10.3389/fpsyg.2015.01860, (CC BY 2.0). https://creativecommons.org/licenses/by/2.0/legalcode

Figure 13.11a Laboratory of Cognitive Neuroscience, EPFL

Figure 13.11b Courtesy of Emotiv and Emotiv EPOC+/ Insight

Index